THE COMING OF THE THIRD CHURCH

Walbert Bühlmann

The coming of
the Third Church

**An analysis of the present and future
of the Church**

ORBIS BOOKS

Maryknoll, New York 10545

1978

Original title: *Es kommt die dritte Kirche. Eine Analyse der kirchlichen Gegenwart und Zukunft.* An Italian edition, in a fuller form, appeared with the title: *La terza Chiesa alle porte,* 1974.

The translation for the English edition was edited by Ralph Woodhall SJ and A.N. Other from the third Italian edition (May 1975), revised and brought up to date by the author, and from the German manuscript.

THIRD PRINTING

Nihil Obstat: Bernard Forshaw, D.D.

Imprimatur: Denis McDonnell, V.G.

Liverpool, 29 January 1976

LIBRARY OF CONGRESS CATALOGING IN PUBLICATION DATA

Bühlmann, Walbert.
    The coming of the third church.

    Translation of Es kommt die dritte Kirche.
    Bibliography: p.
    Includes index.
    1. Catholic Church—History—1965— 2. Catholic Church—Doctrinal and controversial works—Catholic authors. 3. Church and underdeveloped areas.   I. Title.
    BX1390.B8313   1977   282   76-23237
    ISBN 0-88344-0695
    ISBN 0-88344-0709 pbk.

CONTENTS

Part One

The new shape of the world

Part Two
New light on old problems

ABBREVIATIONS

AAS	Acta Apostolicae Sedis, Vatican
AFER	African Ecclesiastical Review, Masaka, Uganda
AG	Ad Gentes. Decree on the missionary activity of the Church
AIF	Agenzia Internationalis Fides (press agency)
CIM	The Clergy Monthly, Ranchi, India
CM	Le Christ au Monde, Rome
EMZ	Evangelische Missions-Zeitschrift, Stuttgart
ET	English translation
GS	Gaudium et spes. Pastoral constitution on the Church in the world of today
HK	Herder Korrespondenz, Freiburg im B.
HThG	Handbuch Theolog. Grundbegriffe, Munich
ICI	Informations Catholiques Internationales, Paris
IDOC	The future of the missionary enterprise, Rome 1973
IRM	International Review of Missions, London–Geneva
JEE	Jeevadhara. A Journal of Christian Interpretation, Allepey, India
KM	Die kathol. Missionen, Freiburg im B.
KMJ	Kathol. Missionsjahrbuch der Schweiz, Freiburg i. Ue
LG	Lumen Gentium. Dogmatic constitution on the Church
LthK	Lexicon für Theologie und Kirche, Freiburg im B.
LV	Lumen Vitae, Brussels
NZM	Neue Zeitschrift für Missionswissenschaft, Schöneck
OR	Osservatore Romanc
PM	Paroles et Missions, Paris
PMV–CI	Pro Mundi Vita, Centrum Informationis, Brussels
PMV–NS	Pro Mundi Vita, Notes Spéciales
PP	Populorum Progressio. Encyclical of Paul VI, 1967
RCA	Revue du Clergé Africain, Mayidi, Zaire.
RM	Rhythmes du Monde, Lyons–Paris
SEDOS–D	SEDOS Documentation, Rome
SEDOS–JV	SEDOS Joint Venture, Rome
SML	Semaine de Missiologie de Louvain
SPIR	Spiritus, Paris
UR	Unitatis redintegratio. Decree on ecumenism
VSVD	Verbum, Rome
ZMR	Zeitschrift für Missionswissenschaft und Religionswissenschaft, Münster i. W.

INTRODUCTION

There is far too much talk about crisis in the Church, far too little about the opportunities we are offered. In the course of history, opportunities have always outnumbered the tribulations; if it were not so, the Church would not have survived. The outstanding opportunity of the present time is the coming of a Church which I would like to call the 'Third Church', that is to say, the Church of the south as distinct from the Churches of east and west. This coming is an epoch-making event within the one Church of Christ. The pattern of the Church, once predominantly western, is breaking up before our eyes; a new migration of peoples now taking place seems to be ushering in a new Middle Ages, this time on a world scale and in the spirit of the third millennium.

We have not yet given sufficient attention to this promising change. In Latin America little is known of Africa, in Africa little of Asia; and in the west, in spite of better information services, we still lack a comprehensive view of what goes on in the southern hemisphere. In the matter of aid for development, we have the well-known Pearson Report. After the first ten years of development aid, Pearson and others have made a study of the aid given so far, assessed results and made recommendations for the second decade. In the field of evangelization, we need what I would call a 'Pearson Report on the Church'. In this field we certainly have books of theological reflection and monographs on areas of concern limited both geographically and thematically, as well as sources of factual information: *Annuario Pontificio, Guida delle Missioni Cattoliche, Bilan du Monde, World Christian Handbook,* etc. But so far, any search for a book giving a general view, assessing the present situation and the prospects, would be fruitless. So I am undertaking the risky venture of writing one — risky not only in scholarship but also in Christian commitment. My task is to hunt out analogous problems in the three southern continents, to indicate common trends, to make more generally known those original solutions which have already been implemented little by little, to deduce from practical developments in recent years what will be practical approaches for the next few years, and to surmise what the future will bring and what the consequences will be for both the southern and the western Church. This should enable us all to explore the new horizons with courage.

I hold nothing against books of documentation, their targets being accurate knowledge of a limited sector or deeper understanding of a particular point. But if we are not to be drowned in a flood-tide of specialized knowledge, or live stranded in spiritual isolation, we also need books that give a bird's eye view. My book, in fact, aims at a satellite view: nothing less will do if we want to take in the three continents in a glance. The perspective is an exciting one but it has its limits: many of the statements made should — one need hardly say — be understood not in an absolute but in a relative sense, even when the words 'mostly', 'as a rule', or 'predominantly' do not actually appear in the text. A study of this kind is bound to include generalizations which take no account of exceptional experience to the contrary. I am here concerned not with any full understanding of specific situations but with inter-continental connections. Nor is this a reference book for all cases; rather it is a work of reflection. The reader must pursue for himself the lines of thought hinted at, and then apply them in his own day-to-day situation.

In Rome, every stone speaks to us of history. Every year, millions of pilgrims, tourists and hippies bring the inspirations and the anguish of mankind into her streets. The Orders and Congregations have gathered together an immense amount of documentation and practical experience in their headquarters and make it available through SEDOS (*Servizio di Documentazione e Studi*) and the meetings of the Union of General Superiors. The universities and special institutes possess accessible libraries and specialists who can be consulted. This city, where among so many Vatican officials the 'care of all the Churches' (2 Cor 11:28) is kept alive, is for all these reasons a favourable place to write such a book. I am grateful to all who have assisted me with suggestions and information. Special thanks are due to P.J. Schlauri who helped with the biblical reflections forming the introductions to chapters 9 to 23, to P.W. Henkel the courteous and ever-helpful librarian at the *Propaganda Fide* library and to Professors B. Häring, Rome, K. Kriech, Solothurn and A. Camps, Nijmegen, who kindly read the manuscript and shared theological responsibility with me to some extent.

In his homily for the 350th anniversary of the foundation of the Congregation for Evangelization, Pope Paul VI emphasized that 'the fire of Pentecost is not extinguished in the living Church of Christ ... even if, in certain moments of crisis and in some testing situations, it remains covered by human ashes'. [1] There is no doubt that, since John XXIII and the Second Vatican Council, in providential coincidence with world events, a new Pentecostal wind is blowing through the Church. Never has she faced a challenge like today's; never before today has she had such an opportunity to become the Church of the world. And this opportunity arises from the coming of the Third Church.

English readers may be interested in a book which foresees English as the international language of the Church, [2] and which deals with countries for which English-speaking peoples have had political and missionary responsibility.

Besides, the fact that within a space of twelve months it was reprinted four times in Italian and three times in German suggests that it must have done something to give people awareness of events in the Church on a world-wide scale. May it help to form missionary consciousness and awareness of the needs of the world among English speakers too.

Walbert Bühlmann, OFM Cap.

[1] OR 22/23.5.1972.   [2] See below ch. IX, p. 182.

Part One

The new shape of the world

Chapter 1

CHANGING PROSPECTS
FOR WESTERN CHRISTIANITY

A. *Migration of peoples in the Church*

1. One glance at a map of the world is enough for Europe
to look dwarfed by giant continents to the east, south and west.
Yet a rapid run over world history will tell us that this dwarf,
by its intelligence and energy, has acted as guide throughout
our planet. Nonetheless, a last-minute glance at the present
shows unmistakeably the phasing-out of European hegemony and
the spot-lighting of new groups of actors now taking the stage:
the peoples of the *Third World*.

Various interpretations are given to the expression 'Third
World'. [1] For our present purposes, the following will suffice:
the First World is the east, oppressed by communism; the
Second is the west, dominated by capitalism; the Third is the
south, threatened by neo-colonialism. The Third World, then,
embraces that group of peoples who are making their débuts
on the stage of world politics. Between them they can muster
a majority vote at the United Nations and are, therefore, much
courted by east and west.

2. Since it is common usage to speak of the Third World,
we are surely justified in coining the phrase: *Third Church*.
The First Church, then, will be the oriental Church, possessing
the rights of the first born (the first eight ecumenical councils

---

[1] Some distinguish sociologically: the way society is divided into the
rich, the middle class and the poor, or capitalists, tradesmen and
proletariat (this distinction is not applicable on a world-scale,
although rich and poor is); others politically: NATO, the Warsaw
pact and the non-aligned; others geographically: east, west and
south. The last is preferable today.

3

were held on eastern soil) but now become, in large measure, the Church of silence. The Second will be the western Church, which in the course of history has more and more come to be thought of as *the* Church without qualification and, by this token, as mother of her offspring in the new world. Finally, the Third Church will be that of the new nations, now entering as a new element into world history and into the history of the Church, who will be the 'surprise packets' of the near future.

3. There are of course other ways in which we could categorize 'three Churches'. From a structural point of view, we could speak of the Roman Catholic Church, the Orthodox and the Protestant. Historically, we could distinguish the early Church from those of the middle ages and the modern period. More significant and closer to our own experience would be to distinguish the 'élite Church' of the apostles and disciples who actually saw the Lord; the first bishops and guides of the community; the charismatics who spoke in tongues; the soldiers and merchants who spread the gospel along the highways of the Roman empire; the slaves who converted their masters; the martyrs who bore witness to the faith in their blood; Christians who joined the community without gaining any worldly advantage but rather exposing themselves thereby to serious risks; also, right from the beginning, sinners like those dissolute, gluttonous, quarrelsome people whom Paul depicts in the first letter to the Corinthians (1:6). Modern historical studies have shown that the condition of the early Church was not as ideal as many like to think.[2] The 'Constantinian revolution' saw the birth of a 'popular Church' which grew in splendour and glory and finally gave shape to the medieval Church, where a whole people was preserved within the womb of mother Church. This Church has been severely shaken for sometime past and now lies at the point of death, about to give way to a greater Church, to a 'world Church'. World-wide in two senses: first, as a geographic entity it does extend to the ends of the world (although no longer battling in serried ranks to achieve 'conquest of the world for Christ'); second, small groups of convinced

---

[2] W. Daut, *Die 'halben Christen' unter den Konvertiten und Gebildeten des 4 und 5 Jahrhunderts* in ZMR 1971, 171-188.

4

Christians are indeed scattered world-wide, experiencing a 'diaspora situation', not bound to historically conditioned institutions, salt of the earth and light of the world (Mt 5:13-14). However, our present purpose is to be concerned not with three Churches following one another in historical sequence but with three Churches alive today alongside one another.

4. According to our view the Third Church is, as a general rule, identified geographically with the Third World, with the tropical zone extending right round the world but also a little beyond the tropics and with the three continents of Latin America, Africa and Asia (including Oceania). This brings us to the much debated concept of 'missions'. We might, to be sure, keep to the strictly theological sense of mission as determined by Vatican II. In that case, the saving mission of the Church is worked out in activities which vary according to their starting points and the circumstances of their exercise: that is to say, in pastoral activity among the faithful, in ecumenical activity and in efforts made to establish Christian unity and, finally, in missionary activity 'in which preachers of the gospel, sent by the Church, going into the whole world, carry out their task of preaching the gospel and "planting the Church" among nations and groups of people who do not believe in Christ'. [3] From the religious and sociological point of view, it is becoming more and more difficult to determine in practice where we are dealing with 'missions' and where not.

Protestant Churches avoided this dilemma in so far as, after the convention held in Mexico City in 1963, they did *not* declare that the missions no longer exist but on the contrary that they exist everywhere: 'Missions in six continents'. [4] At Uppsala in 1968 this conception was further developed: there was firm insistence that the Church is in mission 'wherever human misery, population growth and tensions prevail, wherever

---

[3] AG 6.

[4] Some Catholic authors like Le Guillou and A.M. Henry take this view. Some Protestants express fears: 'When everyone is missionary no one is a missionary. If the mission field is everywhere, the mission field is nowhere' (Bishop S. Neill); W. Freitag warns against the 'ghost of pan-missionism'. Cf. J.T. Boberg (ed.), *Mission in the seventies. What direction?* Chicago, 1972, pp. 115-119.

new forces are on the move, wherever decisions are made on priorities and on the use of force ..., wherever the gospel is not established, especially in centres of power, in revolutionary movements, in universities, in cities, in the relations between industrialized nations and developing countries'; [5] in all such cases, the Church must develop her potential and bring her salvation.

This conception certainly represents a 'forward leap'. It adapts the stale, traditional idea of mission to the contemporary climate. The older persuasion that missions were for Africa and other such place and not for Europe is increasingly questioned by anyone who has lived through a feast day or a Sunday (or even a weekday) in a Third World Christian community and contrasts it with the situation in certain countries of ancient Christian tradition. The fact that some territories are under the Congregation for evangelization and others are not is more an administrative and technical distinction based on historical factors than an ecclesiological one. [6]

This also answers the question whether Latin America should be taken as a mission territory or an established church. Any territory in the Church which is in difficulties and suffers structural defects needs outside missionary aid to overcome its present disadvantage. This is the case in the whole Third Church. At all events, it helps to avoid the less sympathetic distinction between 'young' and 'old' churches.

I think, therefore, that the concept of 'Third Church' may be presented as the basis of a useful working hypothesis. [7] In time, we shall see whether it gains acceptance. To remove the principal objection which will be raised against it, I make the point that 'Third Church' has no derogatory connotation in

---

[5] N. Goodall (ed.), *Bericht aus Uppsala 1968*, Geneva, 1968, pp. 29-31.

[6] We return to these questions later. See, especially, ch. 13 below.

[7] J. Kerkhofs would like to introduce the term 'Churches not belonging to the north Atlantic region', *Zeitschrift für Missionswissenschaft und Religionswissenschaft*, Münster, 1972, p. 161. This corresponds to my way of thinking but is a rather roundabout way of expression. An African priest has found the same expression, independently of me: Anselme Sanon, *Tierce Eglise, ma mère*, Paris, 1973.

the sense of 'Church of the third rank'. It simply expresses the fact that, alongside the Western and Oriental Church, there has arisen a new entity which, by its special characteristics and future expectation, deserves to be denoted and appreciated by its own special name. 'In the third place' means not 'at the end' or 'in conclusion' but rather a new reality alongside what existed before, a fresh peak reached.

5. The Third Church is not something fallen from the sky. It comes as the end product of a historical process, of what we call the history of the missions, of a centrifugal movement, of a certain migration of people within the Church. It is all part of the mystery of the Church.

By 'Church' we do not understand merely a community involved in prayer and preoccupied with its own salvation. The Church began in the strong driving wind of Pentecost and was at once manifested to a crowd made up of people from the whole world. Later, when the Apostles and the Jerusalem community were in danger of yielding to the temptation of the sedentary life, they were overtaken by persecution which scattered them and so gave other towns the chance of hearing the message. Similarly, when the community began to settle in at Antioch, the Holy Spirit intervened and demanded two of their best teachers, Barnabas and Saul for the work of the mission (Acts 13 : 1-3).

Thus began that mobility which remains to this day a characteristic of true Christianity. Every community became a beach-head, a base for the conquest of new territory. The assembly was a preparation for mission. Christians knew themselves as called and chosen in order to be sent. In consequence, Christianity travelled from its land of origin first to Asia Minor and Egypt, then to Greece and Rome. In the course of this advance, it is not the case that Paul followed a brilliant strategic plan of his own: rather, he listened on every occasion and continually to the indications of the Spirit's guidance. [8]

6. At this point, rather than sketch a history of the missions I prefer to put forward a working hypothesis. I would

[8] O. Haas, *Paulus der missionar*, Münsterschwarzach, 1971, 29-31.

say not only that the Church has *in fact* advanced in successive waves so that it has now in some respects reached the ends of the world, not only that, after periods of weariness, it has redevoted itself with new élan to the missionary task, but also that what precisely has enabled the Church to overcome its periods of low ebb and its times of bitter dissension has been its constantly renewed commitment to missionary enterprise. At any rate, it would be easy to prove this in respect of the 16th and 19th centuries. If, in fact, it is theologically true that the Church is 'missionary by nature', and that there can be no genuine renewal without an opening up of horizons for missionary activity, [9] then it should also be possible to prove *a posteriori* the causal connection: renewal *on account of* mission.

Mission entails by definition 'sending' and objectively it implies 'Church on the move'. Movement is inevitably accompanied by fatigue, friction and resistance. The missionary movement embraced all the labours of those missionaries who in centuries past swarmed out of the bridge-heads and bore trials beyond human endurance (in a way that could not possibly be imitated today) in order to preach the gospel in Latin America, Africa and Asia. It is no cyclic movement, no Sisyphean labour but a movement of real progress towards the ultimate objective, the 'Day of the Lord' (1 Thess 5:2) and his perfect kingdom.

Before dealing at length with the Third Church, it could be helpful (especially for readers belonging to this Church) to take a look at the First and Second Churches.

B. *The First Church*

The First Church shows us two faces: that of the Orthodox Church and that of the Church in Communist countries from the iron curtain of Eastern Europe to the bamboo curtain of China, North Vietnam and North Korea.

[9] LG 1; AG 2 and 37. Latourette, Groves and Pastor's *History of the Popes* all record how often the Church, after periods of depression, pulled herself together and then, in spite of unfavourable conditions, achieved good missionary results. But they do not work out the causal link which I have in mind.

1. The Eastern Orthodox Churches in the first sense extend from Russia, Yugoslavia and Greece through the Middle East to Egypt, Ethiopia and South India. They reflect the structure of the Church of the early Christian centuries with strong autonomous patriarchates and with early Christian Christ-mysticism, expressing faith in the glorified Lord and calling unceasingly on God as *Pantokrator,* as Almighty and Merciful, in a liturgy full of feeling. Devotion to the passion of our Lord, which flourished in the middle ages especially through the Franciscan movement, is less developed in the East. Easter is experienced as the supreme feast. Each Sunday liturgy expresses perseverance — in the midst of suffering — in expectation of the coming of the Lord of glory. The western Church, especially now that it is seeking to renew itself by reaching back to the spirit of its origins, has much to learn from the early Christian situation in which the oriental Churches remain rooted.

2. By the same token, however, the oriental Churches have fallen into a state of spiritual isolation ever since the separation from Rome (and because of it). In a sense, they have remained fixed at a point preceding the middle ages. They lack the Council of Trent's renewal of priestly formation. They lack Pius X and the re-introduction of frequent communion. Above all, they lack Vatican II with its renewal of the liturgy, the declericalizing of the Church and a new pattern of relations between Church and state and Church and world.

Recent scholarship has corrected the opinion, once widely held even in specialist circles, that the Christian Orient has made no progress, in theology and spirituality, since the schism. [10] In particular, it is quite untrue that these Churches have abstained from missionary activity. It is enough to recall the wave of Nestorian missions which carried Christianity to Northern Arabia, India and, in the eighth century, as far as China and Indonesia. Moreover, for centuries, the Russian Church spread the faith in Siberia and as far as China and Japan; in the 19th century, this activity reached a climax both in foreign missions and in the formation of missionary conscious-ness at home (with 'missionary associations' and the beginnings

---

[10] P. Kawerau, *Das Christentums des Ostens,* Stuttgart, 1972.

9

of a theology of mission). [11] It is also worth mentioning that Greek Orthodox missionary work was officially started in Uganda and Kenya in 1952; today already it can claim 50,000 Christians and 35 native priests. When Archbishop Makarios visited Kenya in 1971 to open a seminary for priests and to baptize 5,000 catechumens, Radio Cyprus called the event 'the greatest missionary enterprise since the time of the conversion of the Slavs in the 9th century'. [12]

3. In the territory of the oriental Churches there are about ten million Catholics. Their story does not make a golden page in the story of the Church of Rome, since western missionaries tried far too long to force them to adopt the Latin rite, to 'abjure' Orthodoxy and to return to Peter's fold, according to a very narrow conception of Church unity. The Orthodox came to think of them as apostates and the erection of Catholic patriarchates has not, in fact, been a contribution to unity with the separated Churches, as Rome hoped, but has simply duplicated the hierarchies. But many will recall how at Vatican II the bishops and patriarchs of the eastern rites did much by their interventions to ensure that there would be a clearer view of pluriformity in the Church. [13]

4. *The Church of Silence* (it is *we* who are too silent in its regard) has now for 20 to 50 years, depending on the country concerned, been living face to face with its declared mortal enemy. In some places, in spite of acceptance of the Universal Declaration of Human Rights including freedom of religion, the struggle against religion goes on systematically and indiscriminately, using scientific methods; elsewhere, it is more subtle and temporizing. But everywhere, the ruling classes have to admit that religion survives and obstinately crops up again and again.

If bishops and patriarchs keep silence — since the persecution machine requires the Communist hierarchies to wait for

[11] J. Glazik, *Die russisch-ortodoxe Heidenmission seit Peter dem Gr.,* Münster, 1954; id., *Die Islammission der russisch-ortodoxen Kirche,* Münster, 1959.

[12] J. Kraus, *Missionarischer Aufbruch der Kirche von Hellas* in NZM, 1972, 231-239.

[13] J. Madey, *Die katholischen Ostkirchen,* Freiburg, 1973; W. de Vries in *Lexicon für Theologie und Kirche* 7, 1288f.

them to speak so as then to accuse them of being counter-revolutionaries — intellectuals and writers like Pasternak and Solzhenitsyn speak out all the more strongly, sending letters of protest to the Party leaders, to the Secretary General of the United Nations, etc., and risking loss of liberty or exile. Young people too are departing more and more from the Party line. The Church known to them is no 'exploiter of the people' but a victim of the Party, and their spontaneous sense of justice leads them to take her side. It is already said that public enemy number one is not the Church but youth. Inside the Party opinions differ: some seek the triumph of ideology with all the more ferocity while others would liberalize it, not out of a deliberate plan but through necessity since they can no longer resist the pressure from below. At any rate the whole totalitarian system is put in question; that little by little, within the womb of Russian Communism and of its satellites, a new 'Czechoslovak spring' may emerge — a period of thaw — is a possibility that cannot be excluded.

5. In the meantime, a believing people continues to pray and to sing its ancient hymns. Liturgical and theological renewal has as yet no foothold. The bishops try to keep out all 'new ideas', believing that the situation demands preservation of the old order for fear of losing all. Protestant groups, especially Baptists, and Catholic movements like the Focolarini, build genuine cells based on scriptural meditation and Christian renewal. The strength of the Church lies not in high theology but in personal experience of faith, in the decision for Christ which they are called upon to make each day. For this reason vocations to the priesthood and religious life, where permissible, are more numerous than in western countries. Visitors from the West discover more faith in these Churches than among us. Eastern believers, when they visit the West, are disappointed by our materialism and often choose freely to return to their own countries, because there they find more prompting to live in the spirit of the gospel. Pastor R. Wurmbrand, who returned to the West after fourteen years of prison and torture in Rumania, wrote that he was suffering more than when he was in Communist countries. His suffering consisted in his longing for

11

the indescribable beauty of his persecuted Church, following Christ in poverty and nakedness. [14]

6. What will be the future of this *First Church?* In the time of Pius XI, there were dreams of a quick overthrow of Russian Communism and groups of religious were transferred to the Orthodox rite and prepared for the great day. But that day is still to come!

The observation that Communism has failed to extinguish the faith after fifty years of struggle makes us think of a parallel case, that of North Africa, in which a living Church *was* completely extinguished. But this took five centuries. In the present case, we have to ask which will be the survivor. Will the Communist regime, like so many regimes in history, sooner or later fall? In a world which upholds religious liberty, and taking realistic account of the fact that the struggle against religion does not bring any advantages, will Communism finish by changing its ideology and concentrating on economic and political aims? Will it then be the case that the Eastern Church, tested and purified and thus a trustworthy witness, will be able to renew contacts with the Second and Third Church, so that eventually the fundamental notion of human solidarity will circulate freely and develop throughout the world, no longer wearing a Communist straitjacket but winged on its way from Russia by the gospel? Historians of the next centuries will be able to tell. For the present it is worth noting what Spengler said in his *Decline of the West*: [15] Christianity has twice known great movements of thought, in the East from 0 to 500 A.D. and the West from 1,000 to 1,500 A.D. and the third will follow in the first half of the next millennium in Russia.

---

[14] R. Wurmbrand, *Gefoltert für Christus,* Wuppertal, 1969, p. 80; E.T. *Tortured for Christ,* Hodder; B. Mondin, *Cristo ancora clandestino?* Bologna, 1972; P. Roth, *Gläubige und Ungläubige in der Sowietunion* in *Kirche in Not* XIX, 104-122.

[15] *Untergang des Abendlandes,* II, 321.

C. *The Second Church*

1. About ten years ago, the Second Church, though not alone, passed through a brilliant moment in its life, a time of spiritual breakthrough, such as we rarely find in the course of history. The charismatic figure of John XXIII had instantly gained the sympathy of the whole world, Christian and non-Christian. The unexpected announcement of the Council, under the inspiration of the Holy Spirit as he himself testified, received an unheard-of response and awakened unimaginable hopes. He had succeeded in 'opening the windows and letting in a little fresh air'. He had done this by 'showing the world the true face of the Church' and his promises of a 'new Pentecost' were believed. [16] In spite of all difficulties, the Council went much further than Pope John had imagined possible, to judge by the preparatory documents. The bishops of the world showed a growing readiness to face with courage urgent questions in theology and church life, and also a sincere willingness to undertake renewal with regard both to people in the Church and to Church government. This was to be the beginning of a movement expected to lead to a Church which would be freer, more alive, more authentic and at the same time more effective.

2. The euphoric period of openness was followed (typically for the western Church, that is, for our Second Church) by a period of contestation. The Fathers of the Council, in their speeches and behaviour, had presented a new image of the Church, belying former impressions of closedness, regimentation and servile obedience. This shift of public image was confirmed by the Council's openness towards the laity, typical of its general openness, which led to an awareness of lay people's maturity and co-responsibility in the Church. And so, immediately after the Council, many lay people, priests and even bishops began to show increasing impatience and anger when reforms were presumed to be or really were obstructed, when they were too long drawn out or emptied of substance. People believed they could discern a tendency to shunt back on to 'safe' rails the

---

[16] *Acta Apostolicae Sedis,* 1959, 67-68 : *Osservatore Romano,* 24.4.1959 and 11.8.1959; AAS 1962, 69.786-795.

stoked-up trains of thought set in motion by Vatican II, a desire to revoke in actual legislation and in post-conciliar practice what had been promised in theory and in principle. Faced by the dangers of 'liberty' and its evident side effects, many certainly preferred to go back to the security and stability of pre-conciliar times.

'Prophets' arose to make their voices heard against these tendencies. Theologians, individually and in groups, published their declarations of protest. Some lay people followed suit in the press and the other communications media. But the protests seem now to be gradually less frequent and to have given way to a general weariness together with a lessening of interest in religious questions and in 'co-responsibility', since so many in the Church have little or nothing to say. [17]

3. This is not a question of a change of mood but of a serious crisis in the Church, as demonstrated in the religious and sociological researches which have become a regular feature: they reveal clearly a *decline in church life.* The renewal of the liturgy, the fundamental soundness of which cannot be doubted, has generated tensions in the Church but has not brought positive results, statistically speaking. In European countries, attendance at Mass dropped by an average of 10 per cent in the first six years after the Council. The queues at the confessional, once a regular sight in good parishes, disappeared in the course of a few years as the result of very rapid emancipation in moral understanding, while at the same time the frequency of communion increased. The Church as an institution is harshly criticized by 'enlightened Christians', while traditionalist Catholics support her not so much for her message and her religious mission as for her social and humanitarian activity on behalf of the sick, the poor and children. About 80 per cent of Catholics in West Germany, France and Italy see this as the first duty of the Church. [18] There is a marked lack of interest

[17] Among the many analyses published on the 10th anniversary of the opening, cf. D.A. Seeber, *Lehrjahre der Kirche* in *Herder Korrespondenz,* 1972, 525-528.

[18] HK 1972, 281-284; E. Pin and C. Cavallin, *La religiosità dei Romani,* Roma, 1970, p. 66f; cf. Card. Angelo dell'Acqua, *L'evangelizzazione nella diocesi di Roma* in *Le Christ au Monde,* Rome, 1970, pp. 453-465, esp. 455.

in the Church, an unwillingness to take seriously liturgical and other rules (on grounds of evangelical liberty!), neglect of sacramental practice and quiet abandonment of the faith on the part of students and young people. Many priests find religious instruction in secondary schools to be an almost insupportable burden, while chaplains to students in higher education are satisfied if they manage to gather together a small group of young people interested in religious problems, even if they then prove unenthusiastic towards organized Christianity. Catholic Action and the large scale church organizations, the pride of the Church in some countries in the last decade, have largely collapsed. We are left with a large edifice in which nothing much happens. [19]

4. Over and above all this hovers the nightmare of a crisis and, in consequence, loss of vocations to the priesthood and the religious life. To quote one country, by no means the worst but not in a flourishing condition either — France, the 'eldest daughter of the Church': in the eight years from 1963 to 1971, students in diocesan seminaries went down from 5,279 to 2,840 (a loss of 46%, apart from the many theological students who have no intention of going on to ordination); entries into the seminaries have gone from 917 to 354 (down by 61%), ordinations from 573 to 237 (down by 58%). In 1965, deaths among priests exceeded ordinations by 165; in 1970, the gap had increased to 465, to which must be added the 200 leaving the priestly ministry in that year. Italy, heading the list with 42,065 diocesan priests, is for the moment stationary. The strong link with tradition remains. But in the near future a change on the part of young people is expected. [20] In France, it is calculated that in 1975 there will be 31,820 diocesan priests as against 40,994 in 1965. At that rate, we shall reach vanishing point in 30 years. These figures and this prospect were presented to a dumbfounded episcopal conference in 1972 by Bishop Riobé of Orléans. [21] We may hope that things will improve but there is

[19] Regular reports in *Herder Korrespondenz* and *Informations Catholiques Internationales*.
[20] E. Colagiovanni, *Crisi vere e false nel ruolo del prete oggi*, Rome, 1973, pp. 162, 244ff.
[21] *Orientierung*, Zürich, 15 January 1973, 10.

no guarantee (in fact, they may get worse towards the 'end': Mt 24:4ff). In any case, hope does not dispense us from the duty of reflecting and taking measures within the Church. But all these arguments from statistics could easily prove beside the point.

5. No wonder, then, that at times like this prophets of doom intone their Jeremiads over the ruins of Jerusalem, over the Church. Joseph Folliet, to whom the Church in France owes much, looks back sadly to the past progress of French Catholicism, with its numerous conversions, its distinguished writers and its active youth organizations; then, surveying the present situation, he feels the urge to weep and lament. Even the hierarchy stands divided and lacking authority. Protesters and their opponents attack one another to the scandal of the rest of the faithful and many abandon the Church — but where are they going? [22] Others entrench themselves behind their 'orthodoxy'; from behind their defences, they fight off all new ideas and their authors (including the Pope), and in this way they think to save the Church. [23]

6. In such a situation, the only valid order of the day is: 'Objectivity! Recover the middle ground!' But, at the same time, complete honesty is needed. We need the courage to see the *'Church without illusions'*, to face up to reality and interpret it in the light of the faith. H.H. Brunner published under this title [24] 'an experimental report on the period following 7 July 1983'. He supposes (not an entirely utopian supposition) that on that date the Swiss people will have decided, by a referendum, on a complete separation between Church and state. In consequence, now that the ancient bastions of the Church are fallen, he foresees a decline in membership of the (Protestant) Church of 69.2 per cent. The people's Church disappears; on Sundays, the church bells no longer ring and the clergy houses stand empty as a symbol that the parochial era is over. The state takes charge of funerals and other duties which once

[22] *Le temps de l'angoisse et de la recherche,* Lyons, 1972, 6-10.
[23] Besides the well-known Catholic right-wing reviews, cf. J. Eppstein, *Has the Catholic Church gone mad?,* New Rochelle, 1971.
[24] *Kirche ohne Illusionen,* 1968.

belonged to the Church. There remains a Church of the diaspora, groups of committed Christians who gather together to pray, continue to teach one another by correspondence courses or during summer schools and provide one another with the official service of the diaconate as spiritual advisers and teachers.

From time to time Karl Rahner has made similar analyses, not of a future utopia but of the present situation, and has recently collected them in a small book which might perhaps be called his 'spiritual testament'. In his view, we still have remains of a socially structured Christianity in which everything is still arranged homogeneously and hierarchically and personal decisions still lean on (are even replaced by) generally accepted tenets. But he sees this medieval form of Christianity coming to an end and giving way to a communion of those who make a free decision in favour of the faith and who take up a very critical stance towards society as well as towards the Church. Sooner or later the last oases of *petit bourgeois* and peasant life in an era of history nearing its end will dry up completely. Because of variations from place to place in the speed and timing of the process ('the Church out of phase with itself') tensions are inevitable; these must be overcome by mutual respect and acceptance of pluralism; no rigid polarisation must be allowed to take root. One thing is certain: time will tell in favour of this process, so the Church ought to align herself with it and attune herself to it so as not to be floored by it. [25]

7. Will our Second Church, in such disarray, still have a mission in the future? We should have to lose all hope in the resurrection to doubt it. The Second Church is still a reality, by no means a negligible quantity, and 'for a little while' it is still *the* Church even though it took second place during the 1974 Synod of Bishops. To add to our working hypothesis [26] we should here make the point that the more the Church pursues its mission in the world the better it will be able to overcome its internal problems. Introverted lamentations on 'times that are out of joint' lead to no positive result and are not the way to persuade young people to commit themselves to the

[25] *Wo stehen wir?* in *Strukturwandel* 21-48.
[26] See above ch. 1.A. 6, p. 7f.

Church. It is only by opening up new horizons that we invite them to come forward. The present paralysis and crisis will be overcome only by a strongly emphasized and clearly defined 'foreign policy'. The Second Church, as 'Mother Church', must be entrusted afresh with a heavy responsibility: not that of keeping the Third Church under tutelage but of helping it in a spirit of genuine partnership and brotherhood; not of implanting western institutions at any cost but of proclaiming courageously what Christ is doing in the world; not narrowly concentrating on saving 'souls' but struggling for justice in the world and salvation of the whole man. Only such a commitment will make it possible, even partly, to reawaken the interest of those youngsters who at present stand aloof from the Church.

8. The uniqueness of the Christian West will never be sufficiently extolled. For all the various races which came in contact with it during the long migration of peoples it incarnated both the spirit of ancient Greece and Rome and the spirit of the Christian faith. But all this is now a thing of the past. It is fifty years since thoughtful people were frightened by Spengler's *Decline of the West*. The author added a significant note of clarification: 'The title, bearing in mind the decline of the ancient world, means strictly a period in world history embracing several centuries and just starting now'. [27] I do not feel able either to accept or reject a prognosis embracing several centuries. A culture may decline by a natural process of ageing and ebbing away of vitality. Alternatively, it may be cut short violently by the invasion of foreign cultures (as Spengler admits). There is a third possibility: a culture may die through spiritual sickness, a prey to its wild dreams, [28] just as it may, on the contrary, be renewed biologically by an infusion of new blood or re-energised by spiritual and religious factors, since the spirit can always make everything new.

9. It therefore seems to me that the future can best be thought of in terms of the West being relieved of its present responsibilities. In fact our present-day experience is that the

[27] *Untergang des Abendlandes,* I, VII.
[28] H. Sedlmayr, *Verlust der Mitte,* Salzburg, 1955, pp. 232-236.

world's centre of gravity is no longer in Europe [29] and that the Second Church no longer constitutes the focal point of Christianity, although this does not necessarily mean that the West must 'decline'. It is by now an incontrovertible fact that the West has been dismissed from its post as centre of religious cultural unity for the whole of Christianity, a post which derived from the medieval situation and continued to be held despite upheavals affecting the secular history of Europe. However, the West, as a field of religious cultural influence within the Church (no longer medieval), remains in existence. It must and will survive because, together with its now world-wide technical culture, it can implant the Christian heritage in an expanded world, and because it is carrying through with courage the transition from Western Church to world-wide Church. [30] All this is the death and resurrection of the Christian West.

D. *The Third Church*

1. Presumably, New Year's Day 2000 will not be marked by any special natural phenomenon. The Greenwich observatory will not record a shock wave. But that particular New Year will certainly see some very special celebrations. Champagne corks will pop in greater numbers than usual; the speeches and messages will be longer and more carefully prepared than on other New Year's Days. Certainly, in the years after 2000, experience will have left indelible marks in the consciousness of mankind. Twentieth-century man was different from the man of the previous century. Third millennary man will differ from man in the second (of this type, we are the epigones). A favourite exercise for futurologists consists in picturing mankind, technology, economics, world politics and even the Church in 2000, since by then movements now well under way may have run their course. [31]

---

[29] See below ch. 4. B., p. 80ff.
[30] Rahner in LThK 1, 18-21; id. *Europe the Church for others?* in *International Review of Missions,* Jan. 1973.
[31] Besides the works of Jungk, Greiwe, Resch, Herburger, Kahn, cf. A. Greeley, *Religion in 2000,* London, 1971; V. Milani, *Tra 28 anni . . . il 2000.*

2. There is one among these finishes which it is easy to anticipate on the basis of present trends. We presuppose, of course, that in the meantime there is no unforeseen world catastrophe and no extraordinary change in man's religious attitude (he is, after all, a free agent). It is this: we are in the middle of a process of change as a result of which the Church, at home in the western world for almost 2000 years will, in a short time, have shifted its centre of gravity into the Third World, where its adherents will be much more numerous. The situation can be expressed in figures as follows:[32]

	1900	1965	2000
Millions of Christians in western developed countries (Europe, N. America)	392	637	796
Millions of Christians in southern countries (Asia, Africa, Oceania, S. America	67	370	1118

The distribution in percentages of Christians is as follows:

	1900	1965	2000
First and Second Church	85%	63%	42%
Third Church	15%	37%	58%

The forecast is easy to substantiate, for our generation certainly is experiencing a migration of the Church into the southern hemisphere.

The shift is even more marked in the particular case of the Catholic Church:[33]

Catholics (in millions)

1960	N. America	Europe	Africa	S. America	Asia	Oceania
	47	250	23	192	33	3
	51.5%		48.5%			
2000	80	300	175	592	80	7
	30%		70%			

[32] D.A. Barrett, *AD 2000: 350 million Christians in Africa* in IRM 1970, 39-54; cf. also *L'explosion démographique et l'avenir de l'Eglise* in *Pro Mundi Vita, Centrum informationis,* Brussels, 1970/40.

[33] Since Barrett calculates the number of Catholics in 2000 only for Africa, and since other specialists in Church statistics could give

The preponderance of Catholics in the southern hemisphere appears clearly in the following diagram:

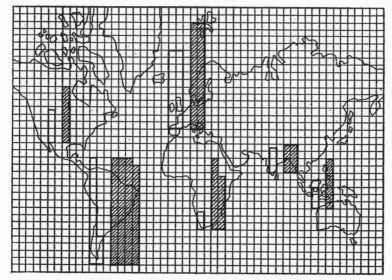

Catholics by continents in 1960 *and in* 2000
(Key: ☐ = 10 m. 1960 ▨ = 10 m. 2000)

3. The causes of this shift in population are easy to discern: the western and oriental Churches are static, registering only a slight increase in population and no new conversions, while they do experience losses. (D.B. Barrett, who made these calculations, has taken account of numbers leaving the Churches. Hence, he calculates that in Europe in 1965 87% of the whole population was Christian, against 77% in 2000; in Russia, he counted 70% of the population Christian in 1900 against 26% both in 1965 and in 2000). The Third Church, on the other hand, is flourishing — and doing so in countries where the demographic explosion is massive (especially in Latin America) and in countries where the number of newly baptized is greater (particularly in Africa). The figures are worth inspecting in greater detail.

me no other data, I have made approximate calculations myself on the basis of *Bilan du Monde,* I, 31 and *U.N. Statistical Yearbook,* 1972, 10.

4. The demographic explosition in Latin America results in the following population figures:

1930	108 millions
1965	243 millions
2000	638 millions

The unique situation of this continent is revealed by the contrast with the others. Between 1930 and 1965, the world population increased by 58.69%. This is broken down as follows: Europe about 25.07%, Asia 62.94%, Africa 89.02% and Latin America 125.00%. Latin America has easily the highest level of demographic increase in the whole world.

5. In Africa the population increase, together with adult baptisms, produces the following table (in millions):

	1900	1930	1950	1970	2000
Catholics	1	6	14	45	175
Protestants	1	4	9	29	110
Orthodox, Copts	2	5	8	14	32
African independent	0	1	3	9	34
Total	4	16	34	97	351

6. This migration of the Church towards the southern hemisphere is, then, an indisputable fact, an important event in Church history and, at the same time (this the most important consideration), an *outstanding opportunity*. Only meanness on the part of western Christians could tempt them to complain of losing prestige to the Third Church. In making this gravitational shift southwards the Church is turning towards the 'peoples of antiquity', realizing in the process that world history did not begin in Europe, that Latin America, Africa and Asia are more ancient and much more interesting in a way (from the point of view of the history of culture and the origins of man) than the West.

The Church is gravitating towards 'young peoples' which impress visitors by the high proportion of youth in their populations. While western countries are preoccupied with the problems of old age (including that of the advancing years of so many of the clergy), we find that 43% of the population in Asia and S. America and 44% in Africa are under 15 years of age. Two thirds of the population of the three continents are under 25.[34] The young Churches of the south are Churches of youth.

The Church is gravitating towards 'dynamic peoples' in the spring-time of their new (modern) life, remarkable for their initiative, optimism and freshness on the world scene.

Finally, and most important, the Church is gravitating towards the poorer peoples. And there she finds the opportunity not only to become in a real sense the 'Church of the poor'[35] but also to have some experience of the goodness, humanity, simplicity and integrity of poor people. Perhaps, through this shift, the Church will be able to speak like Mother Teresa when she received the Pandit Nehru Peace Prize in 1972 from the president of India: 'The greatest gift I have received is the way I have been enriched by knowing and appreciating the poor. They are marvellous people.' What an opportunity for the Church! In any case, the Third Church is the Church of the future as well as the future of the Church!

7. Whereas the First and Second Churches have lived their separate lives rather on parallel lines, for reasons which are understandable although unfortunate, there have always been close vital links between the Second and Third Churches. This solidarity, the maternal relation of the Second Church towards the Third, must not be suddenly denied and cut short; it must be established on a new footing.[36] The Third Church must not remain a kindergarten for mother Church nor a poor house for the exercise of her charity. If in profane matters we are realizing more clearly the interdependence of all in the world, this is equally true of the Churches. They need one another: the Third needs the Second for support and the Second needs the Third for renewal. In profane matters, the great tasks facing the world are ceasing to revolve on an east-west axis and are beginning to relate to a north-south axis:

[34] World Bank, *Trends,* Table 1.4; United Nations, 1970, Report X.
[35] See below ch. 5.B.3.d., p. 120-122.
[36] See below ch. 13.B., p. 273-281.

political rivalry between the two super-powers is beginning to give place to common economic aid from the rich world to the poor. A similar shift of attention is to be observed in the Churches. The Second Church will no longer find her true purpose in life primarily in herself but rather in setting up the conditions necessary for the life of the Third Church, enabling the latter to be Church in the full sense, that is, a sign of hope and salvation for the Third World in a hemisphere full of poverty and sickness, of non-Christian religions and seekers for truth.

Here I would make a forecast, more in the form of a question than of an assertion. In the course of the third millennium — who knows? — a Church historian may compare the eastern Church to the morning star, silent, glittering, ever full of hope, the western Church to the moon which, after a night almost as luminous as the day, is now growing dim and the Third Church to the sun, newly risen on the horizon, ruling the day.

My reflections have been confirmed by two events in 1974: the Synod of Bishops, a triumph for the bishops of the Third World to the surprise of all, and the UN General Assembly at which the new states, by their majority, are increasingly imposing their will, so that men say, 'The Third World is on the point of becoming the First'.

Chapter 2

HISTORICAL PRELUDE

A. *The experience of freedom*

1. The history of the world began with the emergence of man as a living being who strives consciously and freely to shape his own destiny. But world history, as a special subject and scholarly study, dates from a much more recent period. In fact, what was first called 'world history' was simply the story of Europe and European conquests in the other continents. So much so that young Indians and Africans had to imbibe English or French history in school and regurgitate it in examinations. In former millennia, when each culture lived in isolation within its own boundaries and considered itself the centre of the world, things could hardly have been any different. But for this point of view to be cultivated still, after the Age of Discovery and after Europe has, for the first time in history, brought all countries and all men to the knowledge that mankind constitutes one single society, betrays a narrowing of horizon nowadays quite inexcusable. The humiliation of the second world war, the subsequent decolonization and finally the realization that war in Korea, Cuba or Vietnam threatens a catastrophe of world proportions, so that in the second half of the twentieth century the fate of everyone is bound up together — all this was needed before men could be convinced that 'there exists a world history forming a united complex of events and that the history of each region . . . unfolds within the horizons of world history'. [1] World

---

[1] *Saeculum Weltgeschichte*, I-IV, Freiburg im B., 1965-71, pp. viif. How seriously 'world history' is taken here appears already in the first volume, which treats in detail of the primary centres of high culture, Mesopotamia, the Nile valley, the Indus valley, the valley of the Yellow River, the high cultures of Polynesia and ancient America (237-448) and only then comes to mention the countries at the east and west ends of the Mediterranean. Similarly: F. Valjavec (ed.), *Historia Mundi*, I-X, Bern, 1952-61.

25

history worthy of the name — eschewing the 'Europocentric' outlook — can now at last be written.

The Church cannot claim to have been a shining exception in this matter. On the contrary, she has shown even worse self-centredness. In the first millenium, Church records dealt with the whole Church and with its efforts at missionary expansion which brought about the formation of the western Church. Then, from the time of the schism of 1054, the eastern Church was left out of account; later the Protestant Churches of the Reformation were deliberately ignored and the splendid history of the 'foreign' missions was left to specialists in that field. The remainder was chosen, presented and interpreted in strongly triumphalist fashion.

2. *Decolonization* took place in two periods each lasting about twenty years: Latin America, 1810 to 1830, under two great fighters for liberty, San Martin and Bolivar, and Asia and Africa, 1945 to 1965 (the latter is our particular concern here). Although the pre-conditions and the progress of liberation varied from place to place (we do not need to describe them in detail) all showed surprising features. In India, for instance, the foundations were laid in the previous century: the Indian National Congress was founded in 1885, when struggle was already in the air, as an instrument of agitation within the scope of the constitution. But in spite of strikes, boycotts and demonstrations occurring for decades, England was not prepared to negotiate freedom in India. Again in 1942 there were revolts, with 940 deaths and 60,000 arrests. It was only in 1947 that India and Pakistan gained their freedom, but then it happened very rapidly. [2]

On the other hand, Tanganyika, the best behaved child within the family of British peoples, only began to think of national freedom in 1954 when Julius Nyerere founded the Tanganyika National Union. The following year he presented the British government, through the UN, with a request for the independence of his country, to be made effective in the course of twenty years. But things were moving so fast that Tanganyika gained internal freedom in 1960 and full autonomy

[2] M. Edwardes, *A history of India,* London, 1967.

in 1961. In 1956, a group of Congolese asked for freedom for the Congo in a similar manifesto, to be made effective in thirty years.

Finally, General De Gaulle was preparing the sort of surprise of which he alone was capable. Drawing a lesson from the French experience at Dien Bien Phu in 1954, he made a journey through Africa in 1958 and, anticipating all demands, offered freedom to all French colonies. 1960 goes down in history as the 'year of Africa', since in the course of it seventeen new states were born in the ancient 'dark continent'. [3]

3. Thus only in these two post-war decades has the world really become the home of free peoples. In 1775, two thirds of the world population lived under colonial domination; in 1945, the population of the colonies still represented 45% of mankind. But by 1970 the percentage had dropped to 3%. The organizers of the United Nations had never imagined such a rapid development. In 1945, 51 states assembled as foundation members of the UN and the headquarters then in construction was planned 'with foresight' for 70 states. But on the twentieth anniversary of the foundation the number of member states had risen to 114; with 6 exceptions the 63 new members came from the Africa-Asia block. By 1972, the total had reached 136. [4] The face of the world really has been changed. Between 1945 and 1965 there has been a complete change of colours on the political map of the world.

4. This new world is indisputable fact. But among those who pass judgement on it, looking back over the events of the last century, there are sharp differences of opinion. Not a few of the white people who have to withdraw claim to know that Africans are immature and absolutely incapable. They foresee a dark future and are sure that 'the African cities, which the white man has planned and constructed and made into decent places for men to inhabit, will in time be swallowed up again by the jungle. In some places, the desert will return; in others, the primitive forest will overwhelm the sky-scrapers. In the

[3] Cf. Bühlmann, *Afrika gestern, heute, morgen,* Freiburg, 1960, pp. 96-131; P. Gheddo, *Il risveglio dei popoli di colore,* Milan, 1956.
[4] The United Nations, *The next 25 years,* N.Y., 1970, 4.

end, everything will be back where it started. Colonial administration will have come and gone and, with it, political freedom because Africans do not know what to do with it. . . '[5]

The opposing point of view puts all the blame on white people and keeps alive the memory of atrocities. There is no denying that these occurred, during the earlier periods especially. Even as balanced a historian as J. Höffner says of America under Spanish rule: 'The new world suffered enslavement and extermination so cruel as to make one's blood run cold'.[6] The critic A. Rüstow is of the same opinion: 'This long chapter is the cruellest and bloodiest in the annals of history before 1933'; he adds that the accounts of other colonies would be no less shameful for us Europeans.[7] With regard to Africa, B. Davidson thinks that Leopold's rule in the Congo between 1874 and 1887 was worse than a century of enslavement. He does not find it surprising in the circumstances that Africa has remained backward; the wonder is that it has survived. His comment on the colonialists' judgements is: 'The less intelligent a white man, the more stupid the black man seems to him'.[8] With regard to Asia, it will suffice to mention the humiliation inflicted on free China by western powers with their Unequal Treaties.[9]

As always happens, a page has been turned in our history, and the once honourable expression 'colonization' by which western powers described their overseas exploits has been in practice completely replaced by 'colonialism'. There are two sides to the coin in any historical analysis of European hegemony during the past centuries.

5. Meanwhile, students of the Third World looking for new emphases in the writing of history are bringing to light the

[5] L. Barcata, *Schreie aus dem Dschungel. Afrika — Aufstieg oder Untergang,* Stuttgart, 1961, p. 9. The film 'Addio Africa' is on the same theme.
[6] *Christentum und Menschenwürde. Das Anliegen der spanischen Kolonialethik,* Trier, 1947, p. 11.
[7] *Ortsbestimmung, der Gegenwart,* Erlenbach, 1950-2, II, p. 313. On all this see Bühlmann, *Die Rechte der Person under der Nation und ihr Bedeutung für die Mission,* in NZM 1957, pp. 192-207, 241-255.
[8] *Erwachendes Afrika,* Zürich, 1957, pp. 72, 92, 100, 106.
[9] Cf. below ch. 4.A.6, p. 70f.

precolonial periods. Africa, as well as America and Asia, has a cultural history — even though as little as thirty years ago serious writers produced books such as *'Savages of Africa'*. [10] For example, the royal dynasty of Uganda can be traced back to the 15th century and perhaps as far as the 13th; there was a kingdom in Benin from the 12th century, with an artistic tradition which survives to the present day; the Ghana kingdom in the Sudan reached its apogee towards the middle of the 9th century with a court life of much pageantry, an army of 20,000 men and territory extending for 2000 kilometres. [11]

K.M. Pannikkar, the first Asian to study the European presence in his continent, caused a stir by the way he distinguished light and shade in European influence. Western masters (and missionaries) have been forced to recognize that many things were not as they believed. [12] History faculties in Third World universities are well equipped. History reinforces national awareness, gives it a serious purpose and helps the new people find its way through the uncertainties of the modern world. The same can be said of young Churches and their histories.

6. The young nations have not only celebrated their independence; they have also acquired a new awareness of themselves. At first they were no more than Europe's shadow and were necessarily involved in the wars and crises of that continent. Now they are masters of their own destiny. They were once treated as objects, as manoeuvring space in which others made history; now they emphasise the fact that they are subjects of their own history. First they were objects of discovery but now they discover themselves, and the self-discovery is far more important and more exciting. Formerly, they were treated as merchandise, as means to an end; now they act as persons and pursue their own ends. They used to suffer estrangement and alienation, feeling the gap between what they were and what they wanted to be (like white people); they have now discovered or re-discovered an identity of their own.

[10] M. Briault, *Les sauvages de l'Afrique,* Bibl. Scientifique, Paris, 1943.
[11] *D. Westermann Geschichte Afrikas und Staatenbildungen südlich der Sahara,* Cologne, 1952.
[12] *Asia and western dominance,* London, 1953.

True world history, then, began only after the pageant of past millennia had been performed in the national costumes of local history, and after the last few centuries had been presented in the trappings of a spurious world history. Only later shall we know for sure whether the pageant can now proceed as genuine world history. The producer does not give us a preview of the script; if he did, the performance would lose much of its interest.

7. In the meantime, young peoples try to learn and act out their new roles. They want to make their presence felt at home and abroad. They do all they can to strengthen national awareness, and do so with much more panache than our dispirited patriots. In schools, the flag is run up each morning to the strains of the national anthem, which is also played at the end of every performance in the local cinema, etc. Countries and cities either give themselves new names or restore ancient names (Gold Coast becomes Ghana; Sudan — Mali; Ceylon — Sri Lanka; Léopoldville — Kinshasa; Batavia — Djakarta, etc.) so as decisively to wipe out traces of the colonial past. National feasts, ministerial visits, prestige buildings and slogans are all aimed at bolstering self-esteem and imbuing the people with a fresh awareness and hope for the future.

8. We can also bear in mind, as a corollary, that these nations will make their contribution to the world community. With their politics of non-alignment, they have already played no small part in reducing confrontation in the cold war and in preparing China's entry into the United Nations. Their literature throws light on some fundamental aspects of human existence: the mystique of poverty and commitment to work for others (S. America), the tradition and experience of 'négritude' (Africa), the pre-eminence of the spiritual (Asia). H. Günther says: 'The poetry of 'négritude' is among the most moving and the most genial of this century. The black renaissance is probably the decisive spiritual event of the 20th century'. [13] By their religious spirit, they are capable of making the modern world in all its

[13] *Die Botschaft Afrikas* in *Welt und Wort. Literatur-Monatszeitschrift*, Tübingen, 1959, p. 103.

complexity more religious. By their humanity and spontaneity, they can free western man from his obsession with work, money and career — as a group of Ivory Coast dancers said: 'White people have shut themselves up in hothouses: we shall take them by the hand with a smile, lead them out and restore them to the human community'.

B. *What is freedom?*

1. During the course of their desperate struggle for independence, the imagination of many Africans and Asians ran riot: 'When the Whites have gone, they will not be able to exploit the country any more. They will not be able to make us pay taxes. Then we shall divide the riches of the country among ourselves. We shall seize all the positions of power and we shall become rich like them. . . . ' But things did not turn out quite like that. After the euphoria of the celebrations, coming back to reality was unpleasant. [14] In many places, the first effect of independence was the closure of factories and businesses belonging to whites and consequently higher unemployment. Then the government found that it had to increase taxes and the country began to know the dictatorial ways of petty officials suddenly become somebodies. The legacy which the young politicians had to take up with their independence proved to be burdensome. They had to begin almost from scratch to make long term plans, to build up trustworthy cadres and to establish monetary liquidity. They had gone to meet freedom with élan and enthusiasm, but on the day after independence they saw their real problems at once beginning to show up. The next chapter is concerned with economic problems; here we restrict ourselves to political questions.

2. All forces are united during the struggle for independence. But when the common enemy has decamped and pulled out, all the old tribal, cultural and religious conflicts flare up again. The struggle to maintain internal unity constitutes one of the first tests for the new regime. Consider the problems

[14] W. Holzer, *26 mal Afrika,* München, 1968, 7-16.

facing Indonesia with 3000 islands extending over 50 degrees of latitude (5550 km) or India with its ancient kingdoms, its many different languages (every banknote is printed in fourteen languages and these are only the more important ones) and 580 million inhabitants, or finally Zaire, as large as India but with only 22 million inhabitants belonging to 200 different tribes: what must these countries do to become cultural and administrative unities? This problem makes it understandable, even if not excusable, that the struggle between Hindus and Moslems in India should have caused an enormous number of deaths and 14 million refugees. It also explains the war in Ruanda in 1964 between the Watutsi and the Bahutu which cost 40,000 lives, and the war in Burundi in 1972 in which over 100,000 died (between 2.5 and 5% of the population). In Bangla Desh, after the victory, the Biharis were massacred *en masse* even though the number of victims was concealed for diplomatic reasons. The list could be extended. We no longer speak of recent events in the Congo and in Biafra, but they could be repeated anywhere in the world tomorrow.

Tribalism, putting sectional interests before loyalty to the state, is gradually quelling the surge of nationalism. According to Ali A. Mazrui, Africans are today less conscious of being citizens of a nation than they were on the day of independence. Political cynicism is spreading because of the lack of economic progress and administrative corruption. Everyone seems to be going back to his corner and Africa seems well on the way to being 'retribalized'. [15]

This is far from Nkrumah's great dream of the 'United States of Africa'. Instead, we observe disruptive jealousy between states, micro-nationalism and a Balkanization of Africa, even though the OAU (Organization for African Unity) has existed for ten years. This body often tries to make up for its internal difficulties by the aggressive tone of its external policy. [16]

Many of the inter-state conflicts (between 1956 and 1967

[15] *Current socio-political trends* in F.S. Arkhurst (ed.), *Africa in the Seventies and Eighties,* N.Y., 1970, pp. 49-53; Traber M., *Das revolutionäre Afrika.* Freiburg in U., 1972, p. 55.
[16] Doundoun Thiam, *Die Aussenpolitik der afrikanischen Staaten,* Düsseldorf, 1966, pp. 12-41.

there were 32 border disputes) can be traced to the colonial period. They were caused by the arbitrary division of related tribes by frontiers drawn by white men at the Congress of Berlin in 1885 and in other treaties. Kilimanjaro, for example, was Queen Victoria's birthday present for her nephew, Emperor William. That is how Africa was treated.

3. The young nations have gone in for excessive military armament to defend themselves against tribalism and neighbouring states. If only the eastern and western powers, while incapable of undertaking substantial disarmament among themselves, would at least refrain from arming the Third World! Instead, they compete in the armament business. Business is business and politics is politics! The international arms trade is one of the saddest features of the post-war period. The international peace commission in Stockholm has published the following figures: arms exported to the Third World cost more than 6 billion DM. While the average national income in these countries increased by 2% during the second half of the sixties, expenditure on arms increased during the same period by 7%. Between 1945 and 1969, 55 wars broke out, big and small, 53 of them in the Third World. [17]

4. The armies have become not merely a power group but, like the trade unions and even more than these, a factor in upheavals. The whole Third World seethes like a volcano. Instability has become a permanent characteristic. Latin America (the most volcanic area!) comes first with 62 regimes overthrown between 1945 and 1970. Only seven out of the 24 states have not experienced a *coup d'état*. Next Africa, with 43 coups (some unsuccessful) in 24 countries between 1950 and 1972. [18] Asia has been more fortunate; but not a few national heroes and founders, instead of finishing in the nation's pantheon, have been exiled or assassinated. [19]

It may well be asked whether these coups, which are going

[17] HK 1972, pp. 119-122.
[18] The list is in Traber, *op. cit.* (n. 15), pp. 144-155.
[19] T. Filesi, *Dieci anni di indipendenza. L'Africa sacrifica i 'Padri della Patria'*, in *Nigrizia*, Verona, 1970, n. 3, 4-8.

off as though in a chain reaction throughout the two continents, are a defensive reaction of the forces of order against corruption and communism or, alternatively, struggle for power within new ruling classes. Or could they be natural phenomena according to the laws of psychological development, due like juvenile schizophrenia to premature overburdening? In this case, what would be the prescribed treatment for individuals and for communities?

5. Freedom, which was received with glad Hosannahs a few years ago, in some places now seems a disastrous caricature. The constitutions of the new states were conceived in large measure on the model of the western democracies. But, in countries formerly ruled by chiefs, sultans and maharajahs, none of the ripe fruits of a sound democratic system can be culled from a newly-planted tree of freedom. Here and there, military heads of government or presidents have assumed as their right a royal or even despotic status. Or else one political party dominates the country, spreading an atmosphere of fear and oppression, so that no one dares to speak or write against it or against the government. In many countries (not only in the Communist ones) much is still very far from what is meant by freedom in England or the United States.

6. On this diagnosis the prospect is not rosy. But who are we to set ourselves up as judges? They might well retort, 'Physician, cure thyself' (Lk 4 : 23) or, 'He who is without sin among you, let him cast the first stone' (Jn 8 : 7). W. Holzer observes: 'Compared with our own wars and revolutions, the revolutionary upheavals of Africa in the last decade have cost less in blood and sufferings, even taking the Congo and Nigeria into account'. [20] Since the pace of everything is faster nowadays (and the communications media are so efficient in bringing events to the notice of all), we probably need to compress a century of our history into a decade and compare this with the last ten years in Africa. We are not likely to get the prize for good behaviour. If we refrain from concentrating on the morbid symptoms (as any diagnosis of course does) we can confidently

[20] *26 mal Afrika,* 11.

34

say that these new peoples have made by no means a poor use of the first two decades of independence. History must be allowed time. The political parties and cadres arose almost overnight in most of these countries, but in time they will gain in cohesion and a more genuine and more efficient democracy will develop, [21] even if human history (as we ourselves know by experience) remains a very human business. One thing remains beyond doubt: if it is true that our western statesmen have no easy task, the tasks facing the leaders of the Third World are cruelly hard and we cannot but admire their courage.

C. *The ultimate liberation*

1. The map of the free world still shows black spots. The South African government is inexorably committed to deleting what it considers to be the black spots by compelling groups of blacks living in white residential areas to move into territory assigned them by the laws of apartheid. But this makes what we consider to be the black spots even blacker, for in our eyes the black spots are the shameful politics of certain white governments which, 200 years after the French Revolution and 25 years after the Universal Declaration of Human Rights, seem still not to admit the fundamental principle of liberty, equality and fraternity.

2. Leaving on one side the small relics of colonial empires which still exist, we shall deal here only with the triangle of Southern Africa. This is the most compact block of 'unredeemed' territory and the most tragic. Here Harold Macmillan's 'warm wind of freedom' has been checked by an ice-cold front. [22] Although their historical origins differ these lands are nonetheless united in a common destiny. They are the Union of South Africa, now with Namibia, annexed in 1968-1969 (the former

[21] D.G. Lavroff, *I partiti politici nell'Africa nera*, Milan, 1971.
[22] Cf. F. Ansprenger, *Der Schwarz-weiss-Konflikt in Afrika*, München-Mainz, 1971; *Dossier sur les colonies portugaises*, Brussels, 1971; Holzer, *op. cit.* (n. 14), 539-627.

UN mandate of S.W. Africa), the two Portuguese overseas territories of Mozambique and Angola, and Rhodesia.

All are alike in one point: they have a white minority dominating a black majority. In South Africa, whites are 18% of the population, in Namibia 16%, in Rhodesia 5%, in Angola 5%, in Mozambique 1.3%. These percentages are continually changing in favour of the blacks, in spite of stepped-up white immigration. If in 1970 South Africa had 3.8 million whites, 2 million coloured, half a million Asians and 14 million blacks, in 1980 the figures will probably be: 4.5 million whites and 20 million blacks.

3. The whites in Southern Africa have no demographic potential; but they certainly have economic potential. Their territories have more natural resources than Canada and the United States together. Economic growth is spectacular and can ride out the sanctions often applied to these countries. So, why this accursed division between the races, and this denial of democratic rights to the black majority? The present situation has deep historical roots, affecting present thinking and emotional attitudes.

In the past white immigrants, particularly the Calvinist Boers, believed themselves to be in the position of the Hebrews in the Old Testament. As a chosen people they had to protect themselves from the pagans. At first, they were disposed to give equal civic rights to baptised Africans. However, towards the end of the 18th century, the distinction between black and white began to replace that between non-Christian and Christian; white racial origin became more important than baptism. It was not until recently, after over half of the African population had become Christian, that arguments based on the mystique of the chosen race ceased to be used. [23] Yet even in 1965, Ian Smith supported his unilateral declaration of independence with the claim to be saving Christian civilization.

4. In South Africa and Rhodesia, the big question is the

[23] O. Niederberger, *Kirche-Mission-Rasse. Die Missionsauffassung der Niederländisch-Reformierten Kirchen von Südafrika,* Schöneck, 1959.

existence of a white population which has no other homeland. The theory and practice of separation of the races pilloried in the writings of black and white authors has accumulated so much hatred that no one believes any more in the possibility of a peaceful solution and there is freer recourse to violence. But excellently equipped police and armed forces will no doubt be able to guarantee the status quo for the next ten years. The white ruling class fears democratization and the principle of universal suffrage. But fear only underpins ideology, strengthens the illusion of white superiority and immunises minds against objective arguments. [24] Outsiders, it is insisted, cannot understand the special situation in South Africa and they waste time on sterile questions of principle. A fair retort would be that only outsiders have the courage and objectivity to see things as they really are and to judge without prejudice. One day I happened to be speaking to a South African lady on the belvedere at Johannesburg and I asked her what she thought about the racial conflict. She replied, 'I see no problem. We live well and so do the blacks. When I was quite new here, five years ago, I thought there were some things wrong. But you soon get used to the situation and you realize that things have to be like this.' You do get used to things, as in a class room you get used to the bad air; only someone coming in from outside notices that it is time to open the windows.

'We are doing a lot for the blacks', they say at every step. But they forget that the blacks are not content with bread and clothes, that they are human beings who wish to decide their own destiny. The proposed Bantu states with internal autonomy are only half a solution. The infertile territories of the black 'homelands' provide neither for agriculture nor for industry. The villages and towns are simply places of residence for the women and children and for the aged. More than 40% of the men who are old enough to work are absent all the time. The white people's economy depends for 70% of its working force on the blacks (and they are cheap labour), but politically these must be kept under. The Franciscan, Cosmas Desmond has thrown light on the situation and on the real state of mind

[24] Thielicke *So sah ich Afrika,* Gütersloh, 1971, pp. 29-45.

among people living in the famous 'homelands'; he observed: 'What I have written will no doubt be condemned. I hope those who read it will share my reaction, one of disgust, fear and shame'. [25]

But the white bulwarks have been shaken. After the coup in Portugual and the subsequent political change in Mozambique, even South Africa and Rhodesia seem to be looking for a way out. Perhaps there is hope.

5. In Mozambique and Angola there was, officially, no racial discrimination (unlike the Anglo-Saxons, the Latin peoples always fraternized in their colonies), but the 'assimilados', blacks who had gained equal rights with the whites on account either of education or of income, were no more than 1% after 500 years of colonization. The two territories, twenty times as extensive as the motherland, have made remarkable progress in the last decade, since international capitalism has given support to many useful projects, the greatest being the two dams at Cabora-Bassa and Cunena intended to produce energy primarily for South Africa. The two territories have been in political ferment for ten years. Portugal spent 40% of her national income and conscripted her young men for four years of military service to maintain 'peace and order', in other words to conduct the last colonial war of the traditional type. This little people, which had once possessed the greatest colonial empire stretching from Brazil to Africa and to the Far East, was not able to accept that that era was finished. While Belgium, France and England withdrew with honour from their colonies, Portugal clung on to its remaining overseas possessions with the madness of despair.

6. In 1965 the president of Tanzania, Julius Nyerere, put forward a constructive plan in a speech in Holland. He said Europe surely had everything to gain from preserving Africa as a peaceful southern flank. But Africa could not live in peace as long as there were colonies. He suggested that Europe ought to put pressure on Portugal, and at the same time offer her economic help, so that she could withdraw without loss from

---

[25] *The discarded people,* Johannesburg, 1971. The book was banned and the author put under house arrest.

her African possessions. He continued: 'We look on the western powers as our allies along this path of peaceful liberation. If this is not to be, which God forbid, then we shall have failed. But in that case we Africans will not be able to allow things to remain as they are. We shall be compelled to free the Portuguese colonies in other than peaceful ways. If that happens, we shall probably get no help from the western powers. If then we were to look elsewhere for help, as we would be compelled to do — I repeat: we would be *compelled* to do — the West would misunderstand us. But we beg the West not to let things go so far. We beg the West to understand us, while there is still time'. [26] The western press derided the president and said that he would have done better to stay at home and think of better things, rather than travel abroad preaching revolution. But, on his way home, he presented his heartfelt appeal for a peaceful solution to President De Gaulle and to the Pope.

Four years later, thirteen African states signed the Declaration of Lusaka, affirming among other things: 'With this manifesto, we declare ourselves convinced beyond a shadow of doubt that all men are equal and have the same right to human dignity and respect, without regard to the colour of their skin, to their race, their religion or their sex. We are convinced that no individual or group has the right to govern another group of healthy adults without their consent. No decree of a Portuguese dictator or law passed by a Portuguese parliament can make Africa part of Europe. . . ' The declaration then indicates facts in southern Africa which constitute violations of these principles and continues: 'As far as the attainment of liberty is concerned, we cannot compromise. We have preferred and still prefer to seek liberty without physical violence. We prefer negotiation to destruction, talking to killing. But as long as peaceful progress is blocked by the attitudes of those actually in power, we have no choice but to give all the support we can to their struggle against their oppressors. . . ' [27]

7. It is impossible to be unaffected by the logic of these

---

[26] J.K. Nyerere, *Freedom and unity,* Dar es Salaam, 1966, pp. 329-331.

[27] Quoted in Ansprenger, *op. cit.* (n. 22), pp. 75-81.

reflections, unless one considers human dignity and the rights of man to be nothing but words. Is this the voice of the one crying in the wilderness? In the meantime the tension was increasing, with the human drama of guerilla wars, refugees and terrorized populations. I visited Tanzania, Rhodesia and South Africa three times — in 1961, 1966 and 1971. Each time I noticed two things. First, the contemptuous way they spoke in the south of blacks and the black states: They were children... You could never trust them... North of the Zambesi, there was nothing but chaos and Communism. (It is of course true that certain heads of state, and certain things that happen, play into the hands of the critics.) There have even been suggestions that a coup in Tanzania would bring peace for twenty years!

Secondly, there is a difference in the bearing of the black peoples north and south. In Tanzania, people are mature and stand before you as genuine partners. In the south, they give an impression of servility, inhibition and psychological under-development, because they have been given no chance so far to be themselves. They lose their reserve only in confidential conversation. Once I managed to discover the true feelings of two of them: at the end of one such conversation I asked if this exchange could be dangerous for them and what, for example, would happen if a white policeman overheard us. They answered: 'We would be in prison tonight.' Then I asked, 'What would happen if blacks came to power?' The reply was, 'We are all of us frustrated and no one can say how we would react.'

The famous writer Alan Paton, then leader of the Liberal opposition, declared in 1958: 'In South Africa, it is too late for a peaceful solution.' President Kaunda once said that whites in S. Africa were in a boat approaching the Niagara Falls.

8. Will things be allowed to go to the limit? The more entrenched one is, the less one is disposed to accept political change. Might is right. It seems Spengler's harsh verdict is being proved right again: 'The world is condemned by history. It has always been on the side of life that is stronger, fuller and more sure of itself... It has always sacrificed truth and justice to power and race. It has condemned to death men and nations

for whom truth was more important than action and justice more essential than power.' [28]

The time could come, and maybe it is approaching, when the mass of black people will suddenly rise and prove more powerful than the thin upper layer of whites who are armed to the teeth. The developing situation in southern Africa could lead to something more than a 'mini-Vietnam'. [29] South Africa (and, until quite recently, Portugal) declared it could not relinquish the bridge-head controlling the south Atlantic and the Indian Ocean: its policy was not the fruit of slogans and ideology but the result of political realism, a response to the threat of oriental powers to the western world. The western powers (in spite of fine words at the UN) shared this view: for economic and strategic reasons, they supported the white regimes and showed that they had not grown out of their colonial mentality. They wanted to keep communism at bay but, through racial separation and social oppression, they were in fact preparing the ground in which communism can best flourish. However, while the western powers were reinforcing their stations, the East did not just stand and stare: Russia is consolidating her position in the Indian Ocean and China has gained a foothold in Tanzania and Zambia. So the position we find ourselves in is crazy: Christians defending the minority and the side of injustice, while communists stand for the majority and for justice. The tragedy has reached its climax. But history teaches that, even if justice does not always prevail, the mass of the people does. The peasants of Vietnam fought for ten years against the strongest army in the world and won. It would indeed be a disaster if things come to a head in southern Africa. Whites would find their worst expectations come true, because they had not come to terms with reality in time.

9. Recent events leave us ground for hope. Governments are feeling pressure from below, from young people who reject the sort of capitalism their elders have left them, who abhor

---

[28] *Untergang des Abendlandes,* II, 635.
[29] A. Jaffe in *Newsweek,* Nov. 1972: *Africa's mini-Vietnam, Mozambique;* R. Gibson *I movimenti di liberazione africana,* Milan, 1974.

white supremacy and who live spontaneously in brotherhood with all men. [30]

Even black freedom fighters, called 'terrorists' and 'Communists' by whites, far from seeking vengeance have shown an astonishing will for peaceful collaboration. If the negotiations in progress succeed in finding a political solution and are not driven on the rocks by white intransigeance, then this 'hopeless case' could turn out to be the glory of the black race. It would go down in history as a model of generosity: *realpolitik* would become 'realistic policy'.

D. *Mission in the free nations*

1. For the Church's mission, it is a new experience to be facing the new nations. With a few exceptions, missionary activity has gone hand in hand with colonization for almost two millennia. No matter how we interpret the underlying relation between the two orders, it is self-evident that political expansion and the Church's expansion in the world have covered the same ground, geographically and chronologically. The cradle of Christianity was in Palestine, a Roman colony. In the first centuries the new religion spread along the roads of the Roman empire. Later it spread throughout the colonial realms of Spain and Portugal. The great century of Christian expansion (1815-1914), of which K.S. Latourette wrote enthusiastically that there was nothing comparable in the whole of history, [31] developed almost exclusively within the ambit of English, French, Belgian and German colonies and protectorates.

2. To establish to what extent and in which particular cases this co-existence amounted to union calls for much thorough research and carefully nuanced judgements. We can reject as exaggerated such formulations as: the missions were 'precursor and running dog of imperialism' [32] or 'right from Vasco da Gama

[30] The works quoted in n. 22 were published to alert public opinion. Ansprenger's report was published by the scientific commission of the Catholic working party on development and peace.

[31] Latourette, IV-VI: *The great century.*

[32] T. Ohm, *Asiens Nein und Ja zum westlichen Christentum,* München, 1960, p. 186.

42

to the end of the second World War, the missions were disfigured by their union with aggressive pretensions to dominion'. [33] But the missions cannot be completely cleared of the charges. Certainly, we now know that many Bulls sent by Popes in the 15th and 16th centuries to the Portuguese and Spanish monarchs sought to give a gentler, more humane character to colonial ventures; nonetheless Alexander VI, in *Inter cetera*, 1493, 'with the authority Almighty God has granted us' did entrust the new worlds to the two kings and their successors 'for all time' so that they might 'subjugate the barbarian peoples and bring them to the faith'. [34] From then until the last colonial undertaking, the conquest of Abyssinia in 1935-36, the Church never raised a formal protest against colonisation. In the meantime, *Propaganda Fide* has repeatedly and clearly warned against mixing missionary activity with politics and has advised missionaries to be on their guard against any kind of nationalism. [35] But it is precisely such warnings that reveal that everything has not been not as it should. There are places other than China — the extreme example — where missionaries, children of their time, entertained European prejudices, nationalism and colonial attitudes which we now condemn. So, 2000 years of evangelization within the framework of colonialism have left on the missions a mark which today meets with condemnation. Whatever the intention of the messengers of the faith, missions looked like the other face of colonialism to the native peoples. Soldiers who conquered the territory, merchants who exploited it, missionaries baptizing and founding schools — all came from the same country, had the same colour skin, spoke the same language and exchanged hospitality. No one could seriously doubt that they were all part and parcel of the same commodity.

---

[33] K.M. Pannikkar, *Asien und die Herrschaft des Westens*, Zürich, 1955, p. 407.

[34] F. Filesi, *Esordi del colonialismo e azione della Chiesa*, Como, 1966, pp. 54, 61, 138, 154 etc.

[35] J. Beckmann, *La congrégation de la Propagation de la Foi face à la politique internationale* in NZM 1963, pp. 241-271. Id. *Der religiöse Charakter von Mission und Missionar nach den Bestimmung der Propaganda-Kongregation* in KMJ 1946, pp. 13-23.

3. Only when the colonial era was over, and the white owners abandoned the country while the missionaries remained, did many people realize that the true function of the latter is independent of colonialism. Besides, the Church had anticipated decolonization. Not only had the schools awakened minds (especially in Africa) and given rise to aspirations for political independence, not only did the first nationalists arise within the ranks of the Christians (especially of the Protestants [36]), not only has the consecration of native bishops anticipated independence, but, beginning in the 50's, bishops in many African countries frequently expressed their views on the problem. The declaration which made the strongest impression was that issued in December 1953 by the bishops of Madagascar. Six years previously the French army there had stamped out, with much bloodshed, an attempt at independence (with an estimated 20,000 dead). Now, the bishops declared that political freedom forms part of the fundamental rights of man and that the Church recognizes the right of self-government as a natural right. The French colonialist press branded the declaration as demagogic and the high commissioner, M. Bargues, said in his New Year message: 'It is deplorable that men who are the spiritual guides of the people should depart from the teaching of Scripture and, in an official declaration, encourage moves aimed at destroying the established order and cutting off an integral part of the Republic. It is to be hoped that this appeal will remain unheard'. [37]

In 1955, when no African state had yet received independence, Pius XII turned his attention to the problem of colonialism and spoke of 'preventative peace making'; he encouraged western powers not to indulge in laments for the past but to solve the problem constructively. In particular, he invited them

[36] Corresponding to their different conceptions of the Church, Catholics aimed especially at training a native clergy, while the Protestants set out to train laymen for responsible tasks in politics, business and the mass media. Cf. E.A. Ayandale, *The missionary impact on modern Africa,* London, 1966, XVIII, 173ff; W.E. Philipp, *The influence of Christian missions on the rise of nationalism in Africa,* in IRM 1968, pp. 229-232.

[37] F. Méjan, *Le Vatican contre la France d'Outre-Mer,* Paris, 1957.

so to act that 'just and progressive political freedom is not denied to these peoples and no obstacles put in its way'. [38]

4. Since then our view of things has become clearer. We still have to free ourselves of certain left-overs from that time and we must stop trying to mythologize colonialism by ascribing it to Providence, like the Pax Romana. From the modern point of view (whatever the understanding of men of other times) colonialism stands condemned even though some of its consequences were good — thanks very largely to the missions. There is nothing objectionable about commercial and cultural contacts but these should not have taken place in the way they did, with the subjugation of whole peoples and the gratuitous exploitation of their raw materials. Along with the most rabid nationalist, Christians should not hesitate to condemn colonialism, so long as and so far as such condemnation can be constructive.

5. As a result of decolonization, it is not only the young states that have started on the way of their new future but also, hand in hand with them, the young churches. Formerly they were 'missions', Churches of the second class, daughter Churches, immature children, apostolic vicariates and not yet autonomous dioceses. Now they have become mature Churches with corresponding rights, responsible for themselves, open to all the opportunities and risks which an adult individual has to face in life. The end of colonialism, like the French revolution and the loss of the Papal States, is an external event which was necessary to set the Church free to develop its true and proper mission. During his journey to Uganda in 1967, Paul VI bore witness to the new situation of the Church in Africa (and in Asia): 'We desire nothing else but to promote in you what you already are: Christians and Africans. We wish our presence among you to be a sign of our recognition of your maturity... You Africans are by this time your own missionaries. The Church of Christ is truly planted in this blessed land'. [39]

6. Decolonization has improved the image of the Church. But that does not mean everything has been put right. The

[38] AAS 1956, p. 39f.   [39] OR 2.8.1969.

Church has to endure the crisis of growth of the world in which it lives. Most of the new states have declared for separation of Church and state — undoubtedly the best formula for countries with a Christian minority. The alternative is for the state to be either Catholic (in Spain, for example, until a short time ago), or Protestant (as it still the case in N. Ireland), or Moslem (as in the Sudan until 1964), or even communist, where there is a will to destroy religion, which shows the absurdity of the formula. [40] Moslem states, which have Islam as state religion, recognize freedom of religion and worship (as postulated by the rights of man) and equality without any distinction based on religion. [41] Of course, practice does not everywhere correspond to theory. Then it may be permissible or of obligation to appeal to the magistrates, as Paul did (Acts 25 : 11f) and as the Catholic Union of India did not long ago, after several neophytes and catechists had fallen foul of laws which several states had passed against conversion; the high court at Orissa declared these laws unconstitutional and quashed the proceedings against the accused.

7. Missionaries (and all white people who remain) are called to undergo a deep psychological transformation. Formerly, they left Europe only to find Europe everywhere. They remained in the protective shade of the frontier posts of European domination, shared the privileges of white people and enjoyed precedence in postal services, means of transport, etc. These advantages have gone. In some countries the tables are even turned: the new holders of power impress on white people that 'We are the masters now', often refuse to take them seriously and try little by little to get them out of the way.

In older times, the missions were characterized by an exotic sense of distance; now the once interminable sea journeys have

---

[40] President Nyerere puts these considerations forward and then adds: 'Religion does not concern the state as such; but the state has to guarantee its citizens, as religious beings and religious communities, full freedom to practice their religion': *Freedom and Socialism*, Dar es Salaam, 1968, 12-19.

[41] *Les Constitutions des Etats africains d'expression française*, Paris, 1961. J. Funk, *Die Religion in den Verfassungen der Erde*, Steyl, 1960. T. Filesi, *Islam e libertà di culto nelle constituzioni dei paesi dell'Africa del Nord*, in OR 12.9.1972; OR 30.7.1972.

been replaced by a few hours in an aeroplane and the primitive life of the mission territories has been gradually brought up to European standards. But psychological distance and absence from home are more oppressive than harsh living conditions. Those who cannot accept this with courage and understanding would do better to leave the country rather than go on living in it with hidden resentment and risking discredit to the Church.

8. Sometimes governments anticipate the decision to leave: they declare individuals or groups *persona non grata,* with all the consequences that follow. Expulsions of missionaries have reached considerable proportions. Expulsion can take different forms: the courteous invitation to leave, the air passage together with the request to leave the country within 24 hours, the non-renewal of a residence permit, endless delays in granting entry visas for new missionaries. But it can also take more forthright forms as in China, N. Korea, N. Vietnam, Burma, Guinea, etc., where new 'missionary deserts' have been created, new 'blank spaces' on the Church's missionary map. In 170 ecclesiastical divisions out of 830 there is now no missionary activity. Often these measures are directed not against missionaries as such but against all foreigners, from whose influence there is a desire to be freed. Motives can vary widely, from a justifiable desire for independence to a certain sensitiveness (if only because strangers are apt to take note of internal difficulties) and even to rabid xenophobia. In the coming years, it is quite likely that these states of mind will become more radical and we shall be taken by surprise with more expulsions of missionaries. At one time only Communist countries indulged in this kind of action; highly religious (non-Christian) states followed suit, and then states gripped by nationalism; now, even 'Christian' governments (of the right-wing variety) do not hesitate to expel missionaries who are not convinced adherents of their kind of Christianity.

9. No country, then, carries any guarantees for the future. It is therefore wise to be as adaptable as possible and to make timely provision so that, if ever missionaries are expelled, the Church can continue to exist. We hear of 'secret plans' in some places. But they are not taken seriously and eyes are opened

only when the bomb explodes. Looking back, a missionary expelled from Guinea has drawn some conclusions. Most of his proposals are put forward in this book. Here is a preliminary summary:

— The governments of the young nations are jealous of their authority. They want to be kept informed of all our activity. We should tell them of our journeys, seek permission for our assemblies and discuss our plans with them.

— We should avoid all triumphalism in connection with our 'good schools', our hospitals and big mission stations. Anything with the appearance of a 'state within the state' excites jealousy. In Guinea, we missionaries passed for a reactionary class of rich men. We need to integrate our works with the state so as to preserve what is essential.

— The most urgent thing to do is this: we must pass on responsibility to native priests and lay-people, leaving the initiative to them even if that has repercussions. It is they who must save the Church in the future. We must just try to help them as long as possible.

— In such circumstances, silence is golden. We should not criticize what is going on. Many things will upset us but it is better to say nothing. Criticism from foreigners is unacceptable.

— We must avoid all illegal financial transactions. We must stop having things sent to us from Europe. We must content ourselves with the living standards of the country.

10. The local native Church, in its pilgrimage after the euphoria of liberation, will experience the disenchantment of coming back to reality, just like the young states. It will attain its new identity through a historical process which is often quite enigmatic. There will be stormy periods and spells of calm; there will certainly be a place for suffering and persecution which, according to the gospel and the story of Christianity, are necessary means of purification.

During the months in which this book was being put together, Zaire was in the news with its conflict between Church and state. The Cardinal and Nuncio were being defamed, the bishops branded as counter-revolutionaries, the independent

48

newspapers and periodicals (mostly Catholic) suppressed, Christian names at baptism prohibited. At last, the Catholic president of the country, which has 40% of its population Catholic, ignored all diplomatic protocol and behaved in a way which had only once been known since the time of Hitler, on the occasion of the Polish president's visit in 1967: he passed through Rome without visiting the Pope. Although none of this can be condoned, it needs to be understood as a reaction against the powerful Congolese Church of the 'good old days' — an adolescent crisis, through which the young state has to pass to maturity and during which the Church can discover its true identity of disinterested witness to the gospel. We must expect similar tensions in other countries, especially whenever the Church is determined to be faithful to its prophetic role. [42] Fortunately, we can subscribe to what P. Beyerhaus writes, after an analysis of three young Protestant Churches: 'Persecution is the most radical form of vexation to which the young Churches are subjected: without outside help, they are compelled to affirm their duty as Christ's Church, facing up to opposition which threatens their very life. In persecution, the young Church faces the question whether being the Church is more precious than peace, material goods, prosperity and life. The choice to be made is between apostasy and martyrdom. Thus the Church comes to experience more intensely its dependence on Christ and its indissoluble union with him... The Churches of Nigeria, Korea and Borneo have become what they are only through martyrdom...' [43]

Another classic example is that of the Church among the Ibo. After the unhappy civil war in Nigeria, all foreign missionaries were compelled to leave. The Church on the spot remained in a strong position with three native bishops, 150 priests, 163 sisters and a people with faith. The awareness that they were on their own led to the enrolling of 450 students of theology in 1972 and to about 1600 novices in the male and female religious congregations. Even in less 'classical' situations, with

---

[42] See below ch. 5.B.2, p. 105.

[43] P. Beyerhaus, *Die Selbständigkeit der jungen Kirchen als missionarisches Problem,* Wuppertal, 1956, p. 280.

fewer advantages to start with as in Guinea and Burma, there are signs that the Church lives on in spite of the difficulties. Deprived of institutions and of financial means, they become all the more similar to the primitive Christian community in faith, hope and love.

This prelude to world history, this entry into the pageant by the Third World and the Third Church, takes place to an accompaniment full of tension. At present we can watch the preliminary placings. History justifies us in expecting that the appearance of this fresh cast will greatly influence future performance.

Chapter 3

THE SECOND LIBERATION

A. *Suffering hunger with dignity*

1. When the heads of the new nations were celebrating independence day with flags flying and festive garb, they knew that a new horizon was opening up beyond the goal they had reached, and that the important part of the journey was just beginning. 'Independence of flag' was not an end but a means to an end, as President Nyerere used to say. It was only the pre-condition for discovering, or re-discovering, a cultural identity, and also for implementing more energetic measures to free the people from disease, ignorance and poverty. In practice, this meant developing health and education services further than the colonial masters had been able to. It meant shaping the economy in the interests of the country and not those of foreign companies. The political revolution had to be followed by an economic revolution, in order to meet the growing expectations of a free people.

2. In point of fact the Third World has come into existence at a favourable time. The western world paid dearly for the passage from a peasant to an industrial economy (consider the appalling conditions of workers in the early stages of industrialization); it travelled slowly and laboriously the road from the water-wheel to steam, electricity and, finally, atomic energy. It began the 20th century with the motor car, continued it with the aeroplane and is ending it with space travel. The young states are coming on stage in this last phase and will be able to cull the mature fruits of technical advance. They have been catapulted from their stone, bronze and iron ages into our atomic age. They emerge from primeval forests and jungles to find

51

themselves surrounded by a display of products of the entire world, splendid and magnificent.

3. But there is a spectre: the dilemma of progress. Are the rich countries not playing the part of Satan when he took Christ to the top of the mountain and showed him all the kingdoms of the world and their glory? We spread before the poorer nations the wonders of our standard of living. For most of them these are unattainable, although a few of the newly rich can buy them by bending the knee to Mammon.

Besides, does our standard of living, with its accompaniment of restlessness, feverish acquisitiveness, competitiveness, urban anonymity, its drugs and its frustrations, really amount to the sum total of everything desirable? Is the only possible pattern for development really that of heaving poor countries out of the plain of their traditional way of life and forthwith depositing them on the dizzy heights of mature western consumer society with no chance to acclimatize gradually? [1]

For centuries people in the Third World (before it was so called) lived and survived. They accepted pain, sickness and death, endured hunger before the harvest as something quite natural and feasted after the harvest with exuberant joy. All were equally rich, equally poor, and within the community each person was more or less able to live out his life unpretentiously. It was a great experience for the missionary, and still is, to make contact with people of this type in the African villages: 'These people are contented with trifles. For them a visit like that is a real event. When you go into their homes they are over-joyed. They bring gifts, rice and eggs, and are particularly happy when you fondle the children's heads. They are marvellous children, light and agile. A friendly look is enough to make them radiant like a light newly lit. I was touched to see so many children and not a single toy...' [2] Even among the uprooted poor in the *favelas* of Brazil and the Indian slums, one gets the impression of being among happy people — one could almost say privileged. It is easy to engage them in conversation for

---

[1] W. Rostow, *Stadien wirtschaftlichen Wachstums,* Göttingen, 1960.

[2] B. Heim, *Pro-Nunzio in Kairo berichtet so über seine Besuche in Ober-ägypten,* in *Schweiz Kirchenzeitung,* Lucerne, 1972, p. 36f.

there are none of the inhibitions of higher society. They react with a smile. They make us say to ourselves: 'These people are living the gospel without knowing it'. Christ must have had such people before his eyes when he said, 'Blessed are the poor'. But with progress we get cupidity, selfishness, the break-up of families, criminal behaviour and revolution...

4. Nevertheless, neither the romanticism of tourists nor the idealism of certain critics of society can stop the development now under way or even slow it down. It is irreversible. Poor people now know of the possibility of a better life and strive for it with insatiable desire. Just as the average western family has wound its way uphill to the washing machine, the television set, the motor car and holidays, just as the missionary has improved his standard of living with a solid house, a water pump, a refrigerator and holidays at home, so there are 2000 millions of people who want and must have their medicines, schooling, clothes, tinned food, bicycles and entertainments. Progress is a mark of the times and everyone who can joins in. Any idea that these masses of people can be left to exist in human 'nature reserves' is out of the question as a solution and, even if it were not, would have to be rejected as too easy a way out. It has to be accepted that progress will spread by contagion over the whole surface of the earth, and the problems involved must be overcome. Through the escalation of his ever growing desires man is brought to frustration, and with that (but on a higher level) he finds himself face to face with the authentic problem of the meaning of life and his longing for the infinite, to use a more ancient form of expression.

5. Independence has not been fruitless. For all the criticism which can be made, and for all the continuing shortcomings, the real achievements cannot pass unrecognized. Anyone re-visiting these countries after a few years will notice immediately that there has been a change (in some districts at least). Not only are the capital cities and airports cleaner, for reasons of prestige, but there are new industries, new research centres, a developing agriculture and many new schools.

A classic example illustrating all these changes is Goa.

From the stagnancy of the old Portuguese possession, it has become a dynamic centre of development. A few figures: [3]

Goa	1961	1971
Primary schools	476	1047
Secondary schools	119	558
University colleges	—	10
Patients in hospital	11,648	41,514
Out-patients treated	56,623	545,141
Co-operatives	—	404

Roads, an indispensible requirement for the economic development of any country, have been built almost everywhere and great international road-building schemes have been implemented. The Panamerican highway joining all the states along the Andes has been complemented by a Transamazon route. In Africa, the north-south connection exists and work is in progress on the cross route from Mombasa to Lagos. Work started in 1969 on an Asian highway along a 23,000 miles route from Istambul to Singapore and by 1972 most of the countries involved had completed their stretch.

6. Travellers in India are continually surprised by the number of canals, small artificial lakes and pumping-stations. These, with the help of fertilizers, Philipine rice and Mexican wheat seed, make two or three harvests possible, each bigger than the one harvest used to be. Thus the *green revolution* has proved more than a slogan and the disturbing spectre of world famine [4] of a few years ago has been kept at bay, at least for several decades. Until five years ago, the Philippines had to import half their rice; now they are exporters. In India, the production of grain increased from 10 million tons in 1960 to 18 million in 1969, and in Pakistan from 4 m. to 7 m. Food production in the Third World is increasing faster than the

[3] *Ten years of liberation*, Goa, 1971.

[4] L.J. Lebret, *Suicide ou survie de l'Occident*, Paris, 1958; also J. de Castro, *Weltgeissel Hunger;* W.D. Paddock, *1975 wird keiner mehr satt;* R. Dumont and B. Rosier, *Nous allons à la famine;* Reports of the congress of the FAO 1974.

population and it is thought that until 1975 no developing country will have to increase its food imports. Of course, it only needs a great drought or a flood (both disasters quite unpredictable in tropical regions) to upset all calculations.

7. The principal aspects of development can be expressed in figures as follows: [5]

Percentage of children of school age receiving schooling:

	1950	1955	1960	1965
Africa	15.1%	21.0%	28.6%	35.0%
Asia	25.8%	30.6%	38.1%	53.2%
S. America	39.8%	46.9%	57.1%	58.2%

Calories compared with 100% in adequate diet:

	1959/61	1970
Brazil	102%	109%
Central America (except Mexico)	91%	92%
S. America (except Argentine and Uruguay)	90%	96%
N. Africa	95%	99%
The rest of Africa	100%	105%
Middle East	96%	99%
East Asia	92%	97%

Average income in dollars:

	1960	1969
Asia	90	109
Africa	105	123
S. America	319	374

8. Compare these last figures with those for the average income of the poor(!) regions of Southern Europe: 1960: 321 1969: 496. You will realize just how relative is progress in the Third World. Deprivation is still firmly rooted everywhere. Being foreigners we rather close our eyes to this, feeling our

[5] World Bank, *Trends,* 2.2; 2.3; 3.2.

consciences far from clear. Yet help is just not available for so many who are struggling to escape from poverty, who would like to have a house instead of a hut, a plough instead of a stick, clean water instead of contaminated water. In S. America, in Africa and in Asia, you are warned, even by natives, against giving anything to beggars, to cripples or to the mothers with their babies beside the roads. You feel ashamed not to give anything. But to give is to be submerged by a wave, and anyway your small gift serves only to prolong by a day a human life not worth living. In defence, you look away from the misery — in defence, that is, of yourself not of the sufferers. And you pass by on the other side, like the priest and levite on the road to Jericho.

These personal impressions can be related to the United Nations social survey of world problems (restricted for the sake of brevity to Asia). [6] It gives the number of young people under 14 (this youth so full of hope) as 754 millions; the number of homeless persons increased during the sixties by 50% in India and by 100% in Pakistan; in Asia there are more than 480 million city dwellers (more than the whole population of S. America or of Africa). As a result of this rapid increase, conditions in the cities have worsened beyond all description. At Calcutta, half the population lives in the slums. The elementary services — water, sewage and transport — are totally unsatisfactory. Only the better conditions in certain countries (Japan and Singapore) raise the annual average income to 109 dollars; in fact, four-fifths of the population have less than 100 dollars a year to live on.

Ten years ago Senegal was considered a model of development. Fr L. Lebret, founder of IRFED in Paris, had made surveys and started a twenty-five year plan to be carried out in stages. There were to be investment, a network of advisory centres, and flying squads equipped with tractors and bulldozers, all inspired by a mystique of creativity in progress. But the reality still falls far short of the plan's expectations, and that not only because Fr Lebret has died in the meantime. . .

[6] United Nations, 1970, Report 3-25; A.J. Fonseca (ed.), *Challenge of poverty in India,* Delhi, 1971.

9. The euphoria has worn off not only for the new states but also for western countries. Ten years ago, a kind of crusading spirit in support of the poorer countries was gripping the imagination. 'Aid for development' was a fashionable expression and an enormous number of books were written on the subject. It was hoped that a concerted attack could break the back of underdevelopment. Since then it has become clear that, underneath the promising appearances, an immense gap was opening up which forces development to take time. And so, for the second decade of development, a more modest aim is proposed, that of helping the 25 countries on the lowest level of development, i.e. with an average income less than 100 dollars, industry producing less than 10% of the gross national product and more than 80% illiteracy. These 25 countries have a total population of 140 millions, less than 10% of the population of the Third World. We are to concentrate on these and restrict ourselves to them. We are indeed becoming modest! Archbishop Helder Camara was not wrong when he spoke of the 'miserable conclusion to the first decade of development'. [7]

B. *Being disgracefully rich*

1. The blame for this meagre success falls on many shoulders. The first to beat their breasts should be the rich countries who have simply not done their duty. The UNCTAD conferences in Geneva and Delhi asked developed countries to give 1% of their gross national product in aid to developing countries. But the third conference at Santiago in Chile in 1972 calculated that aid had reached only 0.74% on average, and the 3000 delegates from 141 countries who took part in this 5-week-long conference failed to find any new incentive offering hope of further progress. On the contrary, it is clear that the gap between rich and poor countries is increasing not decreasing. Moreover, during the conference a US lunar probe was in full swing and the world press gave much more prominence to that than to UNCTAD; a reporter rightly observed that for the western countries the moon is closer than the Third World.

[7] Kerkhofs and Henry (ed.), *Dialogue d'aujourd'hui — Mission de demain*, Paris, 1968, p. 213.

While the tables given above show that poor countries have increased their average income by around 10 dollars, development in rich countries is as followers:

	1960	1969
Italy	928	1401
West Germany	1578	2192
USA	3200	4241

If things continue at this rate, in the year 2000 the industrialized countries of the west will have 1500 million inhabitants with an average annual income of 5000 to 10,000 dollars, while the 4500 million inhabitants of the Third World will have an annual income of 500 dollars. [8] Clearly a world like that would be bad for everyone.

The flow of capital towards the poor countries, in most cases investments subject to harsh conditions, caused the recipients to pay 80,000 million dollars in interest in 1971; this is a large slice of the national income. In spite of the progress they have made, the developing countries' share in world trade has fallen from 32% in 1951 to 18% in 1970. Their exports consist mainly of raw materials: wool, rubber, sugar, coffee, copper; and although prices fluctuate from year to year, upsetting all plans, taken as a whole their prices (except for petrol) have remained stationary for about twenty years while the prices of commodities they import from industrial countries have been continually rising. [9] In practice this means that a peasant in Pakistan, Senegal or Colombia must give a quarter to a half as much again of his jute, ground-nuts or coffee as he did ten years ago to buy a watch or a bicycle. It has been well said that there is no need for rich countries to give more; they should simply take less.

2. But exhortations seem to have little effect. On the contrary, there is a noticeable loss of interest in aid for development, while discontent is growing. [10] Certain 'prophets' see signs

[8] HK 1972, pp. 63-66.
[9] World Bank, *Trends*, 5.5; 5.7.
[10] F. Duve, *Die Eskalation des N-S Konflictes*, in M. Greiwe (ed.), *Herausforderung an die Zukunft*, München, 1970, pp. 319-328.

that the great powers will become less interested in the Third World, owing to the lessening of cold war tension and the rivalry that goes with it. They notice the field of manoeuvre for the strategic balance of power shifting from the surface of the globe to outer space, and reducing the need for bases in the Third World. Moreover as developments in chemistry continually produce more synthetic products, dependence on raw materials from the Third World lessens. This could lead to a new isolationism, with the great human masses in the tropics regressing, willy nilly, to their pre-colonial autarchy and trying to survive by whatever means are at hand. [11] I would hold this to be too cheap a solution. The western world cannot renounce the enormous market constituted by the Third World, and the awakened masses of the southern hemisphere will not let themselves be pushed off the bandwagon of the one-world now that it is under way. It is no longer a question of accepting or rejecting the shared destiny of the one world: this one world is a *fait accompli*. As Mrs Indira Ghandi has said: 'It is not a question of seeing whether the developed countries can afford to help the developing countries but whether they can afford not to.'

3. Developing countries, too, have their share of responsibility for the present state of affairs. The fruits of economic help are largely swallowed up by a too rapid population growth; they are also wasted by a parasitic class of new rich. At meetings of international organizations at Brazzaville in 1962, I heard it said that Africa was going the way of Latin America — the classic example of a vicious distribution of wealth, with a small class of rich people contrasting with a mass of poor. Whereas Asia has had some kind of capitalism from ancient times in the form of maharajahs and great landowners, in Africa the land belonged to the tribe, wherever it was not occupied by white settlers, and every member of the tribe had the same opportunities. But now, even in Africa, social divisions have become a fact: on the one side, the poor people; on the other, politicians who in one way or another get hold of the money and put it in safe keeping abroad, senior employees or associates of foreign firms which

[11] H.H. Brunner, *Kirche ohne Illusionen*, Zürich, 1968, pp. 139f.

need a native façade for their business, and the bureaucrats in civil administration who charge high prices for their 'services'.

Brazil is not the only country of which it can be said (as has been said by a group of bishops and provincials of religious orders in a recent declaration) that the economic miracle benefits scarcely 20% of the population and makes the rich richer and the poor poorer; in the last ten years, this 20% of the population has increased its share of the national income from 54.4% to 61.1%, so that a reduced percentage of the population enjoys more than half the national income. Similar examples can be found in Asia, so much so that it is said the green revolution, by helping the few, does nothing to prevent the red revolution. [12]

4. On corruption among the ruling classes, R. Dumond had some disturbing things to say over ten years ago. F. Behrendt agreed with him and spoke of a 'vicious circle of sterility and frustration in this bankrupt type of development politics'. [13] More recently, Nobel prize-winner G. Myrdal has remarked that while developed countries are moving towards social equality, inequality in developing countries is increasing and becoming entrenched — in clear contradiction to the fine speeches made by heads of state. Wealth is in the hands of privileged groups, who know how to turn aid from the government or from foreign institutions into grist for their own mills and can prevent the state from undertaking really decisive social reform; meanwhile the masses lie around passively, mute and apathetic. [14] He has written page after page on the phenomenon of corruption: 'Where parliamentary rule is operative, much time and concern is devoted to this subject. At intervals, newspapers conduct anti-corruption campaigns, laws are passed, means of control are set up, police detachments are directed against the crime and investigations are made. From time to time, some functionary, usually a subordinate, is prosecuted and punished and in some cases a minister has to resign. Nevertheless, everyone in all these countries is convinced that corruption continues to pros-

[12] R. Kurzrock, *Asien im 20 Jahrhundert,* Berlin, 1972, p. 128.
[13] R. Dumond, *L'Afrique est mal partie,* Paris, 1962; R. Behrendt, *Soziale Strategie für Entwicklungsländer,* Frankfurt, 1965, p. 450.
[14] *Polit. Manifest* 49-76.

per and is actually increasing among high functionaries and politicians. . .' [15] There is truth in the saying that these countries are underveloped not economically but administratively. President Nyerere, one of the incorruptibles, has seen this and repeatedly stressed it since as long as 1966, after he had analysed numerous failings in state government; according to him, the great misfortune of Africa is no longer colonialism but the new castes of corrupt rulers, who are more concerned with their own interests than with those of the people. [16]

Occasionally, in Africa and India, I used to remark that I had never in my life greased palms but still managed to make my way. What I said seemed beyond understanding, so inveterate is the habit of paying the nurse for medicine, the teacher for passing an exam, the official for a signature. Exploiting one another is just part of life.

Is corruption, then, a passing phase? We must hope so, even though it still thrives in western countries too. In the meantime, the need to make money is so great that everyone has an eye to the main chance. Money can be a fascinating new experience. Where the nation has not yet built up a healthy sense of patriotism and public spirit, we may have to deal with people who act not as individuals or as citizens of the state but rather as members of a clan, defrauding the state with a quiet conscience in the interest of the tribe. [17] Once I asked a rich Indian to explain how China had managed to overcome its underdevelopment in twenty years, when India had not succeeded even with the advantage of more external aid. He replied that China had a strong regime, while India had freedom which could be abused. Besides, China and Japan possessed a stronger community conscience: 'We Indians are ready to betray our country for money. We business men think only of our profit,

[15] Op. cit. 222-235, esp. 224; Traber, Das revolutionäre Afrika, Freiburg in U., 1972, pp. 24-29.

[16] The Standard, Dar es Salaam, 8 July 1966. See further Nyerere, Freedom and Unity, pp. 82, 92, 264, and Freedom and Socialism, p. 95.

[17] Ntite Mukendi, Nos élites et la conscience civique, in RM 1969, pp. 179-187; L. Stucki, Kontinent im Aufbruch. Südamerika auf dem Weg ins 21 Jahrhundert, Bern, 1971, pp. 305f, 173.

while the Japanese want to make Japan great. It is a thing I have often noticed in business relations with them'.

5. The real root of the evil lies in the poor people themselves, although they are not to be blamed for this. It is in their apathy, their incapacity to shake themselves and really want a better life. The attitude has been formed in the course of millennia of malnutrition, enervating tropical climate, and religious attitudes of submission to fate. It cannot be changed overnight. They would like to make progress but lack the energy. The Latin American situation has been described as follows: the *campesinos* lament, 'We are poor, because it is the will of God'; workers shout, 'We are poor, because the Yankees are exploiting us'; the capitalists grind their teeth, 'We are not succeeding, because Communists are behind all the trouble'. In other words, no one feels responsible for the state of affairs. Similarly, you hear people say, 'Give us 50,000 immigrants from Israel and the country will change'. But this would not be real development. At the most, it would produce a dominant caste, while the people continued to live a subordinate existence, like the pariahs in India or the Arabs in Israel.

True development cannot be given or imposed but must be sought and achieved by the community in question. It is well known that *community development* and the sensitizing of the poor necessary to this purpose are the two pillars of the process. There is much theoretical writing on this subject but, as far as practical achievements are concerned, there are only a few bright spots here and there. Mgr Salcedo, with his *Accion Cultural Popular* and his study centre at Sutatenza in Colombia, has done much since 1947 to bring young people to have confidence in themselves, to wish for a better future and to build it. During a lunch, he said: 'Underdevelopment is not in the stomach but in the head; the thing is to create a new mentality. Injections of money from abroad are no use unless they are followed up by autonomous development'. It is only when such reflections are put into practice, and leaders who are close to the people (like Archbishop Helder Camara and his 'Project Hope' at Recife or Mgr Bambaren with his *Pueblos Jovenes* at Lima) are able to inspire groups of young people and encourage them not to wait passively for the state to do something, not to wait for miracles or assistance but to roll up their sleeves and build village schools, excavate aqueducts, connect up the electric power — it is only then that we find the Archimedean point at which we can lever up this world of underdevelopment. [18] Without this self-help, this self-motivated activity, the finest projects remain foreign bodies in the system, façades, 'modernization without development'; [19] they come to nothing almost as soon as the instigators, who are usually strangers, have disappeared.

6. Today, after much enthusiasm for revolution, it is recognized that violent revolution attains its end only in a very qualified way. True, there is institutional violence incarnated in feudal lordships, military governments and international commercial arrangements which seek, by all possible means including violence, to maintain 'peace and order'. In practice this means disorder and established injustice, which can rightly be eliminated by any legitimate means. For many people, the range of means available extends from democratic negotiation through sit-ins, demonstrations and confrontations to guerrilla warfare and *coups d'état;* then to the ultimate solution of all-out revolution and insurgency, bloodbaths and Molotov cocktails — or else to the ultimate failure of being crushed by tanks.

No one except those who profit from injustice can doubt that unjust structures are to be changed. But revolution, in the traditional sense of the word, is not in most cases the best means to this end. Latin American theorists propose as an alternative *Promocion popular.* Starting from the present pyramid of the S. American population, with a wide base of the deprived and under-privileged and a sharp apex of the 20% well-to-do, it is clear that nothing basically is changed by a removal of the power group at the top. It would simply be replaced by another power group, while the uneducated masses remained at the bottom. It is necessary to start from the latter, seeking to shake them, form and educate them to self-help, in

[18] Stucki, *op. cit.,* p. 13f.
[19] Norman Jacobs, *Modernization without development: Thailand as an Asian case study,* N.Y., 1971.

the hope that, becoming more aware of their situation, they may get closer to the ruling class and eventually assume for themselves the responsibility and duty of changing structures. [20]

7. It is both interesting and encouraging to view the laborious work of progress of the present time in wider historical contexts. It needed about a century, from 1750 to 1850 including the French Revolution, to bring the populace to the point of acquiring full political rights. It needed another century and the Marxist revolution, set on course by the communist party manifesto in 1847, to obtain a more or less healthy economic situation for the western workforce. Mankind has paid a high price for the two revolutions. Both could and should have developed in a more 'ideal' way; in fact they occurred as they did, with all their faults. The good ideas of both have survived while harsh realities have been forgotten. Looking back, historians recognize historical necessity in each.

Shall we need another century to achieve on a world scale the social equilibrium so laboriously arrived at within businesses and single countries? If so, we are only at the beginning of the process. And will time be on our side? Things move faster now than in the former hundred year periods and popular awareness is far more acute than in the first decades of the Marxist revolution. Will the two economic systems of communism and capitalism fight it out in the world arena so that in the end one alone survives? Or will they both complete the moderate reforms necessary to meet both economic realities and the requirements of human dignity? Will intermediate models be developed (like African socialism in Tanzania) [21] in order to redeem the human masses of the Third World from the condition of the poor Lazarus and sat them at table with their more prosperous brothers? [22]

[20] K. Lefringhausen and F. Merz, *Das Zweite Entwicklungsjahrzehnt 1970-1980,* Wuppertal, 1970, pp. 62-66.

[21] It is becoming more and more evident that, if the experiment in Tanzania succeeds, it will be a valid model and a great hope for all developing countries. Cf. Rostra Theologica, *Entwicklungspolitik am Beispiel Tansanias,* Berlin, 1971.

[22] *Populorum Progressio,* no. 47: 'It is a question of building a world in which freedom is not an empty word and where the poor Lazarus can sit at the same table with the rich.'

What is more, charitable hand-outs are no longer the answer. After the successful 'conspiracy' of the oil producing countries, who knows whether the producers of coffee, sugar, copper etc. will not be tempted to try similar manoeuvres? It would indeed be a sad thing if raw materials became weapons in the hands of the more powerful instead of a help to all. Or is this perhaps the inevitable boomerang reaction to the way Europe has acted in the past?

Be that as it may, this present generation of the First, Second and Third Church ought to recognize as it own the task of bringing the development process to a happy conclusion. In 2050 or sooner, we shall be judged on this. The difficulty of the task must not be taken as an excuse; it is a stimulus and a challenge. The enormity of having three continents so rich in resources as S. America, Africa and Asia still living in such shameful poverty must be wiped from the face of the earth. A glance at history gives us ground for thinking the task will be accomplished. We are faced not by complete chaos but by a world which little by little can be improved.

Chapter 4

SALVATION FROM THE EAST?

A. *The historical mission of China*

1. As we come to the end of 25 years in which world politics were dominated by continual rivalry between the two super-powers, USA and Russia, and by the overriding need to maintain the 'balance of terror', the fact of China suddenly becomes the centre of interest. This almond-eyed people remains enigmatic and, if we are not entirely mistaken, will cross the threshold of the third millennium as the greatest power and will seek to play a leading role during its course. Napoleon's prediction, 'When China awakes, the world will tremble' and the 'yellow peril' of which Kaiser Wilhelm II spoke at the beginning of the century seem now to be becoming reality. China with its 5000 years of civilization, the 'middle kingdom' until now closed in on itself for geographic and other reasons, has at last recognized its hour of destiny and is on the point of taking up its post in 'world history'. Numerically, with its 773 million inhabitants, it is more significant than Africa (334 million) and Latin America (283 million) taken together. It seems to have succeeded in capturing the world market in ideas. [1]

2. This is all the more surprising in that China was, until recently, as unknown as the moon. The journalists who managed to visit the country between the cultural revolution and spring 1971 could be counted on ten fingers — as many as the astronauts who have walked on the moon. More than unknown, China was isolated and discredited. With the victory of the

---

[1] Mehnert K., *China nach dem Sturm*, Stuttgart, 1972. Besides Mehnert, Kurzrock, Böttcher, cf. P. Gheddo, *Dove va la Cina?* Milan, 1972; A. Peyrefitte, *Quand la Chine s'éveillera*, Paris, 1973.

communist troops over Chiang Kai Shek's armies and the proclamation of the People's Republic in 1947 recognized by only
a few western states, a 'bamboo curtain' descended, drawing a
veil over events of which we have had no precise news to the
present day. The massacres of 'saboteurs' and 'counter-
revolutionaries' ordered by popular tribunals between 1949 and
1954, judging by a statement of Mao Tze Tung himself, [2]
counted 800,000 victims; but according to various foreign
experts the figures are anything between 10 and 15 million.
With the decree against counter-revolutionary activity, there
began a systematic struggle against the missions. All foreign
missionaries were expelled, including about 5000 Catholic priests,
laybrothers and sisters, often after a process of abuse, show-
trials, ill-treatment and imprisonment. All this helped to blacken
the picture of China and to make credible the reports that spoke
of murder, violence, poverty and famine. China was now totally
closed in on herself and subjected to the mill-stone which would
grind all the grains into one flour.

3. But everyone sensed that a situation of this kind could
not last for ever. In an election speech in 1968, Richard Nixon
declared: 'It is not possible for almost a billion of the strongest
inhabitants of this small planet to live in disdainful isolation'.
With the happy idea of ping-pong diplomacy and the official
visit of the President to Mao in February 1972, the spell was
broken. There was an explosion of enthusiasm for China after
the twenty years of anti-Chinese propaganda: the fight had
been against the system; the Chinese people were found to be
human. One state after another accorded recognition to this
giant of a brother celebrating its admission to the United
Nations to frenetic support from the small states of the Third
World. But now all who can — journalists, politicians and
business men — visit China and return enthusiastic. Here are
some of their testimonies: 'A fascinating experience' — 'No
other country has struck me as so healthy a place as China.' —
'I am very impressed by China. The Chinese are trying to build
a new society which will deserve to be called "communist" in
the best sense of the word.'

[2] Kurzrock, *Asien im 20 Jahrhundert*, Berlin, 1972, p. 34.

Of course, a question mark hangs over many features of the Chinese scene. Recent reports tell us the people are not as firmly behind the government as was thought. The opposition of young people, their unwillingness to work and their increasing demands seem to give rise to difficulties. There are those who just do not believe in the miracle of the Chinese revolution. [3] The future will soon reveal who is right. In any case, rarely in history has the world's attitude to a people changed so radically as it has towards China. A parallel could be drawn with the way the world revised its judgement on Christianity after the Edict of Milan in 313. The accommodation between Church and state which began with that date is today seen with more critical eyes than in the past. What will history say of the negotiations between Peking and Washington?

4. No one doubts that the feelings of cordiality, rejoicing and mutual respect with which Nixon and Chou En Lai toasted each other and held their conversations were genuine. But the ideologies and economic systems as well as aims in world politics of the two powers are so different that this could hardly be the start of a genuine friendship. Amalrick speaks of hypocritical approaches based on utilitarian considerations. [4] It is easy to guess the motives of the two communist giants in their rivalry for the friendship of the American giant. Russia is afraid of ideological competition and strategic threats from China. Conversely, China fears encirclement by Russia and Russian allies (India, Vietnam and eventually the Philippines) and, with good reason, takes seriously the possibility of a surprise attack from Russia before she herself can build up an adequate nuclear

[3] J. Domes in Kurzrock op. cit., p. 47: 'So the China that has emerged from the cultural revolution is not the China of the young enthusiasts of the revolution. Anyone who pays attention to the reality of Chinese society today and not to the propaganda statements of the mass media, will not find a 'new society' under the leadership of an old man of high quality as a theoretician and determined in its shape by 'millions of revolutionary followers' at his side. He will find, rather, an old society, shaken in its structures but in no way fundamentally changed, led by a coalition of coldly professional military manipulators of power, flexible diplomats and planning bureaucrats fond of pragmatic decisions.'

[4] A. Amalrik, L'Union Sovietique survivra-t-elle en 1984?, Paris, 1970, p. 94.

68

arsenal. Thus both see the need to protect their flanks, and for this purpose are ready to draw closer even to capitalist America.

At all events, the pattern of world relations has been changed. The small pre-war triangular arrangement (London-Paris-Washington) gave way first to the two-power confrontation of the post-war period (Washington-Moscow) and then to the greater triangle (Washington-Moscow-Peking). [5] To this pattern, two more powerful points are added, Japan and united Europe (assuming this union becomes effective). Thus, the world is becoming a political, economic and military 'pentagon'. To this we can now add the Arab block. From now on, we have the prospect of living in a polycentric world, and this cannot but be favourable to a better balance of forces.

5. But, to return to the subject of China, Mao has struggled with tenacity to free his people from all forms of oppression. He has been reacting against an unworthy form of existence, which has kept China prostrate for far too long. In the 'Unequal Treaties' of the last century — unequal because imposed on China rather than negotiated on an equal footing — treaties only finally abolished in 1942 during the war, the country had to suffer so many attacks on its sovereignty from the western powers as to accumulate within itself enormous stores of hatred and bitterness. With the defeat of the Nationalist (and American) army, the yoke of foreign interference was finally broken. China became the inflexible enemy of the USA and its interventions in the Third World. From the beginning, China held out for the unconditional withdrawal of American troops from Korea and Vietnam and set about fanning the flames of anti-Americanism wherever possible. Her entry into the UN, 15 November 1971, was a triumph over the 'American conspiracy'.

In the same uncompromising way China conducted a struggle for freedom from Russia, when the latter sought to interfere as it had done successfully in the satellite states. The 'great leap forward' was a way of breaking with Russia and branding the Russians with 'communist heresy', with being a

[5] W. Böttcher, *Das grosse Dreieck Washington-Moskau-Peking*, Stuttgart, 1971.

'capitalist and welfare state'. It encouraged the Chinese to accept the withdrawal of Russian capital and technical aid, with the consequent temporary stagnation, in order eventually to achieve the same results by their own resources in full independence.

A third liberation was that effected by the cultural revolution, that is liberation from bureaucrats and petty bosses. The revolution had eliminated the caste of great lords but others had slipped into their places. The evil of a corrupt bureaucracy was taking hold like a tumour and called for a radical cure and the 'permanent revolution'. The office-desk pyramid was razed and the bureaucrats packed off to work in villages and mines; all administration was decentralized and freedom and initiative were restored to the people.

6. It is in this context that we must understand the liquidation of the missions. They were not entirely without blame in the matter of the humiliation suffered by China in the past. Through the Unequal Treaties they had obtained advantages and privileges. Missionaries enjoyed a sort of extra-territoriality. They were, as a rule, under the French protectorate. They had thefts within the missions severely punished. They were able to expropriate pagodas and have them made into churches. They could get rid of local authorities with whom they were dissatisfied. Christians considered themselves to a certain extent exempt from the laws of the state, in so far as they were people of the mission. The ancient Chinese archives contain hundreds of volumes on difficulties with missionaries. This gave rise to a profound sense of xenophobia. [6] All this does not excuse the way the missionaries were treated, but it does explain why they were ostentatiously humiliated before the popular tribunals. The accusations were highly exaggerated but not entirely without foundation, as is clear from the comprehensive account by J. Schütte in a well-documented book on the subject: 'The Catholic missions in China were not agents of a foreign power;

[6] P.A. Cohen, *China and Christianity*, Cambridge, 1967; cf. also J. Beckmann, *Zum Wandel vom positiven zum negativen Chinabild in Europa*, in NZM 1966, pp. 126-128; id. *Die stellung der kathol. Missionare zur chinesischen Kultur*, in KMJ 1942, pp. 41-67.

nor were they the vanguard of imperialist aggression. But to protect and secure their rights as well as the life and property of missionaries and Christians, they depended on the western powers, putting themselves under the protection and juridical sovereignty of a foreign state and calling on its aid in their difficulties and disputes... Through clauses of the Unequal Treaties which were imposed, often after unjust wars, by the western imperialist powers on the unarmed Chinese empire, the missions secured privileges and special rights and, on occasion, made imprudent use of them... Incidents provoked by missionaries and Chinese Christians not only often led to repression and severe punishments but were also exploited by western powers as pretexts for extending their political interference and widening the scope of their imperialist pretensions, in selfish and unjust ways'. [7] At all events, the missions found themselves in the same boat as the western powers and came to appear as a Trojan horse through which foreign hegemony had penetrated the country. So with the end of colonialism they could only expect their own like end.

7. The idea of self-help and self-reliance became the leading idea. It was proclaimed by mural displays in the streets and in the schools: 'Do not be a weakling'; 'Other people need you'. Such slogans over a period of twenty years have created an unequalled readiness to work. Mao believed from the beginning in the unlimited strength of the masses: with a hundred million hand carts and a hundred million baskets it is possible to move mountains, without as yet having the more sophisticated technical means available. China, once technically underdeveloped and appearing in the UN report of 1949 below Pakistan and Indonesia, has now reached a stage of development and self-confidence, from economic, military and ideological points of view, which compels the admiration of visitors and makes her

---

[7] J. Schütte, *Die katholische Chinamission im Spiegel der rotchinesischen Presse*, Münster i. W., 1957, p. 179. B. Wirth, *Imperialistische Uebersee- und Missionspolitik, dargestellt am Beispiel Chinas*, Münster i. W., 1968. Fr Lebbe was one of those prophets who recognized and criticized a false position in good time: cf. the book much criticized by ex-missionaries: J. Leclerq, *Vie du P. Lebbe*, Tournai-Paris, 1965.

a prototype of underdevelopment conquered. The battle against famine is won and supplies are assured for future emergencies. If the standard of living is not yet comparable with that of the West, still the Chinese people has never been as well off as now. Since 1952, the average income has increased by 50%, while the cost of living remains low.

8. The military position is an achievement for self-reliance. China has not only built up ground forces of three millions and a navy which is the third biggest in the world, but is already an atomic power and could soon be in a position to strike at all points in the USSR. For this reason, if ever war broke out with Russia, it would be fought with conventional weapons, would last long and end in victory for China. This is the opinion of Amalrick, a Russian, who was accused of anti-patriotic activity for his book and deprived of his liberty. He thinks war will break out between 1980 and 1985 and that, just as Rome and Constantinople fell, so Moscow itself will be taken and the Chinese people will emigrate in force. [8] Mehnert, however, thinks that the Chinese have their eyes on America rather than on Russia, much as the barbarians had their eyes on Rome when the empire was about to fall. [9]

9. The hero of all this development is Mao, once commander of the communist army, philosopher of the revolution and leader of the greatest people on earth. Admiration and enthusiasm for this now aging man, especially among the young, has spread throughout the world. [10] This introverted Chinese thinker, who cannot speak any foreign language and has only three times ventured out of his own country, has more followers in the world than any living figure. As events have proved, he has succeeded in giving heart to this giant people, in overcoming individualism and egoism and in reawakening concern for the

[8] Amalrik, *op. cit.* (n. 4) pp. 98-100.

[9] In Böttcher, *op. cit.* (n. 5) p. 188.

[10] Pro Mundi Vita, Notes Spéciales, Brussels, no. 22: *La jeunesse chrétienne et Mao Tse-tung* (with bibliography); W. Schilling, *Einst Konfuzius – Heute Mao Tse-tung. Die Mao-Faszination und ihre Hintergrunde,* Weilheim Ebb., 1971; RM 1971, no. 2: special number on China and Mao.

common good. People work, work, work — not for the sake of gain but for the glory of Chairman Mao and for the socialist fatherland. But just as egoism always finds its way back in again and as the individual needs continual conversion, so also the nation will need a new cultural revolution from time to time.

Mao's Bible, the Little Red Book (containing maxims taken from his speeches) works psychological miracles. Ordinary workers and learned teachers both live by it. By 1968, 740 million copies had been distributed. Mao's fundamental idea is faith in the future. Looking back puts us in chains; looking forward frees our energies. Only the signs of the time must determine our route of march. He holds that the consciousness of the people is like a blank sheet of paper; without caring about the great history of the past, we must be able to write on it with today as our starting point. With this mentality, the Chinese put themselves in the vanguard of mankind to whom the future belongs. So Maoism appears as a secular religion for the betterment of the world. Differently from Marx, who aimed at transforming social structures so that thereby the 'new man' might result, Mao begins with the transformation of man who will improve the world by faithful and modest dedication. We could quote texts which, leaving aside their lack of explicit faith in God, could well have come from the better manuals of ascetics.

Mao has been called the second Moses, leading his people into the new land. [11] He has been compared to Dom Lou Tseng-tsiang, former president of the Chinese council of ministers, who later became a monk. With all the differences between them, they both had the same ideal of abnegation in the service of the people. [12] E. Snow's last book contains declarations that the seventy-six year old Mao made to his friend: 'Soon I shall see God. It is inevitable. One fine day, everyone must see God. . . I am a simple man, a solitary monk, who travels through the world with a leaking umbrella'.[13] It is hard to avoid the impression that these could have been the words of John XXIII. In

[11] PMV *op. cit.*, no. 6.
[12] RM *op. cit.*, 57
[13] *Die lange Revolution*, Stuttgart, 1973, pp. 196, 201.

fact, with all necessary qualifications (we could be misunderstood here), the two could be compared for their spontaneous approach to the world, their asceticism, their simplicity, their rejection of the bureaucratic mentality and their faith in the future. It is a pity they could not have met face to face.

10. Unless after the death of the present rulers, all rather aged, there is a radical change of direction (national pride would probably prevent a change of course), China will assume the role of spiritual guide among peoples of the Third World. In that case, the communist army's victory at Hsuchow in January 1949 will be not only a turning point in Chinese history but will also go down in world history as the beginning of victory for all those peoples who want to recover their dignity and self-confidence.

At this point many readers will recall the horrors of the first years and the cultural revolution and will object, with good reason, that all that was against human dignity. The Chinese rulers were obsessed by their grand aim. They would not be satisfied with a paper revolution and did not intend to use kid-glove methods. They shrank from no means that could free them of the enemies of the revolution. The cruel methods used were aimed precisely at shocking people and making them aware of the radical nature of decisions taken. Here we may ask how far, in situations of extreme oppression for whole peoples, it may be necessary (and therefore permissible) to have recourse to violence as a temporary solution (presuming, of course, that massacres are excluded).

At all events, with this violent effort China has become a model of how to overcome underdevelopment without bowing the knee to foreign powers and accepting dependence on them. This is what fascinates many countries, because they are still suffering the consequences of white hegemony and supremacy and want to free themselves of this trauma. It is not, of course, possible to transplant everything in the Chinese model, since it is not possible everywhere to count on a people being so hard working, frugal, disciplined and intelligent.

On the occasion of China's entry into the United Nations the head of their delegation, Chow Kuan Hua, said China had

74

no intention of becoming a third great power alongside Russia and America but would continue to belong to the ranks of the small powers, in order to fight with them against the hegemony of the big two. China's aim would be to set in motion a world crusade for the liberation of the poor and oppressed. [14]

11. These words were followed by actions. In spite of her own poverty, China still does a lot, and in particular adopts a *specific form* of aid, for development. At the third UNCTAD conference in 1972, China alone was able to inject a note of hope in the general atmosphere of depression. The Chinese representative proclaimed 'the principles on which China offers aid to other countries', including the following points:

— The sovereignty of the states receiving aid is fully respected. Aid is not tied to any political conditions. China does not demand any privilege in return.

— The country receiving aid is not brought into dependence on China. The aid received ought rather to be directed towards achieving economic independence.

— Technical assistance always includes technical education for personnel of the country receiving aid.

— Specialists sent by the Chinese government live under the same conditions as native specialists.

— China offers long term loans without interest, in order to preserve developing countries from heavy indebtedness. (This does not, of course, exclude economic dependence as far as the acquisition of consumer goods is concerned.) The classic case is the aid offered for the construction of the railway in Tanzania and Zambia. The help given by 20,000 or more Chinese exceeds anything done by western volunteers for development or even by missionaries. They live in Spartan conditions in their camps, isolated from the people. They work like ants. They train Africans and they are ahead of schedule.

And yet, in the field of development, China has scarcely rolled up her sleeves. Economic development will go on much

[14] Cf. L. Trivière, *Formose après son retrait de l'ONU*, in Informations Miss., MEP, Paris, Dec 1971, 1-23.

faster now that relations with the outside world have been restored to normal. One western country after another hastens to exhibit its own products; half way through 1972, the great pavilions at the Shanghai and Peking industrial exhibitions were booked up until 1974. The shrewd Chinese will study western products carefully, as the Japanese have done, and then they will make better products themselves at better prices. The profit will not finish in the hands of private business men: a small part will go to the consumer, while the greater part will go to the development of production. Thus silent preparations are going on which will lead in a few years to the explosion of an economic bomb: China will flood the world with her products not, as Japan, in competition with the capitalist countries but rather as a brother to the poor countries of the Third World. Making offers such as no western country has ever made, China will gain their sympathy. That will be the time for competition on a world scale. The winner will not be the strongest but the most disinterested. Can capitalist countries win in such a contest?

12. The time has come not only for the USA but also for the Church to review her relations with China. The communist regime began at an unfortunate conjuncture in ecclesiastical affairs. In 1949, in order to save Italy, Pius XII had recently prohibited all co-operation with communists under pain of exclusion from the sacraments. [15] As a consequence of this call to battle-stations, the Nuncio in Peking, Mgr Riberti had no choice but to warn priests and bishops to beware of communism and to encourage the Legion of Mary in its desperate and heroic resistance. [16] When in the sequel the regime, in accordance with its general policy, [17] demanded that the Churches should observe the three autonomies: self-government, self-support, self-propagation, [18] this appeared in Catholic circles as

[15] AAS 1949, 334, renewed by John XXIII; AAS 1959, 271f.

[16] Wei Tsing-Sing L., *Le Saint-Siège et la Chine*, Allais, 1971, pp. 211-223.

[17] See above A.5, p. 69f.

[18] These three 'selves' had been demanded by Protestants for a long time: P. Beyerhaus, *Die Selbständigkeit der jungen Kirchen als missionarisches Problem*, Wuppertal, 1956, p. 40.

equivalent to a break with Rome; Protestant groups had no difficulty in agreeing. However, about 1000 Catholic priests supported the new regime. From their ranks, 45 bishops were consecrated without the consent and, in fact, against the repeated protests of Rome. [19] Even John XXIII, who had peace and unity so much at heart, felt constrained to define the situation as one of schism. [20]

Paul VI, who has begun to appreciate the new possibilities, has frequently implied that he would like to resume relations with China. During his visit to the United Nations in 1965, he spoke appreciatively of the Chinese struggle and of the way Chinese youth are fighting enthusiastically for a better life. [21] During his visit to the Far East in December 1970, he sent a message from Hong Kong to China which was not so much as mentioned in the Chinese press but was interpreted as a good sign. The Nuncio at Taipeh has been recalled for a rest. We must wait to see how things develop.

One hope must be given up, and that is the hope of starting a new missionary period in the traditional sense and of seeing the surviving missionaries returning to the missions from which they were expelled. [22] Such a attachment to the old structures would be a false start and could prejudice all attempts at a new approach. There must be a readiness to take up any possible opportunities with a new understanding based on the situation in the country, and with new forces. We should make Chinese Christians living abroad (740,000 Catholics with 678 priests) interested in their homeland. Perhaps too, if the great neighbours India and China could establish more friendly relations, we could send Indian priests and laypeople into China. After the re-union of Hong Kong and Taiwan with China (clearly only a

[19] Cf. the three letters to China of Pius XII: AAS 1952, 153-158; 155, 5-14; 1958, 601-614.

[20] AAS 1958, 985.

[21] AAS 1967, 68-71. At the ILO in Geneva, the Vatican representative, Mgr Luoni, in June 1973 referred again to China as a model for the overcoming of underdevelopment.

[22] Hence, it appears anachronistic for the Annuario Pontificio to give these dioceses and apostolic vicariates. It nourishes the false idea that the expelled bishops might some day return.

matter of time) there will be a relatively strong contingent of Christians who will have their part to play. In any case, now is the time to appoint a commission to plan this work, since 'China represents a challenge to the Church, possibly a unique challenge. Here is a giant country, in which 20% of humanity are living. China is not Russia, with a long Christian tradition in its literature and its history. It is not Africa, where the Church meets deeply rooted animistic cultures. It is not Latin America, with its rather special Christian traditions. Nor is it the world of Islam where the living God is called Allah. In China, religion faces a society which has known secularization for centuries, where the results of centuries of Christian missionary work have been swept away and where people are living in a period of traumatic experiences. China is a unique opportunity for preaching the gospel'. [23] The Catholic Church is still not reaching these 770 millions; Radio Veritas does not broadcast any glimmer of the light of the gospel. [24] Groups of enterprising people are sensing a new atmosphere and organizing meetings for study and conferences. Here, the 'children of this world' are again 'wiser than the children of light'. In the US, there are 500 specialists on China, 1000 post-graduate students are working on theses about China and 10,000 are learning chinese. [25]

13. For years past, the Chinese priest Wei Tsing Sing and others have been defending the view that, in the case of China, Rome should abandon its insistence on close union between a local Catholic Church and an external centre of unity. He would have Rome offer reconciliation and recognition to the bishops and priests of the Chinese national Church (those, that is, who have survived the cultural revolution) and thus regularize ecclesial relations. [26] Others are against this proposal as a betrayal of the expelled missionaries and those Chinese bishops and

[23] L. Ladany, *Christliche Mission in Rotchina?*, in KM 1972, pp. 148-152; R. Rush, *Religion in communist China,* N.Y., 1970.

[24] Cf. below ch. 18.8, p. 348.

[25] Böttcher, *op. cit.* (n. 5), p. 185. N.P. Moritzen and B. Willeke, *China - Herausforderung an die Kirchen,* Erlangen, 1974. PMV and the Luthern World League: colloquium on faith and the Chinese experience, Louvain, 1974.

[26] Cf. n. 16 and Trivière in n. 14.

priests who remained faithful to Rome at great cost. [27] The expelled missionaries have suffered a trauma and, with their consequent anti-Chinese attitude, cannot give credence to any reported improvements. I do not think they and the priests faithful to Rome would have any good reason to harden themselves against any attempt at a solution; if they did, they would be like the elder son who was scandalized by the feast given to the prodigal.

Here, for the first time in this book but not for the last, we raise a question of principle: must we accept only the perfect solution or can we be satisfied with a modest beginning, allowing time for historical growth and development? Do we want to preserve the principle of exclusivity, insisting on presenting an 'either- or', or are we prepared to take account of an irreversible state of affairs and compromise? Many of those pro-regime priests and bishops may have thought they must in conscience embark on a course of action which Rome, at the time, could not approve but which later, in other circumstances and with other considerations in view, she might be able to ratify. Without casting any doubt on the primacy of jurisdiction in itself, the bishop of Rome, taking account of special circumstances, could refrain from its full exercise, as he has often refrained in past centuries. It is not a matter of 'all or nothing' but a matter of doing what we can and saving what we can.

It could happen — one can hope it will — that from her own experiences within communist China the Church will learn much of value for her presence and action in other countries. [28] In that case, China would indeed have hurt the Church but the suffering would have been salutary. God, in his providence, has frequently used the scourge of temporal power to enlighten his Church and confirm her in her true mission. Mao might well appear in the same historical gallery as Robespierre, Garibaldi and others.

---

[27] I. McGrath, *Trivière's China and the Vatican: a rebuttal,* in *Columban Intercom,* Hong Kong, 1972, n. 3, 6-8.

[28] Cf. below ch. 5.B.4, p. 125.

B. *The world's new centre of gravity*

1. Alongside the model of China, the doggedness of the North Vietnamese and the hard work of the Japanese lead us to look for 'salvation from the east' or, at any rate, to see the centre of the world of the future shifted into Asian territory.

Already in ancient times it was recognized that the smaller fighter could defeat his stronger adversary with shrewdness and surprise tactics. But in the whole of military history there has never been anything as extraordinary as the Vietnam war. It is understandable that France should have had to beat a retreat with her colonial army. But when the Geneva treaty dividing the country at the Seventeenth Parallel did not restore peace and President J.F. Kennedy directly involved the United States, leading the the notorious escalation to which Nixon put an end without winning the war, things had come to an incredible pass. On one side the people of North Vietnam with a territory and population half that of pre-war Germany but supported by foreign aid had struggled for thirty years, first against Japan, then France, after that against South Vietnam and finally against the United States: on the other side, the *direct* involvement of the American super-power which between 1965 and 1972 unloaded 72 million tons of bombs on Vietnam — three and half million more than the total used in the second world war. And yet this unequal contest produced neither victor nor vanquished but only the more or less honourable withdrawal of the Americans. It calls to mind the marvellous stories of the Old Testament, where the God of the covenant protected his little people against powerful enemies — except that in Vietnam it was not the God of the covenant but foreign aid backing up the decisive will of a people seeking its own liberation. Here again we meet the Chinese philosophy of will and dedication as an invincible guarantee of victory. The war in Vietnam was to be a test of the strategy of the people's war. [29] The test had a positive result and proved its worth in spite of all the sacrifices. There are bound to be repercussions.

[29] D.S. Zagoria, *China's strategy,* in A. Casty (ed.) *Mass media and mass men,* N.Y., 1968.

2. America was victorious in two world wars, 1914-1918 and 1939-1945, and thus attained a prominent position in world politics. But she has not been able to win this 'third world war' and finds her political predominance threatened. Her career in policing the world has clearly passed in zenith and will continue to decline.

The second world war left a great gap: England, which had controlled all the sea passages with Gibraltar, Suez, Aden the Cape of Good Hope and Singapore, had to withdraw; her colonies became independent states; world politics came more and more to be characterized by the cold war between the two super-powers. Then America, as Kennedy put it, found herself placed, by destiny rather than choice, on sentry duty at the frontiers of the free world. Anti-communism became her prime motive in all things. The Marshall plan had aimed to rebuild a strong Europe to oppose a possible invasion from the east. The Truman doctrine offered military and economic support only to states willing to oppose communism. In Vietnam the strategic safety of the whole of south-east Asia was at stake, since after South Vietnam, according to the 'domino theory', Laos, Cambodia, Thailand, Malaysia, Singapore and finally Indonesia and Australia would fall victim to the advance of communism. From the economic point of view (given that strategy is merely the armed escort of economics) these great human masses had to be protected as markets, and the exploitation of their raw materials assured. There was also the need to safeguard free passage through the Straits of Malacca which carry 98% of the trade between the Indian and Pacific Oceans including oil from the Perian Gulf for the USA. [30]

After the fall of South Vietnam and Cambodia, has the 'domino theory' become a reality? Communist guerrillas are already operating in the other states of south-east Asia and the large Chinese populations in Malaysia, Singapore and Indonesia cannot conceal their sympathy with greater China, even if they are not yet ready to change their standard of living for that of

[30] F.V. Drake, *Why we are fighting in Asia?*, in Casty *op. cit.*, pp. 207-212; R.F. McNair *Must America police the world?*, in *The Plain Truth*, California, April-May 1970, 2-6.

China. In any case, America will not lightly intervene: the antipathy of Americans to foreign wars cannot be ignored, any more than the antipathy to the Yankee nourished in other peoples. In too many places in the past, America showed herself quick to support any reactionary regime provided it offered proof of a clearly anti-communist attitude and would protect American interests and investments. [31] This period is coming to an end. Like France and England, twenty years ago, America will have to give up dominating the world; in tomorrow's world, her only possible honourable stance will be based on the promotion of progressive reforms and *free* commercial relations with respected partners. These are the lessons of Vietnam.

3. It would be mistaken to conclude that America's star is setting. It would be right to say that she will have to take account of rivals in a new polycentric world. After Russia, the first rival to arise is the loser in the second world war, the passive witness of America's first atomic bomb, Japan. Almost 100 years after making the acquaintance of western civilization, 25 years after the overwhelming defeat which led everyone to think that this proud empire would have to reconcile itself to a modest existence, Japan is back in third place among industrialized nations. It is merely a matter of time (probably ten years) before Japan overtakes the Soviet Union. It will take less than 30 years to challenge US predominance. This is the prediction of one of America's futurologists in the economic sphere, H. Kahn. [32] Kahn sees the basis of Japan's explosive development in the spartan frugality of the Japanese, their exemplary industriousness, their absolute loyalty to the community and their burning zeal to cut a fine figure before the world and to make Japan great. To that must be added co-ordinated planning between the state and private industry, almost complete abstention from re-armament, and a favourable relation with the Pacific hinterland, from which Japan draws necessary raw

[31] Myrdal G., *Politisches Manifest über die Armut in der Welt*, Frankfurt, 1970, pp. 258, 328ff, 372f, 448ff, 452. Cf. also the well known book by W.J. Lederer and E. Burdick, *The ugly American*, London, 1959.

[32] H. Kahn, *Bald werden sie die Ersten sein. Japan 2000*, München, 1968.

material and to which she supplies technical experts and business men. Today, Japan gets more from this region by peaceful economic penetration than could be gained by military occupation.

Of course, since Kahn's prognoses, this peaceful conquest is slowing down. In the last five-year plan (1972-1976) Japan has ear-marked twice as much for military expenditure as in the previous period. Her commercial activity is beginning to meet difficulties and to arouse antipathy in other countries. This suggests that that the Japanese must beware lest they go the way of the Yankee in Latin America. Moreover, they have suddenly found themselves menaced by the pollution of their water and atmosphere. Finally, young Japanese do not seem to have the same drive for achievement as the previous generation, nor are they willing to make the same sacrifices, so the system cannot maintain the pace and discipline of the ant-hill. The ministry of labour has been quick to draw the conclusions: a White Paper in 1972 recommended a five-day week, longer holidays, more travel (thus stimulating an unheard-of boom in tourism) and more internal consumption. [33]

But Japanese economic development will continue, even if the tempo is reduced, in a Pacific sphere of influence (the Philippines, south-east Asia, Indonesia, Australia, possibly even China) which will leave the European Economic Community in the shade. In the year Norway said 'No' to the latter, in September 1972, the Japanese prime minister Tanaka visited Peking, resolving centuries of hatred in a few hours of cordial negotiation. The Italian newspaper *Il Tempo* commented on this event in a leading article with the significant headline: 'Ancient Europe — Young Asia'.

4. Japan's meteoric rise, the writing on the wall in Vietnam and the enormous drive of China are unseating yesterday's western-dominated world and shifting the world's centre of gravity eastwards.

Regrettably, the course of events in the world has always had a close relation to military history. The first world war

---

[33] Regular reports in the press and *Japan's role in Asia,* in *Impact,* Manila, 1972, no. 11.

was followed by expansion towards the west. The United States came out of 'splendid isolation', made an active and decisive contribution to the outcome of the war and, from then on, were full participants in the history of the West. The second world war was followed by a southward expansion. The peoples of Africa and Asia, until then merely objects of colonization, manipulation and missionary activity emanating from Europe as centre of the world, gained independence or won it by force of arms and entered into full partnership in the community of peoples. Then, in Vietnam a 'third world war' took place, much smaller than the others in its field of operations but longer in duration and more decisive in its long term historical influence. It was a confrontation not merely between the two parts of the country and the great powers backing them but between two worlds, communist and capitalist. For this very reason, America could not be allowed to win, since it would have hurt the susceptibilities of Russia and China too much; but, equally, America was not forced to accept defeat, since it was time for the Super-powers to make friends. An accommodation of sorts was reached on matters not yet decided; these will be decided in years to come on economic and diplomatic battlefields.

So this military conflict, together with the other two factors mentioned, has brought about extension eastwards. Four out of the five great economic blocks touch the Pacific: the USA, Russia (with the ports of Vladivostok and Nakhodka), Japan and China. In America, as a result of the Vietnam war and also because of favourable climatic conditions, there has been a shift of economic activity from the east coast facing Europe to the west coast facing Asia. Japan is strengthening its commercial links not only with China but also Russia. Russia would like to benefit from Japanese capital and technical expertise for the development of its eastern Siberian provinces. There is talk of a giant oil and gas pipe-line leading to a port on Wrangel Island (to be constructed by the Japanese). This would reduce Japanese dependence on Middle East oil. [34]

Tourism in this area will expand greatly, since all the

---

[34] Th. I., *Japan in neuer Konstellation*, in *Vaterland*, Lucerne, 11.10. 1972.

distances can now be covered in a one-night flight. The Hawaian islands, for instance, can be reached in a flight of four to six hours from all four economic blocks. Thus the greatest ocean will become an inland sea, easier to manage than the Mediterranean in ancient times. Already all the indications are that the Pacific has become the world's most important ocean, that the 21st century will be not only, as Kahn predicts, the 'Japanese century' but also the 'Pacific century' (not only in the geographic sense, it is to be hoped), and that the political and economic centre of gravity of the world has moved from the west to the east.

5. If this is the state of affairs, we shall have to resign ourselves before long to seeing a new shape to the map of the world. Until now, at least in Europe, it was impossible to represent it otherwise than with Europe symbolically in the middle surrounded by the other giant continents. From now on, we shall have to move the two Americas from the left side to the right, put the Pacific and its surrounding states in the middle and consequently move Europe out to the western margin. Europe will retain its intrinsic importance but the pre-eminence it has held for 2000 years, and especially since the Age of Discovery, is lost for ever. Between 1950 and 1975 there has been a decisive change in the shape of the world. One period in history has come to an end and another is beginning.

There was a significant episode at the 29th congress of orientalists held in Paris in 1973. All the representatives of the 'Orient' protested against the use of this term which implies that Europe remains the centre of the world. For Japan and China, the 'Orient' would be the United States. It was decided to adopt another title and call it a 'congress for humanist studies on Asia and North Africa'. However, for practical reasons, I shall continue to speak of east and west — Orient and Occident.

The maps which follow show how the centre of the world has shifted in the course of history:

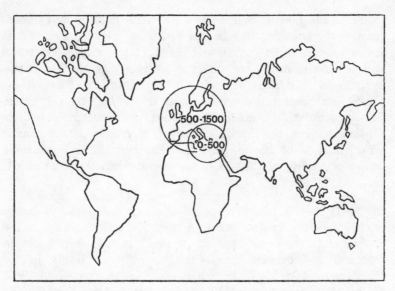

The centre of gravity of the world in Christian antiquity and in the middle ages.

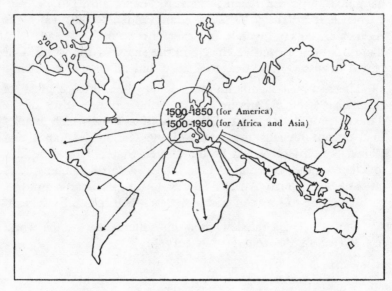

The centre of the world in the Age of Discovery.

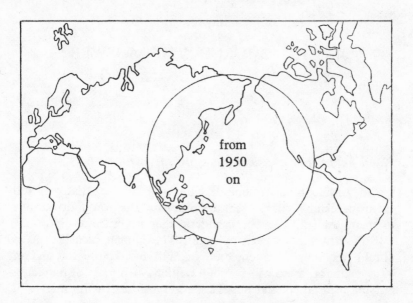

The new centre of the world.

6. We must bear in mind that Rome is no longer at the centre of the world, as she has been almost uninterruptedly from the time of the Roman empire. Classical Greek and Roman culture is no longer, exclusively, the source and basis of world culture, as it has been assumed to be from the Middle Ages on. Consequently, the Church in Rome must reflect deeply on her position in the world of tomorrow. It will not be determined by western history any longer but by the present and future of the new continents. The Church's opportunities are to be sought in local Churches in the south and east. These Churches ought not to be unconditionally bound by the structures evolved within the history of the west. The Third Church is taking up her rightful place; by attending to her own sources and remaining rooted in her native soil she will find her own strength and, at the same time, add to the riches of the universal Church.

Chapter 5

IS THE CHURCH THE ANSWER?

A. *The universal sacrament of salvation*

1. Although one should fight shy of superlatives and exclusive claims, the present condition of the world drives one to them. At least, no one can deny that never before have the world's expectations been so great. The human race has taken untold millennia to reach 3000 millions but before the end of our generation there will be 6000 millions — a mass of humanity nursing aspirations and hopes as never before. In the matter of awareness, we face an entirely new situation: thanks to modern means of communication and the penetration of modern civilization into the remotest corners of the globe, everyone knows of the possibilities of a better life. We are no longer reconciled to our fate; we have been sensitized, organized, stimulated to react. 42% of the 2500 millions in the Third World are under 15: that is to say, 1050 million youngsters are looking wide-eyed at this world of their hopes and longings. In the year 2000 they will be in their prime: what will the next 25 years bring them — and then the next millennium? Hopes fulfilled or disappointed?

2. Messianic movements cropping up all over the Third World in the last ten years show just how strong and impulsive, but at the same time irrational and unrealistic, such expectations can be; contact with colonization and with Christianity destroyed the former equilibrium in consciousness, making it susceptible to any prophet who promises liberation from material, moral, social and political deprivation. Such movements are reactions against a form of existence which has become burdensome to people aware of the advantages of civilization without actually possessing them, and are always accompanied by resentment

88

against the white man who has humiliated them, who dominates and despises them. The feeling of impotence drives people into the religious world and makes them dream, usually under the influence of Old Testament miracles and liberation stories, of a future Messiah who will obtain for them all that they expect. [1] A world lies open before them and they wait for salvation, as thirsty land waits for the rain.

3. The higher the hopes, the greater the disappointment. People had to recognize that independence day did not bring an earthly paradise. Then they heard of organizations and commissions, in rich and poor countries alike, concerned with aid to the poor. When they went to them, they were passed from one to the next with renewed hopes, and all too often with renewed disappointment, while deprivation continued to prevail in the land. The United Nations appeared as the most splendid of these post-war organizations; it did much but failed to satisfy all the hopes pinned on it. A whole series of wars in Africa and Asia could not be prevented and, besides, peace is something more than the mere absence of fighting. There was no controlling the arms race in rich and poor states, and now it is not merely a sword of Damocles that hangs over the peoples but the nightmareish possibility of an atomic mushroom forming at any moment over their capital cities.

U Thant thought that perhaps the most enterprising achievement of the UN was to approve the Universal Declaration of Human Rights; but in fact those rights are not respected in many states. Neither the voluminous reports and innumerable recommendations from organizations affiliated to the UN (ECOSOC alone had formulated 1235 resolutions in 1967) nor an annual budget of 184 million dollars and a staff of 9000 employees from over 100 nations [2] have yet renewed the face of the earth.

---

[1] Out of the copious bibliography on this subject, we might mention the books of Guariglia, Fuchs, and also: H.J. Margull, *Aufbruch zur Zukunft. Chiliastisch-messianische Bewegungen in Africa und Südostasien*, Gütersloh, 1962; H. Schar, *Erlösungsvorstellungen und ihre psychologischen Aspekte*, Zürich, 1950.

[2] The United Nations, *The next 25 years*, N.Y., 1970, pp. 205, 207, 219.

In this world of titanic enterprises, which still cannot solve its own problems, there is a growing sense of paralysis and weariness as well as a seething spirit of rebellion and revolution. If the Redeemer was born at a time under Caesar Augustus 'when the world was at peace',[3] today he must come into a world that is confused and lost and which, therefore, has all the more need of him.

4. At that time, he came into the world. He did good to all men. He opened up the prospect of the kingdom of God to all who believe and hope. He spoke of the Father in heaven who takes more care of every man than he does of the birds of the sky and the lilies of the field, who welcomes the prodigal son with joy and prepares a feast for him. Further, he was not content to speak but translated his words into deeds: he provided bread, cured the lame, forgave sinners. The poor and sinners got on well with him. The rich and respected found him a thorn in the flesh. They felt threatened by him and in the end found a way to get rid of him. If Christ were to return now — how many men would be as he wishes them to be? After his death, he gave his disciples to know that he lived, that he was near them even when he did not appear to them, and that through them he wished to be near all men even to the ends of the earth.

5. So, after him the group of his disciples has continued to exist, as his *Church* (when in this context and in the rest of the book there is mention of the Church, for theological and practical reasons I am thinking in the first place of the Catholic Church but not in an exclusive sense). The Church is a sign of hope held aloft among the peoples, the place of the coming of the Holy Spirit in the world, the voice proclaiming salvation to all who are wretched, the people among whom this salvation appears visibly and who have the distinctive vocation of committing themselves to passing on this salvation to all. It would be necessary to write long hymns on the Church and to the Church, with the literary talent of a Gertrude von Le Fort, to express even inadequately what she means for humanity.

[3] The former reading in the Martyrology for Christmas Eve.

However, more important than what is written about her is the way she presents herself to the world.

6. The Second Vatican Council repeatedly chose to describe her as the 'universal sacrament of salvation' (*universale salutis sacramentum*). [4] Now, it seems, we hardly dare to express out loud so great a claim. In patristic teaching on the Church and in more recent theology 'sacrament' means the whole economy of salvation, with its focal points in Christ the primordial sacrament, in the Church and then also in the seven sacraments. Hence the Council text intends to attribute to the Church an instrumental sacramental causality, both symbolic and efficacious, within the context of God's saving plan for all mankind. [5] 'Salvation' is that towards which all men aspire but which, for the present, no one possesses to the full. The Church preaches salvation through God and brings it to men not, in the first place, as some *thing* but rather as a new relationship with God who is revealed to be favourable to man. Similarly, damnation consists fundamentally not in external circumstances but rather in a deeply rooted disposition of the human personality. Nevertheless, such salvation is not purely spiritual in character but tends to embrace man in his immediate totality as well as in his social and cosmic relations, even if for the moment he remains subject to the dialectic of the 'already' and the 'not yet'. Sin is no longer considered predominantly as an affair of the individual but is increasingly seen as incarnate in structures and in political and social injustices. Consequently, salvation in the fullest sense of the term implies also redemption from these injustices and transformation of the structures towards a better world in the way indicated by the gospel. [6] 'Universal', finally, indicates that this salvation is for all men who are in need of it, not simply for those who are *in* the Church, and for all situations which lack it. So the Church is always 'the universal means of salvation'. This is, indeed, a tremendous claim.

7. Because of this, the fundamental attitude of the Christian

[4] LG 48, 1, 9; GS 45; AG 1 and 5.
[5] A. Grillmeier, in LThK, *Konzil* I, 157.
[6] J. Ratzinger, LThK 5, 78-80; J. Linssen, *The Bangkok Conf.*, in SEDOS Doc., 6.3.1973; The Synod of Bishops, Rome, 1974.

91

is *confidence* which should prove itself in all his actions. True, before Vatican II many preachers and confessors had the reputation of being rather disposed to admonish, scold and prohibit, and even today there are those for whom the windows opened by John XXIII only let in black birds of ill omen. The attitude is understandable and human, since the world still has its dark sides, but it is not particularly Christian. Apart from the fact that lamentation does not drive the ravens away, the Church as sacrament of salvation is not meant to draw up an account of these evil times and issue condemnation but much rather to spread light in the darkness, speak words of hope to the despairing, encourage those who have lost heart, show a way out of impossible situations and thus preach salvation to all men, Christians and non-Christians alike, black and white, illiterates and astronauts, and assure even the ex-commandant of the Auschwitz concentration camp, who knows himself cursed and condemned by all, that there still is one who believes in him, and that in him — in Jesus Christ — he is still offered a chance of salvation. [7]

In many places in Africa, India and Indonesia, this state of mind attuned to salvation can be sensed during Christmastide. The joy of Christmas is expressed in song during great celebrations (often ecumenical) in national stadia or in other public places. They dance in groups all day and night, proclaiming in song and mime to the whole people: 'A Saviour is born for you'. It is after all right to take seriously the promises of the prophets and the gospel story.

8. This tone of confidence is not the same as easy optimism about salvation, or unrealistic blindness to evils present in the world and in the Church. No one is denying sin and Antichrist, nor can anyone who has his eyes open. When Christ speaks, as

[7] Cf. Rud. Höss, *Kommandant in Auschwitz,* München, 1963. Höss was responsible for the gas-chamber death of hundreds of thousands of prisoners. He was captured after the war and hanged on 16 April 1947. In prison, he wrote his memoirs which finished as follows: 'Public opinion will continue calmly to see in me only the bloodthirsty animal, the cruel sadist, the murderer of millions — the broad masses can hardly imagine the Commandant of Auschwitz otherwise. They could never understand that he had a heart, that he was not evil' (p. 156).

if about something very obvious, of the evil spirit who returns with seven like himself so that 'the last condition is worse than the first' (Lk 11:26), when Paul sighs over the man who has not yet come to the experience of faith and grace, and laments that he cannot do the good that he would while he commits the evil that he hates (Rom 7:14-16), when poets speak of the 'curse of evil actions, condemned to conceive and give birth to more evils' (Schiller), it is clearly time to take account of reality and not fall victim to facile utopianism. But in the contemporary world, men of the Church must cry out in a loud voice that, notwithstanding this evil reality, God has said a very definite 'Yes' to human history in Jesus Christ (cf. 2 Cor 1:19-20). Underneath all the sins and all the bewilderment of modern man — superman and underdog, anarchic man, sexualized and demonized man — there lies a profound need of the human heart; historic difficulties are never overcome and finally solved until the need which is manifested in this bewilderment has found true fulfilment instead of merely apparent satisfaction. [8] The Church will always put forward this point of view in any discussion, and so will never join the prophets of doom but will always believe confidently in God's final victory.

All this does not exclude a certain bitterness in life and a certain melancholy. [9] There are plenty of situations which have to be understood in the light of Good Friday rather than of Easter morning. Dag Hammerskjöld, the unrecognised mystic in the United Nations headquarters, saw before him all the unsolved problems in the world and noted in his spiritual diary: 'The third hour and the ninth hour: they strike now, now. Jesus is in mortal anguish until the end of the world. During this time, we must not sleep'. [10] We may not separate the cross and the resurrection, the two poles of the existence of Christ and of the Christian, although in our daily experience we may feel the attraction now of one pole and now of the other.

[8] Sedlmayr, *Verlust der Mitte*, Salzburg, 1955, p. 207f.
[9] K. Rahner, *Weltgeschichte und Heilgeschichte*, in *Schriften V*, 115-135, esp. 132.
[10] Sven Stolpe, *Dag Hammerskjölds geistlicher Weg*, Frankfurt, 1965; K. Kurz, *Zu Dag H. geistlichem Tagebuch*, in *Geist und Leben*, 1965, pp. 185-200.

9. When, therefore, we assert that the Church is present in the zone of hunger, disease and desperation, not in order to exacerbate this desperation and cause it to explode without any good result but in order to transform it in the hope of Easter, the question at once arises how far such a claim corresponds to reality. Can we say that the Church is the 'sacrament of salvation' in Latin America or elsewhere without blushing for shame? In Asia, the most enlightened pastors agree that the Church is still becoming steadily more irrelevant to the needs and fundamental aspirations of the young peoples. These peoples are advancing more rapidly than the thinking of the Church. The Church has, indeed, developed many social services but has not carried out any radical rethinking.[11] In Kerala for example, and elsewhere, by providing schools she has made a decisive contribution to awakening people and introducing them to the modern world. But this becomes detrimental when she remains stagnant in theology and discipline and, consequently, in permanent conflict with the ruling élite, with students and with the workers. Many bishops and missionaries betray a strange impotence. They feel that something is wrong, that something is happening; but they do not know how to react, for example, to the lack of native priests, to the possibility that missionaries could be expelled, to the advance of communism, etc. They have lost the principles of action: they do not know how to respond and cannot devise a courageous and far-seeing plan of action. A general atmosphere of spiritual weariness certainly does not encourage new ideas, but the situation worsens through stagnation and immobility. Would that the Spirit of Christ might intervene and give his Church new courage and new strength!

10. Clearly the Church's response can no longer be proclaimed from high up in the pulpit. (The new architecture has taken account of this!). She would be accused of superficiality, of having her answers ready-made, centuries-old and applicable to everyone without discrimination. Such answers will not do any longer. Real questions, today, arise out of real situations of suffering and experience. The true answers can only come

[11] Tissa Balasuriya, in *Jeevadhara. A Journal of Christian Interpretation*, Allepey, India, 1972, pp. 330-340.

through understanding *with* people and suffering with them. This is the only way they can be recognized as *answers to real and actual questions*. Otherwise they will pass unnoticed. 'It is necessary to immerse oneself with courage and simplicity in the situations as they present themselves. You do not save those who are drowning in the river of current events by standing on some imaginary "river banks of eternity" but only by having the courage to swim in the current'. [12] Ready-made answers and the sense of possessing the truth in a definitive manner have often in the course of the centuries been a hindrance to real meeting with the world. They led to monologue not dialogue. Now we are more modest. Cardinal S. Pignedoli, when he was secretary of the Congregation for the Propagation of the Faith, said at the All India Seminar at Bangalore in 1969 that Christ is, indeed, the answer to all questions but that does not mean that the Church has at her disposal solutions and miraculous resources for all problems; the Church is much rather a seed bed for solutions, animating individuals and societies who have to deal with the problems. [13] A Church taking up this attitude is much more credible to men of today than one continuing to offer the wrong kind of security.

11. This emphasizes that the Church is not something out of this world. To speak of the Church *and* the world is anachronistic. It is more a question of the 'Church *in* the contemporary world', as the pastoral constitution of Vatican II puts it, or else the 'Church *of* the world'. The comparisons Christ used to describe the mission of his Church all point in this direction: light of the world, salt of the earth, leaven in the dough. There are two distinct realities which nonetheless interpenetrate, living one in the other and one from the other, not two 'perfect societies' co-existing and meeting only at certain points of contact and intersection. The Church lives in function of the world and not vice versa. She has to ask where and in what ways the world is obscure, overburdened and in need of salvation, where it needs help. Hence, the world establishes the order of the day: it is in accordance with its needs that the Church must under-

---

[12] Rahner, in *Handbuch der Pastoraltheologie*, I, 224.
[13] *Church in India*, 444.

stand herself as sacrament of salvation. This world in ferment is the Church's (theological) territory: it is not simply the object of her activity, nor even just her partner in dialogue; it is a part of herself in which the joyous message of the gospel is lived out. [14]

This is the way to overcome that wrong attitude to the rights of the Church which in the past has caused missionary activity to be restricted and now even to be called altogether in question — the attitude that treats the good of the Church as more important than salvation through the Church, as if the Church were a rival of the world, as if the purpose of mission were to extend the Church's scope for its own sake, to bring men into the Church and to separate and isolate them from the community they belong to, to build up a powerful Church as a state within the state. Such 'ecclesiocentric' attitudes must be eliminated once and for all, so that the Church may shine forth in the world. [15]

12. According to Toynbee, each culture is challenged and stimulated by facing new situations and is kept alive by this continual process. Harsh climate, overpopulation, class struggle and religious divisions demand a response. But each challenge presents us with the Sphinx's demand: 'Answer or be devoured'. Those who neither answer nor react appropriately will perish. Thus there are cultures which disappear and others which survive, stagnant cultures and self-renewing cultures. [16] The Church is not exempt from this historical law. As we have seen in previous chapters, she is facing unique challenges at the present time: the opening up of western culture to the whole world, the crushing poverty in which so many live and the advance of communism. Another challenge springs from contact with peoples who used to live at peace with their mythologies but are now coming up against modern insecurity; and yet another

[14] W. Kaspar, *Glaube und Geschichte*, Mainz, 1970, pp. 209-223, 240f; J.B. Metz, *Zur Theologie der Welt*, Mainz, 1969, p. 13f, 85 (ET *Theology of the World*, Burns and Oates, 1969); *Kirche für andere*, pp. 22-27.

[15] L. Rütti, *Zur Theologie der Mission*, München-Mainz, 1972, p. 268 and *passim*.

[16] P. Ricoeur, *Histoire et vérité*, Paris, 1964, p. 88f.

from the mass of 'youth who, by their simple presence among us, are prophets of what the future will be'. [17] God has his plans for all these groups and for each individual, plans which can be discerned not in dreams but in the 'signs of the times' (Mt 16:3f). Men of the Church are prophets who have the duty of explaining these signs of the times to the world.

A secular critic of civilization has written: 'Anyone who judged the present situation objectively, with the eyes of a detached observer, would readily come to the conclusion that our prospects are not rosy and that, taken all in all, indications of the future are more against us than for us. However, for those of us who hold ourselves committed to the cause of liberty through fair weather and foul, a threat as grave as this becomes a motive for determining to do absolutely all we can and leaving the rest to history'. [18] If such a man can dare to have so much confidence, how much more the Christian who, as he looks at the three southern continents, can see that the Church has ahead of her even greater opportunities than today for carrying out her mission of bringing salvation. [19]

13. In sharp contrast with this point of view is the attitude of those who speak of the crisis, and plainly the end, of the missions. In the homelands there seems to be growing apathy and neo-isolationism with regard to the missions. [20] The reasons for this are various and need not be treated at length here. [21] Missionaries themselves, in courses during their vacations and in conferences in the mission territories, are wondering about the meaning of their existence. [22] This means that even those

[17] Paul Valéry, quoted by Y. Congar, *Initiatives locales et normes universelles,* Conférence à Rome, 1972.

[18] A. Rüstow, *Ortsbestimmung der Gegenwart,* Erlenbach, 1950, I, 19.

[19] Cf. E. Bolaji Idowu, *The predicament of the Church in Africa,* in C.G. Baeta (ed.), *Christianity in tropical Africa,* Oxford, 1968, pp. 417-436; R.G. Goté, *Prospective de l'Eglise en Afrique,* in *Eglise Vivante,* Louvain, 1970, pp. 331-341; M. Légaut, *Pour entrevoir l'Eglise de demain,* in Lumen Vitae (Fr. ed.), 1972, no. 1, pp. 9-40.

[20] Boberg at al. (ed.), *Mission in the seventies,* p. 148.

[21] Bühlmann, *Die Fragwürdigkeit der Mission,* in KMJ 1967, 4-7: id. *Mission — Ende oder Wende?,* KMJ 1969, 4-10.

[22] *Conference of Religious India,* 1969; the whole conference was devoted to this question.

who incarnate in their lives the meaning of the Church's mission are groping in the dark! At one time, there were few things so surrounded by a romantic halo as missions and missionaries. Now the halo is discredited and demythologized. What remains? Very much indeed. We ought to bring it out into the open. This is not the place for a theological proof of the significance of the missions. Here we presuppose it. [23] Those who do not feel its urgency cannot be expected to pursue it with zeal. But for those who believe in God the Father, in Jesus Christ his Son and in one, holy, catholic and apostolic Church, the raison d'être of mission is beyond dispute; it remains only to discuss, and that profoundly, how the mission of the Church is to be carried out and what methods are to be adopted at the present time. The more decisively we embark on new ways, not persisting in using yesterday's solutions on today's problems, the sooner the significance of mission will become crystal clear. It is certainly no anachronism to go on speaking of mission. We are not, I hold, at the end but rather at the beginning of an extraordinary missionary era. The foundations of world mission were laid in the first half of this century. The post-war period formed a new image of the world and the Council cleared the way for an interior renewal of the Church. The last quarter of the century will show how far the Church is able to take up the challenge and exploit the opportunity this new situation offers.

B. *Human dignity*

The Pastoral Constitution *Gaudium et spes* (the Church in the modern world) had a rough passage: only at the eighth revision did it gain the approval of the Council fathers. Now the passage from theory to practice is even more laborious. First of all, the Church has to learn to make her way *in* the world. The lesson *must* be learned: being 'the universal sacrament of salvation' implies many things not directly connected

---

[23] Kasper, *Glaube und Geschichte,* Mainz, 1970, pp. 259-264: *Warum noch Mission?;* K. Rahner, *Pastoraltheologie,* II, 2, 46-80: *Grundprinzipien zur beutigen Mission der Kirche.*

with the perfect kingdom of the hereafter. Having been oriented in too one-sided a way towards the world to come, with a correspondingly one-sided concern for the souls of men, the Church must now direct herself to man as such, as he is now living in this world. With this in mind let us cursorily recall what has already been said about the world's new shape, so as to show briefly how the Church, alongside her universal preaching of salvation, must carry out her concrete task in the world.

1. *In the free world*

1. Freedom, which is necessary to make a man a man in all his dignity, is far too sublime a gift to be achieved overnight by a change of political flag. It is not given once and for all; it must be won again and again and continually perfected in the course of an individual human life and in the history of a people.

The first task of the Church in the young nations consists in broadening peoples' sights (since pre-conciliar catechisms with their sharp division between worship and life produced a sort of religious self-centredness — as if all that mattered was saving one's own soul), so as to turn the faithful gathered for worship into mature Christians and thus into model citizens of the state collaborating positively and courageously towards solving problems faced by the nation. We must admit this is a peak yet to be scaled. There is food for thought in the fact that peoples 'without religion', like Japan and China, have managed to create a community spirit and bring about spectacular economic progress, while 'religious people', as in India, Latin America and the predominantly Christian élite in Africa, run after their private interests along capitalist lines.

2. Precisely because of these problems in establishing freedom, the Church needs to become a counterbalance or, better, the conscience of the state, exercising a function of social criticism. She has to be the refuge of liberty, the voice of the weak and the oppressed who cannot make their own voices heard. The Church must not be silent where torture is practised, where political opponents are imprisoned, where there are public

executions and where the weak are exploited. She must gain the reputation of being the group of people who will not accept things as they are and who oppose oppression of man by man.

This conception of the Church's duty provokes questions: Will this not, in the end, disguise the true nature of the Church? Isn't this perhaps running away from unanswered problems in theology and Church membership, and from embarassment about fulfilling the Church's true spiritual task? Doesn't this approach incur the risk of incompetent, amateurish interference in the complicated fields of politics and economics? [24] This last reservation was also expressed in the sharp criticisms of many economists (who felt themselves directly called in question and blamed) after the publication of *Populorum Progressio* in 1967 and after the conclusions reached by the World Council of Churches at Uppsala in 1968 about working for radical changes in the structures of society. [25] The Church cannot and may not allow herself to be distracted from her intention by such opposition, which was only to be expected. The synod at Rome in 1971 again confirmed that it is not possible to remain silent on the cries of those who suffer from violence and are oppressed by systems and mechanisms which are unjust; we may not ignore the challenge of a world which, by its perversity, contradicts the Creator's plan. Of course it is not the task of the Church to offer technical solutions in politics and economics, but she has the duty of recalling to men's consciences the demands of the gospel, of protecting man's dignity and his fundamental rights. [26]

Taking up a position on these questions must be counted among the most difficult of the Church's tasks but also the most

[24] HK 1971, pp. 305-308: *Uebernehmen sich die Kirchen?*

[25] Cf. the many contemporary press reports.

[26] AAS 1971, 923-942. Cf. also the activities and publications of the Pontifical Justice and Peace Commission. Bibliography in n. 57. The symposium of the African bishops' conference (SECAM) 1972 has appointed a 'Commission for inner African affairs', to study concrete instances of injustice and oppression and to recommend appropriate measures. A special problem calling for the attention of the Church is the so-called 'fourth world', i.e. the emigrés, refugees and oppressed minorities. Cf. M. Bordeaux, *The Fourth World*, London, 1972.

58501

decisive; she must undertake this task, on pain of passing for
a collection of old fuddy-duddies, irrelevant to the modern
world. On the one hand, it would be wrong to rush into open
opposition; on the other, it would be equally wrong to be silent
through fear and false prudence, like the watch dog that has
not the courage to bark (Is 56:10). The right attitude can only
be found in absolute freedom from worldly bonds and in living
in the presence of the Lord of history.

3. This sounds all very well in theory and in the abstract.
It is possible to find formulas and draw up documents which
meet with general approval. But once we come down to the
concrete and practical, the community divides into the 'prudent'
and the 'courageous'. In the episcopal synod in 1971, some
representatives spoke quite openly about abuses and referred to
concrete cases. Their criticisms were reported in *L'Osservatore
Romano* and thus gained a certain amount of publicity. But the
final document refrained from mentioning concrete instances,
not for diplomatic reasons this time but for the sake of fairness:
in fact, if a start in condemning particular cases were to have
been made in such a document, no country could have come out
unscathed.

The Church's critical social function must be exercised *at
three levels*. The first criticisms should come not from on high
but from the grass roots, from God's people in the neighbourhood, from all citizens but especially from young people since
they have a name for being particularly sensitive to cases of
injustice in the world. Many groups of workers and students in
Latin America, Africa and Asia whose sensibilities have been
aroused are making this type of effort. Next, individual bishops,
and especially episcopal conferences, must be ready to make
themselves heard, [27] not as external observers visiting some
foreign land but as responsible citizens of their own states. For
success in this they need to be absolutely united, or else one
bishop will be played off against another. The civil authority
called in question will not dare to go against a united Church.
This unity, in its turn, depends a very great deal on directives

[27] Reports in HK, ICI, IDOC, etc.

101

2

coming from the supreme authority, Rome. The three levels are inseparably interconnected.

4. This brings us to the problem of the *prophetic* and *diplomatic* functions in the Church. Christ gave his disciples the double directive: 'Be wise as serpents and simple as doves' (Mt 10:16). In a world as complex as this present one the Church cannot always take one and the same direct course. Attitudes and statements must necessarily vary according to circumstances and will sometimes appear contradictory. The selfish nationalism of great powers must be opposed while the exaggerated self-consciousness of smaller peoples must be met with understanding and sympathy. On principle, violence is to be rejected, but we side with those who are fighting for freedom and human dignity. We must denounce injustice and oppression and at the same time do what we can to keep our influence over the oppressors, to dissuade them from continuing their oppressive policy. For these purposes the Church needs both prophets and diplomats (in the good sense which is compatible with the gospel). Each needs to recognize the other and agree on complementary functions.

In Brazil, the two functions find flesh and blood expression in two Church leaders. On one side we have Archbishop Helder Camara, the voice crying in the wilderness, reminding the powerful of their misdeeds, putting his finger on the sore points, awakening the masses and calling them to non-violent revolution. The powerful brand him as a heretic and a communist; they detest him and will not listen. The powerless see him as their own special bishop. Alongside him, we have Cardinal Eugenio Sales, an ecclesiastical diplomat in the best sense, who does not burn his bridges but keeps in contact with the powerful and tries to practise politics as the art of the possible. Camara would long ago have finished in prison if there had not been Sales to defend him, and Sales would have carried less weight in his negotiations if Camara had not made his protest; they need one another. Unfortunately, the marriage of functions does not always work as well as it does in this instance; too often 'prophets' and 'pressure groups' are thought by the official Church to be disturbers of the peace and, therefore, in need of being silenced if possible. Solutions to the immense problems facing the Church and the world can be worked out only by open discussion of them, not by ignoring them in a spirit of cowardice.

Here we have much ground to recover. Some observations made by 30 spiritual guides of young people in various Asian countries are valid also for the other two southern continents: the Church and the majority of her institutions are not directed to the true needs and problems of these peoples; the better students find it more and more difficult to belong to a Church whose guides lack courage and the necessary decisiveness. [28]

2. *A world to be freed*

1. The triangle of southern Africa presents a special case, on which the Church may not be silent. [29] It is fair to say that the bishops of S. Africa and Rhodesia have done and said all they could and all that duty required. In a succession of documents they have declared that the refusal of civil rights to the black majority and the politics of apartheid cannot be reconciled with the Christian conscience. [30] It is to be hoped they will not be wearied by the apparent ineffectiveness of these documents, that in this matter they will keep even more firmly to a common front with other Christians, that white priests will not get too habituated to the situation and, out of regard for their 'white flock' by whom they are generously supported, close their eyes to injustices inflicted on blacks, and that the Church will proceed with even more courage to the necessary changes in her own structure. The two million Catholics in S. Africa and Rhodesia are more than 90% black, whereas the 32 diocesan bishops were still all white in 1974, and there were only three black auxiliary bishops. [31] No wonder then that the

[28] AIF 24.11.1971.
[29] See above ch. 2.C., p. 35-41.
[30] Southern African bishops' conference: in 1970, they published 8 documents on racial questions and in February 1972 a new pastoral letter echoing the bishops' synod in Rome 1971.
[31] AIF 24.7.1974.

black priests and lay people have been openly demanding Africanization since 1971.

2. Things are different in Mozambique and Angola. Unfortunately the anachronism of the political situation was matched by an equal anachronism in relations between Church and state. [32] On the basis of the 1940 concordat and the missionary agreement, the Church enjoyed many privileges: bishops were maintained and paid like governors of provinces, missionaries' journeys from and through the territory were at state expense with first class travel for priests and bishops; missions were considered educational services and supported as such. However, at the same time, the Church was bound and gagged: the bishops had to be Portuguese and with a few exceptions they proved unequal to the occasion, taking up an attitude which is not to the honour of their office. Right up to the coup, they thought that their charge consisted in maintaining a traditional line, in baptizing shoals of converts, in combining with the state to ensure 'peace and order' and in condemning the 'subversive' activity of the 'terrorists', while the best priests and black Christians felt betrayed by the Church and her diplomacy and were torn by the dilemma of remaining loyal to their country (not Portugal) or to the Church.

Two reports show how the local bishops thought along outdated lines. In 1971, a bishop from Angola declared to a 'high school for national defence' in Lisbon: 'After the Jewish people, no nation has shown as clear signs as Portugal of a special vocation from God to be worked out in history... The conquest of lands needed to complete her territory was undertaken not simply for political motives, for building an empire, but rather with the specifically Christian intention of spreading the faith'. In the same year, the official representative of Mozambique at the episcopal synod in Rome, replying to the charges of African bishops, said that, if condemnations were needed, the first thing to condemn was the terrorism and subversion in Mozambique. But the Church should not be

[32] J. Sanches, *Les missions catholiques et la politique de l'Etat portugais,* in *Spiritus,* Paris, 1972, pp. 370-382; id. in SML 1972, pp. 90-107.

concerned with such things and should concentrate on the interior conversion of men. 'We should trust one another. We should leave our brothers in peace and pray for them'. [33]

3. That the Portuguese bishops thought 'in Portuguese' is a fact and should be accepted as such. But that made it all the more desirable that the Vatican, whose word is heard all over the world, should speak clearly and take steps to change the situation. But the Vatican remained silent and Portugal made good use of the silence, borrowing the maxim, *Qui tacet consentire videtur*. Here we may ask: after all the trouble caused over the centuries by the Portuguese *padroado*, [34] was it really worth while to show so much respect for the Portuguese position and so to lose the sympathy of all the black African states? Whereas during the last phase of colonization the Church had adopted a courageous attitude [35] she now ran the risk of destroying the good impression then made. When the White Fathers in Mozambique protested against the situation in the country, with a form of protest that made up for the silence of the bishops, *Osservatore Romano* and *Fides* passed over the matter in complete silence, although they did publish unfavourable comment on the Protestant governments of South Africa and Rhodesia [36] and on communist states. Do we not have an even greater obligation to be objective in judging Catholic governments and to keep our distance so as not to involve the Church in justified criticism? Of course, what matters is maintaining a missionary presence in those countries. But the advice to 'preach the gospel, save souls and not get mixed up in politics' betrays an out of date way of thinking, suggesting that the soul is more than the man, that the gospel is a pious book of meditations with no direct connection with human dignity and human freedom. The salvation of the flock remains, un-

---

[33] SML 1972, 98; OR 24.10.1971.

[34] Full bibliography in LThK 8, 195f; J. Beckmann in NZM 1963, pp. 241-271, esp. 249-254.

[35] Cf. above ch. 2.D.3, p. 44.

[36] The animadversions of Paul VI in *Africae terrarum* 1967 (n. 17-19) were directly primarily against racial discrimination and therefore against South Africa.

doubtedly, one of the first duties of the pastor. But Christ faced up to the possibility that the pastor might be killed and the flock dispersed, in the certain confidence that he would lead them again after the resurrection (Mt 26:32). Sooner or later, these countries will be freed, with or without the Church. But the latter eventuality could turn out to the Church's disadvantage.

I wrote this in the spring of 1974. Liberation has come sooner than expected. Things began to move in September 1973. In that month, the Pope received three bishops from Mozambique. Next Sunday, 16 September, at the Angelus he spoke of Mozambique and other countries which are striving for independence. Soon after, he received the Patriarch of Lisbon and named Mgr E. Muaca as diocesan bishop, the first Angolan to receive such an office. All this led to the conclusion that the Vatican was taking up a new attitude to these two countries. Even so, the coup d'état, when it came, was a surprise and a humiliation. If the liberation does not rebound against the Church, it will be thanks above all to the missionaries who remained close to the people during this Calvary, and now feel more than ever united in brotherly union with the blacks.

3. *The poor world*

(a) *Development aid and/or animation?*

1. Anyone at all in touch knows the Churches have been playing a large part in the struggle for the 'second liberation' with which we were concerned in Chapter 3; in plain fact they have about 50,000 people engaged in development work and make about 1000 million DM available each year for social works in developing countries (more than all the organizations affiliated to the United Nations put together). [37]

We can distinguish three stages in missionary aid for development. In the first, missions open bush schools and dispense medical aid as their response to deprivation — a sort of first aid. After some time comes the second stage: solidly built

[37] *Future of the Church*, 37.

primary, secondary and technical schools, great hospitals and model farms. When the words 'development aid' were first heard, missions could point proudly to what they had already achieved. Now, these institutions must certainly be kept, but we need to go further and pass from positional warfare to war of movement. The watch-word of the third stage is: 'Out of our fixed positions and advance'. [38]

2. The Church must recognize that in external works for development hers is a *subsidiary function*. She intervenes when there is need and as long as there is need, where the state is not yet in a position to take the initiative. Beyond this, missions can only provide timely aid, preparing the ground for development rather than carrying out development. True development can only be brought about by good structural changes, social justice, sound industrialization and favourable conditions of world trade. This is what *Populorum progressio* insisted on. The encyclical devoted only one incidental section (12) to the development of the missions themselves, a point taken badly by some missionaries who thought they were being overlooked. But development *is* a worldly business, in the proper sense. It has its own autonomy, even though it should come under the inspiration of the gospel. It calls for capital aid, for competitiveness and for competent assistance but not for ecclesiastical jurisdiction or the Church's official ministry. Hence, it is a matter for the laity not for the institutional Church. [39]

3. This does not mean that mission's work for development is finished. The subsidiary tasks it performs will still be needed for some time, depending on conditions in the various countries. Its strength will continue to lie in 'grass-roots projects'. Here, as a general rule, the Church will be filling its true role — a spiritual one — of preparing men's hearts and minds for development, animating them. If, then, there is less to do outwardly and visibly in future, we should expect to do much more along the other lines — the lines that determine so much. If aspira-

[38] W. Bühlmann, *Entwicklungshilfe und Mission,* in KMJ 1963, 6-19.
[39] A. Seumois, *Eglise missionaire et travail de développement,* in NZM 1970, pp. 161-174.

tions towards development have not made much headway to date, the real reason for this is that man himself has fallen short — man in his poverty, prisoner of magical religious ideas; tribal man yielding to the temptations of group interests; élitist man who is prey to corruption. [40] In this field, can anyone speak more forthrightly and effectively than the Church? Who is better equipped for the task of creating 'spiritual infrastructures', the will to work, trust and dedication to others? [41]

President Nyerere continually appeals for Church help in this. Once, speaking before a Catholic episcopal conference, he said: 'I ask your help. You have influence over the people. Without you my Declaration of Arusha (on socialism) will remain in the clouds'. Another time, failing to see any priests in a popular assembly, he said: 'I would like to see some priests here, since they carry my ideas to the villages better than government officials'. In another conference, he turned to the missionaries present and said: 'You missionaries can help us in these aspirations. The people of this country listen to you. You priests have great power. Every Sunday, you have so many people in church. Tell them they must pray, but tell them they must also educate their children well and work in the fields. I do not think it wrong to speak in church about working in the fields. If we are made in God's image, must we live in mud huts?' [42]

4. Just as there is a hierarchy of truths, according to which not all propositions about the faith are equally important, [43]

[40] On corruption, cf. ch. 3.B.3-4, pp. 59-61.
[41] Cf. the disturbing description of H. Volken, *Social Justice and community development,* in CIM 1973, pp. 27-32 where he shows how great hopes were aroused 20 years ago with the launching of the 'community development programme'. It was thought that 550,000 villages could be freed from need. The result has been a great disappointment for which the Church is not without blame, since she has not been actively involved and continues to bring up candidates for the priesthood in a theoretical atmosphere distant from the world, and has not been able to make the Christian faith a ferment for making men more unselfish.
[42] W. Bühlmann, *Die Kirche als entwicklungsfördernder Faktor in Africa,* in *Internationales Afrika-Forum,* München, 1971, pp. 549-555 esp. 553f.
[43] UR (Decree on ecumenism) 11.

so also there is a question of the opportuneness of truths (*kairos*) according to which in given circumstances one truth is to be stressed more and another less. It is clear that in the Third World, in its dark night of deprivation, we should speak less (I do not say, refrain from speaking) about matrimonial sins and about Sunday obligation but more and more loudly about the duty of Christians in the world, about commitment to others and the task God entrusted to us in creation, about the mystique of development as the symbolic break-through of God's kingdom. Our millions of Christians should form the vanguard of national aspirations, living cells for the work of nation building. This would cast a little light in the darkness.

(b) *Aid for development and/or evangelization?*

1. In future the missions will probably devote less effort to the traditional works and more to those inspirational activities known as 'animation'. One hopes so. It will still, however, be necessary to devote much money and effort to aiding development, no longer as a private concern of the mission but in concert with other groups, large and small, including Christians and non-Christians. The need for this is so great that it raises fears in some ecclesiastical circles for the *primacy of evangelization*.

Some missionary bishops complain that they can obtain money relatively easily for tractors and for raising poultry and pigs but not for the construction of churches. On the other hand, we hear tell of missionaries who give higher priority to an agricultural development project than to building a church, and who devote themselves so whole-heartedly to this kind of enterprise as to suggest that they are 'neglecting their priestly duty'. But those who think and speak in this way of them should remember that long before these social experiments were set up 20 to 40% of the missionaries in most missions devoted themselves to teaching, with the full approval of the Church. This was a 'priestly work' neither more nor less than modern social activities. Was there not more cause for concern in the days when religion was firmly separated from life, when worship was offered in places unconnected with daily life and the catechists went from village to village with a little book teaching 'nothing but' religion?

In Latin America, where the separation of sacred from profane has developed in a particularly detrimental way, priests complain that there are still too many bishops who seem to take no interest in social questions and are concerned only with keeping Catholic forces united under their own direction. [44] An extreme form of this attitude was expressed in a novel about Camillo Torres, in which the cardinal says to the journalist, 'My duty, Señor, consists in taking care of the spiritual good of those entrusted to me. Life here on earth is a very small matter compared to that awaiting us in heaven. So the rulers must concern themselves with this life, while I take care of the other life'. Valencia (C. Torres) confides to the same journalist, 'It is man who must take his own decisions. It is conscience which makes him able to respond. The voice of conscience could well be the voice of God... I often think that, if Christ came back to this world, no one would dare look him in the eyes... Among the wealthy classes, one protects the other; the others live without protection, without love, while all the time pictures of saints in our churches continue to look down unmoved on the worst social injustices of our centuries'. [45]

2. The question is badly put. It is not a matter of doing one thing or the other, of a dichotomy between evangelization and humanization, between the horizontal and the vertical dimension but rather of different aspects of the one reality: of the hope of Christ's Church in this world, of the two dimensions of the one Church realized in this world by *kerygma* and *diaconia*, preaching and service, worship and social commitment. The same Christian is member of the Church and of the world. There is in him a unity and symbiosis of two functions, stressing one or the other according to the circumstances without excluding either. Each Christian is a witness of the whole Church and assists the Church by expressing as best he can his mission

---

[44] E. Lakatos, *Die Bibelbewegung als Aufgabe der Kirche in Süda-merika,* in *Verbum,* Rome, 1970, pp. 97-107.
[45] W. Horman, *Der Guerilla-Priester,* Freiburg im B., 1969, pp. 79, 105f.

towards the world. It would, therefore, be false and detrimental to give way to mutual suspicion or to take offence at the direction development is taking. Whether we wish it or not, in the future more stress will be laid on development, and if evangelization cannot consent to be the soul of development it will be put on one side.

It is good that there is a general reaction against religious practice separated from life. The Catholic continent of Latin America and the Catholic Philippines must cease to be a scandal to non-Christian peoples by showing the world a false picture of Christ and his gospel. They must play a role in the plan of divine providence by showing the world that Christianity is capable of changing for the better a people and a society. [46] The same must be said of the Church present among non-Christian peoples. The final declaration of the national seminar of the All India association of Catholic students, at Goa, in May 1971, expressed this clearly: 'It is essential that the institutional Church say one thing in clear terms: not to take part unreservedly in the revolutionary movements of our time which struggle for social justice means to betray Christ and to abandon the sacramental life of the Church. We, the youth of India, want a Church of the poor, a Church with no more triumphalism, riches or ostentation in ceremonies, institutions or style of life, a Church appearing as a visible sign of Christian values in a developing country'. [47]

3. The Church in all her various functions is an integral unity. So is man with all his different aspirations; so also is salvation, properly understood, since it is universal. And so, finally, living the Christian life is to be thought of as one indivisible thing. Karl Rahner has some fine things to say about the unity between love of God and love of our neighbour. Instead of warning us against the spread of horizontalism, he has pointed out its close connection with the vertical dimension.

[46] H. Camara, *The Church and colonialism*, London, 1969, p. 23f, 54; C. McCarthy, *Le Filippine e l'evangelizzazione dell'Asia*, in *Civiltà Cattolica*, Rome, 1970, pp. 360-364.
[47] S. Kappen, *Ind. Studenten in der Glaubenskrise*, in KM 1972, pp. 121-124.

The two are not just juxtaposed; they are fused in a real unity. We practise the love of God through love of the neighbour and vice versa: whenever a person effaces himself in genuine love of his neighbour, he has taken a step towards God. The indissoluble union between the two relationships constitutes Christianity's basic conception of man. The Church's prophetic task is to proclaim this union in terms which leave no doubt; the two relations must not be divided, so as to suggest that one of them presents a second, additional obligation, because both occupy the foreground. Rather, preaching should reveal in radical fashion the ultimate dignity and deep meaning of man's relation to the human 'thou' of his neighbour. (This does not exclude explicit teaching about God and faith in him. On the contrary, every Christian knows well there is no *complete* salvation without the vertical dimension; it is not possible to take the horizontal completely seriously without the vertical.) We should be grateful for this insight since 'today we face a new situation. Mankind, with its immense numbers, having achieved a certain concrete unity and contrived new forms of community life, must learn to love in an entirely new way or will perish. At a time when God is being 'disclosed' as no more than an incomprehensible mystery of silence, man is tempted to honour him merely by silence... We are observing the rise of a world that is terribly worldly, which man is creating for himself. It should not be sacralized so much as experienced, and brought to fulfilment in its own depths which are sanctified by God himself, that is, open towards him. In this situation and in this era of change, love of one's neighbour could be a source, a key word, truly decisive and fully relevant... in which the whole of Christian salvation, the whole of Christianity is contained'. [48]

4. So we can do no other than congratulate and encourage those missionaries, laybrothers, sisters and native priests who are deeply committed to co-operation with the people, hand in hand and shoulder to shoulder with them in creating a better life,

[48] K. Rahner, *Ueber die Einheit von Nachstenliebe und Gottesliebe*, in *Schriften 6*, pp. 277-298; id., *Heilsauftrag der Kirche und Humanisierung der Welt*, in *Schriften 10*, pp. 547-567.

inspiring a new confidence, establishing a communion of practical love, making the kingdom of God visible on earth and, clearly, at the same time bearing witness to our wonderful God who is Father of all. During the preparatory phase of the synod of bishops in 1974 there was a tendency to restrict evangelization to the simple proclamation of the gospel, the sacraments and the hope of eternal life. In the event, the bishops of the Third Church spoke clearly in favour of integral salvation; after the thesis (the horizontal dimension) and the antithesis (the vertical) it was time to put forward the synthesis. It is fortunate that, in Africa especially, the schools for catechists are no longer preparing young men in theology and theory alone, in order to send them out as teachers of religion, but instead are giving a complete formation to young couples and then sending them into the villages as germinal cells of the new life — as 'animators'. In this way religion acquires its correct *Sitz im Leben* and can be seen in its true function — that of shaping life according to the joyous message of the Lord.

Hence, we shall no longer make the customary distinction between direct and indirect missionary methods, [49] but will talk of spoken witness and living witness, of explicit and implicit witness or, in Rahner's terms, of categorical and transcendental Christian activity. On this view, to practise evangelization in the right way is also the best way of working for development (since it provides the 'spiritual infrastructures' already mentioned in this chapter). And development work thoroughly carried out is the best evangelization — no more than implicit, certainly, but very effective. Only this unified view will enable us to overcome the crisis of identity in the missions, suffered both by missionaries and by Christians in the home countries. We can transcend the former patterns of thought and their distinctions and find a fresh anchorage in this new form of link-up between the missions and the world and in the Church's universally unifying efforts for the salvation of the world. If the Church does not penetrate the world in this way, as an efficacious sign of the love of God for his creation, then we must not be sur-

[49] J. Schmiedlin, *Kathol. Missionslehre im Grundriss,* Münster i. W., 1923, pp. 322-417.

prised if soon we have a world without the Church and the Church without the world. [50]

(c) *Evolution and/or revolution?*

1. Whatever we may think about it, revolution is a fact of life which cannot be eliminated from the present world. A world-wide revolutionary climate has been created, especially by Mao's ideology and his Little Red Book. In its first ten pages the term 'revolutionary' occurs 42 times. Now that the absurdity of total war has made for a strong feeling against war in general, paradoxically revolution is presented as socially acceptable. The ancient military hero becomes more and more questionable while the revolutionary hero begins to inspire fascination. [51] Many students, even novices and priests, have put up the picture of Che Guevara in their rooms. Revolution is not a phenomenon of the state of prosperity but of deprivation; it is a desperate gesture of defiance by the poor man (or by the rich man in solidarity with the poor, as in Che Guevara's case) against poverty and injustice. A World Bank study has established that violent unrest and revolution in recent times have affected only one rich country, but 48% of those with medium income, 69% of the poor nations and 87% of the very poor. [52] The relation between poverty and revolution is a proven fact which also shows the way to avoid revolution.

2. It goes without saying that we should not bypass available democratic means as steps to reform, that we should not be quick to resort to violent revolution. The latter, however, cannot be simply excluded from the list of permitted resources. The

[50] This is the radical concern expressed by Rütti; cf. also J. Schmitz (ed.), *Das Ende der Exportreligion. Perspektiven für eine künftige Mission,* Düsseldorf, 1971, pp. 70-98; Schooyans M., *Chrétienté en contestation: L'Amérique Latine,* Paris, 1969, pp. 249-274; J. Blomjous, *Christians and human development in Africa,* in AFER 1972, pp. 189-201; SML 1969: *L'Evangile au coeur du développement;* G. Bauer (ed.), *Towards a theology of development. An annotated bibliography,* SODEPAX, Geneva, 1970.

[51] W. Dirks, in E. Feil (ed.), *Diskussion zur Theologie der Revolution,* München-Mainz, 1969, p. 215.

[52] SML 1972, 7. The issue is devoted to the theme '*Missions au temps des révolutions*'.

Church, insofar as she must stand by the side of the poor, needs to give due attention to this phenomenon of revolution in poor countries.

If we search the gospels, we find it is as clear as day that Christians are called to be witnesses of the risen Christ and not agents of revolution. The revolution he brought into the world, inner renewal of man, has nothing to do with violence. The principles of non-violence are consistently worked out in the Sermon on the Mount and Christ acted in accordance with them. With the best will in the world it is not possible to distil from the gospel one drop of violent revolution. The revolutionary finds no explicit justification in the gospel. Christians must have the courage to present models of behaviour which the world cannot offer but which it needs. The Christians must put an end to the escalation of violence.

3. Still, the question cannot be settled quite as simply as that. After all, the Church has for centuries justified the killing of tyrants and spoken of just defence and just war. Why, then, cannot there be a 'just' revolution?

In 1967, Paul VI made a classic statement on this theme in *Populorum progressio*. Speaking of the unhappy situation of deprivation and revolution, he adds: 'and yet we know, revolutionary uprising — except in the case of clear and prolonged tyranny, seriously affecting the fundamental rights of the person and dangerously harming the common good of the nation — is a source of renewed injustices and provokes new disasters. We cannot fight against real evil by means of even greater evil'. [53] He admits, then, even though with the greatest caution, the legitimacy of revolution in exceptional cases. But it was as if he was alarmed by his own courage. The next year, during a visit to Colombia, he definitely withdrew his statement. Or did he? He condemned the way of atheistic Marxism, the way of bloodshed, anarchy and violence as unworthy ways of pursuing our aims, because love cannot take the way of hatred and violence. However, in condemning this type of revolution, he did not have in mind the other type, revolution born not of hatred but of

[53] PP 30-31.

115

love towards the neighbour who has been wronged, revolution seeking to proceed with moderation and prudence: this could represent a genuine Christian alternative to the cruder Marxist revolution. This type of revolution is the subject of the letter signed by eight hundred Latin American priests in a document directed to the episcopal conference and to the association of Christian trade unionists, an 'open letter to our brother Paul'. [54] Between the two extremes of brutal violence and absolute non-violence, there could be an intermediate solution. Simply because revolution and violence are misused, we should not conclude that we must close ranks against all possible use of force. This would leave force in irresponsible hands.

4. The episcopal synod in 1971 dealt expressly with world justice. Bishop Gutierrez Grassier of Bolivia and Bishop Dirivian of India sought clarifications on the theme of revolution and felt we should not identify this with Marxist revolution and then consider the matter closed. But other bishops continued to identify revolution with communism. The working groups did not in fact go beyond the directive to study the theology of revolution. [55] Consequently, in the final document, as distinct from the courageous working paper, the question was in effect put on one side. This was certainly an admission of inadequacy and a sin of omission in face of the harsh reality and the intolerable conditions in which so many men have to live.

5. The World Council of Churches at Uppsala in 1968 did not actually subscribe to R. Shaull's thesis nor did it indulge in an idealization of revolution, but it did admit that, in certain circumstances, Christians 'despair of their ability to get rid of economic injustice by peaceful means and feel obliged to have recourse to violence as a genuine solution. In such cases, violence and passive inaction both fall under the judgement of God... The Christian community has to establish whether it can recognize the validity of such decisions and support them'. [56]

[54] Cf. ICI Sept 1968, 10-13; Oct 1968, 12-22.
[55] OR 22-30, Nov 1971; cf. P. Land, *La giustizia nel mondo*, Rome, 1973.
[56] Goodall (ed.), *Bericht aus Uppsala*, Geneva, 1968, 70, 30.

So the W.C.C. did not make a ruling once for all but left each particular case to the conscientious judgement of Christians and communities involved.

6. In the meantime, ideas about the theology of revolution, political theology and liberation theology are gradually gaining a foothold. [57] It is asserted that theology, in order to recover some relevance, must be deprivatized (it was, in fact, too exclusively concerned with the interior life of Christians and the Church) and must deal with public issues (not in the sense of party politics but in terms of the common good) and with necessary structural changes. In this way, theology would not be politicized in the bad sense but actually depoliticized in so far as historical ties between the Church and the old structures would be weakened. It would mean preaching non-violence no longer merely to the poor but also to the rich and powerful. The same attitude which can drive individuals to say 'No' to the world and retire to a cloister might, it is claimed, today lead a person to put himself at the head of a social revolution, and it would be wrong to deny such 'rebels' the merit of a great love for Christ. [58] In the Missal we read, in connection with Saint Ferdinand the King, that he 'fought against thy (God's) enemies and defeated the enemies of the faith' and, in connection with Joan of Arc, that 'to confound the enemy' she did not 'shrink from facing the perils of war'. From these readings we may conclude that rulers who *today*, whatever 'faith' they profess, despise all Christian and human love are worse than the ancient enemies (Saracen or English), and that to eliminate such evil it may be right to take risks and, precisely by taking those risks, to actuate faith and love. It is fairly obvious that, in this post- or neo-colonial period, the missions will have no part to play unless they can be persuaded to commit themselves deeply in

---

[57] Cf. nn. 51, 52; further: T. Rendtorff, *Theologie der Revolution*, Frankfurt, 1968; H. Peukert, *Diskussion zur 'politischen Theologie'*, München-Mainz, 1969; G. Gutierrez, *Teologia de la liberación*, Salamanca, 1972; G. Adler, *Revolutionäres Laieinamerika. Eine Dokumentation*, Paderborn, 1970.

[58] J. Silone, *L'avventura di un povero cristiano*, Montadori, 1971, p. 31.

the social field instead of indulging in pietism. [59] This is said in the conviction that where a status quo contains no less injustice than could be caused by its overthrow, then it is permissible to undertake a revolution for justice sake, even in the name of Christian love. Then to risk giving one's life for others could become the highest expression of Christian love. [60]

7. No wonder that particularly in Latin America more and more priests refuse merely to administer the sacraments and distribute welfare, but fight alongside workers and students for social justice. There are 'red' bishops and cardinals too who take up an uncompromising attitude, to the displeasure of the traditional classes. [61] No wonder the theology of liberation and of Paschal hope is hailed as the first original achievement in theology in this continent which has been Christian for centuries; it can be considered Latin America's contribution to the universality of the Church. [62]

From theology we turn to the question of forming the consciences of Christians. When all is said and done, prudence must have the last word. Certainly one might in theory conclude that in South Africa, for example, institutional violence has reached such a pitch that there is, theologically, no objection to reacting with violence. However, in the actual situation, facing such overwhelming force, a revolution would unleash an unimaginable blood-bath and leave behind it nothing but chaos. For this reason, revolution turns out to be inadvisable and the best solution seems to be to work patiently at changing mentalities from within. [63]

In this field of action, we have to redeem a mortgage. Any

---

[59] J.C. Hoekendijk, *Zur Frage einer missionarischen Existenz,* in *Kirche und Volk in der deutschen Missionswissenschaft,* München, 1967, p. 319.

[60] J.B. Metz, *Das Problem einer 'politischen Theologie'* in *Concilium* 1968, pp. 403-411; id., *Theologie der Welt,* 99-116.

[61] R. Valdas, *Die roten Bischöfe Lateinamerikas;* J.C. Gonzalez, *Helder Camara, l'arcivescovo rosso,* Rome, 1971.

[62] A. Sepsezian, *Le cas de l'Amérique Latine,* in SML 1972, pp. 59-66, esp. 65f; J.C. Scannone, *Theologie der Befreiung in Laieinam.,* in *Orientierung,* Zürich, 15 January 1973, 2-5.

[63] Cf. AIF 4.4.1973: statement by Archbishop Hurley.

global assertion requires some qualification, but there is no disguising the fact that historically the Church has continually sided with the authorities, that she has been opposed to all attempts to upset the social order and has been slow to understand the dynamic of history. [64] Even today, in certain countries, the Church has not yet found the openness and flexibility necessary to interpret and take seriously God's action in history. But if those in authority in the Church, at least in Christian countries, are not capable of turning the rich into brothers of the poor, it should not come as a surprise if later the poor come to think of the rich as enemies to be eliminated, in a justified defensive action. [65]

8. So much, then, for the variety of present-day theological positions. In spite of the terrible increase of violence and counterviolence in the modern world, now approaching the absurd, and within the specifically Christian vocation which is a vocation to follow Christ stripped of all things, it is still necessary to opt for the way of non-violence. This alone manifests clearly the folly of the cross and hope in the kingdom of God to come, a hope which is utopian and realistic at the same time. Francis of Assisi left his Crusaders' camp and went as a 'hero without arms' (the title of book by Z. Kossak) to the sultan, spoke to him of God and won his sympathy. Martin Luther King, who had the masses at his disposal but mobilized them not for violence but for peaceful protest, paid for his non-violence with his own blood. This is our gospel lived out, our specific contribution, the prophetic models which we need at least as much as those of a Che Guevara or a Camillo Torres. Non-violence is so creative that, more often than not, it takes us further than violence. Where it is not possible to eliminate certain embittered situations, the guilty heritage of generations, the Christian has a hope which no communist can offer, a hope more realistic than any revolutionary initiative. It 'protects man from the temptation of pursuing certain justified this-worldly aspirations towards

[64] F. Houtart and A. Rousseau, *The Church and Revolution*, N.Y., 1971.

[65] This conclusion is reached even by the very prudent P.J. Masson in SML 1972, p. 197f.

a better future only attainable through such violence as will constitute a cruel sacrifice of this generation in favour of another, and will make the future into a Moloch to whom real man is sacrificed in favour of a man who is not real but always on the point of becoming real'. [66]

(d) Documents and/or deeds?

1. The attention tardily paid by the Church to the poor at Vatican II was one of the great surprises at the Council. Cardinal Lercaro (at the prompting, it is thought, of John XXIII) in a famous speech on the 'Church of the poor' noted with regret how, up to that point, not a single draft conciliar text had spoken expressly of the fundamental and central mystery of the Church as Church of the poor; yet one of the central points of the teaching on the Church was precisely that God turned in a special manner to the poor and that he has recommended them to us as a sign of his special presence (alongside the Eucharist); this aspect should have been introduced in all the documents. Cardinals Montini, Suenens and others gave their assent to these reflections and from then on the theme was longer passed over in silence. [67] The Church must not only fight the poverty of the poor but must also change her own structures so as to become poor herself and *be with* the poor who are waiting to meet her and who constitute the riches of tomorrow's Church.

2. Although the Council affirmed that the gulf observable in many Christians between the faith they profess and the life they lead is one of the most pernicious evils of our time, [68] we still cannot say, unfortunately, that the Council speeches on the Church of the poor have resulted in any effective trend towards the Church of the poor. We must hope that we are not here confronted by the 'graveyard peace of theoretical reason' or a concrete validation of K. Rahner's saying: 'It seems that God

[66] K. Rahner, in E. Keller, *Christentum und Marxismus heute,* Vienna, 1966, p. 210.

[67] Bühlmann, *Kirche der Armen,* in *Fastenopfer der Schweitzer Katholiken, Arbeitsmappe Kirchenbau,* Lucerne, 1971, 5-8. Le Guillou et al., *Mission et pauvreté,* Paris, 1963.

[68] GS 43.

and the devil reside in the details, while the preaching of the Church is on the general and universal level'. [69] Modern psychology confirms that theory is not enough to change lives; to form consciences, for 'conscientization', we need action. True, the stimulus given by the Council has not remained without fruit. Individual bishops in Latin America have left their palaces for simple houses, recognizing, in the words of Cardinal Maurer of Bolivia, that 'the Church could possess her wealth and her territory in the past with a quiet conscience but today, in face of the hunger and deprivation of so many people, this can no longer be done without sin'; the vacated properties have been made available for social work. Religious have renewed their constitutions and seek to make the poverty they profess more credible. But the Church, as such, still needs the courage to carry out a radical change of direction. Palaces for nuncios and bishops and rich churches in poor countries are still being built. [70] Candidates for the priesthood, who almost always come from the poorest environments, continue to be trained in seminary hotels for a lord's life and then find it difficult to return to live among the poor. [71] It still seems as if bishops and priests who take the Church of the poor seriously are not viewed with favour and run up against difficulties. Sad to say, at the time when *L'Osservatore Romano* was keeping the Roman priests in the slums at arm's length by repeated criticisms, the front page of this journal fêted a Cardinal (now dead) whose capitalist mentality was notorious with a letter full of praise, as if he were the best bishop in the world. [72]

3. Are we, then, to content ourselves with nothing more than fine documents? Is the Church of the poor nothing but a

---

[69] Rahner, *Strukturwandel der Kirche als Aufgabe und Chance*, Freiburg, im B., 1973, p. 85, 82

[70] Cf. below ch. 20, p. 362ff.

[71] A new way is being followed, here and there, in Latin America. In India, too, Archbishop D'Souza of Bhopal is founding a new kind of seminary, in which theologians learn a second trade so to go out as animators towards a better life in the villages and effect a breakthrough in the Church's presence in north India. Those who know, of course, think the method will not be attractive, since the seminarians will prefer a more comfortable life.

[72] OR 25.10.1973.

beautiful illusion, a rarity, a curiosity given scope only here and there by individual idealists? G. Herburger, in a novel full of utopianism and sarcasm, has shown how Jesus could be represented in 1984 in a factory and in workers' barracks, at the bar and in the place of worship, in rich men's homes and in the crowds, and how 'the greatest figure of western history, now reduced to a cliché and an alibi', [73] could once again become a reality and a challenge. Will poverty remain utopian? Will Karl Rahner be right in what he says about the inability of the Church of today to be poor? 'As far as can be predicted, the Church will not prove capable of fighting this battle with poverty through her own poverty, although this is the way it should be. The Church will not succeed in mobilizing herself to a sufficient extent... The inability to be poor remains. The necessary transformation of consciences, as long as it is not imposed by physical factors, as long as it depends solely on moral appeals, does not proceed with enough speed to accomplish what is really needed in measurable time. We lack the creative imagination; utopia is not as yet effective'. [74] The 'physical factors', which could *impose* a change of conscience, are perhaps nearer than is realized.

4. *Facing the communist world*

1. Now that the cold war is officially at an end and the mortal enemies have shaken hands in Moscow, Peking and Washington, it is becoming easier for the Church, too, to pass from the historic stance of anti-communism to positive dialogue, which had in fact already begun with John XXIII. Even if Christianity and Marxism were irreconcilable from the historic point of view, it remains a fact that the Church's judgement and her general attitude have been influenced to some degree by the political environment of the west. The Church shared the anti-communist fixation, of which Archbishop Helder Camara writes: 'As long as communism appears the greatest evil on earth, as long as the average American persists in the illusion that to die in Korea or Vietnam is to die for the free world —

[73] Herberger, *Jesus in Osaka* (from the book-cover).
[74] *In Neues Hochland*, no. 1, 1972, 52-59.

an illusion because two thirds of humanity do not belong to this free world, since they are living in subhuman conditions and are enslaved by hunger, disease and ignorance — as long as the American middle classes are unable to grasp that the chief social problem of the present time is the growing gap between rich and poor countries, as long as there is no change in mentality and no revolution in ideas, the United States will not be able to face up to its responsibilities as the greatest democracy of our times'. [75]

The growing importance of China in the Third World is a fact which cannot be met by opposition but should be understood and appreciated as a challenge and an opportunity.

Moreover, both Christianity and communism have undergone profound changes since their first encounter. They have learned from one another. Both have reached a point in their understanding of themselves which makes a genuine meeting possible. Today, it is no longer possible to say that the Churches preach 'a God without hope' and communism 'a hope without God'. Today, there are communists who read the gospel. Similarly, it is recognized that Marx's atheism was a methodological atheism and not a metaphysical one: he supposed that God and religion alienated man from himself and brought him to trust in the gods rather in himself — something which is no longer true without qualification. Christians have in the meantime undertaken a 'dedivinization' of the world and today religion helps towards a commitment to the world. Thus Bloch could formulate the paradox: 'Only an atheist can be a good Christian and only a Christian can be a good atheist'. It seems that the period of ideological confrontation between the two is coming to an end and contact will lead to better mutual understanding. [76]

2. When it is no longer a question of structures pitted against structures and 'system against systems, but men meeting

[75] H. Camara, *The Church and colonialism*, London, 1969, p. 85.
[76] J. Moltmann, *Umkehr zur Zukunft*, München, 1970, p. 52-59; R. Garaudy, *L'Alternativa*, Assisi, 1973, 5-21; cf. also *Dialogzeitschrift*, Freiburg im B., 1968 ff and the work of the Secretariate for non-believers.

men, it could happen that we might succeed in giving the communists something they have lost, that is, the gospel as good news for men who have been embittered. As far as ascetics is concerned, they lack nothing. This we do not need to preach to them; rather we could learn from them. But we certainly can show them things which lighten the burden of asceticism, conveying to them something of the Johannine spirit of love, which lessens the harshness of life and can lessen their ruthlessness in pursuit of their aims. The socialist revolutions everywhere have restricted freedom (as an apparently necessary measure to overcome egotism) and have thus extinguished joy. They favour mass sport and subsidize entertainment, but always under firm control. What is lacking is freedom and joy in play. [77]

Visitors to Peking report that all goes smoothly in a city cleaner than New York, but that it is a silent city without any sound of hearty laughter. [78] Things are said to be even worse in Cuba, joie-de-vivre, serenity and cordiality having completely disappeared. 'Even in the poorest parts of the Third World I had visited, I had met people who were warm-hearted and lively, facing the future with confidence, even if they were hungry, unable to read and dressed in rags. But in Cuba I found an oppressive atmosphere such as I had experienced nowhere else'. This was the report of Fr Gheddo after a visit to the sugar island.

The good news cannot be preached to the black buffaloes of India, trotting along indefatigably with foaming mouths in front of their carts. But it can be preached to communist people; in fact, they may be thirsting for it more than appears on the surface. Our strident anti-communism has stripped us of imagination. When we see the determination with which the communists strive to inculcate their ideas among the western and southern peoples, and compare it with the little that we do ourselves vis-à-vis them, we can only beat our breasts and pray for our conversion and for more confidence.

[77] Moltmann, *Die ersten Freigelassenen der Schöpfungen,* München, 1971, p. 18f.
[78] J.A. Michener in a US press release 23.2.1972, on the occasion of Nixon's visit to Peking.

3. Our hope of bringing our message to the communists will increase in proportion as we acknowledge that we Christians have something to learn from them. The way they declare merciless war on unjust structures ought to inspire us too. We are too ready to come to terms with structures. We need to be brought up short by the communists. We could share with them the idea that social injustices are not to be taken for granted, that charity hand-outs are no substitute for justice, that in view of the equal dignity of men privileged classes have lost their right to exist, that the accumulation of riches in a world of poverty is criminal. We need to learn from them simplicity in standards of living, the hard work needed to transform the world, solidarity with the poor, 'hunger and thirst after justice' not simply in an introverted and individualistic sense but also taking account of 'justice in the world' as the 1971 synod taught. The Church was present and still is present in many parts of the Third World by her sacramental life and her works of mercy, but she is not yet sufficiently committed to agrarian reform, to just wages (including those of mission employees) and to decent housing conditions. We must not imitate the brutal methods of the communists but we can imitate their unqualified commitment to eliminating injustice.

R. Italiaander imagines a poor man from the *favelas* of Rio de Janeiro climbing up to the colossal Christ of Corcovado and saying: 'I have climbed up to you, Christ, from the filthy, confined quarters down there, with their stench of urine and typhoid fever, to put before you, most respectfully, these considerations: there are nine hundred thousand of us down there in the slums of that splendid city and the number keeps increasing... And you, Christ, do you permit things like that? Why? Did you not come to help the world?... Christ, do not remain here at Corcovado surrounded by divine glory. Go down there into the *favelas*. Come with me into the *favelas* and live with us down there. Don't stay away from us; live among us and give us new faith in you and in the Father. Amen'. [79] If Christ did go down into the *favelas* in the person of Christians and their priests, that poor man would not become a communist.

[79] R. Italiaander, *Profile und Perspektiven,* Erlangen, 1971, p. 132-134.

Christians and communists could even meet in that poor man's house and, through his friendship, becomes friends together and Christ would be among them.

4. In Tanzania, we can see in progress not only a model case of Chinese aid but also an encounter between the Church and communism. President Nyerere, a believing Christian, is continually explaining to bishops and priests how much is at stake, how it is not a question of practising anti-communism but rather of anticipating communism, of building a society which will not need communism. Here are some quotations taken from his speeches and addresses: 'With regard to the interminable argument between people who are apparently only concerned with religious things and those who devote all their energy to temporal welfare, I find it very regrettable that some members of the first group consider the second group evil and communist simply because it is so concerned about temporal welfare. How can anyone who believes in the Bible blame the others because they are striving to improve the social situation of their neighbour? Even if they do not read the Bible, their actions are good. We should judge deeds according to their worth, not according to the religion of the doer... The Church has a new opportunity in Africa but she could let the opportunity pass her by. When we began to criticize feudalism and capitalism, we did not get the support of the Church. Is it not terrible if we let atheists be the only ones to identify with the poor and be their spokesmen? The socialists are on the side of the poor. Should the Church not be the first to take the part of the poor and disinherited rather than leave this work to the atheists? She should be the guide of the poor. As a believer, I place my hope in the Church. I offer the Christian Church a new chance to identify with God's poor...' [80] He has also urged priests to leave their isolated parish houses and live closer to the people, to share the life of the people, [81] to come down like the Christ of Corcovado into the slums. So far, the

[80] Bühlmann, op.cit. (note 42), p. 554.
[81] Published in Ecclesia, Dar es Salaam, Sept. 1970, Nov. 1970. Cf. also J. Civille, Ujamaa socialism, Rome, 1972 (a thesis for the Accademia Alfonsiana).

126

Church has gone no further than to make declarations, publish fine documents and even to live in fear and disguised opposition. Alongside appreciations of 'African socialism' there has been a reprinting of Pius XI's encyclical *Divini Redemptoris* against communism. In any case, so far, Catholic Christians, unlike Protestant and Moslem groups, have not entered into the popular community movement *Ujamaa*. Will the Church miss this opportunity?

5. The Church must enter the lists against communism. There is no choice. The stronger will prevail. One has the impression that President Nyerere may have invited the Chinese into his country with the hidden intention of facing the Church with an important choice, offering her new opportunities and constraining her to be herself.

Atheistic communism uses violence to gain its ends. Western capitalism needs money to induce man in self-interest to work harder. Could there not be a mixed form, socialist and Christian, in which spirituality, Christian formation and responsible awareness take the place of violence and money? Or is the effectiveness of Christian spirituality to remain for ever limited to the example of the first community in Jerusalem? If the Tanzania model were to fail because Christians, the managerial class in the country, do not make enough effort and because professed Christians in capitalist countries boycott it, then only the two extreme possibilities of communism and capitalism would remain (and the Third World has nothing to gain from either of them alone). The Third World would have lost a hope; the Church would have wasted an opportunity of being the Church for today's world.

However, history — or what Christians call 'providence' — always finds a solution. This is the inspiring lesson of the past. Either a spiritual movement, like Cluny, Francis of Assisi or Vatican II, permeates the Church or else a violent movement comes to the aid of the imprisoned spirit. The French Revolution helped monarchs and countries everywhere to open their eyes, although this came late in the day. Vittorio Emmanuele II helped the Church, at last, to free herself of the Temporal Power. Communism could be called, in Tanzania and elsewhere, to purify the Church by fire and make her capable of her authentic mission. This could be one of the 'physical factors' of Karl Rahner, [82] bringing to light what fails to emerge through a free transformation of consciences. We must leave all this to history and remain full of hope.

[82] Quoted above, p. 122.

Chapter 6

THE CHURCH IN FIGURES

A. *Success after success*

1. Two outstanding Protestant historians of the missions, who are not only descriptive writers but also interpreters, stress how the Churches in the first half of this century have been battered by storms and yet in spite of, or even because of, these difficulties have made great progress. They are thinking especially of the two world wars and the economic crisis occurring in the interval between them. [1] Now we would have to add decolonization with its new dangers. In the Catholic Church, ever since Benedict XV the popes have given strong impetus to the missions by their repeated encyclicals and by systematic subdivision of dioceses; but our own century has outstripped all others, so far as concerns numbers of Catholic missionaries, native priests and dioceses. In consequence, articles and books on the missions have multiplied beyond measure. [2]

2. *Increase of Catholics in the southern continents* [3]

Year	Latin America	Africa	Asia	Oceania
1900	56,579,749	2,378,824	11,442,574	—
1949	145,000,000	14,848,622	26,928,000	1,830,982
1966	226,280,506	31,781,816	43,447,279	3,782,319
1972	253,409,000	41,746,000	49,045,000	4,548,000

---

[1] Latourette entitles his last volume 'Advance through the storm' and Groves returns repeatedly to these unfavourable conditions: e.g. pp. 40f, 194, 342.

[2] A good impression can be had from Streit-Dindinger *Bibliotheca Missionum,* of which the 30th volume was published by Herder in 1975. Cf. also *Bibliografia missionaria,* Rome, 1935ff.

[3] I have used Emmerich, *Atlas Hierarchicus;* for the latest figures (from 31.12.1971) also Secretary of State, *Annuario Statistico,* 1971.

3. Increase of number of priests

Year	Latin America	Africa	Asia	Oceania
1900	14,778	2,961	10,657	—
1949	27,552	10,130	—	3,250
1966	44,791	16,438	26,932	5,453
1972	47,195	17,061	25,558	5,677

4. Increase in number of ecclesiastical divisions

Year	Latin America	Africa	Asia	Oceania
1900	140	47	—	—
1949	308	—	—	45
1966	577	318	471	62
1972	615	356	358	62

5. Increase in number of native priests [4]

Year	Africa	Oceania
1949	1080	3447
1959	2072	6403
1969	3623	9811

6. Increase in number of native bishops [5]

Year	Africa	Oceania
1951	2	31
1961	38	75
1969	133	126
1973	170	144

Between 1952 and 1959, between one and four African bishops were consecrated each year, but

in	1960	9	1963 - 69	5 to 9
	1961	10	1969	16
	1962	12	1970	14

Guida delle Missioni cattoliche, Rome, 1970: includes only the territory subject to Propaganda Fide. No more recent figures have been published.

[5] **AIF**, Supplément N. III/2-5 (1971) and AIF 26.9.1973.

Of the 36 archiepiscopal sees in Africa in 1971, 30 were filled by Africans; of the 37 archiepiscopal sees in Asia, 30 were filled by Asiatics.

B. *Technical and theological critique of ecclesiastical statistics*

1. Statistics seem to offer mathematical security; in fact, they easily lead to self-deception and a too ready belief that all goes well. All the surveys contain a factor of uncertainty which can be reduced but not eliminated. A population census taken in western countries can attain a high degree of certainty thanks to enormous expenditure in money, personnel and organization. But how could the states of the southern continents allow themselves such an outlay? Then there are questions of prestige. There is always the desire to appear better than one is, so the number of illiterates may be falsified, either by those being questioned or by public officials lowly or exalted. Ecclesiastical statistics, which are based simply on the inquiry forms sent to places where the data are collected, have to contend with a different factor making for uncertainty: many priests think the census and the figures for baptism and Easter communions are a bureaucratic waste of time (the purpose of these surveys might have been made clearer if the statistics had been used on parochial, diocesan and national level to analyse development in the local situation and to take appropriate measures with planning and consultation); so, either they fail to reply or else give approximate figures. Much the same is true of some diocesan curias.

2. Anyone concerned with Catholic missionary statistics can detect a peculiar lack of co-ordination between different Vatican departments. It is very difficult, for example, to draw up a comprehensive view of Africa. The majority of the ecclesiastical divisions belong to the Congregation for Evangelization (*Propaganda Fide*) which publishes statistics for these territories alone. Other dioceses, in Ethiopia and Egypt for example, belong to the Congregation for Eastern Churches. Angola and Mozam-

bique were administered by the Secretary of State directly and other countries, Algeria for example, by the Congregation for Bishops. Age-old structures, not yet disturbed even by the reform of the curia!

To meet this difficulty, a central Office for Church Statistics was set up in 1967 and has published figures annually since 1969.[6] These have been received with much satisfaction, and year by year they become more complete and informative. The Office has tried to devise, in agreement with the various departments, a common questionnaire. Unfortunately, it has so far had no success, and missionary bishops already tormented by so many worries must now fill in two different questionnaires (as well as all the usual forms) and send them to two different addresses in Rome. This hardly encourages a quick reply.

3. Although ecclesiastical statistics have their use, they also have their dangers for the pastoral ministry, and these must not be ignored. There could be a temptation to drag people to church and the sacraments, appealing to Lk 14:23, 'Compel them to come in'; figures for catechumens could be embellished (the village catechist is paid on the basis of the number he instructs) and so could figures for baptisms, Easter communions and marriages reported to the bishop and, through him, to Rome; figures could be rounded up; and they could become an end in themselves. The urge to have everything inspected, measured, registered and published threatens to destroy the mystery of the Church: we could know exactly who is in and who is out but the Church could thereby lose its spiritual character and become a merely human organization. D.S. Amalorpavadas speaks aptly of the pastoral heresy, mistaken for zeal, of deceiving ourselves by numbers and running after efficiency — so typical of the west.[7] The really important thing, interior conversion, is not measurable. Missionaries collecting the figures, as well as those who study them, will do well to discern the mystery of God's call behind the columns of statistics and

[6] Cf. the description in *L'Attività della Santa Sede nel 1969*, 800-802; *nel 1971*, 811-813.

[7] D.S. Amalorpavadas, *L'Inde à la rencontre du Seigneur*, Paris, 1964, p. 283.

find a transcendent, spiritual meaning to the numbers on the forms.

4. Today we need to ask ourselves, in all sincerity: 'Who *is* to be listed as a Christian? The number of baptisms can be recorded but not the degree of conversion. A missionary once said: 'I have baptized more than 3000; I have not converted anyone. Only God can do that and even he finds it very difficult'. Should we continue to count all who are baptized and then proceed to live for years in unregularized marriages and cease to go to church? (What we *should* do, pastorally, in such cases is another matter.) From the viewpoint of statistics and in line with the social dimension of the Church, people are considered to belong to the Church if they are baptized and have not formally indicated their will to leave the Church. The people of God here below is, in practice, a people of sinners. Even a serious state of sin does not of itself automatically exclude the sinner from the Church.

Some Protestant Churches give the impression of taking a very indulgent view in this matter: they count among their members anyone who has occasionally shared in their worship and is interested in the gospel. Here we might do well to follow the lead of D. Barrett who distinguishes between evangelization and Christianization. An individual or even a group may have heard the gospel or may even have accepted it without entering the Christian community through baptism and the other sacraments. Those who have simply been evangelized should not be counted among the members of the Church. Further, he distinguishes between Christians who are *affiliated*, that is, those who in virtue of their baptism figure in the baptismal registers, and *practising* Christians, who take part fairly regularly in the life of the Church: the number of the latter, for the Protestant Churches of Africa, would be three or four times less than that of the affiliated. Finally, he distinguishes *professing* Christians, who say they are Christians in the census, but in fact are not; the number of these last amounts to about 50% of the total of affiliated Christians. [8] These marginal Christians, who are ashamed of 'paganism' and sympathetic towards Christianity,

8. *Frontier situation 1-2.*

are found not only in Africa but also in Asia. In Japan, for example, there is a total of 700,000 baptized Christians, but as many as six million call themselves Christian.

C. *The present situation*

I would have liked to publish figures for Catholic and other Christians together. But the new *World Christian Handbook* has not yet been published; so I must restrict myself to the Catholic Church: [9]

Area, population and Catholics, 31 *December* 1973

COUNTRIES	Area — Thousands of Sq. Km.	Population — in thousands	Catholics (baptized) in thousands	% of total pop.
	AFRICA			
Afars and Isaas	22	101	12	11.9
Algeria	2.382	15.772	66	0.4
Angola	1.247	5.914	2.718	46.0
Botswana	600	646	22	3.5
Burundi	28	3.600	1.930	53.3
Cameroon	475	6.167	1.930	24.4
Cape Verde Island	4	284	260	91.5
Central African Republic	623	1.669	293	17.6
Chad	1.284	3.868	202	5.2
Comoro Islands	—	—	—	—
Congo	342	1.004	447	44.6
Dahomey	113	2.912	418	14.4
Egypt	1.001	35.619	143	0.4
Ethiopia	1.222	26.076	175	0.7
Gambon	268	515	337	65.5
Gambia	11	493	11	2.2

[9] Secretary of State, *Ann. Stat. 1973,* p. 16-23. For detailed explanation this year book should be consulted.

134

Area, population and Catholics, 31 December 1973

COUNTRIES	Area — Thousands of Sq. Km.	Population — in thousands	Catholics (baptized) in thousands	% of total pop.
Ghana	239	9.355	1.150	12.3
Guinea	246	4.208	40	1.0
Guinea Equatorial	28	298	235	79.8
Guinea-Bissau	36	509	44	8.7
Ivory Coast	322	4.641	579	12.5
Kenya	583	12.482	2.035	16.3
Lesotho	30	994	443	44.6
Libyan Arab Republic	1.760	2.161	5	02.
Madagascar	589	7.462	1.634	22.8
Malawi	118	4.791	934	19.5
Mali	1.240	5.376	45	0.8
Mauritania	1.031	1.257	7	0.5
Mauritius	2	868	275	31.7
Morocco	447	16.309	95	0.6
Mozambique	783	8.823	1.560	17.7
Namibia	824	673	125	18.6
Niger	1.267	4.304	12	0.3
Nigeria	924	59.607	3.484	5.8
Réunion	3	474	444	93.6
Rhodesia	391	5.900	570	9.6
Rwanda	26	3.984	1.622	40.7
Sâo Tomé and Príncipe	1	78	71	91.6
Senegal	196	4.227	173	4.0
Seychelles	4	56	50	89.3
Sierra Leone	72	2.861	55	1.9
Somalia	638	3.003	3	0.1
South Africa	1.221	23.724	1.629	6.9
Spanish Sahara	266	99	16	16.6
Sudan	2.506	16.901	370	2.2
Swaziland	17	463	42	9.0
Tanzania	945	14.377	2.837	19.7
Togo	56	2.117	409	19.3

Area, population and Catholics, 31 December 1973

COUNTRIES	Area — Thousands of Sq. Km.	Population — in thousands	Catholics (baptized) in thousands	Catholics (baptized) % of total pop.
Tunisia	164	5.509	20	0.3
Uganda	236	10.810	3.544	32.8
Upper Volta	274	5.737	348	6.0
Zaire	2.345	23.563	9.723	41.3
Zambia	753	4.635	932	20.1
Total AFRICA	30.312	378.935	44.135	11.6

NORTH AMERICA

Bermuda	0,05	55	9	16.0
Canada	9.976	22.125	9.420	42.6
Greenland	2.176	51	—	—
St. Pierre and Miquelon	0,24	6	6	96.9
United States of America	9.363	210.407	46.809	22.2
Total North America	21.515	232.644	56.244	24.2

CONTINENTAL CENTRAL AMERICA

Belize	23	132	81	61.4
Costa Rica	51	1.887	1.749	92.7
El Salvador	21	3.864	3.599	93.1
Guatemala	109	5.540	4.835	87.3
Honduras	112	2.781	2.683	96.5
Mexico	1.973	54.303	50.361	92.7
Nicaragua	130	2.015	1.967	97.6
Panamá	77	1.614	1.458	90.3
Total Cont. Centr. America	2.496	72.136	66.733	92.5

CENTRAL AMERICA — ANTILLES

Antigua	1	86	9	11.0
Bahamas	14	199	37	18.4

Area, population and Catholics, 31 December 1973

COUNTRIES	Area — Thousands of Sq. Km.	Population in thousands	Catholics (baptized) in thousands	Catholics (baptized) % of total pop.
Barbados	1	334	25	7.4
Bonaire	—	—	—	—
Cayman Island	—	—	—	—
Cuba	114	8.873	4.202	47.3
Curaçao	1	234	180	76.9
Dominica	1	150	64	42.7
Dominican Republic	49	4.432	4.186	94.4
Grenada	0,34	95	75	78.9
Guadalupe	2	642	324	50.5
Haiti	28	5.200	3.988	76.7
Jamaica	11	1.987	161	8.1
Martinique	1	343	300	87.5
Puerto Rico	9	2.919	2.510	86.0
St. Kitts Nevis Anguilla	—	—	—	—
St. Lucia	1	107	95	88.8
St. Vincent	—	—	—	—
Trinidad and Tobago	5	1.064	366	34.4
Turks and Caicos Islands	—	—	—	—
Virgin Islands (Great Brit.)	—	—	—	—
Virgin Islands (U.S.A.)	0,34	65	25	38.5
Total Centr. Amer., Antilles	238	26.430	16.547	62.6

SOUTH AMERICA

Argentina	2.777	24.286	22.876	94.2
Bolivia	1.099	5.331	4.981	93.4
Brazil	8.512	101.707	90.964	89.4
Chile	757	10.229	8.807	86.1
Colombia	1.139	23.209	22.500	96.9
Ecuador	284	6.726	6.306	93.7
Falkland Is., Malvinas	12	2	—	10.0
French Guyana	91	52	42	80.8

137

Area, population and Catholics, 31 December 1973

COUNTRIES	Area — Thousands of Sq. Km.	Population — in thousands	Catholics (baptized)	
			in thousands	% of total pop.
Guyana	215	758	105	13.8
Paraguay	407	2.674	2.308	86.3
Peru	1.285	14.912	14.290	95.3
Surinam	163	432	80	18.5
Uruguay	178	2.992	2.685	89.7
Venezuela	912	11.293	10.832	95.9
Total South America	17.831	204.603	186.776	91.3
Total AMERICA	42.080	535.813	326.300	60.9

ASIA (MIDDLE EAST)

Afghanistan	647	18.294	—	—
Cyprus	9	659	—	—
Iran	1.648	31.298	28	0.1
Iraq	435	10.413	275	2.6
Israel	21	3.183	60	1.9
Jordan	98	2.555	44	1.7
Lebanon	10	3.055	955	31.3
Syria	185	6.890	196	2.8
Turkey	781	37.933	28	0.1
Total Asia, Middle East	3.834	114.280	1.586	1.4

ASIA (OTHER COUNTRIES)

Bahrain	—	—	—	—
Bangladesh	143	71.614	134	0.2
Bhutan	—	—	—	—
Brunei	—	—	—	—
Burma	678	29.560	285	1.0
China, Mainland	9.561	799.622	—	—
China, Taiwan	36	14.657	300	2.0

Area, population and Catholics, 31 December 1973

COUNTRIES	Area — Thousands of Sq. Km.	Population — in thousands	Catholics (baptized) in thousands	% of total pop.
Hong Kong	1	4.160	262	6.3
India	3.475	583.336	8.747	1.5
Indonesia	1.904	125.561	2.633	74.6
Japan	372	108.346	359	0.3
Khmer Republic	181	7.643	18	0.2
North Korea	121	15.087	—	—
South Korea	98	32.905	854	2.6
Kuwait	18	883	20	2.3
Laos	237	3.181	37	1.2
Macau	0,02	262	30	11.5
Malaysia	336	11.754	326	2.8
Maldives	—	—	—	—
Mongolia	1.565	1.359	—	—
Nepal	—	—	—	—
Oman	—	—	—	—
Pakistan	804	66.749	360	0.5
Philippines	300	40.219	32.758	81.4
Qatar	—	—	—	—
Saudi Arabia	—	—	—	—
Sikkim	—	—	—	—
Singapore	1	2.185	88	4.0
Sri Lanka	66	13.364	925	6.9
Thailand	514	39.787	161	0.4
Timor, Portuguese	15	639	188	29.4
United Arab Emirates	—	—	—	
USSR (in Asia)	16.831	62.674	—	—
North Vietnam	159	22.481	—	—
South Vietnam	174	19.367	1.873	9.7
Yemen	2.940	17.452	10	0.1
Total Asia (other countries)	40.530	2.098.847	50.368	2.4
Total ASIA	44.364	2.213.127	51.954	2.3

Area, population and Catholics, 31 December 1973

COUNTRIES	Area — Thousands of Sq. Km.	Population — in thousands	Catholics (baptized) in thousands	Catholics (baptized) % of total pop.
EUROPE				
Albania	29	2.347	—	—
Andorra	—	—	—	—
Austria	84	7.521	6.823	90.7
Belgium	31	9.757	8.726	89.4
Bulgaria	111	8.619	—	—
Byelorussian Sov. Soc. Rep.	—	—	—	—
Czechoslovakia	128	14.578	10.262	70.4
Denmark	44	5.067	26	0.5
Estonian Sov. Soc. Rep.	—	—	—	—
Finland	337	4.656	3	0.1
France	547	52.130	45.293	86.9
Germany - Democratic Rep.	108	16.980	1.507	8.9
Germany - Federal Rep.	249	61.967	29.246	47.2
Gibraltar	0,06	27	20	73.4
Great Britain	231	54.691	4.998	9.1
Greece	132	9.019	46	0.5
Hungary	93	10.411	6.401	61.5
Iceland	103	212	1	0.5
Ireland	84	4.576	3.416	74.6
Italy	301	54.908	53.809	98.0
Latrian Sov. Soc. Rep.	—	—	265	—
Liechtenstein	—	—	—	—
Lituanian Sov. Soc. Rep.	—	—	—	—
Luxembourg	3	350	327	93.1
Malta	0,32	322	304	94.5
Monaco	0,01	25	22	86.7
Netherlands	41	13.438	6.151	45.8
Norway	387	3.961	11	0.3
Poland	313	33.361	31.252	93.7
Portugal	92	8.564	8.457	98.7

Area, population and Catholics, 31 December 1973

COUNTRIES	Area Thousands of Sq. Km.	Population in thousands	Catholics (baptized) in thousands	Catholics (baptized) % of total pop.
Rumania	238	20.828	—	—
Russian Sov. Soc. Rep.	—	—	—	—
San Marino	—	—	—	—
Spain	505	34.873	34.400	98.6
Sweden	450	8.137	65	0.8
Switzerland	41	6.456	3.134	48.5
Ukrainian Sov. Soc. Rep.	—	—	—	—
USSR in Europe (other reps.)	5.571	187.075	—	—
Yugoslavia	256	20.956	6.771	32.3
Total EUROPE	10.510	655.812	261.736	40.1

OCEANIA

Australia	7.687	13.138	3.287	24.7
Canton and Enderbury Is.	—	—	—	—
Caroline and Marshall	1	91	37	40.6
Cook Islands	0,49	25	3	12.0
Fiji	18	551	47	8.5
Gilbert and Ellice Is.	1	70	28	40.6
Guam	1	115	92	80.0
Marianne	—	—	—	—
Nauru	—	—	—	—
New Caledonia	95	119	82	68.9
New Hebrides	15	90	14	15.9
New Zealand	269	2.964	432	14.6
Nive Island	—	—	—	—
Papua New Guinea	462	2.563	710	27.7
Polynesia (French)	4	120	40	33.3
Samoa (American)	—	—	—	—
Samoa (Western)	3	186	37	19.8
Solomon Islands (British)	28	179	35	19.6

Area, population and Catholics, 31 December 1973

COUNTRIES	Area	Population	Catholics (baptized)	
	Thousands of Sq. Km.	in thousands	in thousands	% of total pop.
Tokelau Islands	—	—	—	—
Tonga	1	92	14	15.6
Wake Islands	—	—	—	—
Wallis and Futuna Islands	0,20	9	8	90.3
Total OCEANIA	8.509	20.312	4.866	23.9

SUMMARY BY CONTINENTS

AFRICA	30.312	359.709	41.746	11.6
North America	21.515	228.687	55.337	24.2
Central America	2.733	91.341	77.589	77.1
South America	17.831	192.000	175.820	91.6
AMERICA (total)	42.079	513.028	308.746	60.2
Asia (M.E.)	3.834	108.534	1.745	1.6
Asia (F.E.)	40.529	1.997.215	47.300	2.4
ASIA (total)	44.363	2.105.749	49.045	2.3
EUROPE	10.509	647.691	260.303	40.2
OCEANIA	8.511	19.652	4,548	23.1
THE WORLD	135.774	3.645.829	664.388	18.2

D. Conversion of the world to Christ?

1. These figures by themselves could bring a smile of satisfaction to our faces, since we belong to the strongest group among Christians and to the largest community among world religions. But a comparison or two should bring us back to due modesty. In 1971, the world was Catholic to the extent of only 18.2%. (Broken down by regions, the proportions were: Latin America 89%, Europe 40.2%, Oceania 23.1%, Africa 11.6%, Asia 2.3%. [10]) All Christians together, in 1966, were only 30.9% of the population of the world, [11] after 2000 years of missionary labours! And now for another shock: in the near future, because of the demographic explosion, the proportion will not improve but will worsen in favour of the non-Christian majority. Assuming present trends continue, experts predict that if Christians were 34% of the world population in 1900 and 31% in 1955, they could be only 16% in 2000. [12] This prospect of becoming a more and more reduced fraction of the mass of humanity in spite of all our missionary work — in other words, the prediction that the world will not be converted — can disturb present-day Christians and paralyse many. What is the purpose, then, of continuing the missions? Are the hopes and dreams that the world would one day become Catholic (or at least Christian) just words written in the sand? The goal towards which we were so enthusiastically advancing has suddenly become a mirage. The image of the Church which we had built up is shattered.

2. Apart from defeatism, which cannot be a Christian attitude, we can react in two ways with regard to our missionary obligation. Both could be called extremist. A typical and enthusiastic example of the first would be John Mott (1865-

---

[10] *Ann. Stat. 1971*, p. 135.

[11] H. Emmerich, *Atlas hierarchicus*, Mödling, 1968, 65.

[12] H.R. Weber *Gottes, Arithmetik in der Mission*, in *Kirchentreu und kirchenfern*, Wuppertal, 1967, p. 69. He based himself on J.C. Hoekendijk, *On the way to the world of tomorrow*, in *Laity*, Geneva, 1961, no. 11, who puts it forward more as conjecture than precisely calculated. D. Barrett, however, holds that the percentage should be 31.2%

1955). As general secretary of the YMCA and, from 1921, as president of the International Missionary Council, he spoke and wrote untiringly of evangelizing the world in this generation. [13] Of course, he meant evangelizing in the sense of of the first announcing of the gospel, not of its effective working out in the full Christianizing of the world. But he had mobilized the forces and hoped to be able to say to Christ during his life-time: 'Your orders have been carried out!' There is the same enthusiasm among the Protestant sects, especially the Pentecostal movement. They feel driven by the Spirit to bear witness everywhere, not to limit themselves in missionary work to co-operating with already existing young Churches (they criticise the World Council of Churches for advocating this) but seek to found new Churches which always become missionary in their turn. In this way they hope to keep pace with the demographic explosion and even outpace it. In their eyes the fantastic growth of mankind calls for a similarly fantastic growth among Christians. [14]

But others ask whether the Church really needs a 'fantastic growth', whether the world is not rather in need of peace, justice, food for everyone, rather than an increase in the number of Christians; the quantiative mentality could be a manic or a magical mentality. They recall that the Church is a sign; they speak of the 'holy remnant' of the Old Testament (Jer 40: 11; Is 4: 3-4) and of the little flock of the New (Lk 12: 32). They take things as they find them, accepting ecumenical co-existence for all the great religions without thereby neglecting the particular function of Christianity. Besides, they maintain, redemption means a promise of salvation for all, depending on the mercy of God not on the success of ecclesiastical forces; it is to be realized in the centripetal movement of the eschatological

[13] His well-known title: *Evangelization of the world in this generation*, 1900; on the Billy Graham movement, see CM 1973, 322-336, 398-405; cf. also the reports on the Congress at Lausanne, 1974.

[14] Cf. the complete July issue of IRM on 'Church Growth' reacting to and reflecting on the opinion of D. McGavran, *Wrong strategy: the real crisis in Missions,* in IRM 1965. The World Council of Churches takes a sound middle position on principles (330-334) and refers to the Institute of Church Growth, Eugene (Oregon, USA).

pilgrimage of the peoples towards God's holy mountain, not in the centrifugal movement of missionary expansion; the latter has too often shown an un-Christian intolerance towards the extra-Christian world, and has thus shockingly debased the pure and simple promise of salvation [15] which that world stands in need of.

3. The solution, as always, lies between these two extremes — in a combination of both in the light of faith. If we consult the Scriptures, we find with surprise that when Jesus spoke of the growth of the kingdom of God he did not refer to a quantitative development but to a qualitative expansion outwards of what lies within, under the figures of light, salt and leaven. Even the grain of seed producing a hundredfold did not refer to a numerical multiplication but to a marvellous development of the word of God *within* man. On the other hand, the Acts of the Apostles often stress, rather surprisingly, how the number of the disciples grew (6:1), how in that day 3000 souls were added (2:41), how the Lord every day added to them those who were to receive salvation (2:47), how a great number were gained for the Lord (11:24), etc.

Both tendencies, then, can appeal to Scripture. Undoubtedly, a certain increase is needed so that the Church can be a sign. But the decisive element is precisely the character of being a sign, a quality, the power to radiate light; it is not quantity, which can degenerate into a sluggish mass, sedentary and self-satisfied. According to modern theology, the mission of the Church is not to secure the salvation of 'souls which would otherwise be lost' or to bring the greatest possible number into the Church as the ark of salvation; rather it has the aim of building up the Church as a sign of salvation for all and of gaining new witnesses to the grace of God already working in the world [16]. If it was a matter of numbers, we would be fighting a lost battle. But if the decisive thing is the power to radiate

[15] J. Jeremias, *Jesu Verheissung an die Völker,* Stuttgart, 1956, develops these biblical and theological considerations in a very radical way (without, however, excluding mission in the traditional understanding).

[16] On this theology see below, ch. 10.B.4, p. 231.

light, then we have a marvellous task to fulfil. In India today there are about nine million Catholics, almost as many Protestants and 600 non-Christians. In 2000 there will be about thirty million Christians and 1000 million non-Christians. When we are faced with similar proportions, we must have the courage to say: 'A million Christians more or less count for nothing; what will matter is what those thirty million mean to the thousand million non-Christians'.

4. Moreover, these estimates of future population have some very shaky foundations. [17] Until a short time ago, the population of Japan increased annually by two million but now it is almost static. Even China, the largest nation, has, in the course of a few years, brought its population growth under control. [18] The demographic explosion may well have lost its virulence within a few years.

Besides, it is nowhere written that Catholics or Christians must continue to increase as they have in recent decades. Apart from changes in external circumstances, new pastoral thinking will have its consequences. In Latin America and also in Africa and Asia, baptism is less indiscriminate. On the occasion of the baptism of a child, for instance, parents are invited to a three-day course of renewal. Baptism is refused where the parents' marriage has never been regularized over the years and they have long ago given up going to church. We have played about too long with unreal membership of the Church but now the truth is surfacing. Also new theological thinking on the baptism of infants will have its effects. [19] The centre of interest in the care of souls has shifted from sacramentalization to evangelization, from individual baptism to the building of a genuine Christian community capable of bearing witness. This

[17] In Rome, I spoke with three specialists on Church statistics. None had given any thought to the question of the proportion of Christians in the year 2000. They merely referred to the difficulties in making any such calculations.

[18] On China, see below ch. 15.b.3, p. 319.

[19] W. Kasper (ed.), *Christsein ohne Entscheidung, oder sollen die Kirchen Kinder taufen?*, Mainz, 1970; D. Boureau, *L'avenir du baptême*, Lyons, 1970; D. Grasso, *Dobbiamo ancora battezzare i bambini?*, Assisi, 1972.

and other reasons have led in some countries to a rapid fall in the numbers of baptisms. In Zaire, for example, where baptisms of children of Catholic parents should correspond to a birthrate of about forty per thousand, the rate of baptism has suddenly fallen in half the diocese to below twenty per thousand and in many to less than ten. This cannot fail to affect Church statistics.

The future, then, is in God's hands (and in man's free will). But Church history teaches us two things: growth in maturity in a minority Church brings, as a consequence, numerical increase while growth in maturity in a majority Church leads in most cases to a numerical diminution, which is a healthy readjustment in which many nominal Christians discover that following the Lord exacts a price which they are not ready to pay. [20] But intensive and extensive growth are not to be understood as alternatives. They stand in a living relationship of mutual interdependence. As long as the Church understands herself as a movement directed outwards, there is no ground for alarm in discovering that her visible nucleus represents a minority. [21]

5. In this minority situation, the biblical principle of representation assumes a great importance which has been brought to light by modern theology. [22] It is based on the social constitution of man. No one is a self-contained individual sufficient unto himself. Everyone is moulded and constituted what he is, even in God's sight, by what his neighbours are. Everyone is both threatened and supported by others. Thus humanity is constituted as a communion indivisible in destiny, both in profane and in salvific history. The vicarious function of Adam, the election of Israel, the importance of the apostles and of Mary — all these are continued in the function of the

---

[20] Weber, *op. cit.* (n. 12), p. 69.

[21] J. Schmitz, *Die Weltzuwendung Gottes,* Freiburg i. Ue., 1971, p. 50; further H. Küng, *Christenheit als Minderheit,* Einsiedeln, 1965; F. Murray, *What can Church statistics tell us?,* in NZM 1971, 118-125; J. Bishop, *Numerical growth, an adequate criterion of Mission?,* in IRM 1968, pp. 284-290.

[22] Klaes N., *Stellvertretung und Mission,* Essen, 1968; Kasper W., *Glaube und Geschichte,* Mainz, 1970, p. 271f; L. Scheffczyk, in LThK 9, 1036.

Church for the world. In dependence on the work of Christ, justified man intercedes for sinners and unbelievers and the Church as a whole lives and prays, believing, hoping and loving on behalf of all. From this perspective, we no longer speak of co-existence with the non-Christian world but (better) of an attitude of pro-existence (as Küng suggests), and of an intercession before God on behalf of the whole universe. The election of an individual, then, is no restriction of God's salvation but, on the contrary, makes that salvation more accessible to the world.

This vicarious action is asked of all Christians, even when they live far away from non-Christians (as in the case of St Teresa of the Child Jesus). It does not shut the believer up in his room or in church to pray to God but drives him precisely in the other direction, outwards, to bear explicit witness to the kingdom of God before all the world. It reaches its climax in mission. But, even here, we come across historical situations [23] in which he must be content to represent his people in silence. He will find in the principle of vicarious representation the reason for perseverance and courage when he faces rejection of the missionary message. 'This perseverance is the expression in history of God's patience and longanimity towards men... Here we may understand how the Church ought to behave towards peoples which will not be converted. Only the sovereign freedom of God can convert peoples and bring them to the Church; what will always be needed is our engagement to vicarious representation, right to the limits of our capability'. [24]

[23] For example, see ch. 7.C.2, p. 160f.
[24] Klaes, *op. cit.*, p. 104.

Chapter 7

THE THIRD CHURCH
IN THREE CONTINENTS

I do not intend to repeat for each continent what has already been said in general terms. Nor do I wish to anticipate the more panoramic and synthesised view to be expounded in later chapters. But it can be helpful to relate these general viewpoints to local situations, to bring out some typical features underlying the history of each continent and to see the Churches in the particular context of their continents.

A. *Africa's hour*

1. Africa, continent of giant rivers from the Nile to the Niger, from the Zambesi to the Zaire (the Congo), of great deserts and disastrous droughts, of healthy plateaux and malaria-ridden depressions (still so much in need of investment), is the nearest continent to the Christian west but it has for long been strangely remote. Asia was traversed by missionaries and explorers as long ago as the 13th century. America was discovered late in the 15th century and a hundred years later was served to a considerable extent by missions. But Africa remained the 'dark continent' almost to the beginning of this century; only three points were known and retained the interest of the world: Suez, Dakar and the Cape of Good Hope, ports of call on the sea routes to the other continents.

2. Christianity has sought to christianize Africa in three successive waves. [1] Three times the gospel message has been

---

[1] Cf. Bühlmann, Hastings, Groves.

offered. The first wave lasted six centuries, the second three, the third up to now one century. The results of the first two periods of mission have been almost completely lost. Is the present one the final decisive opportunity for the Church in Africa?

During the first wave, Christianity gained a footing in North Africa from Egypt to Morocco and southwards as far as Ethiopia and the region of Chad. In the fifth century in North Africa there were about 500 Catholic bishops and as many Donatists. The African Fathers made a notable contribution to the Church's theological heritage. In the long run, however, only the Copts of Egypt and Ethiopia managed to resist the victorious march of Islam.

The second period began with the penetration of Portugal in the Congo, in the region of the Cape and in east Africa. For three centuries Christian communities were founded, native priests were ordained and there was even a black bishop named Henry. In 1532, King John III of Portugal reported to Pope Clement VII that the whole Congo was Catholic — an enormous exaggeration, of course, although the results were considerable. Later, however, the missions were overwhelmed by the advance of Islam in the east; in the west they fell victim to political intrigues between Portugal, Spain and Holland and had their home base undermined by the French Revolution; the result was that in the first decades of the 19th century the Africa mission presented a picture of devastation.

The third wave began a good century ago and, after heroic sacrifices by the missionaries, fanned out over a great expanse of territory and obtained remarkable results.

3. Africa has suffered more humiliation than other continents. In the time of the old Greek and Roman empires, Moors were known as slaves. In the 16th century, the western powers renewed their interest in Africa principally as a quarry for slaves. It has been calculated that about 30 million slaves were transported to the new world. It was usual to depict them as typical idolators. Sources of the period repeatedly declare that they were absolutely ignorant of God, that they lived like beasts;

they were lecherous, thieves and liars and they ate like animals. . .[2]
From the 18th century there was a 'doctrine', now known to
be complete nonsense both ethnologically and exegetically, that
they were the accursed sons of Ham. At Vatican I, a group of
missionary bishops proposed to compose prayers for black
Africa, beseeching God to free that continent at last from the
curse of Ham. During my first stay in Africa, twenty years
ago, I found African pupils with these ideas in their heads;
the one thing they longed for was to become white.

Such a mentality is not changed overnight. The only
wonder is how quickly, in fact, the changes have come. One
of the first educated Africans, Dr Aggrey of the Gold Coast,
cried out to his people: 'My African people, we are created in
God's image. They wanted us to think of ourselves as chickens,
but we are eagles. Spread your wings and fly'. The poets of
négritude sing to themselves and their readers that black is
beautiful. They speak of white devils and exclaim with conviction: 'white as sin'. It is quite understandable that some
Africans, more than Asians, suffer from an inferiority complex
and compensate in ways disagreeable to us.

4. The two great decades of the African Church lie between
1952 and 1972. The number of African Catholics then tripled
from 12.5 million to 36 million. Similarly, native priests
increased from 1400 to 4200; and the number of African
bishops actually rose from two to 147. It is no exaggeration to
say that so great a success in so short a time has never been
recorded before in the history of the missions. Africa, last of
the continents, has suddenly overtaken the others and won the
prize. If we bear in mind that this was also the period of
decolonization and of Vatican II, we have to admit that we
are dealing with a particularly eventful period of history, which
will presumably have lasting effects. External observers are
struck by the colossal progress made by the Catholic Church.
B. Sundkler, former Lutheran bishop of Bukoba in Tanzania,
writes: 'The story of the development of the Roman Catholic
Church and its priesthood in Africa in this century is astonish-

---

[2] Bühlmann, *Afrika*, Mainz. 1963, 11-17; J. Jahn, *Wir nannten sie
Wilde. Aus alten und neuen Reisebeschreibungen*, München, 1964.

ing, one of the wonders of the dramatic history of world missions. . . The spread of the Church was guided by a global strategy. Strategy and planning, not improvisation, is the strong impression given by this development'. [3] Of course, we shall see that not all that glitters is gold. Apart from difficulties between Churches, in some places relations between Church and state are likely to be a serious problem in the years to come.

5. The reasons for this great success must be sought, first of all, in the mission schools. It could almost be said that going to school was tantamount to becoming a Christian. Malicious tongues explained it thus: people wanted instruction, progress and career and so they made use of Christianity. That is only a partial explanation. Beneath it all, there is the African's deeply religious pre-disposition. His sense of God, on whom he knows he is completely dependent, is the light by which he sees, the air he breathes, the skin in which he lives — not merely the clothes that cover him partly. The African does not simply believe in God and the spirits of his ancestors but lives, in the full sense of the term, under the eyes of the creator, the hidden cause of all other causes. Anyone denying this would not be considered normal in Africa. [4] Religion so penetrates social life that an adequate description would involve a study of clan structure.

But African religion is not 'religion of the book'. Leaving aside for the moment Islam, there are no sacred books, great founders of organizations spanning the regions. With the decline of tribal tradition in modern times, African religion is in danger of disappearing. Pagan has come to mean the same as savage. But experience has shown that men, like ants, can be tenacious in rebuilding the broken structures of society. [5] So, when the religious man of Africa has sought a new religion, Islam or

---

[3] B. Sundkler, *The Christian ministry in Africa,* Uppsala, 1960, p. 76, 78; C.P. Groves, *The planting of Christianity in Africa, IV, 1914-1954,* London, 1958, p. 193.

[4] So affirms an African, Amadou Hampaté Ba, in G. Dieterlen, *Textes sacrés d'Afrique Noire,* Paris, 1965, p. 9; J.S. Mbiti, *African religions and philosophy,* London, 1969, 1-3.

[5] J.C. Froelich, *Animismes,* Paris, 1964, p. 231; E.G. Parrinder, in C.J. Blecker *Historia Religionum II,* Leiden, 1971, p. 630.

Christianity, he has taken with him many of his former attitudes, many more than missionaries usually recognize. Faced by the advance of secularism, [6] African bishops do not miss an opportunity to emphasize that an irreligious African goes against the whole of African tradition.

6. A word must be said here on the spread of Islam. It is the strongest religious community in Africa: in 1970, according to Barrett, there were 145 million Moslems, 104 million 'pagans', 97 million Christians. But the Moslem drive has been greatly exaggerated. Twenty years ago people were still saying that all the northern regions of Nigeria and Cameroons were Moslem. Now we know that it is only the ruling classes that belong to Islam. Colonial powers like England, Germany and France had treated Islam with the utmost respect for tactical reasons and published exaggerated figures. As late as 1958, the British governor of Tanganyika said that 65% of the country was Moslem, whereas it has now been made clear that Moslems are no more than 20% of the population. [7] The advance of Islam southwards began to slow down towards 1930 and came to a halt about 1950. [8] Moslems did little to promote modern schools and neglected the education of girls (it can be shown statistically that the Islamization of African countries varies in inverse proportion to the spread of schools); consequently, Islam has been facing a real crisis ever since black Africa entered the modern era.

7. No one who visits Africa can forget the experience. These singing and dancing people who are so cheerful, spontaneous and emotional — and therefore unpredictable too, who transform huts into homes, work into rhythmic movement and worship into real celebration, must have something to offer the

[6] On secularism, see ch. 14.B., p. 301ff.

[7] V. Haelg, *Islam und christliche Missionsarbeit an der ostafrikanischen Küste* in F. Renner (ed.), *Der fünfarmiger Leuchter*, St Ottilien, 1971, II, 153-180, esp. 166.

[8] D.A. Barrett, *Frontier situations for evangelisation in Africa*, Nairobi, 1972, p. 8; J. Lanfry, *Rencontres ou rivalités?*, in *Petit Echo* (White Fathers), Rome, 1974, no. 2, 84-95, replies exhaustively to fashionable exaggerations.

Church and mankind. Twenty years ago, Daniélou was saying that the Church must expect a liturgical renewal from Africa, with a more expressive Christian art and a revival of sacred dance. [9] Youth Masses give us some inkling of this. So it is easy to understand the Catholic Church paying special attention to this continent. In 1957, Pius XII published his encyclical 'On the Catholic Missions in Africa', *Fidei Donum*, in which he described a situation difficult but full of hope and urged the whole Church to intensify its aid. 'The slightest delay is full of dangers'. In 1967, on the occasion of the tenth anniversary, Paul VI sent his own mesage to Africa, *Africae Terrarum*, in which he renewed and amplified the appeal of *Fidei donum*. Two years later he made the African journey which caused such a stir, in order to make his moral support clear to the continent and to the whole Church. [10]

B. *Latin America's hour*

1. That Africa's hour has struck as far as the missions are concerned has been known for decades. But Latin America was long thought to be a soundly Catholic continent, politically unstable certainly, but without problems for the Church. Yet it became clear during the pontificate of Pius XII that all was not well, so much so that a cardinal once said, 'When the Pope thinks of Latin America in the evening, he cannot sleep that night'.

Everyone felt something must be done, but no one knew where to start. Hence the foundation of the various institutes of religious sociology (CERIS, DESAL, IBEAS, DESEC, etc.). In 1955 the bishops formed CELAM (*Consejo Episcopal Latino-Americano*) and the religious, who were the majority of the clergy, CLAR (*Conferencia Latino-Americana Religiosa*). All these have sought to turn the searchlights on Latin America and make the whole world aware of the situation there; surveys have been made and plans of action worked out. Latin America is now outstanding for precise information, programmes for social

[9] J. Daniélou, *The Salvation of the Nations.*
[10] On this visit, see above ch. 2.D.5, p. 45.

154

and pastoral action and formation for priests and laypeople. Now, at last, all know that this is the hour for Latin America too. [11]

2. It is only in the light of history that we can understand the present position with all its contradictions — the tension between links with tradition and the fulfilment of present tasks. The Portuguese and Spaniards arrived in the continent in the heyday of the Inquisition and of anti-Reformation attitudes. Within forty years they had subjugated and decimated the Indians of high culture and driven the nomads back into the virgin forests; they integrated the remainder in the course of time through mixed marriages and finally brought them under the influence of the missions. (They did the same with the negroes introduced later.) Today pure Indians are no more than 12% of the population. [12] There was in fact a transplantation of Iberian Catholicism. The secular and regular clergy needed were provided at first by those two countries, though later by others. In the second half of the 19th century groups of European immigrants poured in, not usually accompanied by their own priests; consequently the clergy problem remains unsolved to this day, notwithstanding appeals from successive Popes. [13] The outcome of all this is a Catholicism characterized by strong links between Church and state and between Church and the owners of the large estates; there is marked clericalism; the people cling to baptism, first communion and ecclesiastical burial, but beyond that they see their religion as the cult of saints, processions and vows and will have recourse to any means, including spiritualism, to obtain 'graces' and miracles. In the end, it is not man at the service of God but religion at the service of man in his selfish ends. [14] In any case, here we see taken to

---

[11] Cf Schooyans, Laurentin, Stucki, Apporto; further W. Promper, *Priesternot in Lateinamerika,* Louvain, 1965; F. Houtart — E. Pin, *L'Eglise à l'heure de l'Amérique Latine,* Paris, 1965; E. Pironio, *Verso una Chiesa pasquale,* Rome, 1974.

[12] M. Hartig, in LThK 5, 647f.

[13] W. Promper, in LThK 6, 810-812.

[14] L.A. De Boni, *Lateinamerika swischen Aufstand und Diktatur,* in *Kirche in Not,* 46-64, esp. 47-49; Schooyans, *Chrétienté en contestation,* Paris, 1969, p. 85-91.

an extreme the policy of baptizing in the mass, in the hope that the second and third generations will give rise to better Christians. On the contrary, when the first conversion miscarries, a second is less likely to come later; once a whole population becomes bound by tradition, hardened within Catholic structures, it is that much more difficult to shake. This is what makes the care of souls so difficult here, compared with Africa where the dynamism produces clearly perceptible successes.

3. We cannot speak of Latin America without mentioning its particular social situation. Most of its countries were once dominated by an oligarchy of rich men: great landowners and, more recently, industrialists and men of commerce, supported by politicians and generals. But the situation is changing. 'Conscientization' has awakened large sections of the population; bishops and priests make their contribution; [15] generals are no longer simply dictators for the defence of the rich but carry out revolutions — even left-wing ones as in Peru, where until the coup of 1968 about 90% of the national income ended up in the hands of 2% of the population. Revolution has been tried in all its forms by guerrillas and *tupamaros;* for many students and teachers, communism has become a demonstration of genuine patriotism. In the meantime, only the police and armies manage to hold back an even greater explosion. S. America is richer in volcanoes than any other part of the world: a symbolic fact.

4. Right in the middle of this turbulent period came some new events: the new ways of John XXIII which put in question much in ecclesiastical behaviour, then Vatican II and, above all, the second Latin American episcopal conference at Medellin in 1968 which tried courageously to apply the principles of the Council to the realities of the continent. [16] For the first time it was realized that the local Church in Latin America has responsibilities of its own and cannot simply look to 'Mother Church' for care and tutelage; the exploitation of the masses was unmasked and there was a clear resolve to take the side

[15] On 'conscientization' see ch. 3.B.5, p. 62, and ch. 5.B.3.c.7, p. 118.
[16] CELAM, Bogotà, 1968, *Documentos finales de Medellin.*

of the poor; the inadequacy of previous clericalist structures was uncovered, and it was recognized that the Church can tackle her present task only by discussing it with lay people and inviting them to take their share of responsibility. The formation and training of basic groups became the watchword. These, it was hoped, would gradually arouse the mass of people to religious and social action.

The Medellin documents are magnificent, a real event for the Church of Latin America. It was whispered that the undoubtedly conservative majority had given in and accepted the texts only because they had no alternatives to propose, but had been sabotaging the execution of them right from the start. [17] Whatever the truth about this, it remains a fact that after Medellin something was changed. The idea of basic groups did not remain sterile. The Church in Latin America no longer consists only of sumptuously adorned cathedrals and places of pilgrimage visited by the masses: it consists also of committed young Christians who make a decisive contribution to progress, of peasants who preach the gospel, of family men who sacrifice their free time for the community. Here and there, the Churches are full again on Sundays; people who, until yesterday, only prayed to St Anthony, St Philomena or St Wendelin, now gather to meditate together on the Bible. The spirit of Medellin has been given concrete expression in documents from bishops, priests and groups of lay people; these have gone very far and could be used as models on the other sides of the Atlantic and Pacific. They show how a local Church has become aware of itself after centuries of dependence and has found its own solutions. The experiments and pastoral experience of Latin America are more significant than the theology of liberation and can, with better reason, be taken as the contribution offered by the continent to the universal Church. In any case, Latin America is being watched and it knows it. That is a source of inspiration.

5. In spite of this promising reawakening, a sense of disappointment has again fallen on this Church. Did we hope for

---

[17] L. Stucki, *Kontinent im Aufbruch. Südamerika auf dem weg ins 21 Jahrhundert*, Bern, 1971, p. 65f.

too much? Will the mass of the population not let itself be aroused any more? Have we got down to work too late, in the sense that, now the Church is talking and acting, the population is no longer willing to listen? Perhaps *promociòn popular* [18] works too slowly and cannot match the pace set by the violent revolutionaries?

The most serious problem is still the clergy. About 50% of the priests still come from Europe and North America, and everyone knows that these countries cannot go on sending replacements. In the last ten to twenty years a whole series of quite palatial seminaries have been built, in order that Latin America should at least have the structures needed to form her own priests. John XXIII wrote to *Adveniat* that he hoped Latin America, through this programme, would be in a position not only to meet her own needs but also to put at the disposal of other countries a reserve of missionaries who could not be suspected of colonialism. [19] The intention was a fine one but the results have been disappointing. Many of these seminaries are empty; others have been turned to other uses. Too many priests have given up their ministry: more than 200 a year since 1969. [20] And these losses were from among the best educated and the most committed, those who had been inspired by the first wave of enthusiasm after the Council. At the same time, the population will double in the course of thirty years.

In Brazil and other places, already 80% of the population are left on their own, either because there are not enough priests or because their methods are not adequate. 'The Church baptizes her people and then abandons them' is the judgement of those who know the situation. The sects recruit members among these 'flocks without shepherds'; for this we must thank God, since they help the people to understand and conduct their lives in the light of the Bible. Many districts are inaccessible for six months in the year because of bad climatic conditions. But the Protestant pastors, lay men who have received a short but effective training, live on the spot. We too have at our

[18] See ch. 3.B.6, p. 63.
[19] Promper, *op. cit.* (n. 11), p. 288.
[20] Secretary of State, *Raccolta 1969*, 56. *Ann. Stat.*, *1970*, 67-77.

disposal in the basic groups men who are capable and trust-worthy, who would be suitable for the priesthood, but they are married. In some cities, for instance in Sao Paulo, priests have been systematically visiting skyscraper blocks with 500 or even 1000 inhabitants (enough for a parish each) and have gradually assembled a good number in a common room for Mass. Thus the Church has gone to the people in a way which meets a basic demand of the new pastoral policy. Naturally, priests are exhausted by this kind of work. In the blocks they have dis-covered trustworthy men who would be ready to work at the weekends as priests in their own neighbourhood *but* they are married and 'the others, who are not married, are not up to it. It is a pity'. Some bishops are tempted, and encouraged in this by the theologians, to present the Church with a *fait accompli* by ordaining the men, in spite of the negative decision of the 1971 synod. This, once again, comes down to the problem of choosing between the ideal solution and a working compromise, as in the case of the Chinese national Church. [21]

6. In spite of all the setbacks and daunting situations, the re-awakening of the last ten years will not be held up but will make faster progress. Confident as I am of this, let me quote the words written by P. Werenfried in a circular letter after his journey in Latin America: 'The progress of the kingdom of God is undeniable, especially in Brazil. Christ lives wonderfully in many pastors, holy priests, heroic sisters and active lay people whom I have met in hundreds. In spite of some lamentable states of affairs there is no reason for despairing of this continent, where the poor are not communist and the communists are not poor. It is not the precipitate destruction of old structures but only the convincing preaching of the gospel of divine sonship that can set in motion this process of ascent and descent, lifting up the poor to their full human dignity and awakening in the rich the spirit of poverty, making rich and poor alike into new men who are called to create by their own efforts the new structures which Latin America needs. Meeting these people whom God has freed by the Christian witness of our friends both from the *favelas* and from the ghettos of luxury housing,

[21] Cf. ch. 4.A.13, p. 78.

in order that they might know and love another — meeting these builders of a new age has been my greatest consolation'.

C. *Asia's hour*

1. Some mission strategists would think it absurd to say that this is Asia's hour in the mission,field. The great cultures of the east have always been a laborious harvest for the Church.[22] But if we neglect Asia, we leave a question mark over the Church's missionary claim. Asians are now 54% of the world's population and the proportion will probably rise to 60% in 2000; a Church which recognizes her mission 'to the ends of the world' cannot reconcile herself to being absent from that immense population. Asia is overwhelming: not only as Christians but simply as men we feel confronted by the crushing weight of a super-power; we seem to suffocate in the human masses of the cities and lose ourselves in unending distances as we travel through the country, apparently condemned to succumb like Napoleon and Hitler in their campaigns in Russia. We feel inhibited from writing on Asia, so much difference is there between near, middle and far east; Tibet, the roof of the world, and the many islands are so different, not only from the geographic, political and religious point of view but also from that of mission history. It seems impossible to unite them all under a common denominator. [23]

2. One thing however we can safely say: Asia is the most religious of the continents. All the great world religions have their cradle here. The three monotheistic religions — Judaism, Christianity and Islam — arose in western Asia and the more moralistic religions with their doctrines of cyclical return and rebirth — Hinduism, Buddhism, Confucianism and Shintoism — in the east. This is not merely a historical fact but is true in present-day experience as well: visitors from the west are

[22] K. Klostermaier, in J. Schmitze (ed.), *Das Ende der Exportreligion...*, Düsseldorf, 1971, p. 46.

[23] There are hardly any books on 'Asia' although there are countless monographs. So I must go by my own impressions and conversations on my journeys and not attempt to give a bibliography.

surprised and impressed by the intensity of the religious atmosphere which they meet at every step. This is so, whether we go into the innumerable mosques, temples and pagodas with their magnificent traditions of art and culture or among the masses of pilgrims who show their faith with flowers and lights, with their bows and lifted hands or squatting in profound recollection. It is felt too when we are in contact with individuals in their homes, in the streets or even in air-flights where we suddenly find ourselves in uninhibited religious conversation. As religious persons meeting religious persons, we feel united with them.

3. At the same time — this is the great mystery — Asia is the least Christian of the continents. There the Christian lives in a minority situation and can easily develop a sense of inferiority. The 49 million Catholics form 2.3% of the population but to this must be added the 11 million Protestants and 3 million Orthodox. If we discount the 30 million Philippine Catholics, the percentage falls to 0.95%. After so many centuries, the missions have barely left the starting post. Like the Greeks, Huns and Mongols, Europeans have occupied India (and other parts of Asia) but these political events have passed over the country — like hurricanes or like the changes of seasons, mere phenomena in the physical order — without leaving a scratch on the spiritual integrity of Hindu culture. [24] The same could be said of Christianity: it has succeeded in conquering individuals but not in transforming any people or religion from within. Is this because the Portuguese, unlike the Spaniards in America, set up only bridge-heads and fortresses throughout their enormous empire to protect their market places and their churches? They controlled the oceans but not the land. Even St Francis Xavier passed from place to place but did not succeeded in effecting a systematic penetration inland; nor did those who followed him. Even in the last century, missionaries in India and Indonesia established themselves for preference at points controlled by the whites and their soldiers, as in the cantonments of India; they did not fan out as in Africa.

[24] Surendranath Dasgupta, *A history of Indian philosophy*, I, Cambridge, 1969, VII.

The unavoidable question remains: Why was this so? The other continents became Christian one after the other. Even black Africa, in 2000, will probably be 57% Christian. [25] Why is Asia, the greatest and most religious of the continents, almost a forbidden hope for the Church? When we speak of Christian and non-Christian, we should, of course, bear in mind that a more appropriate term for western countries might be 'post-Christian': economic and political life is hardly permeated by the gospel and the Church as a historical reality is steadily losing ground among the people. Some honest Asians ask us which countries are nearer the spirit of the gospel, India or the United States, Thailand or England, Burma or France? In the western states, we find social injustice, terrible world wars, organized crime and uncontrolled capitalism; in the eastern countries (with exceptions, of course) we find in their place a spirit of mildness, search for peace, feelings of brotherhood, nights of prayer and the silent acceptance of lives in poverty. The spirit of the gospel is clearly on the side of those who do not know the gospel. This makes all the more pressing the question: Why ever do they not accept the gospel?

4. Christianity has a significant institutional presence all over Asia, except where Moslem or communist influence prevents it. This presence has a long history in the middle east, in south India and in some other places. Perhaps for this very reason, it retains something of an historical and static character. Structurally speaking, in the last 150 years the Church has been solidly built up in many places. One example: when in 1817 Mons. A. Pezzoni became Prefect of the immense territory of north India, he had at his disposal two Capuchin missionaries; one lived in Patna, one in Agra and he himself in Delhi. [26] Since then, schools have been founded, churches built, hospitals opened and new dioceses formed. In the last twenty years, the Capuchins have been able to retire and entrust one diocese after another to Indian clergy; they have retired into small groups and they are waiting, as one of them said, for the last sacraments

[25] D.A. Barrett, IRM 1970, 39-54.
[26] B. da Poppi, *Mons A. Pezzoni, Missionario e Missionologo (1777-1844)*, Rome, 1956, pp. 10-17.

and a happy death. The mission is dead: the Church lives on. But of course, apart from the buildings, the Church lives on only in Christian communities which are small and poor; only a few districts like Ranchi, Goa, Bombay and Kerala have substantial groups of Christians. The small state of Kerala, with an area which is 1.19% of India, has 37.5% of the Catholics, 60% of the priests and 77% of the sisters of all India, [27] which means that Christianity is very weak in the rest of India. In Indonesia Christians were able to join in the national movement in good time. And so, in spite of being a minority group (2% of the population) they were considered a constitutive part of the new nation at its birth. Japan had an hour of grace in the 17th century, when there were between one and two million Catholics including not a few noblemen. Then letters to Europe said, 'If we can have enough missionaries, Japan will be Christian in ten years'. [28] But persecution and 200 years of isolation from the outside world destroyed this hope. A second hour of grace followed the second world war. In the years 1947 to 1951, Catholics increased by 42.51%, in 1951-1956 by 44.38%. Then in successive five year periods, the increase went down to 30.74%, 15.70%, 7.29%. Finally, in 1971-2 the increase fell to 0.35% In this country of the future, Catholics are 0.3% of the population and all Christians together 0.8%. In this country, which is a model for Asia, the Church should be a model to other countries. Unfortunately it is still too introverted, too lacking in courage and dynamism.

From Asia, Daniélou expected a contribution towards the renewal of contemplation and mysticism for the advantage of the whole Church. [29] The expectation seems to have been justified as far as western countries are concerned [30] but less so in Asia itself. The absence of the contemplative element has been one of the most serious deficiencies in Catholic missionary work. There has been deep dedication to action and activities;

[27] *Directory of vocations*, IV.

[28] J. Schmiedlin, *Kathol. Missiongeschichte*, Steyl, 1924, p. 278.

[29] J. Daniélou, *The Salvation of the Nations*: 'The whole of the east is like a single immense monastery, only waiting to put its great longing at the service of the true God.'

[30] On eastern influence in the west, see ch. 10.B.3, p. 245ff.

the missions have earned gratitude for their schools, organization and efficiency but have not been recognized as masters in the spiritual life. Christianity was taught from the catechism but there was little talk of experience of the divine. In India, the homeland of contemplation, not 1% of the nuns live in contemplative communities and the very few male *ashrams* (Kurisumala, Shantivanam, Thirumaha, etc.) have not as yet any real following. The All India seminar of 1969 requested with urgency the construction of places of meditation, where it would be possible to draw from the springs of the oldest tradition of the life of poverty in close union with nature and with the people around, so as to put these treasures at the service of the message of God's kingdom. [31]

5. There is no mistaking the fidelity and dedication of the Christians of Asia. The Goanese, the Eurasians and others form very faithful communities, and have proportionately more vocations to the priesthood and more nuns than people in other continents. Vietnam has had 300,000 martyrs in the course of long persecutions; a bishop declared: 'Here they are quite ready for martyrdom. Everyone would be ready to die for the faith, without giving it a thought'. This seems no exaggeration. And yet, proud of their glorious past, they forget to adapt themselves to present needs. [32]

These Christians, their priests, even the missionaries themselves must be taxed with a certain lack of missionary courage. They stay enclosed within their little communities, as if afraid of the enormous task before them, as if somehow protecting themselves from the overwhelming power of Asia. Is this because of the introverted character of Asians, who are tolerant and more disposed to co-existence than to missionary expansion? Or is it caused by the fact that in many places Christians come from the poorer classes, like the outcastes of India, and feel they do not have the right to approach others? It is true that in

[31] E. Zeitler, *Indiens Kirche zwischen gestern und morgen*, in *Priester und Mission*, Aachen, 1972, pp. 105-109; Abhishiktananda, *Towards the renewal of the Indian Church*, Ernakulam, 1970, shows the priority of the spiritual for the renewal of the Church in India.

[32] P. Gheddo, *Cattolici e Buddhisti nel Vietnam*, Milan, 1968, p. 211.

India, because of the difficulties foreign missionaries experience in getting entry permits, a wave of missionary activity is going on now; the Christians of the south are sending many priests and nuns to the north and Kerala alone has sent 11,065 priests and nuns to other Indian states. [33] But this does not yet amount to a real missionary campaign. Those who are sent devote themselves to the care of small communities of Christians and nothing more. It could be said that these 'missions' to the north are an excuse for failing in mission, that they are not really the missionary drive they are thought to be. In 1969, less than 5% of the priests and only 0.1% of the 30,000 nuns in India were dedicated to authentic missionary work, while 45.8% were occupied in school work. And yet north India would be a marvellous mission field for nuns who have the courage, imagination and dedication needed for the decisive task of the Indian Church. They need to abandon the 19th century model and discover the tasks assigned them by the post-conciliar period. [34] Questions are being asked: the first All India consultation on evangelization, held in Patna from 3 to 8 October 1973, the Indian episcopal conference at Calcutta and the Asian conference at Taipeh, both in 1974, make it perfectly clear that something is brewing.

6. And high time too! Anyone with his eyes open can see that the Church in Asia is facing a new opportunity. The present is creating entirely new conditions. Whereas formerly Asia was characterized by the continuity of a society firmly based on religion, society now is in the throes of transformation. Urbanization creates masses who are rootless and, at the time, organized and self-aware. The votes of the outcastes are being canvassed. The media are spreading news everywhere. The model of Asian traditional life is being undermined. [35] Even the religions are beginning to be sensitive to the new atmosphere. Criticism is making headway; not everything is believed. Newspapers are suggesting that the thought complex Maya-Mukti-Nirvana-Karma has undoubtedly produced a galaxy of saints but, at the

[33] *Directory of vocations,* V.
[34] *Conference of religious,* 116f.
[35] M. Edwards, *A history of India,* London, 1967, p. 319f.

same time, a people of pygmies with their eyes closed to the problems of life and defenceless against hunger, sickness and external attacks. To put this right, it is suggested, a new materialistic philosophy is needed. [36] Secularization would make men free. The equation between Indian and Hindu is no longer accepted. Family ties are also weakening. The great mass of students go through a sceptical phase and many of them, after overcoming their insecurity and frustration, begin to raise questions again and freely open themselves to any good news. Asia is at the dawn of a new day.

7. Faced by opportunities like these, the Church cannot continue in its limited way of life and be concerned only with internal problems. In the course of history, the Church has always travelled along the new highways opened by soldiers. Now the world's highways are converging on Asia. The Church can either be reduced to an insignificant ghetto minority or can undertake an entirely new mission in the strength of the risen Christ. 'Yet now Christ is risen from the dead' we can affirm with Paul (1 Cor 15:20). Therefore the Church will *not* let this historic hour pass her by.

Mission a thing of the past? The whole configuration of the world of today seems to refute this. In the inter-war period, it became clear that Africa's hour was sounding. For twenty years now, we have become aware that it is Latin America's hour too. Finally, the time has come to speak of Asia's hour, [37] although this is no reason for forgetting the other two continents. I say it once again: We are not at the end of the missions but rather at the beginning of a new and extraordinary missionary era. We face a quite exceptional global call to actualize the mission of Christ in the world of today.

[36] *The Times of India,* New Delhi, 29.10.1972.
[37] It is pleasing to be able to report that the Indian missionary institute PIME at the General Chapter 1971 decided to dedicate themselves, with the highest priority, to the evangelization of Asia. Cf. S. Stracca, *Un Institut donne la priorité à l'évangélisation des non-chrétiens,* in CM 1972, 130-134.

Part Two

New light on old problems

Chapter 8

MISSIONS BEFORE THE PEOPLE'S TRIBUNAL

Twenty years ago we were shocked and outraged not only by the expulsion of missionaries from China but also by the defamatory, though not all entirely false, charges thrown at them by the local press and radio, and quite often by the public tribunals: the missions hospitals were set up to murder adult Chinese with knives and syringes, while the orphanages were for killing babies; infants were baptized by the thousand and killed at once, their bodies being dug into the gardens like manure, their eyes torn out to make medicines and their bone-marrow extracted to make nutrients; the mission schools, being aimed solely at winning strong young men over to the imperialist cause, used only foreign teaching material, subjected the pupils to anti-communist propaganda (Chinese hymns celebrating freedom were never sung) and in the compulsory religious instruction injected them with the poison of imperialist culture; the missionaries' reports depicted a China of orphans, pigtails, bandaged feet and opium; the missionaries themselves lived in palaces (while paying unfair wages to their employees) and let native priests and nuns live in hovels. [1] Thus a humiliated people gave full vent to its repressed hatred.

We must expect the growing influence of China in the Third World to spread a few of these ideas abroad. My concern at present is not with this but with whether *we* can claim the right to criticize the missions. Mission, in spite of its divine origin, is still a human enterprise in its execution and is therefore, in principle, open to criticism. After being idealized and romanticized, the missionary is beginning to lose some of the

---

[1] J. Schütte, *Die katholische Chinamission im Spiegel der rotchinesischen Presse*, München i. W., 1957, pp. 326-344, 359-364, 232-253.

brightness of his halo. [2] This book cannot help criticizing certain missionary situations. Can we claim a right to do so or not?

A. *Critique of the past*

1. The severest criticism has been directed against missionary methods in Latin America. It still is, although the writings of R. Ricard and K.S. Latourette have brought about some tempering of it. The conclusions of a recent study on Mexico are valid for other countries: there is insufficient reflection; groups of missionaries, instead of co-operating, are divided by rivalry; there has been no attempt to enter into really explanatory discussion with the old religion or to find truly native forms of expression for liturgy and doctrine. [3] The old institutionalism still holds sway to this day. One of the sharpest critics, Ivan Illich, introduces a book as follows: 'In each chapter, I attempt to question a particular certainty. Each chapter treats of an illusion expressed in a particular institution. Our institutions create certainties. If these certainties are taken seriously, they destroy the heart and put the imagination in chains. I still nourish the hope that my statements, angry or deeply felt, troublesome or harmless, will provoke at least a smile and, hence, a new freedom, even if that freedom costs something'. [4]

2. In Africa, too, the 'dear negroes' had sharper eyes than they were credited with. Criticisms of the missions and missionaries are not all present day outbursts of nationalism. Unchanging views on seven decades of the Protestant mission in Ghana, collected by H.W. Mobley, [5] can hardly lack validity, and they can point a lesson for Catholic missionaries too: missionaries

[2] P. Gheddo, *Processo alle missioni*, Milan, 1971.
[3] J. Baumgartner, *Mission und Liturgie in Mexico*, Schöneck, 1971, I, p. 411f.
[4] I.D. Illich, *Almosen un Folter. Verfehlter Fortschritt in Lateinamerika*, München, 1970, p. 8. On 'institutionalism' cf. ch. 7.B.2, p. 155.
[5] H.W. Mobley, *The Ghanaian's image of the missionary*, Leiden, 1970, pp. 73-151.

kept their distance from the people, living for preference in hilltop residences; universal brotherhood in Christ was indeed preached, but in practice aid was given with a paternalistic and superior air, so that black people suffered in an intangible way from their colour; African tradition was condemned without being studied (there were, to be sure, missionaries who studied it for many years and published learned works on it, but they were isolated individuals) and Christianity simply suppressed the African religions, replacing the spontaneous piety of the African — so closely linked to the mysteries of life — with arid devotions remote from life; marriage became ringed around with notions of sin... [6]

Professor Ayandale of Nigeria, author of a book making similar criticisms, [7] intervened at the first international congress on missionology at Driebergen, after many white representatives had expressed themselves in a way he considered too critical of the missions: 'Even if *you* came to us within the framework of colonialism and did not preach the gospel in all its purity, that has not prevented *us* from receiving the gospel and genuinely living it'.

3. In the case of Asia the same criticisms are made, but what is stressed is the deficiency in spirituality and the western forms imposed on Christianity. T. Ohm has expounded this criticism in two books and arrives at this conclusion: 'We continually hear that the missions need more money, more schools, more churches, more adaptation... These certainly are real needs... But we shall not convince Buddhists, Hindus and Moslems unless we are more spiritual and more alive in the spirit than they'. [8] To non-Christians, becoming a Christian meant belonging to the west, eating flesh, drinking alcohol, acting like a bad child who denies his own father, that is to say, India and Indian culture. Radhakrishnan asked: 'Who

---

[6] Cf. also S. Hertlein, *Christentum und Mission im Urteil der neoafrikanischen Prosaliteratur*, Münsterschwarzach, 1963.

[7] *The missionary impact on modern Africa*, London, 1966.

[8] *Asiens Nein und Ja zum westlichen Christentum*, München, 1960, p. 220; cf. his previous book, *Asiens Kritik am abendländischen Christentum*, München, 1948.

has the right to destroy what he will not take the trouble to know? Trampling in the dust what is sacred to the soul of the people, what has been built up by the wisdom of centuries, is spiritual vandalism. We can only ascribe such a thing to blind prejudice, to a pitiful kind of ignorance'. [9]

'Up to the present, evangelization has been left to chance, trusting to the good will which may be present here and there, without method and without general planning' writes D.S. Amalorpavadas, who has been trying for some time to introduce more system and planning into the Church in India. He attributes attachment to the old methods in the young Churches to their anxious preoccupation with orthodoxy: 'They cling unbendingly to the juridical and institutional structures, taking as their rule of conduct the codex of canon law, the Index, Denzinger, the *monita* and instructions of the Holy Office, instead of the gospel and biblical, patristic and pastoral theology'. [10]

B. *Forward-looking criticism*

1. In this second part of the book, where I try to draw conclusions from the new shape of the world for a new perspective on its problems, I cannot avoid criticism. I would like to underline at the outset, once for all, that I do not intend, in spite of all this, to cast doubt on the magnificence of past missionary performance. One would have to be colour blind to see nothing but black in the story. With all their faults the missions can point to achievements in history, and in the present day, which compel the admiration of honest visitors; closer acquaintance has dispelled the prejudices of more than one. Rolf Italiaander, for example, in one of his better known books brought the African mission before a true people's tribunal;

[9] P. Thomas, *The renascent Hindu attitudes towards Christianity,* in *The Living Word,* Alwaye, 1972, pp. 410-432, esp. 417-421; also in M. Dhavamony (ed.), *Evangelization, dialogue and development,* Internat. Theolog. Conf., Nagpur, 1971, Tome 1972.

[10] D.S. Amalorpavadas, *L'Inde à la rencontre du Seigneur,* Paris, 1964, pp. 65, 235.

the proceedings come to a head with the charge: 'The more I reflect on the work of missionaries, the stranger it seems to me. These people, driven by a neurotic urge, have destroyed a people's philosophy of life, without putting anything in its place...' [11] But in another book, ten years later, he admits he has been converted: 'The longer I reflected on my experience, the clearer it became to me that the missionaries must be judged to have made a positive contribution, even from the view point of a liberal Christian'. [12]

Just as mission as an enterprise carries conviction and wins approval, so too do the missionaries when one meets them — young people with their courage, dedication and closeness to the people, older people with their peace and serenity, looking on the sacrifice of their life as something quite unremarkable. As a mere writer, I confess to not being worthy to unloose the sandals from the feet of so many missionaries. The Protestant theologian H. Thielicke once met a Catholic missionary in South Africa who, in spite of all prejudices, believed in black people; he writes: 'The hope in faith overflowing from this young Father has a certain grandeur and is very moving. It quite puts me to shame!' [13]

2. All this cannot and must not hinder us from being critics, in the sense of exercising discernment between good and bad, between good and better. For this purpose, one who lives at a distance can take a wider view and has the advantage over one who is immersed in the mission, defending his own work and exposed to the well-known danger of professional bias. There is a general tendency in the Church to defend the traditional, to remain attached to 'what has proved its worth', to avoid new risks, to disregard situations coming to a head, to concede points only when absolutely obliged to or when they cease to carry much weight. [14] Here criticism should help

[11] Italiaander, *Der rubelose Kontinent: Africa,* Düsseldorf, 1958, p. 624.
[12] Italiaander, *Profile und Perspektiven,* Erlangen, 1971, p. 7. The whole book, with its 'profiles', will help to overcome many clichés about the missions, through presenting convincing figures.
[13] H. Thielicke, *So sah ich Afrika,* Gütersloh, 1971.
[14] Rahner, *Strukturwandel der Kirche als Aufgabe und Chance,* Freiburg im B., 1973, pp. 29, 52f, 55 etc.

towards a clearer perception of when and how best to do what has to be done. W. Kaspar writes: 'Negative criticism, well understood, does not have deleterious effects but releases a force for freedom. The scales fall from men's eyes suddenly and they see reality in a new light. They realize that things could and should have been different. This opens up possibilities and makes room for action. In the past, unfortunately, Christian preaching has aimed to be a calming rather than a rousing influence. Not wanting to excite people, it has often become boring and uninspiring'. [15]

In the following chapters, then, criticisms will be directed not against men but against situations, not as condemnations but as judgements. I draw conclusions from new situations; I indicate possibilities for new forms of action and I shall delineate certain utopias. [16] I shall do this without reserve, in all openness, since it is truth that makes us free (Jn 8:32). I shall speak not as one throwing stones at the Church from outside but as one who lives in the Church. Since I have had the advantage of being able to travel, to see, hear and read a good deal and also to hear the voice of outsiders, I shall inquire about whatever could be to the advantage of the Church. I hope I shall work not against the Church but for her, engaging in the type of debate within the Church which is the right and duty of committed Christians. [17]

[15] W. Kasper, *Glaube und Geschichte,* Mainz, 1970, p. 236f.
[16] Cf. 9.A.12, p. 188.
[17] On 'contestation' see below p. 212.

Chapter 9

FUNCTIONS IN THE CHURCH: STRUCTURE AND SPONTANEITY

On this rock I shall build my Church.

(Mt 16:18)

A. *Eternal forms?*

1. *Central administration in the Church*

1. The best-known image of the Church and the Papacy for the last hundred years has been that of a rock, firmly resistant to the waves and unchangeable through all the storms. The imposing basilica of St Peter and the massive walls surrounding the Vatican have served to symbolize this.

But the biblical reality concerning Peter and his messianic community is a little different. It is true this community will never succumb, but it certainly will be shaken by storms: it is precisely this which will prove it to be founded on rock and not on sand. The complementary image, more topical today, is that of the tempest-tossed boat with the disciples on board terrified and saved only through Christ (Mt 8:23-27). Even Peter, the rock, had so little faith that he was in danger of drowning when he went to meet Jesus on the water (Mt 14:24-33). He was so far from understanding God's plans for his Son that Jesus addressed him threateningly: 'Go far from me, Satan. You think not according to God but according to men' (Mt 16:23). He had so little courage that in the hour of testing he abandoned and denied the Lord, even if later he repented bitterly and after the resurrection was again called by the risen Lord (Mt 26:69-75; Jn 21:15-17). Even after that he was

175

so inconsistent in preaching the gospel before the pagans that Paul had to resist him to his face (Gal 2: 11-14). A man with such precedents would hardly be 'papabile' today. But Christ cast a veil over all these weaknesses and kept Peter and his community in the one faith to this day.

There is no trace here of the unchangeable rock and the Church as a bulwark. More than any other institution the Church has changed in external form from gospel times to the present and yet has remained herself.

2. After a static period, the Church is once again in a phase of change which will have historical importance. Twenty years ago anyone who ventured to predict that within a relatively short time the faithful would be able to eat and drink up to an hour before communion, that Mass would be celebrated in the language of the country, that priests leaving the ministry would be able to marry in church and receive the sacraments, that there would be prayer meetings and Bible study in the company of Protestants, that Friday abstinence in the old form would be practically abolished . . . such a man would not have been thought a prophet but a dreamer. And yet, what was timidly formulated as *postulata* at the first international congress on mission at Nijmegen in 1959 and at the first international congress on missions and catechesis at Eichstätt in 1960 [1] has become reality more quickly and more widely than any one could have imagined. This is the situation we must take account of.

3. On the other hand, a clear tendency towards calling a halt has asserted itself in the Church in the last few years. There is a desire to bring the flood waters back into well defined channels, to re-integrate the divergent forces into a unitary system, to restore to canon law its lost importance. It is felt that the Church is now renewed and that mutable forms must now be stabilized again.

Such a trend is understandable as a tactical pause. It is a fact that there are very many people in the Church who have not been able to keep up with the developments going on; they

---

[1] J. Hofinger, *Katechetik heute,* Freiburg im B., 1961; (ed.) *Mission und Liturgie,* Mainz, 1960; *Teaching the Faith,* Sheed and Ward.

176

are confused and would like to 'die in the old faith'. There are also people living in the Vatican who think all this disturbance over renewal has led to nothing except destruction, secularization, and surrender of the gospel to sociologists and psychologists. They think dialogue is never constructive but only complicates matters and holds things up; at one time we accepted the word of the superior as the will of God; we need firm guidance and not experiments which are doomed to failure from the start... It is only human to have some concern for these people, who would rather be on a firm rock than in a pitching ship. But we are not, for their sake, permitted to bring renewal to a halt.

Renewal is a continuous process, just as life renews itself all the time, or else arterio-sclerosis sets in as a sign of the approaching end. The Council was not a finish but a fresh start, a thrust forward, after which the post-conciliar Church must go bravely on her way. [2] God is not a God of 'eternal rest' but of eternal life. It falls to the hierarchy, given their special share in God's mission, to discover precisely in which changes God is at work today. [3] John XXIII expressed this beautifully (and with theological soundness): 'We are not here on earth to be curators of a museum but to cultivate a garden full of flowers and life. It must grow into a wonderful garden'. Certainly, the interior renewal is positive. But we live at a time when the speed of the train has been surpassed first by the automobile, then by the aeroplane, the jet, the missile. (In 1972, Pioneer X, on its way to Jupiter, touched a speed of 52,000 km per hour.) Scientific publications annually include some 30,000 specialist reviews with up to two million original articles, carrying on research of enormous scope. In the circumstances, it is impossible to maintain that the Church *is*, from now on, fully adapted, and that her discipline, structure and theology will need no more changes. [4]

[2] K. Rahner, *Das Konzil — ein neuer Beginn,* Freiburg, 1966; cf. also id. and H. Vorgrimmler, *Kleines Konzilkompendium,* Freiburg im B., 1967, p. 28.

[3] H. Cox, *God's revolution and man's responsibility,* London, 1965, p. 99f.

[4] H. Küng, *Structures of the Church,* London, 1965; J. McKenzie, *Amstruktur im Neuen Testament,* in *Concilium,* 1972; Kasper, *Glaube und Geschichte,* 1970, pp. 355-442.

4. Rome, the city steeped in history, needs to be warned by the lessons of history. It has always shown a tendency to remain sceptical about the progress of science or to reject it outright. It is enough to recall the case of Galileo, the series of doctrinal statements on evolution, freedom of religion, conscience, etc. Only after much shuffling has the Church gradually discovered the kernel of truth in various radical reform movements and appropriated it.

In particular, the institutional Church has found it very difficult to accept the modern democratic mentality.

The Papal States were governed as an absolute monarchy. From the early middle ages, it was emphasized that all authority is granted 'by the grace of God' and is responsible only to God (and the Church), not to the people. In recent centuries, the Church has always been on the side of monarchical authority and has, in principle, supported efforts to suppress the democratic movement at birth. Only during Vatican II did she decisively move out of the castles of princes and renounce, as a matter of principle, the privileges deriving from the alliance between altar and throne. [5]

Even if the democratic model cannot be applied in all points to the Church (because here all authority does come ultimately from Christ) and even if the voice of the bishops carries a weight qualitatively distinct from that carried by any vote taken among the faithful, this by no means implies that the faithful and the priests have a merely consultative function in pronouncements and decisions of the Church. In the time of Christ, these problems had not arisen. Then the only known form of government was monarchy, from bedouin chief to emperor. But it would be humanly and ideologically mean-minded to disregard the fact that Christ gave his Church a basic constitution meant to be efficient, functional and as adaptable as possible to any age. Today, when every authority must be justified by its own competence and ability to give wise guidance, and is to be enriched by general participation, when the personalities of great rulers

[5] F. Kern, *Gottesgnadentum und Widerstandsrecht im frühen Mittlelalter. Zur Entwicklungsgeschichte der Monarchie,* Darmstadt, 1954. A. Gnägi, *Katholische Kirche und Democratie,* Einsiedeln, 1970, pp. 166-169, 228-231.

are being eclipsed by concern for the personal development of all, he would surely wish the whole people of God to have a much greater co-responsibility in his Church. [6] In dealings with the Third Church, where the birth of new states has brought old and young, men and women the same democratic rights in places where clericalism and paternalism used to reign supreme because of the strength of tradition among missionaries, central administration should intervene not to impose curbs but to relax them, giving encouragement wherever energies may be flagging. [7]

5. Roman authority has reacted diffidently to scientific progress, viewing it in a conservative spirit. The same attitude has been adopted, though more forthrightly, towards theological progress. During the first meeting of the International Theological Commission held in Rome, 1969, Karl Rahner showed clearly how these authoritative interventions during the last hundred years have, indeed, been a real defence of the faith but a sterile defence, not aiming at a positive integration of new problems. This task of integration has fallen to men who were rather suspect at Rome. 'Almost everything said by the Roman departments on biblical questions in the hundred years previous to Vatican II has become obsolete and is not taken into account by anyone now'. [8] At a time when we are witnessing the birth in western countries of a pluriformity of theologies seeking to serve the interests of the faith, and when in the Churches of the south the gospel is no longer merely 'translated' but is also preached in completely new spiritual contexts, the central authority of the Church needs to be a universal collective genius to give a just appraisal to all developments and not strangle them at birth.

6. This brings us to the nerve centre, the question which exercises us most in this polycentric world; it can be formulated

[6] Rahner, *Strukturwandel*, pp. 127-130; E. Nickel, *Der Mensch von morgen und die Religion*, in A. Resch (ed.), *Welt, Mensch und Wissenschaft morgen*, Paderborn, 1972, pp. 229-231; R. Guardini, *Das Ende der Neuzeit*, Würzburg, 1965, p. 71; L. Rütti, *Zur Theologie der Mission*, München-Mainz, 1972, pp. 307-317.

[7] PMV-CI 1970/33: *La jeunesse occidentale et l'avenir de l'Eglise.*

[8] *Glaubenskongregation und Theologenkomission*, in *Schriften* 10, pp. 338-357.

something like this: How far is centralized organization good and necessary in the Church; to what extent is it a qualified good which should now be dismantled? When I use the term 'Rome' in a pejorative sense, I have no intention whatever of calling in question the hierarchical Church or the papal primacy in themselves, but only some forms they have evolved in the course of time and which have become problematic in the present new configuration of the Church and the world. The bishop of Rome's function as source of unity remains intact. He has acted for the unity of the Churches much more effectively than the UN Organization has ever acted for the unity of nations. But this in no way invalidates the principle of subsidiarity and should not obscure the fact that, historically, unity has developed from below upwards. Canon law and liturgy were rooted in living local communities only later recognized by the centre and transmitted to other Churches. The patriarchal system arose when the bishops of a region, in the interests of greater unity and effective action, yielded some of their rights to one bishop as their leader. [9] Central administration cannot claim any creative role. It would be wrong to expect of it any creative activity. It should be quick to recognize creative elements in local Churches and slow to make decrees from on high.

7. The western Church, in particular the Roman Church, finds herself today in something like the situation of the primitive Church among the Jews, for we too must beware of handicapping with the trappings of history the arrival of the new 'Church of the Gentiles', the Third Church. We have the opportunity of becoming the Church for the whole world but we must pay the price, that is, strip ourselves of western bias. I would make three points here:

Rome is no longer Rome as she was in the time of the ancient Romans or during almost two millennia in which the Roman Catholic Church was the Church of the west. Rome is not now at the centre of the world but rather on the edge.

[9] W. de Vries, *The origin of the Eastern Patriarchates and their relationship to the power of the Pope,* in T.E. Bird (ed.), *Archiepiscopal and Patriarchal autonomy,* N.Y., 1972, pp. 14-21.

Peter, indeed, remains for ever the foundation of the Church. But the contingent circumstance that he lived and died in Rome must not be made too much of, as if the Catholic Church stood or fell with Rome. In the middle ages, Popes repeatedly lived elsewhere — for 70 years in Avignon; who knows what the future will bring? Certain hymns about Rome give an impression of ecclesiastical nationalism and sound bombastic in the ears of non-Romans, as when Pius XII, the son of a family of Roman patricians, apostrophized Rome as 'the eternal city, the universal city, capital of the world, the city *par excellence,* city of which all are citizens, seat of the Vicar of Christ, towards which the whole Catholic world turns its gaze'. [10] After the end of English colonialism, the Anglican Church lost much support: Anglicans in India and elsewhere no longer like to belong to the Church *of England.* For this reason, they have changed their name in many places. Even Vatican II changed the draft text which said the Church, one, holy, catholic and apostolic subsists in the 'Roman Church' and substituted 'in the Catholic Church'. Strictly speaking, the 'Roman Church' (the 'Church of Rome') is a local Church, part only of the universal Church, although Rome's bishop is at the same time head of all the bishops of the Catholic Church. [11] Many episcopal conferences now call themselves, for example, 'the Episcopal Conference of Tanzania'. And their headquarters, they call simply the 'Catholic Secretariat'.

Latin, as the language of the Church, has come to the end of its historical function. Even the desperate salvage attempt by means of *Veterum Sapientia,* in 1962 — about which later John XXIII himself smiled — did not manage to ensure that teaching in seminaries should be in Latin. [12] In Vatican II, for technical reasons, it was both necessary and helpful to continue to use Latin. Even episcopal synods had to do the same, until in 1971 certain bishops presented a *fait accompli* and spoke French or English. If it is no longer possible to save Latin even in western countries, much less can we demand that African and Asian candidates to the priesthood should study the langu-

[10] AAS 1946, 18.
[11] LThK, *Konzil* I, pp. 173-175.
[12] AAS 1962, 129-135.

age, since it has no connection with their own culture. For this reason, some seminaries have simply cut it out of the programme. So we have to face the fact that tomorrow's priests will not know Latin. Yet, for a world Church, a language which can serve as a bond of union is of immense importance. Attempts made with artificial languages like Esperanto will probably not succeed. But since English is now spoken as a first or a second language by 30% of mankind, throughout all the continents, the Church must disregard the fact that it is a 'Protestant' language and make an effort to ensure that priests, religious and others learn it. So within a number of years it could become the Church's language, in place of Latin. One does not need the gift of prophecy to foresee that in 2001, at the latest, *Acta Apostolicae Sedis* will be published in English.

The composition of the *major ecclesiastical bodies* should correspond more than it does with the present membership of the Church. In the matter of the college of cardinals Pius XII, in his Christmas message, 1945, announced that it would be made more international and as a first step appointed a cardinal from Asia, Thomas Tien. [13] He and his successors have followed this policy consistently. But in the Roman curia, with the exception of the Congregation for the Evangelization of the Nations, the Third Church is still badly represented. The same disproportion is to be observed in the Pontifical Commissions: in the one appointed on 3 May 1973 to study the role of women in the world and in the Church, the western Church is represented by 21 members, Latin America by two and Asia, Africa and Oceania had a consolation prize of one each. In this respect, the International Federation of Christian Family Movements of the World Council of Churches has shown a better understanding of the realities of the modern world and has drawn conclusions with more courage. For the seminar 'Family 1974', the world was divided into twelve regions, of which only three, eastern Europe, western Europe and North America, belong to the old Church; the other nine are in the southern Church. Each region was to send eight married couples who were to meet not in London or New York but in Tanzania, to pass several days in

[13] AAS 1946, 14f, 104.

the socialist village communities and then assemble at Dar es Salaam not to listen to academic lectures but to exchange ideas in various forms of group dynamics; thus they could be open to inspiration so as gradually to reach final conclusions leading to concrete and decisive action.

8. This brings us back to the problem of centralism. Should these commissions not work more at the regional level to guarantee genuine participation by various parts of the world and to allow for varying circumstances? Should decrees on concrete questions in the Church not be adapted to different situations in different countries? Apart from the fact that central administration — in spite of journeyings by prefects and secretaries — is not in direct contact with real life, does not feel problems deeply and tends to think questions resolved and disposed of by issuing decrees, the simple requirement that a decree must be valid for the whole world ensures that it remains on an abstract level, far from living reality; or else, if it is put in concrete terms, it will do violence to some situations because these differ so much from continent to continent. Two examples will serve to make this clear.

The *pastoral norms on general absolution* [14] have highlighted the problematic nature of such decrees. In the western Church the confessional is rapidly becoming less and less frequented, and people are trying to preserve the essentials of the remission of sins by using penitential liturgies; in the southern Churches of Latin America and Africa there are many Christians, few priests and a tradition of ritualistic piety. But instead of according due recognition and space to the new penitential liturgies — which are already favoured by many western Christians and could prove so suitable for the southern Churches if their use were encouraged — these pastoral norms provide textbook theology permeated by the fear of mortal sin; there are two incidental quotations from Vatican II and the Bible but ten quotations from documents of earlier centuries, and a dozen or so clauses and warnings apt to make scrupulous priests even more scrupulous as well as causing disappointment and resistance

[14] AAS 1972, 510-514.

in the more open. Christ used a different tone in calling men to conversion and the Christian world is looking for a different message from the Church.[15] However, from what we hear, many bishops, especially in S. America, give a fairly generous interpretation to the decree, so that it has opened some doors.

9. The *document on the Eucharistic prayers* is being received with less criticism but not with complete satisfaction.[16] Clearly, order should prevail in parish masses, the Church's unity should express itself in a certain unity of prayer form, and abuses must be removed, especially when they distress people. But abuse is no reason for throwing away legitimate freedom and for prohibiting the use of any but the four Eucharistic prayers of the Roman Missal. I am not putting in a plea for the groups of young people in the western Church who want something different in their prayers and celebrations from what suits our cold and objective adult taste. I am speaking rather for the Third Church which is genuinely characterized by spontaneity, as F. Heiler affirms in his classic work on the prayer of these peoples.[17] Catholic missions suppressed this spontaneity with their stereotyped and pre-fabricated prayers. Moreover, the 'independent Churches' and sects owe their enormous success in Latin America, Africa and Asia in large part to their spontaneous liturgical celebrations.[18] These exuberant and usually non-sacramental celebrations could well be fitted into the framework of Christian life. But what happens? The metropolis decides, as in the days of European hegemony, that the whole world is to be restricted to the four Eucharistic prayers. The Holy See is driven to issuing this document 'by pastoral concern for unity'. But unity is not to be conceived on the lines of

---

[15] Cf. Rahner, *Bussandacht und Einzelberichte,* in *Stimmen der Zeit,* 1972, pp. 363-372, where he defends the sacramental nature of such penitential celebrations.

[16] AAS 1973, 340-347.

[17] F. Heiler, *Das Gebet,* München, 1921, p. 58f: 'The prayer of primitive peoples is the direct expression of deep, spiritual experiences; it rises spontaneously out of need or a feeling of gratitude. Overpowering excitement breaks out in free expression as lamentation and prayer, praise and thanksgiving...'

[18] See below, ch. 9.B.3, p. 203f.

imposed uniformity but rather as unity of faith and love beyond the forms which are conditioned by time and place. Latin was long defended with the same argument based on unity, until it was recognized that unity does not depend on Latin. Every respect is due to the four Eucharistic prayers. They should be used and will be used everywhere. But there was no need, for their sake, to prevent other Eucharistic prayers worthy of the name arising under the guidance of episcopal conferences. For years now, in India and Africa, popular Eucharistic prayers adapted to local culture have been drawn up, always with the consent of the bishops. In India they turned on the theme of love and light, in Africa on life. [19] All these have now become 'non-ecclesial'. Christians in those countries find themselves faced by a difficult choice between loyalty to the authority of the Church and loyalty to their native cultural inheritance. Although the documents very clearly express the will of Rome, we may be reminded of the saying that Rome does, indeed, make the laws but does not make a tragedy out of it when they are transgressed and is frankly surprised when they are taken seriously. . .

10. We must now consider the Vatican system in itself. Every central administration is built up according to specific sociological laws proper to itself; so it is always in danger of carrying on through its own impetus and of serving its own interests, of surviving through a certain common solidarity, of subsisting in a collective routine and being a bulwark of conservatism. It tends to handle individual cases not according to their particular needs but in the light of precedents, according to abstract law. It is convinced that the whole world ought to dance to its tune. This brings a loss of contact with reality, betrayed by the generalised formulas used even in letters. Private initiative is impeded. Everyone is there to carry out orders for his superiors. No one should think; or, at most, everyone should think like his superior. No one should make himself

---

[19] Cf. the special number on the liturgy of Paths Margah, Poona, 1968; further, De Cuyper, *The future of the liturgy in India,* in CIM 1969, pp. 525-536. For Africa, cf. A. Shorter, *An African Eucharistic Prayer,* in AFER 1970, pp. 143-148; ib., *Three more African Eucharistic Prayers,* in AFER 1973. pp. 152-160.

conspicuous. Everyone should adapt himself to the system, the errand-boy system. There is no sense of brotherhood in performance of genuinely personal tasks, but one of course presents a united front when dealing with the external world. Outsiders are not accepted; they should not interfere. The careerist has a distinctive mentality. L.J. Peter considers he has proved scientifically that, in any given hierarchy, an employee tends to rise to the level of his own incompetence. In a lower position, he would have been a good worker but he has been promoted and, without knowing it, has passed the threshold of his competence and reached the stage of incompetence. 'I have observed that most people delude themselves about their own capabilities. I see incompetence triumphantly prospers everywhere.' Only those who have not passed the threshold of their incompetence do a good job. The incompetent higher officials seek to multiply their subordinates in order to enhance their own section's importance and mask their own incompetence. [20] The book exaggerates a great deal, but it must contain a considerable core of truth or it would not have become a best-seller in the United States.

11. It cannot be claimed *a priori* that the Vatican administration must have been preserved from such human weaknesses by the special assistance of the Holy Spirit. Although we may expect greater dedication from employees who are priests, there is no ground for supposing that priestly ordination confers a competence exceeding that of the layman. Moreover, in this case there is no check on the administration's activity, no parliament with an opposition party totting up points against. Religious have the advantage of being able to replace the whole management every six to ten years, and to promote right from the bottom to the top anyone they consider most suitable at the time. [21] But immobility reigns in the Vatican system. It accepts individuals only one at a time into its internal workings, and these must adapt to the system or they will be rejected.

[20] L.J. Peter and R. Hull, *The Peter principle*, N.Y., 1970; J. Folliet, *Les institutions de l'Eglise visible*, in *Le temps de l'angoisse et de la recherche*, Lyons, 1972, pp. 135-137.

[21] Also in orders and congregations the relation between centre and periphery is better. All seek the best way together.

The ecclesiastical hierarchy is doubly stressed since it is tied to a system of honorific titles: it ascends from lay employees and sisters to the Reverends, the Monsignors (who can be minor officials of first, second or third grade, subdivided in their turn into first and second class; or they may be major officials), then to His Most Reverend Excellency the Secretary and finally to the *Eminentissimo e Reverendissimo Signor Cardinale Prefetto, il Porporato*. [22] Compared with former times, this system of titles has been simplified a little but obviously has not yet been adapted to the mentality of the ordinary Christian of the present day.

In spite of lengthy decrees on the reform of the curia, with new names of offices, transferred responsibilities and the founding of new departments (often without clear delimitation in relation to existing bodies), [23] it is generally agreed that the real reform of the curia is still to come. The periphery is losing interest in the centre and the centre is handicapped by its own structure. People lament the fact that the Pope, the spiritual head of the Church, has to operate behind a façade of this kind. Between 1870 and 1929 (the end of the Papal States until the Lateran Treaty), the 'Roman question' was one of the great problems of Christianity and in treatises and congresses Catholics were tireless in protesting in favour of the 'prisoner of the Vatican'. Now a new meaning has been given to this phrase 'prisoner of the Vatican': it means the 'spiritual head ringed around by the bureaucracy'. A whole series of books and novels have taken up this theme and dream about a Pope freely and spontaneously leading the Church, recognized and honoured as head of the Christian community, beyond all differences. [24] Is it only fantasy or is it the expression of a wide-spread popular mentality?

[22] Cf. the style of the *Annuario Pontificio* and in OR.

[23] *Regimini Ecclesiae,* in AAS 1967, 885-928, and the practical applications in AAS 1968, 129-176.

[24] Cf. Silone, West, Herburger, Seeber; further, M. Serafian, *The Pilgrim,* N.Y., 1964; R. Schneider, *Der grosse Verzicht,* Insel Verlag, 1950; G. Bomans, *Der Jordan fliesst nicht in den Tiber;* F. Leist, *Der Gefangene des Vatikan,* München, 1971; G. Zizola, *L'utopia di Papa Giovanni,* Assisi, 1973; H.U. von Balthasar, *Der anti-römische Affekt,* Freiburg, 1974. Besides the attacks of Peyrefitte,

12. The future will certainly find a solution to this: forms which have developed in the course of history will change and will be adapted to new situations. Whether a 'Chinese cultural revolution' will be needed, as malicious tongues suggest, or whether a 'touch of the hand of the Holy Spirit' will be enough is another question. [25] More than once in history, the Pope has lived as a prisoner and has always come back free.

In this context, I would like to sketch a Utopia, not in St Thomas More's sense (his island-state in which all social evils were overcome was meant to be pure fantasy), but in the sense of modern economic planning, where Utopia is used as a thought model and working hypothesis to get us out of our present ruts and make possible what at first sight seems impossible because we are unused to it. In this sense, Utopia unexpectedly becomes more effective and more realistic than any realism incapable of a leap in the dark.

I ask, then, whether we should not give up trying to manifest and strengthen unity in the Church through centralized administration and disciplinary uniformity, by human means, that is, and instead regard unity as something deeper, more sublimely and biblically expressed as *koinonia*, [26] and trust to the action of the Holy Spirit to achieve it (this does not exclude 'human' relations and human exhortation). I go on to ask whether, in view of the new polycentricity of the world and the maturity of the six continents, the times do not call for some radical decentralizing, to give the regions more responsibility and a chance to work out their own Christian life. Both the western world and the Third Church are suffering from the rigidity in Church structures, which present all too clearly an image of power rather than of service. [27] These structures give an impres-

---

Hebblethwaite, Davis, Illich (in R. Laurentin, *Flashes sur l'Amérique Latine,* Paris, 1968). Cf. also P. Lombardi, *Concilio. Per una riforma nella carità,* with a chapter on the Roman Curia (pp. 203-215). A reply in OR 11.1.1962 rejects the charges as 'private opinions' and extols the *'alte benemerenze e magnifico lavoro per la Chiesa e per le anime'* of the Curia.

[25] J. Silone, *L'avventura di un povero cristiano,* Mondadori, 1971, p. 52.
[26] See below, ch. 22.
[27] *Church in India today,* All India Seminar, 1969, New Delhi, 388f.

sion of 'spiritual aggression by a foreign agent' who holds all the keys; they help to constrict many bishops of the Third Church within a legalistic, traditional and clerical framework. [28]

Both the United Nations and the World Council of Churches have their co-ordinating centres for each continent (Santiago and Porto Rico for Latin America, Accra and Nairobi for Africa, Bangkok for Asia). Within the Catholic Church, continental episcopal conferences have been set up (CELAM for Latin America, SECAM for Africa and Madagascar, FABCI for Asia). Logically, then, we ought to devolve more powers on these bodies. Matters so far decided centrally in the Roman Congregations (nomination of bishops, regulation of the liturgy, proclamation of Saints and Blessed, decisions concerning Catholic schools, etc.), could be dealt with by these continental centres, although we must avoid falling back into a new and worse bureaucracy. This could be the source of new efforts and pastoral co-ordination. CELAM offers a practical example of how such a body can be in a position to understand and face the problems of a continent. Why should Africa and Asia not develop dynamic bodies of the same kind?

As in ancient times the 'pentarchy' formed of the five patriarchates of Rome, Alexandria, Antioch, Jerusalem and Constantinople made up the one Catholic Church, so now, in a way adapted to the much greater scale of modern times, we could have something similar uniting the five (or six) continents. 'Rome' would lose something thereby but the Pope would gain and would become free to fulfil his great role as inspirer, co-ordinator, and court of appeal and, above all, as preacher of the faith, the visible and efficacious sign of the unity of all the Churches. Under these conditions ecumenism too — nowadays hampered less by papal primacy than by what is understood by the term 'Rome' — could in the end attain its object.

At the synod of Bishops in 1974, Archbishop A. Lorscheider,

<hr>

[28] Amalorpavadass and Balasuriya in Nagpur 1971: HK 1971, 570f; G. Boudreault, *L'Eglise dans la révolution japonaise*, in SML 1972, pp. 108-122, esp. 112; PMV-CI, 1970; Kongo-Kinshasa 41-43, 59; P. Gheddo, *Cattolici e Buddhisti nel Vietnam*, Milan, 1968, p. 350; D.S. Amalorpavadas, *L'Inde à la reconcontre du Seigneur*, Paris, 1964, p. 318f.

in the first general *relatio*, said frankly that the idea of the hierarchical Church as the centre of all rights and all powers has impaired and still is impairing efforts to spread God's kingdom. Before that, at the European Episcopal Conference at Augusta in 1973, Archbishop Benelli, Substitute to the Secretary of State, stressed that the Pope's primacy of jurisdiction over the whole Church is indeed of divine right, but also admitted that the centralization of power at Rome was the result of human circumstance and, objectively, something abormal. [29] We can surely, then, count on some concrete steps towards a change in the prevailing regime.

The crisis facing the Church is such that only our instinctive attitude of self-defence prevents us seeing it in its true proportions. Those who wish at all costs to preserve the structures developed through the centuries are full of anguish. Others, who see that the structures are threatened but think it worth while sacrificing them for the greater spread of the gospel, are full of confidence. It is not possible to put a brake on the rapid changes; they will accelerate still more. But amid all the turmoil there will remain the community of Christ's disciples who have received the faith in the Father and his Son and who bear it through the world as a sign of hope for all. This is what is contained in the promise of indefectibility to the Church. Thus, this crisis becomes a challenge and an altogether special call to us. [30]

2. *The Congregation for Evangelization (de Propaganda Fide)*

1. It was a blessed hour in the history of the Church when, in 1622, Gregory XV, 'by divine inspiration' (like John XXIII announcing the Council!), founded the Congregation for spreading the faith, in order to stimulate (alongside re-union with separated Christians) the evangelization of the world recently discovered and to co-ordinate and guide this work. There was

[29] OR 29.9.1974; HK 1973, 383f.
[30] So writes M. *Légaut, Pour entrevoir l'Eglise de demain*, in LV 1972 (Fr. ed.), p. 11f; ib., *Introduction à l'intelligence du passé et de l'avenir du christianisme*, pp. 404, 1970.

an enthusiastic response on all sides. Joseph de Tremblay, the grey eminence of Cardinal Richelieu, wrote that the news was received in France with incredible joy and that he thought this was the most important initiative of the Holy See since the time of St Peter. [31] In its first hundred years the Congregation certainly did produce an explosion of new ideas and fresh stimuli. It strove tirelessly to keep the missions free from ties to Spanish and Portuguese power, to promote a native clergy and to obtain better educated missionaries. In the ups and downs of its history, recently presented in three big volumes, [32] it touched a high point of achievement under Card. Van Rossum (1854-1932). He knew how to read the signs of the times, and collaborated closely with Benedict XV and Pius XI in preparing the missionary encyclicals *Maximum illud*, 1919 and *Rerum Ecclesiae*, 1926. He fought to free the missions from European bias by improving the formation of native clergy and ensuring their rapid promotion to the episcopacy. Among other things, he called Fr R. Streit, one of the most eminent Catholic specialists on the missions, to Rome. Van Rossum's work was a turning point for the missions and opened the door to a new era.

2. At the time of Vatican II, some asked if the existence of this Congregation could be justified. Surely the young Churches must feel offended and discriminated against by the fact of remaining subject, unlike other Churches, to a special Congregation, a sort of colonial ministry? Was the Council not tending towards a theological integration of mission in the life of the whole Church? [33] Should this not have implications, then, for the administrative side too? Should not *all* the Roman congregations operate within a missionary horizon? If so, the existence of one specific Congregation for mission might prove a mere alibi. Is not *Propaganda* inclined by all the weight of its history towards a territorial concept of mission(s), and to supposing that Europe and America are active agents of mission while Africa and Asia are passive recipients? Does it not tend to keep

[31] J. Metzler, *Sacrae Congregationis de Propaganda Fide memoria rerum 1622-1972*, Freiburg im B., 1971ff, I/1, 85, 116.

[32] *Op. cit.*

[33] Cf. G. Caprile, *Il Concilio Vaticano II*, vol. IV-V, Rome, 1965/69.

close relations with the missionary institutes and so incline towards selecting bishops from their ranks? Is it not conceived in the spirit of Canon 1350: 2 'Care of the missions is reserved uniquely to the Apostolic See'?

These questions merit closer consideration. Meanwhile *Propaganda Fide* continues to exist, for practical reasons if for no other, since the young Churches prefer to remain within its jurisdiction; it is simpler for them to despatch all their business here than to trail from one congregation to another according to the business in hand (which surely indicates a need to simplify procedure for the other bishops too). Yet is it unthinkable that *Propaganda* might in future transfer all its administrative business to other congregations? Then, along the lines of the Secretariat for Christian Unity and that for Relations with non-believers, it might transform itself into a Secretariat for non-Christians and a centre for sharing ideas. It would then be a body of specialists studying methods both in dialogue and in evangelization (since the two must go together if they are to be credible) and would be able to give fresh heart and deeper theological backing to the Church's missionary effort; it could also co-ordinate inter-church co-operation. With such a change of structure, questions of territorial competence would constitute a minor problem. [34]

3. The weakness of *Propaganda Fide* may perhaps be attributed to its having too much administrative business. Each year it has to deal with about 6000 cases. These dissipate its energies and leave little time for planning and research. However, an improvement is making itself felt. The systematic advancement of native clergy and native bishops will remain a glorious page in the history of *Propaganda*. But at the Council it behaved in a decidedly conservative and sterile way, making its weight felt principally by trying to get acceptance for a schema full of directives, mostly juridical, when most of the bishops had spoken in favour of a more dynamic decree on mission. In the post-conciliar period, it has intervened mostly

[34] A. Seumois, *Le problème de la réorganisation territoriale la S.C. de Propaganda Fide*, in *Omnis Terra*, Rome, 1972, pp. 315-329. On the future of co-operation between local Churches see below, ch. 22.

with exhortations to be prudent, not be infected by European ideas, to try experiments with caution rather than with courage, to give more attention to St Thomas Aquinas than to professors like... [35] However, Mons Pignedoli at the All India Seminar in 1969 formulated a new policy, proposed a continual rethinking of methods and promised the support of *Propaganda* for every renewal in the sense of Vatican II and for clearer teaching about the local character of the Church. [36]

In the meantime, responsibility in this congregation has been entrusted to representatives of the Third Church, so that Latin America in the person of Cardinal A. Rossi, Africa in that of Archbishop B. Cantin and Asia in that of Archbishop D.S. Lourdusamy can be heard at the top. Since 1973, there has been an official liaison group consisting of representatives of *Propaganda Fide* and 18 major superiors to promote dialogue, exchange information and deal with certain problems together. In addition the plenary assembly desired by the Council is functioning.

4. But, notwithstanding these innovations, it is felt that the Congregation remains imprisoned by the limits of the system. Consultors are mostly treated as people of little account. The commissions still do not work efficiently. On the whole the Congregation responds well to its first duty of being a 'administrative instrument' but is still trying to face up to the second duty wished on it by the Council, that of being 'an organ of dynamic management, making use of scientific methods and of means adapted to the needs of our times, taking account of present-day research in theology, methodology and missionary pastoral practice'. [37]

Here, there is still much to do to stimulate and co-ordinate missionary pastoral centres in the Third Church, to extend planning and to draw up priorities as well as dealing with individual cases, to multiply contacts between missionary re-

[35] Writing to the group on priestly formation at the AMECEA conference: *Priestly formation in Africa after Vat. II,* Nairobi, 1967, p. 60f.

[36] *Church in India today,* All India Seminar, 1969, New Delhi, p. 445f.

[37] AG 29. Cf. P. Gheddo, *Processo alle Missioni,* Milan, 1971, pp. 14-17.

search centres of the Second Church and to invite prominent theologians to work together on definite themes.

Even if *Propaganda* has not yet fulfilled all directives in the ten years after the Council — but which body could claim to have done this? — still its long history extending over 350 years gives good reason for hope. [38] Think of all the thrusts forward it has made during this time, the initiatives it has adopted and the leading ideas it has developed. In the last ten years, it has not only shared in changes in the Third Church but has itself contributed to the changing situation by strengthening the eastern Churches, by nominating native bishops and by rooting Christianity in the soil of local culture, Asian and African. *Propaganda* is still firmly set on the same road and is not repudiating the consequences of its own actions. No matter what structural and methodological changes it may have to undergo in future, no matter what adjustments it may have to make to its programmes of work, it will always remain the Church's leading instrument for stimulating and co-ordinating her drive towards 'expansion', understood in an ecclesial not in a geographic sense. Its major concern will still be that of ensuring that the message of Christ is brought to the whole world, so that every man whose 'soul is naturally Christian' may hear it and rejoice. [39]

3. *Legates of the Pope of Rome*

1. There is, perhaps no institution in the Church so exposed to the cross-fire of the critics as that of the Pope's legates, the nuncios, internuncios and apostolic delegates. At the Council, Bishop J. Ammann, speaking in the name of other bishops, asked whether this institution was really part of our intangible Christian tradition or whether it was one of the shadows hiding the true face of the Church from men of today. He thought the same function could be entrusted to men selected by the episcopal conferences and the diplomatic task should simply be left to

[38] Cf. Metzler (ed.), *S.C. de Prop. Fide memoria rerum 1622-1972*, Freiburg, passim.
[39] W. Bühlmann, *Vergangenheit und Zukunft der Evangelisierung*, in Metzler, *op. cit.*, III/2.

laymen. [40] Later, the Council wanted the duty of these legates to be 'more exactly defined in consideration of the pastoral ministry of bishops' and, further, wished these legates to be 'more broadly selected, from different regions of the Church' (no longer, therefore, only from Italy), so as to express the 'truly universal character' of the Catholic Church. [41] The fact that criticism has never been silenced, in spite of repeated declarations from the Vatican that the function of the legates is both necessary and beneficial, [42] means that the institution is not working well.

2. The various forms of this institution [43] as it now exists are described juridically in *Sollicitudo Omnium Ecclesiarum*, 1969. [44] According to this document, nuncios still claim the position of doyen of the diplomatic corps — on the basis of the Congress of Vienna in 1815; otherwise they are pronuncios or internuncios. They are the Pope's representatives to the local Church and to the state; all relations with Rome are handled through their channels. Their duty is to make union between the local Church and the Apostolic See closer and more effective, to be interpreters of the Pope for the good of the country, to work for peace and development in the world and for collaboration between peoples and, finally, to represent the interests of the Holy See to governments. In questions concerning relations between Church and state, they are advised (not required) to take counsel with bishops and keep them informed.

On considering this 1969 description, Cardinal Suenens observed that it gives the impression that a local Church is only a kind of administrative district, supervised by the hierarchy in parallel with the nuncio. He proposed to entrust the diplomatic function to laymen and to choose a prelate of the country to act as liaison officer with Rome for ecclesiastical questions. [45] There

---

[40] Printed in Y. Congar et al *Discours au Concil Vat. II*, Paris, 1964, pp. 149-152.

[41] *Christus Dominus*, 9, 10.

[42] Pope Paul, e.g. in OR 10.1.1972; 22.6.1973; Mons. Benelli in OR 2.3.1972.

[43] K. Mörsdorf in LThK 4, 766-773.

[44] AAS 1969, 473-484.

[45] ICI 25.4.1969; *Doc. Cath.* 21.12.1969.

is general agreement that the Council thought the nuncio's sphere of operation should be more restrictively defined. But, as things have turned out, it has been extended in a document which displays a certain distrust in regard to the synodal and collegial action of bishops. [46] In particular, the local Church is denied all real share in the nomination of bishops; everything is based on canvassing by means of whispered conversation and gets done under a cloak of strict secrecy, preventing any fraternal exchange of ideas; so that, in the end, the only thing that counts is the opinion of the nuncio. [47]

3. An office so liable to contestation needs to be entrusted to an exceptional personality (of the calibre of a Roncalli) to be able to gain the confidence of the local Church. But there is too much criticism of personalities (I confine myself to what is being said in the Third Church). No one doubts that they are likeable people but much fault is found with their competence and their capacity for identifying with the situation. The majority have gone through the pontifical diplomatic academy and have had a legal training. But there is a dearth of understanding of the country, often accompanied by a complete ignorance of the language, of theology and of all preparation for mission work. They live isolated in their residences, with a secretary who is just as isolated and a few nuns to keep house. They represent Rome's point of view abroad: that is their right and their duty. But they should also, with equal firmness, make known at the centre the point of view of the local Churches, defending the local experiments, so as to effect a real osmosis between Roman directives and the real situation of the local Churches. Yet this very seldom happens, because of its possible effect on career prospects. For this reason, they are rather quick to denounce 'suspect' things to Rome — so much so that a new etymology has developed out of recent events: it is said that *nuntius* derives from *de-nuntiare*. This one-sidedness can be parlty attributed to the fact that most of them are still Italians. Judging by the Annuario Pontificio of 1973, 15 out of 16 legates in western countries were Italian, while in the southern countries

---

[46] *Motu Proprio* on the duty of legates of the Roman Pontiff, with commentary by K. Ganger and H. Schmitz, Trier, 1969, 18, 32, 36.

Italians were 43 out of 63. So in this respect there has been some progress in contacts with the Third Church, although it must be said that these posts are little sought after, for reasons of climate and politics, and are readily left for non-Italians. But the time has come for Italy to relinquish her dominating role in ecclesiastical diplomacy, just as England and America have retired from the political and commercial domination of the world. The times are against any kind of monopoly. W. Promper thinks of the palatial nunciatures in Latin America which rival the American embassies (although recently there has been a noticeable trend towards a simpler style of life and in some cases the nuncios have exchanged their palaces for simple houses) and considers the nuncios have applied the brakes to every conciliar initiative. He is of the opinion that we can never give sufficient weight to the harm done by these representatives of the curia in hindering the development of the Church in Latin America. [48] Without subscribing to this harsh judgement, I must admit I do not hear many very positive judgements (there are a few honourable exceptions).

4. Other criticisms concern the essential nature of the institution as such. These legates, with their juridical status as diplomats, give the Church the appearance of a political power. In Asia, where Christians are in the minority, non-Christians cannot tell whether the Church is a religion or a state. The existence of a Vatican state insisting on the dignity of the Pope, the administrative character of Church institutions, the analogies with state administration and the existence of Papal embassies hardly contribute to clarifying the situation and explaining the mystery of the Church. [49]

It remains an open question whether this system promotes real unity in the Church or, rather, makes it more difficult and brings extra tensions, as when nuncios deal directly with the government over the heads of the bishops, or even against their explicit will, and take up rigid positions in the defence of Catholic

[47] HK 1972, 266-268, 421f.
[48] *Eglise Vivante*, Louvain, 1970, p. 370f; 1969, pp. 309-311.
[49] Gheddo, *op. cit.* (n. 28), p. 239.

institutions. Between 1960 and 1973, legates in the Third World increased from 39 to 63 and are still increasing, and the same number of nations have accredited ambassadors to the Holy See. These figures raise the question whether the price in manpower and in expenses is too high for the good that comes of this arrangement, whether the same results could not be obtained in a simpler and more appropriate way — for example, by giving authority to the episcopal conferences to nominate official representatives for negotiations between the Vatican and the governments. The Vatican could intervene with flying envoys in more serious cases.

4. *The bishops*

1. Bishops have a role in the direction of the Church and a responsibility which must be exercised by them only.[50] Vatican II developed the theology of the episcopal ministry considerably. In the analytic index to the conciliar texts it holds the second place preceded only by the word 'Church'. Much is expected of bishops. The good or bad estate of the Church depends very largely on them. It is only human nature that not all respond equally to the hopes placed in them. They need understanding and encouragement. If we take account of the fact that the majority of native bishops entered their ministry at an early age [51] and often had to be chosen from among 30, 20, 10 or even less priests, it becomes understandable that not all can be outstanding bishops.

2. They are still to some degree victims of the past, when the episcopal ministry was thought of as an absolute monarchy. Some are still not used to collegial behaviour. There are great missionary countries where, as yet, there are no councils of priests or of laypeople. There is an instinctive fear of pressure from below: 'Do you want to put a rope round my reck?' asked a bishop. They impose their own ideas; proposals from com-

---

[50] There is a good exposition of these tasks and their theological understanding in the new Directory on the pastoral ministry of bishops, Rome, 1973.

[51] See the statistics below in this chapter, p. 201.

missions wait endlessly for approval. They identify their point of view with the will of God. 'He opposes all changes in the diocese and assumes without any discussion that any change ought to be to his taste'. The finances of the diocese remain a taboo subject but take up more of the bishops' time and interest than pastoral concerns. They are absorbed in administration and management of the diocese, so much so that often they busy themselves with trivialities and want to act as parish priest in every parish. They cannot keep up with their theology and so ought to maintain contact with specialists in theology. Instead they show a remarkable fear of meeting any, and will not take part in seminars until they have managed to overcome their 'agoraphobia' and have had some good experience of 'modern theologians'. Alongside some very fine bishops there are too many who are petty and mean, legalistic and authoritarian, conservative and clericalist. [52] Their attitudes are extended downwards by many priests. In one place, the sisters complained to me that they had asked the bishop for permission to read the gospel themselves at the community mass, since the old chaplain who was half blind read with difficulty, using a magnifying glass, but the request was refused. One priest, after an operation, asked permission to celebrate the Eucharist seated but the bishop told him to wait until he was completely cured. A convent of contemplatives, in the same place, showed me broken window-panes and statues, on which students in the Catholic college had vented their anger against the bishop.

3. Episcopal conferences are meant to make up for the shortcomings of individuals but need more practice in doing so. Experts from various countries have told me: 'Individual bishops are good people. But they lack courage, imagination and the gift of leadership'. 'What they say to me in private conversation does not commit them to saying the same thing at the episcopal conference; when it comes to drawing the practical consequences,

---

[52] There is documentation for these statements in, e.g., HK 1972, 483; *Orientierung*, 31.1.1973, p. 19; *Jeevadhara*, Allepey, India, 1972, p. 348; PMV-CI 1970/30, 29f; B. Willecke, *Mission — worauf es heute ankommt*, in *Thuringia Francescana*, 1972, 354-365, esp. 358; B. Nkuissi in Bühlmann, *Afrika*, p. 130; PMV-NS 27: *Le recyclage des évêques*.

making a decision and taking responsibility, courage fails them'. 'They look too much towards Rome, instead of looking at the problem and listening to the Holy Spirit'. But gradually things are improving. Some episcopal conferences have called in theologians to prepare their seminars. Others have followed courses in management. There should also be courses in group dynamics, at which they could learn how to stimulate real dialogue at their meetings and how to engage in genuine discussion with courage and frankness.

4. One particular problem is set by the bishop's long term in office. Only exceptional men can stay fresh and preserve a spirit of initiative while spending twenty or more years in the same office. The rest get worn out but carry on out of a sense of duty. They feel, as those around them certainly feel, that things are no longer going as they should. But it is not easy to draw the practical conclusion.

Vatican II put an end to the mystique of the indissolubility of the link between the bishop and his diocese. 'If diocesan bishops and those in canonically equivalent positions find they are not equal to the demands of their office, because of advancing age or for other serious reasons, they are strongly urged to resign their office, either on their own initiative or at the invitation of the competent authority'. This directive from *Christus Dominus* was made more precise in *Ecclesiae Sanctae*: 'not later than at the completion of the 75th year'. The new Directory for Bishops adds another reason for resigning, that is, too much difficulty in adapting to new situations. [53] There is a healthy tendency towards lowering the retirement age. Formerly, a bishop could spend a great part of his time at Confirmations, visiting parishes, going on a round of solemn receptions and making decisions on his own. Nowadays, he will find himself soon exhausted by the demands of his office, so that in posts so full of responsibility it really is necessary to bring in fresh men of the highest quality. A group of twelve German theologians have made a theologically reasoned proposal to reduce the period in office of residential bishops to eight years. Obviously,

[53] *Christus Dominus*, 21; *Ecclesiae Sanctae* I, art. 11; Directory for bishops, 38.

the length of the period is arguable. They would permit a second period of office only in exceptional cases, where there was some extrinsic reason arising out the ecclesiastical situation. Such rotation in office would bring a notable increase in efficiency. [54]

In the Third Church, where the average diocese does not dispose of hundreds of priests but only a few dozen, it would be more difficult to find suitable candidates. Nevertheless, the question can and should be taken seriously in the hope that able men would arise. In Africa and in Asia, the majority of the native bishops entered the episcopal ministry at an early age, proof of extraordinary courage in the Church. African bishops, for example, were ordained at the following ages: [55]

Age at consecration	Number of bishops	Percentage
less than 35	9	7.3
between 36 and 40	35	28.5
between 41 and 45	39	31.7
between 46 and 50	26	21.2
between 51 and 55	11	8.8
over 55	3	2.4

The majority, therefore were consecrated between 35 and 45. This means that, as things are, they will remain in charge for 30 to 40 years, which could be disastrous for the African Church. The first step to take would be to arrange a compulsory sabbatical year for bishops, during which they could renew their spirit in calm, study, meditation and prayer. The age limit of 75 for service in this ministry will come to be considered as a first step only. Development in the future will be much more flexible. There will be a tendency to take as respected models those bishops who, in an evangelical spirit, are willing to return to the ranks, dedicating themselves in all modesty to another task suited to their strength and thus rendering a marvellous service to the diocese. The age limit does postulate rational

[54] *Befristete Amtszeit residierender Bischöfe* ('Limited periods of office for residential bishops'), in *Theolog. Quartalschrift Tübingen*, Münsten, 1969, pp. 105-116.

[55] AIF, Supplément n. VI (1971) 10.

application of the principle of the true good of the Church. In this context, it is worth mentioning that in some developing countries all employees are pensioned off at 45 or 50.

B. *Models of a living Church*

1. Whenever man gets inflexible and risks being stifled by structures, religious or profane, which oppress him, a healthy natural reaction makes itself felt — the urge towards spontaneity, play, free time and rejoicing. These things are all connected. Moltmann asks: 'Why are we so lacking in perception? What have the old Pharisees and the new zealots done to us by legalizing a revolution yet remaining conservatively timid in respect of freedom, joy and spontaneity? There is nothing good and sound which is not created out of the élan of joy and the passion of love'. He thinks the Churches, now they have been relieved of some of their former social tasks, should plug the gaps in men's increasing leisure time, stimulate creative imaginations, rehabilitate spontaneity (now so discounted) and make even the act of worship into a new source of spontaneity. [56] Harvey Cox, the well-known author of *The Secular City,* has pointed out this other aspect of things with acute sensitivity in *The Feast of Fools.* [57] Industrial man, he says, with all his hustle and bustle has lost his imagination and his ability to make merry; his celebrations are all too insipid and formalized. But now post-industrial man has put in an appearance, with a life style that values play, imaginative celebration and uninhibited rejoicing. [58]

Those who have their eyes and ears open do not need to read these things in books; they can observe the hurricane of rejoicing (which finds outlet, for example, in a play like 'Elvis on Tour') as spontaneity everywhere gets the better of fixed forms. It is vital for religion to recognize these signs of the times, accept them, and give fresh life to its own structures.

[56] J. Moltmann, *Die ersten Freigelassenen der Schöpfung,* München, 1960, pp. 7, 75.
[57] H. Cox, *The Feast of fools,* Cambridge, 1969.
[58] On this cf. J. Huizinger, *Homo ludens. Vom Ursprung der Kultur im Spiel,* 1956; cf. also statements by K. Rahner, R. Guardini etc.

2. Non-Christian religions, like Islam and Hinduism, also risk losing their young people if they cannot make traditional forms more lively and attractive. The classic case, here, is Japan. The phenomenon of the 'new religions' of Japan has attracted the attention of sociologists, students of religion and politicians, and already there is a copious bibliography on the subject. [59] In the course of millennia, the ancient religion of Japan has often broken fresh ground only to return later to formalism and support for the establishment, so losing immediacy and vitality. But a massive explosion took place after the war. In little groups, usually under the guidance of prophetic figures, people sought to reawaken the slumbering inheritance of the old religion, giving it new forms with creative freedom, and taking inspiration from the needs of modern man. These new forms do not exclude participation in traditional worship but go beyond it, providing opportunities for new forms of prayer, personal encounter and social activity motivated by the inspiration of the moment. In 1965, these new movements had about 37 million adherents. Thus, secularization need not be the end of the road but can give rise to new religious requirements, which must of course be met with absolute creative freedom.

3. The first to feel the natural force of this spontaneity have been the Protestant Churches, themselves the product of an exodus from the structures but structured in their turn. Those which until now had been rather contemptuously termed 'sects' are being taken increasingly seriously, because their extraordinary success shows that they are responding to a real human need. In their little groups, each person can open himself without shame among people of his own kind. He hears the word of God in his own very special situation, he is infected by the religious fervour of the group and infects others in his turn. People who used to feel insignificant, bored and frustrated in the official Churches now no longer feel harnessed to an over-intellectual theology or held in check by patriarchal structures; rather they feel unconditionally accepted on the basis of their own religious experience.

[59] H.B. Earhart, *The new religions of Japan. A bibliography*, Tokyo, 1970; cf. PMV-CI 1970/34, 27-33.

The Pentecostal movement, for instance, in the sixty years of its history, has registered a growth no one could have imagined. In Brazil, Chile and other places, it has more adherents than the other Protestant denominations put together. Through this movement, even European intellectuals have discovered levels of human existence hitherto unknown to them. They base their life on an unshakeable faith in God's word. They pray with confidence and believe that even today there are miracles of conversion and of healing of the sick. They sacrifice 10% of their earnings to the movement. They hold that they are the primitive Christian community; they are those who are still guided by the Holy Spirit. It is easy to criticize them, but that is not the way to grasp the meaning of a movement which is at the cross-roads: it may be gradually integrated with the traditional Churches so as to enrich them with elements of renewed Pentecostal faith or it may continue on its own way in the confident hope of outnumbering all the Protestant Churches by the beginning of the third millennium. [60]

As far as Africa is concerned, B. Sundkler first called attention in 1948 to the (Christian) 'Bantu prophets', and listed 800 independent native Churches in South Africa alone. In the second edition of the book, he was able to speak of 2,200 such Churches. [61] D. Barrett knows of 6000 of them in Black Africa. He describes their extraordinary dynamism and thinks their present nine million adherents will become 34 millions by 2000. [62] These prophets come mainly from among traditional Protestants whose Churches have been literally decimated by these new movements and who see their salvation in the greatest possible openness and in contact with the new forces in a spirit of understanding.

4. The wave of spontaneity has penetrated even the solid structures of the Catholic Church. I am not thinking only of the

---

[60] W.J. Hollenweger, *Enthusiastisches Christentum*, Zürich, 1969; J. Kraus, *Neuer missionarischer Aufbruch urchristlicher Charismen?*, in VSVD 1971, pp. 27-33.

[61] B. Sundkler, *Bantu prophets in South Africa*, London, 1961.

[62] Barrett, *Schism and renewal in Africa*, Oxford, 1968; Parrinder, *Religion in Africa*, N.Y., 1969, p. 162, 228f, 235.

204

pentecostal movement among Catholics, which has spread from the United States to Europe and some countries in Asia. Its adherents believe in the 'new Pentecost' promised by John XXIII and are convinced that, in this great crisis for the Church, the Holy Spirit comes to the aid of his faithful and makes them feel his presence and special activity. [63] Besides this, in Latin America and other places, there are all types of spontaneous groups and basic groups which meet with Bible in hand — the Bible which until ten years ago was a characteristic of the sects and to many Catholics was equivalent to the Koran. [64] They meet for renewal and to understand their mission in the Church. Thanks to these groups, Latin America has been quite changed in the course of a few years; there, far more than in Europe, one is conscious that change is afoot. The various organized movements — Cursillos, Christopher Movement, Better World, Focolarini, etc. — are all expressions of one movement, spanning the continent and generating real Christians, committed and full of initiative. [65]

The outstanding movement in Africa is *Jamaa* in Zaire. This was founded by the Franciscan Father Tempels, when he began to listen rather than teach, replacing traditional catechism teaching by discussions on scripture; out of this were born the free meetings for prayer which are now widespread and entirely led by laypeople. It is held to be the 'most charismatic and least institutional movement'. [66]

---

[63] *New Covenant*: monthly publication serving the Catholic charismatic renewal, Michigan, 1971ff.; E.D. O'Connor, *The Pentecostal movement in the Catholic Church*, N-D Indiana, 1971; J.L. Suenens, *A new Pentecost?*, London, 1975; and the congress of the movement, Rome, Pentecost 1974.

[64] Beltramino, *Un'esperienza*, 111f.

[65] *Op. cit.*, also W.J. Richardson, *The modern Mission apostolate*, N.Y., 1965, pp. 262-295; E. Kakatos, *Die Bibelbewegung als Aufgabe in Südamerika*, in VSVD 1970, 97-107; D. Barbé, *Demain, les communautés de base*, Paris, 1970; M.F. Perrin Jassy, *La communauté de base dans les Eglises africaines*, Kinshasa, 1970.

[66] A. Camps, *New ways of realizing a Christian togetherness in non-western countries*, in *Internationales Jahrbuch für Religionssoziologie*, Cologne, 1969, pp. 182-194, esp. 192; J. Fabian, *Jamaa. A charismatic movement in Katanga*, Evanston, 1971.

5. What are we to say about the spontaneous ecumenical groups? Taizé, with its charismatic leader Roger Schutz, gathers young people of all nations and all denominations for days of prayer. It is preparing a council of youth. [67] What are we to say of the Jesus Revolution, which arose among the most rejected youth, and has caused a sensation in the States from California to the east coast? Walls which used to be covered with placards of pop-stars now give the place of honour to pictures of Christ. The disc, 'My sweet Lord' is a world best-seller and the film, 'Jesus Christ Superstar' is making the rounds of the world. In the place of drinking clubs and discothèques there are 'houses of Christ' and 'Catacombs'. In 'Christian night-clubs', you see fresh-faced girls without make-up and serious young men, who talk together about Christ and bear witness to him in the streets. G. Adler, who has studied the success of this movement, asks himself: 'Did traditional worship in the great Churches leave enough room for affective needs? Are worshipping communities perhaps too bourgeois, so that a young person of unconventional appearance would immediately stand out as a strange element in the community? Have reforms of the liturgy and similar initiatives been too unaware of group dynamics?' [68]

What are we to say, finally, about those movements and groups, which have no specifically religious character — politically involved student peace movements, international youth gatherings, Beatles and hippies, and all those thousands who make months-long journeys every year to India? It is difficult to put them in categories. But all have in common that they are looking for meaning in life; they feel a need to be taken seriously and understood, a need for joy, freedom and spontaneity. [69] What an opportunity for the message of Christ, who came into this world in absolute freedom and spontaneity to offer all men the possibility of a new start.

6. What will come of these movements? Will they find

[67] R. Schütz, *Ta fête soit sans fin,* Paris, 1971.
[68] G. Adler, *Die Jesus-Bewegung in den Vereinigten Staaten,* in *Perspektiven der Zukunft,* Freiburg im B., April 1972, 13; Billy Graham, *The Jesus Generation,* Hodder and Stoughton, 1971.
[69] PMV-CI 1972/41: *Nouvelles formes de vie communautaire.*

room within the traditional Churches? Can they be 'regularized'? Or is their life too forceful and original for any legislation? Paul VI, who has so often shown the sympathy he feels for these young people, and for what is lively and spirited, will not allow this spontaneity to develop outside Church and parish structures. Tension between the two sides is unavoidable. Sociologists tell us that religious communities (the analogy extends to the Church and its constituent parishes) begin with spontaneous swings, a phase in which the founder gathers his first adherents, a community is born with one heart and one soul and all decisions are made together as the occasion demands. Then follows the experimental phase, in which an 'order' and a 'group memory' slowly develop; new questions, as they present themselves, are resolved on the basis of preceding modes of behaviour. At last, the 'rule' is born: in the nature of things, this cannot have quite the same influence on successive generations as the charisma of the founder. So we enter the institutional phase with its many norms, fixing everything; this keeps superiors from the danger of blundering and from having to make decisions at their own personal risk. New adherents now must simply accept these norms and fit themselves into the system. Authority is stressed, the *status quo* is maintained and the brake is put on new initiatives. In the long run, there are only two ways open: either there will be an attempt, in small groups, to revive the spirituality and the inspiration of the sources, leading to renewal in the community as a whole, or else there will be a 'successful' defence against renewal, the sign character of the community will be lost, it will grow old and weary, ready to go down to the tomb together with a generation bound to tradition.[70]

Tension between charisma and institution is not only unavoidable but also necessary. Each needs the other. Institution without charisma becomes rigid and hard and survives, at most, thanks to its own scaffolding. Charisma without institution bursts like a soap bubble, exhausts itself in contestation and fails to fulfil its proper function in society. The two tendencies need to recognize one another and to support one another generously.

[70] G. Scarvaglieri, *L'Istituto religioso come fatto sociale,* Padua, 1973; R. Hostie, *Vie et mort des Ordres religieux,* Paris, 1972.

So, Karl Rahner says, 'The Church of the future will be built up from below through basic communities of free initiative and free association. We should do our best not to put obstacles in the way of such development but to promote it and guide it along the right lines'. He goes on to say that such groups must have the right to constitute themselves, as a sort of parish within the parish, and still be able to work in every way for the unity of the Church in its pluriformity. [71] Even in the diocese of Rome, the importance of these spontaneous groups is recognized. A socio-religious enquiry has shown that 10% of the young people questioned belong to groups of this kind; this led to the conclusion that traditional religious practice, that is, belonging to the Church by virtue of family or social tradition, is seriously threatened but that these spontaneous groups bring new hope. They must, therefore, be encouraged as long as they do not degenerate into sectarianism or anti-clericalism, in fact in order precisely to avoid this degeneration. [72]

The living God makes the Church share in his own inexhaustible fullness through ever fresh insights. The present state of ecclesiastical discipline is the result of growth and of many reactions to past situations. In a period as qualitatively new as ours is, we shall not find satisfaction in solutions deriving from past situations. We must let ourselves be drawn into dialogue with present trends and receive with gratitude, as promptings and help from God, the inspirations of those who feel the pulse of the times. [73]

Charismatic movements run the risk of breaking away from the Church. Should we, then, only build on safe ground and quench charisma to avoid the risk? History teaches that when such movements have indeed finished in heresy and schism the fault has never been on one side alone. This is the reason for the rehabilitation of Huss, Luther and others. [74]

[71] *Strukturwandel*, pp. 115-126.

[72] E. Pin et al., *La religiosità dei Romani*, pp. 69-71; A. Dell'Acqua in CM 1970, 456f.

[73] R. Picker, *Pluriformes Christentum*, Freburg im B., 1970.

[74] W. Nigg, *Das Buch der Ketzer*, Zürich, 1962; Kasper, *Glaube und Geschichte*, Mainz, 1970, pp. 235f, 280f.

In West's novel, Pope Cyril says, 'I hope and pray for a great movement, a great man, who will shake us and bring us back to life, for example a man like Francis of Assisi. What does he stand for? For a complete break with the pattern of history, a sudden and inexplicable renewal of the primitive Christian spirit. . .' [75] Today, we know that Francis was not so much the original creator of his Order but rather one who understood the trend of his time towards poverty, community, fraternity and joy in nature, who accepted the trend and made it into a movement in the Church. We again need a Francis who would understand the breaking out of spontaneity and, with a peaceful and smiling face, find room for it in the Church. Otherwise, we could end up in a tragic schism where there would be the established prayers recited within the Church and, outside, the charismatic Church celebrating the God of joy.

C. *Contestation in the Church*

1. According to many sentries who stand guard during the night, all the evils in the Church arise out of contestation, out of the fact that children are no longer obedient to their parents, Christians to their parish priests, religious to their superiors or bishops to Rome. For them, contestation is a synthesis of all anti-Church attitudes. This kind of obedience and humility is illustrated at length in sermons and books of ascetics.

For better understanding, we need a more precise concept of contestation. It is undeniable that the term con-testation is connected with the biblical keyword *testimoniare — martyrein*. Paul repeatedly uses the stronger form *sym-martyrein* (literally, 'con-testation'), when he is speaking of conscience and of the Holy Spirit testifying something to me (Rom 2:15; 8:16; 9:1). Testifying or witnessing is something more than simply informing. It implies a sharing and self-commitment to something. For present purposes, I would describe contestation as follows. It consists in a community effort to change by legitimate means

[75] M.L. West, *The Shoes of the Fisherman*.

a status quo which is out of date. Subjectively, those who take part in contestation are always in the right, even when it is arguable objectively whether the status quo really needs changing or whether the means used are legitimate. Contestation goes beyond face to face dialogue; it has become a public event. It is, in the first place, *for* something and only then as a means to an end *against* something, that is, against conditions which are to be changed.

2. We can go to no less an example than Jesus Christ himself to understand contestation. How he branded the scribes and Pharisees, the elders of the people and the high priests, that is to say, the *legitimate* authorities of the chosen people! Reading Mark and beginning at chapter two, one has the impression that he systematically cured on the Sabbath, thus seeking the occasion to provoke these castes. He tells them to their faces that publicans and prostitutes will go before them into the Kingdom of God (Mt 21:30-32). He hurls condemnation after condemnation (Mt 23:1-36). This is Jesus in contestation. He paid for it with his life. He was judged and condemned by both civil and religious authority as a criminal and was punished 'between two other malefactors' (Lk 23:32). [76]

According to Phil 2:5, we ought to imitate the attitudes of Jesus. We have generally limited ourselves, one-sidedly, to considering his self-abasement, his *kenosis* in the sense of humility. Henceforward, we must certainly also consider his courage in going against laws, structures and institutions (in so far as they are opposed to the Spirit). Contestation must not only be reluctantly tolerated; it must be taken as an essential element of the Christian life, alongside *kenosis* and in harmony with it. *Kenosis* without contestation would be too easy; contestation without *kenosis* would not be genuine and, sooner or later, would finish in frustration. Both will be taken seriously when they go together. Christ put his *kenosis* into practice, when he took part in unsuccessful contestation and accepted the death

---

[76] A. Holl, *Jesus in schlechter Gesellschaft*, Stuttgart, 1971 (ET *Jesus in bad company*); cf. on this subject, articles by Y. Congar, A.M. Henry, B. Häring in SPIR 1969/38 and the special number of *Concilium*, 1971/8.

of a persecuted prophet. Would it have been better to avoid contestation and be more 'prudent'?

3. From this point of view, the present situation of the Church varies from continent to continent. Many hold that contestation in the Church is a typical product of the western Church. They fail to see that it appears in Latin America as a sign of a Church which is alive again. [77] In Africa, contestation made its first appearance in a book, published as long ago as 1956 and then a sensation, in which thirteen African priests advanced some criticisms of the Church as colonial and western oriented. [78] In recent years there have been strikes in the seminaries. In general, however, the Catholic Church, differently from the 'independent Churches', has so far taken a strong line. Bishops and Cardinals have repeatedly and publicly made declarations, obviously from a concerted plan, that they had no need for contestation, that they would not be manipulated from Europe or from America or have Africa used as a testing ground for new European or American ideas. In spite of all this, contestation lives, and African countries have given open expression to criticism on the practical training of priests, on episcopal authority, on western liturgy, on the law of celibacy, etc., [79] although laypeople have remained rather silent up to the present. In Asia, contestation appears only in those countries where Christians form a relatively strong group and are not struggling for survival, that is, in India, Ceylon and especially the Philippines. For the rest, Asians appear tolerant and passive, although in radical political movements they show other traits. Unlike what happens in Africa, here it is laypeople, especially students, who are organized and active. Even sisters are beginning to take part in contestation. Reviews with titles like 'Forum', 'Quest', 'Outlook', directed towards groups of priests and laypeople, keep the issues in question alive. [80]

[77] Cf. above, ch. 7.B.4, p. 157.
[78] *Des prêtres noirs s'interrogent*, Paris, 1956.
[79] H. van Pinxtern, *Il fenomeno della contestazione in Africa*, in *Concilium* 1971/8, pp. 80-89; A. Yungu, *Ciò che un vescovo congolese pensa della contestazione e delle sue conseguenze in Africa*, in CM 1970, pp. 417f.
[80] T. Balasuriya, *Contestazione nella Chiesa in Asia*, in *Concilium* 1971/8, pp. 90-97.

4. If Christ, then, engaged in contestation in the true sense, there can be no contesting the right to do so. At most, limits are to be set to its exercise. Pope Paul VI has said: 'We do not contest the need for contestation, this requirement in the way of renewal. It is legitimate and necessary on many grounds and within defined limits; but it should be done with moderation'. [81] To the director of *Informations Catholiques Internationales*, he declared: 'The Church is the object of contestation. But it must be done with love'. [82] In a letter from the Secretary of State, 25 June 1971, to an international gathering of Catholic journalists we read: 'When we are faced by opinions infringing on doctrine and moral principles, we are obliged unfortunately to recognize that it is no longer a question of that public opinion which the Church needs to keep alive the dialogue among her members and which is a presupposition of her thought and action.' When the letter goes on to add that this public opinion cannot enter into competition with the directives of the hierarchy, we have certain reservations to make. We should not immediately brand certain persons as anti-Church simply because in their contestation they do not please a member of the hierarchy or because at times they poke a little fun at specific instructions; all cases are to be judged according to the circumstances. Everyone in politics has to face public criticism and, if he is intelligent, learns much from the opposition. The Church must not leave too little scope for free public opinion. Public phenomena must be publicly assessed. Cardinal Maurice Roy, in his letter on the occasion of the tenth anniversary of *Pacem in Terris*, included for the first time among the fundamental rights of man the right to dissent for conscience's sake. [83] A Church that wants to be worthy of faith and efficient in criticism of society must allow increasing space for public opinion in her ranks. Of course, the seriousness of criticism is not necessarily related to its bulk, and its credibility does not depend on the tone of voice used. [84]

[81] Quoted by Y. Congar in SPIR 1969/38, p. 126.
[82] ICI 15.6.1973, 2.
[83] *Riflessioni del Card. M. Roy*, Polyglott Press, Vatican, 1973, pp. 49, 56.
[84] J.B. Metz, *Zur Theology der Welt*, Mainz, 1969, p. 113 (ET *The*

History shows that if criticism is stifled and apparently silenced in the Church, it will produce unhealthy complexes, as happens in the case of individual persons. It will certainly crop up again in a more acute form and in the end it can only be met by an open enquiry and an honest consideration of the points at issue. [85] Rosmini's book, which was put on the Index, denouncing the growing lack of contact between clergy and people and the dependence of the spiritual power on the state, and calling these and other evils 'the five wounds of the Church', is only one example among many. [86] A Church which is conscious of being always on pilgrimage, and knows itself to be made up of sinners and thus ever in need of repentance and renewal, [87] will not be disposed to reject all criticism from the start but will examine it all with humility and will accept whatever is soundly based.

Besides, contestation flourishes only when hardened positions need to be challenged. The ground is cut from beneath its feet in proportion as reforms are implemented. This has been shown in the experience of some religious communities. Young members are today much calmer than a few years ago, because in the meantime the stumbling blocks in the shape of old fashioned structures have been removed.

5. When contestation, in the manner described, is lively and the faithful do not leave everything to the parish priest as 'good parishioners', it can be taken as the mark of a mature Church. As young people have to win independence during a period of maturation, and usually cannot achieve this without criticism and resistance, so it is too with the Christian who has to attain his position of autonomy and co-responsibility in the Church. It is not worthy either of a man or of a Christian to

---

theology of the world); E. Baragli 'Opinione publica' nella Chiesa?, in La Civiltà Cattolica, Rome, 1973, pp. 547-599; G. Deussen, Ethik der Massenkommunikation bei Papst Paul VI, Paderborn, 1972.

[85] O. Köhler, Bewusstseinsstörungen im Katholizismus, Frankfurt, 1972.
[86] New editions of the book 'The Five Wounds of the Church' have appeared in Italian and German.
[87] LG 8.

be nothing but an agent for others. Anyone who forms convictions, through his own experience of faith, his own special knowledge or through dialogue with other Christians, which he believes could be useful to the particular Church he belongs to, has the duty to make them clear and to declare them at the right time and place, even at the risk of not being willingly heard and not appearing in a good light because of this. We can, therefore, speak of a duty of contestation: *parrhesia*, open and honest speaking, is a key-word in the New Testament. We need to reflect much more on it at the present time. The slave did not possess freedom of speech; he had to agree. But we, as free men, as children of our Father, can speak freely and confidently before him and, consequently, before men and in the Church. We have nothing to fear. [88]

[88] J.V. Kopp, *Freimütiges Gespräch in der Kirche,* in *Das Neue Buch,* Lucerne 1962, p. 8: 'How can a Church enter into really open dialogue with the new world that is arising, if she does not practise free speech in her own ranks?'.

Chapter 10

THE GREATER CHURCH: *ECUMENE*

*I have not found so great a faith in
anyone in Israel* (Mt 8:10).

It is a surprising and surely significant fact that Jesus never praised the faith of the Jews, repeatedly reproved his disciples for their lack of faith and exclaimed with impatience, 'Have you not yet understood?... For how long must I endure you?' (Mt 8:26; 14:31; 17:20; 28:17; Lk 9:41). On the other hand, he did praise the faith of the Roman centurion (Mt 8:10) and of the Canaanite woman (Mt 15:28), that is to say, the faith of 'pagans'. Those who lay claim to hereditary rights are compelled to recognize that not only are people from east and west invited but they, the children of the kingdom, are driven out (Mt 8:11-12).

The former fact is a reason for rejoicing, since it means that faith and grace are not bound to any structures. The latter is a cause for examination of conscience, since those who think they are safe within their exclusive institutions and look down on the others with disdain are in danger of being put to shame by the others.

A. *Ecumenism with non-Catholics*

1. In ecumenical matters, our history is not one to be proud of. The many groups of Protestants fought among themselves. Catholics and Protestants openly declared themselves enemies, excommunicated one another and wrote vitriolic 'scientific' works against one another. Christians and their catechists hounded one another and believed they had accom-

plished heroic acts in setting fire to one another's schools. [1] For Protestants, Catholic missions were 'an evil threatening the country, like alcoholism'. [2] Catholics were worse than cannibals, because they could not be converted like the latter. [3] Today it is hardly believable that the Protestant world missionary conference at Whitby in 1947 counted political Catholicism, together with communism, fascism, and Islam, among the totalitarian powers responsible for disturbing the peace of the world. [4] We, in our turn, acted and spoke in just as un-Christian a way about them. The history of the missions bears witness, with thousands of examples, to the 'scandal of division' and the 'grave prejudice to the holy cause of preaching the gospel to all men' of which the Council speaks. [5] Instead of giving non-Christians the choice of saying Yes or No to Christ, we have degraded this option into a choice between many rival Churches, often equivalent to a choice between the English, French, Belgian or American powers.

2. Thank God, the charismatic Pope John XXIII brought about a sudden reversal here. The 'Johannine era' has been immensely effective in southern countries as well as in the west. Ecumenism, which began among Protestants with the Edinburgh conference in 1910, suddenly became a reality to us Catholics as well. (In accordance with the purpose of this book, I deal with ecumenism between Catholics and Protestants, not between Protestants, and only as related to the Third Church.)

The history of ecumenism can suitably and fairly be called the story of a great discovery. [6] It was a mutual discovery. Like the apostles at night on the lake, we have learned to see one

[1] Fuller treatment in Bühlmann *Ecumenism in Africa* (in English) in AFER 1971, pp. 234-255.
[2] E. Halden, *The culture policy of the Basel Mission in the Cameroons,* Lund, 1968, pp. 64-67.
[3] V. de Moor, *Leur combat,* Paris, 1937, p. 134.
[4] E. Kellerhals, *Das Anliegen von Whitby,* Basel, 1947, p. 13f.
[5] AG 29, 6.
[6] St Meier-Schomburg, *Die ökumenische Dimension von Kirche und Mission,* in VSVD 1972, pp. 186-209: the history of the ecumenical movement as a history of discovery (pp. 188ff).

another no longer as 'ghosts' but 'as the Lord' (Mt 14:26-27). We have begun to see the Church in a new light and have noticed that the others at times put us to shame by their faith. The Council emphasized and praised the 'riches of Christ and the works of virtue in the lives of the others'; [7] missionaries in Africa and Asia have had concrete experience of this in their meetings for study and prayer which have become customary. Reports on these meetings are expressed in terms like the following: 'What do we, priests who have taken part in this dialogue, think of the Lutherans we have met? In a few words: we admire them. We have seen them for what they really are, good, honourable, intelligent men. We feel closer to them. We know that the prayer rising from their hearts is the same as that rising from our hearts, because it is Christ's prayer, "That we may be one"'. [8] 'These meetings do an immense amount of good. They remove many prejudices. We learn to know one another. We discover Christians who are convinced, upright and deeply religious. We see how close we are and how tragic, but nevertheless real, is the division between us'. [9] Whereas hitherto our knowledge of one another had been peripheral and had stressed the things that divide and separate us, now we have found the central thing which unites us and we rejoice that our eyes have been opened.

I do not need, here, to describe the ecumenical enthusiasm in Africa and Asia and the wide scope of the changes it has brought about: the community liturgical celebrations, the common work on the Bible and other forms of collaboration in various fields. [10] All this has come as a gift from heaven, a new spring for those countries. Even in Latin America, where 80% to 90% of the Protestant missionaries belong to radical evangeli-

[7] UR 4.

[8] V.J. Donavan, *A Protestant-Catholic dialogue*, in AFER 1962, pp. 41-49.

[9] D. Nothomb, in *L'oecuménisme en Afrique*, CIPA, Rome, 1966, p. 67.

[10] Bühlmann, *op. cit.* (n. 1); *Internazionale Oekumenische Bibliographie*, Mainz-München, 1962ff; SML 1970: *Oecuménisme en Mission*. On common work on the Bible, see below ch. 18.5, p. 345f.

cal groups distinguished by fierce anti-Catholicism, who call the Catholic Church the great harlot, contacts are being multiplied and a certain degree of co-operation is developing. [11] At the very least, acquaintance with their lively activity has shaken us up and helped to convert us from centralism, clericalism and parochial sacramentalism to true evangelism through a laity with Bible in hand.

3. But at the end of the first decade of ecumenism, 1960-1970 (the Secretariat for Christian Unity was founded in 1960), we are clearly faced by a crisis. In 1970, articles appeared with titles like: 'Crisis for Ecumenism?' (Civiltà Cattolica, January 1970), 'Is Ecumenism dead?' (American Ecclesiastical Review, June 1970), 'Has Ecumenism lost its drive?' (Concilium, April 1970), etc. After the opening of the dialogue and the explosion of good will on both sides, we seem to have come unexpectedly to a full stop. Dialogue cannot be an end in itself. It must tend towards 'the restoring of unity among all Christians'. [12] But when it comes to the point, we seem to be frightened of taking definite steps. The crisis reached a climax in 1972 when SODEPAX, the Geneva Commission on social questions, development and peace set up in 1968 by the World Council of Churches and the Vatican, was re-organized and reduced in scope when Rome, reacting against a working paper, said 'no' or at least 'not yet' to the invitation to enter and take a full part in the World Council of Churches. Cardinal Willebrands made this reference to the reasons for the decision: 'The confused situation in Catholic theology, the crisis of authority and certain attitudes to ecclesiastical discipline in individuals and whole groups make our hoped-for adhesion more difficult'. [13]

---

[11] Hollenweger, Enthusiastiches Christentum, Zürich, 1969, pp. 492-496; V. Hayward, Latin America — an ecumenical bird's eye view, in IRM 1971, pp. 161-185. Of all Protestant missionaries only a third belong to Churches in the World Council.

[12] The title of the conciliar decree on ecumenism: Unitatis redintegratio.

[13] Doc. Cath. 1972, 525; CIM 1973, 15-16: Ecumenical activity 1971-72; HK Sept. 1972, p. 438; M. Renver, Grave Crisi nei rapporti ecumenici: la normalizzazione di SODEPAX, in IDOC April 1972, pp. 31-36.

Clearly, this structural question was raised prematurely. We cannot cancel out in a matter of ten years all the differences that have arisen during the four (or nine) centuries of separation or all the accumulated distrust. In the Catholic Church, owing to John XXIII and the Council, a real change of mentality is widespread, but the many Churches in the World Council present a less homogenous picture. Persons committed to ecumenism are still readily suspected of disloyalty to their own Churches. So further basic preparatory work is needed. After a phase of expansion, we are going through a rest period, which has its uses in the life of the Church, as in the life of any organism.

4. On the other hand, progress in ecumenism cannot be regarded as over. It would be very difficult to restart the movement once it had been halted, since we could not count on another charismatic drive like that imparted by John XXIII and the Council. Ecumenism carries with it its own dynamism. If we become satisfied with the new status quo arrived at, with the immediate objective of ecumenism — which was to bring the separated Churches together to pray, reflect and act in union, while maintaining their respective doctrinal understanding of themselves — if we did not seriously aspire towards its ultimate end — which is the restoring of full unity — then we would be in danger of losing in the meantime all we have gained. External circumstances help us, or even compel us to take this final end seriously. The second decade of ecumenism in which we are living will be decisive, one way or the other, for the whole movement.

The younger generation are pushing in the direction of world ecumenism. Young people fraternize without concern for confessional differences. Roger Schütz writes about them: 'They go where they find life. They have received a mainly technical training and they insist on quick practical results. They will not tolerate for long the indecision of the old institutions. They are conscious of their own dynamism and claim it has proved to be credible. They would not be satisfied with an ecumenism which was meant merely to cover up our embarassment in face of divisions. The time has come to go into action, modestly but

219

in a practical way'. [14] We must not allow ourselves to lead an ecumenical double life, speaking highly of it and then letting things remain as they were.

Many young people in the Third Church are even less concerned about the divisions between the confessional camps. Even if their roots are in the anti-ecumenical past, still they are less sensitive to the weight of the ancient structural divisions. What count for them are the larger religious groupings, Christianity, Islam, Hinduism; they consider the distinctions within Christianity insignificant. Besides, all the young states find themselves confronted by the central problem of creating national unity. Wise heads of state have often exhorted Christians not to be focal points for division but rather a ferment of unity. After all, the Christians of those countries can no longer afford, as a minority, to present themselves before the non-Christian block as an array of between five and fifty different Churches. They ought therefore to take the lead with far-reaching imaginative plans for fraternal collaboration, as recommended by the Council, 'through common profession of faith in God and in Jesus Christ before the nations, through co-operation in the technical and social fields as well as in the religious and cultural fields . . . not only among private persons but also . . . as Churches or as ecclesial communities'. [15] The challenge of the modern world to the Church, and serious reflection on our missionary task, impose on us the grave duty in conscience to abandon our introspective and retrospective outlook for a more forward-looking and open one, with a credible presentation of the Christian message for the world.

5. This can only come with a *kenotic* attitude in all Churches. How many considerations of prestige, how much determination not to give ground, lie hidden behind the assertions of 'truth we may not depart from'! Within the World Council of Churches certain groups are hardening, refusing to proceed to full unity of the Protestant Churches at national level as has happened in many African and Asian countries. J.C.

[14] R. Schütz, *Dynamik des Vorläufigen,* Freiburg, im B., 1967.
[15] AG 15.

Hoekendijk brands these groups as 'heretical structures' and 'pseudo-ecumenical associations' which continue to 'pervert mission into confessional propaganda'. [16] Will the day come when the Catholic Church can unite with these national Churches? At last, we hear less of the naive idea that we are the *beati possidentes* and the others need simply to reflect on their position and be converted. We all need to come closer to our common centre, to Christ and his message, to find genuine unity. We need to move from an ecclesiology which is extremist and exclusive to a Christology. Only self-renunciation in the Churches, with regard to their many historic forms, will bring the Church self-realization. [17]

6. I take for granted the many opportunities to work together in the fields of schooling, health, development and politics, etc. In the strictly religious field, [18] I refer to a few of the more modern possibilities.

First, we have to consider what may ruin collaboration, *proselytism*. In the joint statement of the Secretariat for Christian Unity and the World Council of Churches in 1971, this is defined as a perversion of witness. No Church should be prevented from bearing witness to its faith before the world. Proselytism, which is to be condemned in itself as well as for the sake of ecumenism, occurs when Churches, in bearing witness, seek their own selfish ends and make use of means of attraction which do not belong to the gospel. I would not want to deny that the transfer of some Catholics to Protestant movements in Latin America, in the past at least, could be genuine conversion from formalistic Church membership to a life according to the gospel. On the other hand in Africa, and especially in Asia, there is a veritable wave of conversions in the opposite direction, due to the particular situation of the Protestant Churches. For practical considerations and for reasons of principle, these have become africanized and asianized more

---

[16] Hoekendijk in *Kirche und Volk in der deutsche Missionswissenschaft*, München, 1967, p. 330f.

[17] H.J. Margull, *Theologie der missionarischen Verkündigung*, Stuttgart, 1959, pp. 18-23, 45-47.

[18] Bühlmann, *op. cit.* (n. 1), pp. 128-138.

radically than we have. In some countries, they have formed a national union of Churches. These factors have led to a certain confusion and to a loss of organization and efficiency. Many Christians finding themselves in dispute with their minister, or having to pay him a rather high due (whereas among us it is rather the Christians who receive from the Church), seek to become Catholics. 'Conversions' of this kind need careful examination. In some parts of India and Indonesia, the majority of converts come from other Christian Churches. Now this is surely not the purpose of our presence in a continent with such a small minority of Christians. Instead of rejoicing about such minor, individual successes, we should be taking constructive measures to promote Church unity with the aim of making our communal witness stronger before non-Christians.

7. Every Church has its limitations and defects. Instead of trying to make profit out of others' losses, we should be helping one another to bring about *aggiornamento*. In Lower Egypt, twenty years ago, the Franciscans began to visit the Coptic population, poverty stricken and completely abandoned by their priests. They rendered small services and instituted talks about religion. Where formerly 10,000 a year were abandoning their faith, now at least 20,000 are having their faith renewed. The Catholic liturgy is celebrated for them, but the main intention is to return them to the Coptic Church and good relations have been established with the Coptic clergy. It is simply an effort to bring the 'sheep without shepherd' back to Christ without confusing them and without making them decide for or against either Church. [19]

The average Protestant minister, especially in the Independent Churches (the sects), is less well educated than the Catholic priest, native or foreign. [20] A lower level of education makes for an inferiority complex, fear and compensating aggressiveness and fanaticism, the enemies of all ecumenism. All Churches have an interest in better education for the clergy.

[19] P. Franzidis, *L'oeuvre copte franciscaine en Basse-Egypte,* in SML 1970, pp. 171-176.

[20] B. Sundkler, *The Christian ministry in Africa,* Uppsala, 1960, is a classic on this subject.

At Witbank in South Africa, a Protestant, F.H. Burke has been working since 1946 in a Bible school which he founded to serve the 'prophets' and 'bishops' of the Independent Churches. To reach a wider circle still, he has organized correspondence courses since 1961. An excellent means of building bridges to these Churches. [21]

Since 1972, six Anglican theology students have been living and studying at the Catholic seminary at Roma in Lesotho. For political reasons, it was no longer possible to send them to the Anglican seminary at Umtattatin, South Africa. Eucharistic celebration is separate; everything else — prayer, studies, meals, school and recreation — is shared. This enforced solution seems to be turning out well so far. The exchange of students and teachers, beginning here and there, needs to be continued more generously. As occasion offers, we ought to have the humility to accept help from one another. Why should all the Catholic Copt theologians be sent to the Ethiopian College in Rome, when the Coptic theological faculty at Haile Selassie University in Addis Ababa enjoys an outstanding reputation?

8. There are two other noteworthy fields in which solutions imposed by necessity deserve recommendation: religious instruction in common and shared churches. Formerly the Churches always had their own schools in which to provide for the instruction of their young people. But since the nationalization of schools in many countries the children are scattered in dozens of schools throughout the cities. Often the Churches have the right to give religious instruction, but how are they to find enough catechists to visit all the schools? On the principle that some general Christian education is better than nothing, Christians in Dar es Salaam in 1969 joined in the following experiment: all the Christian children in any given class have one catechist who will be Catholic, Lutheran or Anglican as agreed in each case. As a text they use the Bible and a good Catholic catechism, leaving aside some questions like those dealing with first communion and confession which are treated separately for Catholics outside school. In the second half of the course,

[21] W.J. Hollenweger, *Auf den Spuren dynamischer Gemeinden,* Zürich, 1971, pp. 243-251.

when the children are mature enough to understand the doctrinal differences between Churches, religious instruction is still given separately, as in the past, [22] It is impossible to avoid all friction, but given some adaptation the common work continues. Where there is already a good ecumenical atmosphere and where adult Christians are ready for it, we must encourage this mutual help.

The second field is that of shared churches and shared worship. At least in remote places, where the various churches have only small groups of adherents and where the minister can be present only once a month, it is advisable to prepare only one place of worship, co-ordinating the visits of ministers and inviting all Christians to attend the celebration every Sunday — without inter-communion. The Ecumenical Directory considers occasional sharing in Protestant worship 'for good reasons' to be permissible; it also allows shared churches (worship under the same roof). [23] It would be a great step forward if episcopal conferences would give a generous interpretation to this directive, in the light of local situations. During World War I, the Lord's Supper was celebrated in the trenches, in prisoner-of-war camps and under bombardment at night, without regard to confessional loyalties. It was the mark of a single community united in a common destiny. Can such things happen only under the pressure of physical danger and not under the pressure of the modern world?

9. We now have two structural problems to discuss. For the present, they constitute utopias (in the sense of working models) but much depends on them in the attainment of the ultimate ends of ecumenism.

Because the new shape of the world is polycentric, I have recommended decentralization of the Roman curia. I now make the same recommendation on ecumenical grounds. No one imagines that the larger Churches could be united with and fully integrated in the Catholic Church of Rome with its present central administration. Unity could only be effected within a framework of administrative pluralism, which would

[22] *Ecclesia,* Dar es Salaam, Dec. 1969.
[23] *Directorium ad ea quae a Conc. Vatic. II de re oecumen. promulgata sunt exequenda,* Rome, 1967, no. 59, 61.

have to be permitted. Consider the case of the oriental Churches, which are of concern to the Third Church in the Middle East, Ethiopia and south India. It is agreed that in the matter of doctrine, there are practically no obstacles to union. The old difficulties that used to exist were largely terminological and philosophical. [24] Division still exists today principally because of prolonged geographic isolation, historically conditioned structures, strong links with the state and, above all, fear of Rome (not of the Pope) — a fear not without foundation in view of the centuries of efforts to Latinize and subjugate by *Propaganda* missionaries. Re-unification could take place on the basis of a decentralized union of the Churches such as did exist in the first millennium (and cannot, therefore, be against the constitution of the Church). [25] In proportion as theological thinking on the subject of the local Church and on that of the collegiality of bishops is not confined to conciliar texts but is also put into practice in Church administration, this fear will be seen to be unfounded and the way to unity will be clear for the oriental Churches and for other separated Churches.

10. Karl Rahner develops a more advanced utopia. According to him, the old points of controversy have lost their relevance. The most urgent need is to develop among all the Churches a 'theology of the future' which will have something to say to the world of today and tomorrow on actual conditions of modern living. [26] Moreover, he considers that the divisions are still operative merely for historical and socio-religious reasons. Confessional relativism is likely to go on increasing. Faced by great problems and common tasks on a world scale we cannot afford to be divided as Christians. From this situation, we ought to draw the theological conclusion that we should not regard

[24] M.A. Tekle-Haymanot, *La Chiesa etiopica e la sua dottrina cristologica,* Rome, 1974.

[25] G. de Vries, *Dialogo tra Oriente ed Occidente nella Chiesa d'oggi,* in *Unitas,* Rome, 1972, pp. 249-263, esp. 257-59; id., *Die Propaganda und die Christen im Nahen asiat, und afrikan Osten,* in Metzler, *Memoria rerum,* I/1, 561-605. On the 'local Church' see below, ch. 13.

[26] Rahner, *Oekumen, Theologie der Zukunft,* in Schriften 10, pp. 503-519; J. Moltmann, *Umkehr zur Zukunft,* München, 1970, 13.

doctrinal differences, although they are real, as divisive factors in Church structure but should tolerate them for the time being within the one Church, in the hope that in time they will be lessened. Hence, we should build up a structural unity before we attain full doctrinal unity, hoping that, within the structural unity, doctrinal unity will gradually mature. [27]

Since this proposal will have to wait a long time before it is taken into consideration at the highest level in the various Churches, it is all the more desirable that it should have some experimental success at local level. Some countries already have a united Protestant Church, for example, the Church of South India since 1947, the United Church of North India since 1970, the Church of Christ of Zaire since 1970, etc. In a country where Protestant-Catholic ecumenism is well developed, might an episcopal conference not take the courageous step of considering the adhesion of the Catholic Church too and of carrying it out with Rome's approval? This would, by no means, be equivalent to denying the Church's own identity but would mean agreeing once again to a compromise on a pragmatic basis, instead of acting on the principle of 'all or nothing'. [28] It would mean accepting doctrinal and disciplinary differences for a period of transition, in the hope of coming in time to a more satisfactory solution. At all events, this pragmatic attitude would be more realistic, more open to the opportunities and, hence, more Christian than the rigid juridical and doctrinal position which pushes the prospect of unity into the infinite distance.

11. In W.C.C. circles, from the time of New Delhi, 1961 and, especially, Uppsala, 1968, the idea of a universal ecumenical council is still being discussed. In such a council, all the Christian Churches would have representation not merely as observers but as full members empowered to seek out the way towards unity and, if appropriate, to make decisions on it. Whether this council went down in history as the Third Vatican Council

[27] Rahner, *Zur Theologie des ökumen. Gesprache,* in Schriften 9, pp. 34-78; id., *Strukturwandel,* pp. 109-114.
[28] Such compromise as might be justified also in the cases discussed above, ch. 4.A.13, p. 78f and ch. 7.B.5, p. 158f.

or, perhaps, the Second Council of Jerusalem would be of secondary importance. The Catholic Church, still digesting Vatican II, is liable to react unfavourably for the present. [29] But we must not set limits for the Holy Spirit. Since he communicated his inspiration to John XXIII against all precedent and all expectation, he can always transform a Pope anew into a carrier of his ever renewed inspirations.

12. In the meanwhile, the Third Church is left with the task of doing the foundation work and making modest progress towards the final success of ecumenism. For this purpose, as a summing up of what we have said, we could offer the following recommendations:

— Language schools for new missionaries could be organized together, both for practical reasons and, especially, to offer opportunities for ecumenical living together over a certain period.

— Temporary exchanges of students could be arranged between theological colleges. Professors could be invited to give courses lasting a few months.

— Monthly meetings could be held, in the form of 'partage évangélique', 'révision de vie', pastoral reflection, 'celebrations of fraternity'. This also goes for sisters, pastors' wives and other women mission workers.

— Book-shops could be managed in common in the cities, with inter-denominational staffs and books representative of all Christian literature.

— There should be shared places of worship in remote places and all Christians should be encouraged to share in the worship of other Christian groups.

— The problem of religious education, especially in cities, should be dealt with on an ecumenical basis.

— In social projects and political activities, we should not first make our plans and *then* invite other Churches to take

[29] N. Venturini, *Vaticano III o Gerusalemitano II?*, in *Popoli e Missioni*, Rome, May 1972, p. 38; H. Mühlen, *Morgen wird Einheit sein. Das kommende Konzil der Christen*, Paderborn, 1974.

part; we should all act together right from the start of planning.

— We should spread the Week of Prayer for Christian Unity and give it publicity, so as to give evidence to non-Christians of unity among the Churches.

— All kinds of study centres should be organized together: for the study of Islam, for pastoral planning, etc.

— The translation and shared distribution of Holy Scripture should be the favourite child of ecumenism.

— We should collaborate decisively in our use of the communications media: television, etc.

— At home, we should disseminate missionary information together, using modern methods.

B. *Ecumenism with non-Christians*

1. *Copernican revolution in theology*

1. We are familiar with ecumenism among Protestants and between Protestants and Catholics, but the term is also used loosely to indicate new relations between Christians and non-Christians. Each of these is a great step towards the abandonment of mean and blind attitudes which have characterized Christians in the past.

In no other field has the European superiority complex had more detrimental effects than in the matter of assessing non-Christian religions. The cultural superiority felt by the Greeks, who regarded all other peoples as barbarians, and the religious superiority felt by the Jews, who called all other peoples *goyim* or pagans, combined and reached their climax in the middle ages. The Christian religion became synonymous with culture. All who were beyond its pale were branded as savages, pagans and idolators. Christians were so dazzled by the light of their own religion and their own culture that they could see only

---

[30] I. Auf der Maur, *Kirchliche Verlautbarungen über die nichtchristlichen Religionen,* in KMJ 1966, pp. 31-43; J. Beckmann, *Weltkirche und Weltreligionen,* Freiburg im B., 1960, p. 17, 73. On the results of this blindness to other cultures, see above ch. 2.A.4, p. 28.

faults in other religions and other cultures. One need only recall that ecclesiastical documents right up to Pius XII always spoke of 'infidels', of those who 'serve pagan idols' and who 'know not God'. [30] It was only with John XXIII that a new way of speaking suddenly made its entry.

For us Christians, who thought we possessed all truth, it is a great humiliation to have to admit that for 500 years, from the time the non-Christians entered our range of vision, we have lived in serious error in their regard. Our air of superiority was certainly not according to Christ's will.

2. Missionaries, ethnologists and students of religion have gradually discovered the religious world of the non-Christians and made it known through innumerable publications. The communications media and modern tourism have brought an infinitude of fresh information and have multiplied direct contacts. With the loss of Europe's political hegemony Christianity, as the religion developed in that continent and preached from it, has lost its position of external pre-eminence. Suddenly, we have discovered that there are many religions which take themselves as seriously as Christianity. We have realized that two thirds of humanity — formerly distant colonial peoples without importance but now our partners with equal rights in the world of today — are not Christian. In the circumstances, the question of their salvation was bound to come up again. A theology which could find no answer except to condemn two thousand million people (not counting the millions of non-Christians in mankind past and future) would finish by condemning itself. A God who limited his salvation to members of the Christian Church would be an arbitrary, malevolent demon. The question could not be left to missionologists, living on the fringes of theology proper; it had to be dealt with by every theologian worthy of the name. In fact, it has become one of the most debated questions in the last ten years. [31]

3. As far as the salvation of the individual is concerned, it has always been admitted that the prevenient and assisting

[31] W. Bühlmann, *Die Theologie der nichtchristlichen Religionen als ökemenisches Problem,* in *Freiheit in der Bewegung,* Festschrift O. Karrer, Frankfurt, 1969, pp. 453-478.

grace of God would not be lacking. But, where pagans were concerned, this statement was always intended in the sense of an eventual possibility and not of a real likelihood. We could gather innumerable quotations from missionary literature speaking of 'thirst for souls' and of 'the desire to rescue souls from hell'. Christian thought has been too long and too intensely preoccupied with the severity of God's judgements and too little with the inexhaustible riches of the grace of Christ. Now, it is no longer possible to speak of the universal salvific will of God, a will which is in some way securely effective (1 Tim 2:4), if we go on to make the salvation of millions of men depend on explicit faith in Christ, that is, on the human efforts and on the very uncertain successes of the missions. Salvation was won once for all by the one who gave himself as a ransom for the many. The event of Christ is the great event in world history, transforming it into a history of salvation. That event is inserted into the cosmos, into humanity, and it creates a new mode of existence, the 'supernatural existential' of Karl Rahner, making it possible for every man to make an effective response to God's continual offer of grace about which there can be no doubt. Man, wherever and whenever he exists, lives and breathes in the era of redemption accomplished. No one who directs his life in the way of ultimate values can be doing this simply in the 'natural' order; he must be in the order of grace and, therefore, of salvation. But, since this grace offered and granted in each case is the grace of Christ, non-Christians do possess unconsciously — in a non-official way not externally recognizable, because not backed by the visible signs of the sacraments — but nevertheless effectively the grace of Christ. In this sense they are already in some way Christian and — once again, with Karl Rahner — they can be called 'anonymous Christians'. [32]

4. Vatican II recognizes this real possibility of salvation for non-Christians. Moreover, it speaks with appreciation of the non-Christian religions. [33] It does not, however, touch on

[32] Cf. Bühlmann, op. cit., pp. 458f, 469f.

[33] Nostra aetate 2; cf. in this connection LThK Konzil II, 405-495; K. Müller, Die Kirche und die nichtchristlichen Religionen, Aschaffenburg, 1968.

230

the all-important question of the significance in salvation history of these religions and of their position in God's saving plan. Consideration had not matured enough for this to be made the subject of universal doctrinal treatment, and it was left for further theological discussion.

Today, most Catholic theologians reason as follows. If man is willed by God as a religious being, at one and the same time corporeal and spiritual, it follows that he will embody his religious feelings and desires in external actions. These actions, in their turn, will take concrete shape in community rites and functions arising out of accepted convention and building up into tradition as time goes on. And if man, in order to gain salvation, must follow his conscience, and if conscience directs him to the rites received from his ancestors, that is, to a religion, we must conclude that he ought to live according to that religion. But then, we can continue, that religion is foreseen and willed in God's salvific plan. It is, to be sure, unthinkable that men of God as a whole could be completely in error in the decisive questions in life. Hence, we can interpret religion as a way of salvation made possible by God himself. The presence of deviations, deficiencies and extravagances in these religions does not put in question their positive value, since the unworthy things present in Christianity and its history have a no less demonic look. 'Paganism', then, must no longer be seen as the work of the devil. It is not evil in itself, to be destroyed root and branch; it carries out a function intended by God. It is an ante-chamber to the Church, a Church by analogy, a religious space in which the one and only God dwells and works the salvation which he prepared, in Jesus Christ, for all mankind. Consequently, regarding non-Christian mankind, we can speak of a universal (or general) history of salvation which is to be taken very seriously and suffers no derogation by the fact that the particular (or specific) history of salvation was made visible first in the people of Israel and then in the Church of Christ. These three stages in the story of salvation are not mutually exclusive; together they constitute the one salvific plan of God and show the continuity of his saving action. [34]

[34] As defended especially by Rahner, Heilsbetz, Schlette, Feiner.

5. This is, of course, a prophetic explanation of religion, a new constructive view of the world, a revolution in the field of theology. Rahner thinks that the recognition of 'obedience and fidelity to conscience' as the true dividing line between salvation and perdition, with all that follows this insight, marks a much more important stage in the development of the Church's thought than, for example, the teaching on collegiality in the Church. [35]

Christianity, then, is not to be taken exclusively as the one, unique true religion, like the sun around which all the rest turn. Before and alongside Christianity, there are and have been religions with their own 'revelations'. [36] Thus, we need to study the religious phenomenon in itself. Within this general phenomenon, Christianity represents a particular and unique form, being the ground (to continue metaphorically) on which light and warmth (from God who mercifully operates within every religion) have engendered a life which is especially varied and flourishing. This conception does not depreciate the uniqueness of the salvific action effected by Christ but, on the contrary, accentuates it; for it does not merely confer a pre-eminence on the Church he founded but also relates to the event of Christ all the other religions in God's one salvific plan. (One might say that this amounts to inclusive (of other religions) exclusiveness in the Christian claim!) Today, as in the beginning, there exists no name under heaven through which we can attain salvation (Acts 4:12) except that of Jesus Christ; he, however, is already present and active in all religions before the arrival of the missionary.

6. Of course, this view does not eliminate the tension between theology and practice. It is strange how the statements of missionaries in the same country about 'their pagans' can differ. Some speak only of supersition, magic, witchcraft, immorality and devil worship, others of their sense of justice and their religious disposition, of noble men, holy pagans. The

---

[35] His observations on the problem of 'anonymous Christians', in *Schriften* 10, pp. 531-546, esp. 535f.

[36] *Revelations in Christianity and other religions,* Studia Missionalia XX, Rome, 1971; J. Neuner (ed.), *Christian revelation and world religions,* London, 1967.

proverb that a man finds what he is looking for is a partial explanation of this divergence. Without attention and sympathy, we cannot know the better side of paganism.

The Franciscan Basetti Sani, famous for his studies on Islam, had this experience. At first, in his lectures and writings he upheld the theological thesis that Mohammed could not have been in good faith and was an instrument of Satan, who used him to construct an anti-Church and to set up Allah as an anti-God; that was what needed unmasking. Then, in 1947, a moment of grace intervened. He was living in the Upper Nile district and one evening saw a group of poor Moslems absorbed in prayer. A flash of illumination came to him and suddenly he found himself full of respect and love for these prayerful men. From that moment he began to see and expound things differently. Now he thinks God used Mohammed in his salvific plan to free many peoples from polytheism and reveal to them the fundamental truths of the Old Testament as a preparation for Christ (even if Moslems have not, in fact, seen the connection, any more than the Jews). Unfortunately, the Church was not capable of understanding Islam from within and for thirteen centuries opposed it violently, by arms and in teaching. [37]

There is no need to idealize non-Christian religions to justify this new theology. Our own Christian experience is often quite different from 'being called to be children of God (1 Jn 3:1). And yet that is what we are. The tension between theology and practice is part of our daily life and must be endured in faith before Christians and non-Christians.

7. Much has changed in the last 10 to 20 years. Not only have we learned, after centuries of lost time, to make a fair assessment of non-Christian religions, but we are also experiencing their influence in the world. L.S. Senghor thinks that, after the French revolution bringing the modern world political rights, after the communist revolution winning men economic rights, a third revolution is about to occur: in reaction against the materialism of both capitalist and communist, it will reintegrate moral and religious values in the modern world. In

[37] G. Basetti Sani, *Il Corano nella luce di Cristo,* EMI, Verona, 1972, pp. 9-43.

233

this revolution, he adds, coloured people (and hence mostly non-Christians) will play a great part. [38]

In fact, if religion has again become a drawing-room subject, this is due not only to figures like Adenauer, De Gasperi, Kennedy and De Gaulle but also to coloured representatives at the United Nations and in their own embassies practising their religion in all serenity. If in western countries, inside and outside the Churches, there is renewed evidence of a search for peace, meditation and meaningful prayer, this must be attributed in part to the influence of eastern religions. Christians can find their faith enriched by non-Christians; who would have thought it ten years ago or dared to suggest it? And yet, 2000 years ago, Christ emphasized it: 'I have not known faith so great in Israel.'

2. *The pastoral way*

1. The new theology of non-Christian religions is a time bomb, which will very soon reveal its harsh consequences for the work of missionaries. If their work is not merely self-centred propaganda for the Church but the product of faith and theology, then changes in theology cannot fail to leave footprints on it.

We have already felt the shock in our terminology. Recent years have seen the disappearance of a whole series of traditional expressions: negroes, savages, colonials, pagans... If 'pagan' in popular acceptance and also according to the Encyclopedia Britannica means 'one who worships false gods or a false god', then we must now say that there are no pagans in Africa. At most, we may use the expression between inverted commas, because we have not yet found a suitable substitute. The terms 'non-Christian' or 'non-Christian religions' are equally unsatisfactory: Moslems, Hindus, etc. complain at being given a negative designation; but for practical purposes, we have to go on using them for the time being because expressions like 'the religious traditions of humanity' or 'primitive religions' are appropriate but too generalised. In the same way, the terms 'mission' and 'missionary' have themselves become suspect and

[38] L.S. Senghor, *Nation et voie africaine du socialisme*, Paris, 1966, p. 69.

234

are not so readily used. The reality they intend is not being abandoned but it is interpreted and formulated in new ways. 'Christian presence', 'dialogue' and 'witness' are preferred. They say the same thing in a fresh way.

2. Modern theology is blamed for having quenched missionary fervour by eliminating the motive of saving souls. This is simplistic and false. In Africa, the movement towards Christianity continues as before. In Asia and north Africa, conversions among Moslems, Hindus and Buddhists have always been the exception: Christians there were recruited among the outcastes, the untouchables, animists and primitive peoples. Even among these, it is true, there are now fewer conversions; but that is not because of modern theology but rather because, in the era of nationalism, it is harder to go over to the 'foreigner's religion'. In any case, the All India seminar came to the conclusion that modern theology, well understood, is no obstacle to evangelization but a great spur. [39]

The need to evangelize grows out of the maturity of the Christian life, based on God's saving plan. The mature Christian realizes that being called to the Church does not mean, primarily, assuring one's own salvation in a self-centred way; rather it means living for others. It is a call to personal generosity in shouldering, in a first stage of vicarious representation, 'with Simon of Cyrene, the cross of Christ in its world-wide dimensions, the burden of the whole of history, in the service of true life'. [40] Then, in a second stage of representation, he will bear public witness to what the Lord has done for his people. Witness communicates to another not merely some *information* (as is the case with the words of a teacher or expert) but the Christian's own *self* and his most personal conviction of faith; by this communication of himself and his conviction he urges the other to make his decision. [41] The whole theology of vocation in Old

---

[39] *Church in India today,* New Delhi, 1969, p. 333.

[40] J. Ratzinger, *sub voce* 'Stellvertretung' in HThG II, pp. 566-575, esp. 574. On representation and the Church's mission, see above ch. 6.D.5, p. 147.

[41] K. Rahner: Theological observations on the concept of witness in *Schriften* 10, pp. 164-180.

and New Testaments (the prophets, Israel, Mary, the apostles) shows that vocation does not mean a singling out for marks of preference or privileges, but rather a commission to work for the salvation of others. [42] Clearly, one who has not yet reached the maturity of Christian life continues to be concerned simply about the salvation of his own soul. He is like a man who has escaped from poverty and lives well without thinking of the fate of his fellow citizens who remain poor. Readiness and courage in bearing witness, or 'missionary zeal', have always been the criterion for judging a Christian's stage of development.

Missionary witness for the benefit of the 'anonymous Christians' is still called for. The theological conviction that Christ is already present and active in them makes mission possible and makes 'pagans' accessible to the message. We do not bring them something strange from the outside; we discover to them Christ already in them and unveil him to their sight, giving life a new meaning for them. This *incognito* of Christ, by its own dynamism, demands explicit Christianity. The seed has no right not to want to become a plant. The embryo, by an intrinsic law of life, tends to come to the light of day, to become a fully conscious and mature man. In the same way, grace secretly present in non-Christians tends to become manifest; it moves towards embodying itself sacramentally and thus towards the fullness of love and life. Mission and missionaries place themselves at the service of this incarnational dynamism. [43]

After all, these religions themselves aspire to fullness and redemption. With all the respect we owe them, we must admit that they do not yet know the coming of the kingdom of God and the liberating message of the redemption brought about by the one who sacrificed himself for us. Hinduism and Buddhism are fundamentally pessimistic religions. Everyone is the product of his own *karma,* the summation of the good and bad actions of preceding lives and, at the same time, creator of *karma,* present and future. Everyone shapes his own destiny and must redeem himself, if necessary in the course of further lives. There is no

[42] On the theology of election, cf. LThK 2, 280-283; F. Kamphaus, *Mission,* in HThG II, 160-64; cf. also above ch. 1.A.5, p. 7.

[43] Rahner, *op. cit.* (n. 35); id., *Anonymes Christentum und Missionsauftrag der Kirche,* in *Schriften* 9, pp. 498-515.

help from outside, no benevolent God. *Karma* is incorruptibly rigid, just and cold. [44]

It is in this situation that the gospel message must resound: there is one who *has redeemed* us; we do not need to attain moral perfection *before* attaining salvation, since salvation comes as a gift to us sinners. If the gospel is to be presented to communists as good news for the embittered, [45] for Hindus and Buddhists it is glad tidings for ascetics.

3. It is beyond doubt, then, that the Church still has a missionary role to fill. But how? In putting the question, I am thinking in the first place of Asia where mission is more urgent and, at the same time, more problematic than anywhere else. After four centuries of presence, our success has been so meagre that we must admit this is not the way ahead. We must have the courage to judge the situation realistically and dare to make a radical change of direction. In so doing, we would have little to lose and much to gain. If we go on enclosing ourselves in the ghetto, for fear of being otherwise absorbed by Hinduism, we are adopting an attitude unworthy of the Church and one that has no future. A missionary working is a Moslem country wrote to me a short time ago that he was thinking of building a two-storey orphanage, in a country where only the missions have solid two-storey buildings and where orphans have so far been accepted in the patriarchal families. He hoped thus to gain a few Christians. I could not but oppose such a trick. Even when there is a proposal, as in India, to raise the percentage of priests engaged in missionary work from five to ten in the course of five years, the situation cannot really be dealt with by a simple quantitative increase. What is needed is a qualitative change, an entirely new missionary approach. [46] Much was said at the All India Seminar about evangelization and dialogue with other religions. The episcopal conference has its own commission expressly for mission. It is aware of the opportunities of the

[44] S. Radhakrishnan — C.A. Moore, *A sourcebook in Indian philosophy*, New Jersey, 1967, XXIX.

[45] See above ch. 5.B.4.2, p. 124.

[46] P. Le Joly, *Un plan pour l'évangélisation d'un grand pays de mission,* in CM 1972, pp. 386-397.

near future and is on the lookout for a new approach but knows it is not yet ready to attempt one. [47]

Hitherto, the Church has remained completely outside the world of the Moslem, the Hindu and the Buddhist. Genuine meeting has not yet taken place. The Church has been present only in her own institutions, and these inspire fear in people of other confessions; as they look like power structures, they have been taken for Trojan horses and have put people on the defensive. It is time for the Church to accept a more modest form of presence, to cease being cast in a historically conditioned mould, and to allow herself to be inspired and animated by the Lord Christ, coming to meet us from the future.

4. One new approach (not to be adopted suddenly to the exclusion of all others but to be used to complement present efforts and be practised more widely with time) is precisely the one based on the conviction that God has given wisdom and special revelation to all human groups, [48] that Christ is already at work in all religions. The loftiness of Old Testament revelation and the uniqueness of the New Testament are misunderstood if taken in isolation: they are not lonely monoliths rising over the vast landscape of humanity. God does not discriminate against anyone. The awareness and the experience of being in the same boat with all men (in the fundamental religious attitude) open up new and richer horizons both for Christians and for non-Christians. No one can avoid the profound influence of other religions. Religion is coming to be seen everywhere as the supreme value, as the question of life and death, as the search for the real meaning of life. All religions meet today on a very wide front. Ecumenism, co-existence, dialogue, a more profound outlook and, above all, a new synthesis are necessities. If religion is what it claims to be, a way for men towards their ultimate end, it seems that, at the basis of all religions, there must be one religion, the transcendental religion, which is expressed concretely in the many religions. In the beginning, a

[47] *Church in India today,* All India Seminar, 1969, pp. 329-343; Archbishop E. D'Souza, *Oughtn't we to go the intellectuals today?,* in *Conference of religious,* India Gen. Assembly, 1969, pp. 44-54.

[48] Cf. n. 36.

man knows and appreciates the value of his own religion and seeks to live well (which does not mean fanatically) according to its dictates. Gradually, however, he comes to a point (which we have now reached) where he can recognize other religions and be glad to meet them and enter into dialogue with their representatives. He continually finds in the other the religious man. There is scope for an osmosis or cross-fertilization, not through theoretical demonstrations, apologetics or catechizing but through living witness and exchange of religious experiences. Here is the new opportunity for Christianity. It must not make its *a priori* claims from without, as in the past; it can only enter into an honest exchange and competition, in the confident hope of being discovered and recognized, in God's good time, as the supreme form — concrete and historical — of the transcendental religion; the uniquely clear sign of the presence of the God who shows us benevolence. [49]

5. As in our relations with Protestants, so also with non-Christians we can practise the kind of ecumenism described here only if we adopt a *kenotic* frame of mind. We cannot continue with a sort of conquering missionary strategy, snatching individuals from their former religious environment and inserting them into the Latin Church. We can no longer just elaborate a doctrinal system and expect individuals to renounce all previous religious experience in exchange for the system. We can no longer present ourselves as an institution, formed and deformed by history, offering men a stark alternative of acceptance or rejection. But we can present ourselves as simple bearers of the message, and this will, of course, gradually make clear the invitation to join the institution, that is, the community of those who think alike. Christ, like Buddha and Mohammed, did not wish to found a new religion but to take seriously the existing religion and to reform it. The gospel of Christ brought freedom from human regulations, and directed men towards the heavenly Father and the kingdom to come, but did not demand a break

[49] R. Panikkar, *Kerygma und Indien*, Hamburg, 1967, pp. 9-47; id., *Religionen und die Religion*, München, 1965; C.J. Blecker, *Christ in modern Athens*, Leiden, 1965; H. Dumoulin, *Christlicher Dialog mit Asien*, München, 1970; Le Saux, Griffiths and P. Gerlitz, *Kommt die Welteinheitsreligion?*, Hamburg, 1969.

with the synagogue. Christ came not to eliminate the preceding religion but to complete it (Mt 5:17). We must show a like generosity. If Christianity is meant to represent in anticipation the fullness that will come at the end of time, it cannot be meant to give life to only *one* religion, still less to set one spirituality against another. It must be meant as the revelation (or unveiling) of the mystery hidden in all the religions of the world. 'But the price of this is death — as the necessary presupposition of resurrection — death not only of the other religions but also of our own, that is, of Christianity in its present form'.[50] The Church must not only teach and give but must also be ready to learn and receive. She does not yet possess the anticipated eschatological fullness but lives in a real incarnational state of need. In this new frame of mind, the Church will be capable of dialogue with the Asian religions.

6. All this has practical consequences. Until now the missions have been in danger of merely following up minor successes and concentrating all their energies on them alone. It did not seem worth while to engage in religious dialogue with others: 'But it would not lead to conversions.' Many missionaries have time on their hands during the week. During two stays in India, I have quite casually entered into many religious conversations on the road or on flights, and I have always been surprised by the openness and pleasure with which Hindus, Moslems and Sikhs spoke of their religious experience. It has been a help to me and I think I have helped the others a little. One day some Catholic missionaries were discussing whether to go out a little more and do mission work by house-to-house visiting, in order to start a religious dialogue. One answer was: 'Impossible. They do not want it. The most that would happen is that they would wonder if we fancied one of the women'. There was a catechist present who until a few years earlier had been a minister in a Protestant sect. He thought differently: 'It *is* possible. I spent years going from house to house. I asked about the family. I prayed with them. I left the New Testament with them. I was always welcome in poor families. Only in some rich families was my visit not always welcome'. When the dis-

[50] R. Panikkar, *Kerygma und Indien,* Hamburg, 1967, p. 9f.

cussion touched on the poor success of the Church in India, the blame was thrown on others as usual: 'They are proud. God reveals his truth to little ones and hides it from the great. . .' We ought to ask ourselves whether it was not we who were too grudging in our previous behaviour to them.

With these new methods, we need to accept a certain syncretism, as a transitional stage which could, however, last quite a time. We must first lead people to Christ as to a great prophet (even the apostles only gradually came to realize who he really was) for we cannot present him to them from the outset as the one unique religious teacher. We must allow people time for their journey to Christ and his Church. Thanks to the biblical work of Protestants, millions of Hindus already know him; whole books could be filled with sympathetic presentations of him by leading Hindus. [51] One characteristic of modern Hinduism is its openness to social problems, with a corresponding interest in Christianity. Clearly, there is a danger that it will absorb elements of Christianity without finding sound expression for them. [52] We ought to face this danger fearlessly, since those who are in the stronger position have nothing to fear and whoever has Christ has the better opportunities. Fundamentally, it is much more important for Hinduism to become more Christian than for us to convert a few Hindus.

In this way, the Church will increasingly become a more open society. Until now our boundaries have been clearly defined. We know exactly who is in and who is out. From now on, we shall have to take more seriously those who are in the ante-chamber, the sympathizers. Looking at their partial identification with the Church we shall have to pay attention in the first place not to what is still lacking but to what is already present. [53] Here again, we must accept the principle of a positive compromise in place of a sterile exclusivism. [54] We must evange-

[51] St Samartha, *Hindus vor dem universalen Christus,* Stuttgart, 1970.

[52] P. Antes, *Das Neue im modernen Hinduismus,* in ZMR 1973, pp. 99-116.

[53] L. Rütti, *Zur Theologie der Mission,* München-Mainz, 1972, pp. 326-328.

[54] Cf. above, n. 28.

lize and preach Christ with all possible means even if visible success, in the sense of making Christians by fully inserting them in the Christian community, has to wait. We cannot do violence to the absolute freedom of God and of men.

When we do come to the baptism of an individual, this should not entail a final break in his loyalty to his social, cultural and religious past. As Hinduism is, in the first place, a form of social community and leaves plenty of room in matters of faith, we could in the future think of 'Catholic Hindus'. These would be persons or, preferably, whole families who have become Christian but continue to celebrate Hindu rites, interpreting them in a new way and receiving Christian sacraments in addition. This presupposes a certain spiritual maturity; but without such maturity there can be no progress in India. [55] In full awareness of having passed from the provisional to the definitive in religion, they could still recognize the legitimacy of their former religion and so licitly participate in its forms of expression, just as the apostles continued to attend the synagogue and celebrated the Eucharist in addition. [56] There are already individual Hindus, Moslems and Buddhists living as Christians in this way and opening up completely new horizons for Christ's presence in Asia. [57] The once isolated experiments of Fr De Nobili are about to celebrate their resurrection.

7. All this is going to need further elaboration in the spiritual laboratories, and must also be popularized. The Vatican Secretariat for non-Christian religions faces a fascinating task here. Under the new direction of Cardinal Pignedoli it will certainly be equal to tackling it. Alongside the secretariat *for* religions, there now exists a working group *of* religions. In 1970, it organized a first meeting at Kyoto in Japan with 340 representatives of forty nations and ten religions; another meeting

[55] H. Staffner, *Conversion to Christianity seen from the Hindu point of view*, in CIM 1972, pp. 3-15.

[56] W. Bühlmann, *Die Kirche Afrikas swischen dem Apostelkonzil und dem Vatikanum II*, in *Concilium* 1966, pp. 174-184, esp. 181.

[57] P. Löffler, *Die arabische Welt als Testfall der Mission?*, in EMZ 1972, pp. 49-58; J. Jesudasan, *Ghandian perspectives on missiology*, in *Indian Church History Review*, Mysore, 1970, pp. 45-72; K. Baago, *The post-colonial crisis of Missions*, in IRM 1966, p. 331f.

was held in 1974. We have not only a shared responsibility towards the outside world in working for peace and progress in the world but also common internal problems, the encounter with secularism [58] and the safeguarding of the religious conception of life in tomorrow's world.

There is increasing talk of a kind of parliament of religions. There are Hindu gurus and Moslem sheiks who would gladly have the Pope as head of such an assembly, recognizing that only he has the authority to bring together the major religions. [59] We do not know what surprises the future has in store for us. There is one obvious difficulty in the fact that the other religions are not hierarchically structured like the Catholic Church and would have difficulty in delegating representatives. They lack figures, like John XXIII, who are representative of the whole group and can set afoot changes of mentality within it.

8. More important than official talks is the fact of living the new attitudes and expressing them concretely in experiments at local level, in small groups, in *ashrams,* in small communities. Of course, we need to change attitudes and prepare people for this. I have asked many Indian religious communities if they had contacts with gurus, if they practised Yoga and meditation techniques. My question brought reactions of stupefaction, akin to ours twenty years ago if we were asked whether we could learn or accept anything from the Protestants. An inquiry conducted in India showed that priests and brothers with degrees had completed their studies as follows: 356 had degrees in western philosophy, 308 in theology, 98 in natural sciences, 12 in Indian philosophy, 2 in missionology and 2 in Indian studies.[60] We need to reverse the priorities. We need many more specialists to prepare the way for the right approach by the Church in Asia.

[58] See below, ch. 14.B., p. 302.

[59] A Parliament of Religions took place as early as 1893 in Chicago: cf. D.H. Bishop, *Religious confrontation. A case study: The 1893 Parliament of Religions,* Leiden, 1969, pp. 63-76.

[60] *Survey of religious vocations in India,* CRI, New Delhi, 1968, p. 6.

For this purpose I again offer some concrete recommendations: [61]

— Just as it is obvious (or should be) that all missionaries ought to learn foreign languages, so also they should study the religions with which they will have to deal.

— They should complete the theoretical study of these religions by living for a few months in a monastery or some similarly religious environment. They need to learn to know them from within.

— A number of the missionaries (not just isolated individuals) should specialize in more profound study of the religious systems in question and their meditation techniques.

— We need to encourage experiments in Christian *ashrams*, as a simple spiritual presence of the Church.

— We should experiment in mixed *ashrams* (Hindu and Christian).

— In the cities, we should have religious centres open to Christians and non-Christians, not only to provide religious information but also for prayer meetings based on Christian and non-Christian religious texts.

— We should live a simple Christian life in villages where there are as yet no Christians and help the villagers to improve the tenor of their lives.

— We need to organize public meetings on the problems we share: problems of young people, experience of God, etc.

— An annual week of prayer for all believers, on the analogy of the week of prayer for Christian Unity.

— Priests, brothers and sisters in Christian institutions, schools and hospitals should plan their work to make time for systematic house-to-house visiting, so as to get into religious conversation with relatives of pupils and patients.

— In preparation for Christmas and Easter we should

[61] Bühlmann, *Die folgen der theolog. Neubewertung der nichtchristlichen Religionen für das Missionsapostolat in Afrika,* in KMJ 1966, pp. 60-67.

distribute, together with other Christian Churches, leaflets explaining the meaning of these feasts.

— We could request the state universities to institute a chair in Christian theology and, in return, invite representatives of other religions to teach in our seminaries.

— We should invite non-Christians to take part freely in our liturgy and prayer meetings.

3. *Eastern religions in the west*

1. It is a characteristic of our time that spiritual men of the east are being attracted by western secularism while the secularized men of the west, who can no longer believe or pray, experience once again an elemental need for peace, meditation, the experience of God, the link with nature, patience in suffering: in short, they feel the need for typically eastern spirituality.

In the east, we meet western pilgrims everywhere from Pakistan to Bali, not the addicts flocking there in search of drugs nor the insatiable tourists shepherded all over Asia by their guides, but young people who spend months or years taking courses in meditation, living very poorly in Indian style and becoming Indians with the Indians as far as they possibly can. The frontier crossing, Lahore — Amritsar, between Pakistan and India, is open one day a week and 200 to 300 hippies pass through it each time. In India there must be more than a hundred gurus and sadhus from western countries; some, like the German Benedictine Sister Shraddhananda in the Hindu monastery at Paunar, intend this as a searching experiment as Christians, an adventure in faith; others have abandoned the Christian faith, or rather have never properly known it, so they are not really abandoning anything but are gaining much within Hinduism.

2. Yet these are outnumbered by people living in the west who have become enthusiastic about oriental religions, whether they accept merely their meditation techniques and remain Christian, and even become better Christians, or whether they change officially to the other religions. In Federal Germany,

3000 German citizens belong to the German Buddhist Union and 16,000 profess Islam. [62] In all the big cities of the United States, there are temples, monasteries and centres for Buddhist meditation achieving most unexpected success in the study and practice of the spiritual life. In America it is possible to speak of a 'boom' in Zen, which has won the sympathy of young people seeking to escape from the prison of the social establishment. In England, which for a long time controlled the Buddhist countries, the attraction of Buddhist ideas is felt even more strongly — according to the ancient law of the spirit, that the conquerer is always influenced spiritually by the conquered. Here the influence makes itself felt not so much through established centres but (by a kind of hypodermic injection) through cheap pocket editions and radio and television programmes. Its influence is also growing in modern psychology and psycho-therapy. After the discovery of the unconscious as the main-spring of our behaviour, it seems, sadly, that Buddhism manages to control it through meditation better than Christianity.

Hinduism, again, makes an impression through its travelling gurus. The Divine Light Mission, founded by the fifteen-year-old guru Maharaj Ji, already has centres in 45 states, while another guru, Maharishi Mahesh Yogi, teacher of transcendental meditation, is in process of organizing 3500 centres throughout the world, every one of which is to train 1000 teachers. This is to ensure that there will be a teacher for every 1000 persons, so that higher thoughts, better action and interior and exterior peace can be brought to the whole world. In 1972, during a visit to Fiuggi in Italy, I found 2000 young people from 38 countries sitting at his feet for three months. Some of them, including Catholics, told me that in this way they had managed to free themselves from drugs and that they lived contentedly and at peace without alcohol or nicotine. I asked the guru if he had heard the gospel and what he thought of it. He replied:

[62] H.J. Petsch, *Religion aus dem Untergrund,* Freiburg i. Ue., 1972; *Neue relig. Subkulturen in den USA,* in HK 1971, pp. 523-529; M. Mildenberger, *The impact of Asian religions on Germany,* in IRM 1973, pp. 34-42; E. Benz, *Buddhismus in der westlichen Welt,* in H. Dumoulin, *Buddhismus der Gegenwart,* Freiburg, 1970, pp. 191-204.

'I do not teach any religion. Each has his own religion and should remain in it. Religion is a seed which only grows into a tree through meditation. I teach the technique of meditation and concentration'.

In the USA in recent years 175,000 persons have acquired the practice of this transcendental meditation; the US army, on the basis of favourable opinions from psychologists, has recommended it to soldiers.

3. The visible part of this movement is only the tip of an iceberg. The rediscovery of religion and meditation is still spreading among the young especially. Perhaps this is a gigantic challenge to the Church. So far it has happened mainly outside the Church, like the movement towards spontaneity, rather as a reaction against a certain failure in the life of the Church. Will the Churches make their voices heard more in this movement in future? It is time to lend an ear not only to what the Spirit is saying in the Churches, but also to what he is saying to the Churches from without (cf. Acts 2:7). The Churches are in a face-to-face situation with non-Christian religions in their own homelands. The comparison provokes reactions in the non-Christians as well as in those who go to them to learn. The movement can no longer be ignored; it can only be entered into and used for the good of the Christian religion and of religion in general. At Fiuggi I spoke to a Catholic girl who told me that after the course she was returning to America to hold courses on meditation for Catholic nuns. In the Capuchin novitiate in the Swiss province, a guru teaches meditation technique for a month. In Japan, there is P.E. Lassalle's Christian Zen centre. Jean Dechanet's book on Yoga for Christians[63] has had a wide circulation. All bookshops now display and sell many books on non-Christian religions. The process of contagion has had irreversible results. We must continue on this way. Not only in Asia but also in western countries, the thesis (Christianity) and the antithesis (non-Christian religions) will lead to the synthesis, mutual enrichment.

[63] J. Dechanet, *Christian Yoga*, Burns & Oates, Search Press, 1960/73.

Chapter 11

A BURNING ISSUE: THE PRIESTLY MINISTRY

Do not think too highly of yourself...
(Rom 12:3)

A. *A sinister crisis*

1. The division of the Church into priests and lay people, which seems so natural to us, does not go back to Christ. New Testament sources present a picture which is much richer and, at the same time, more flexible. Paul speaks in two classical texts of the various gifts which can be conferred on members of the community: the gift of being apostle, of prophecy, of ministry, of teaching, of service and distribution of alms, of healing the sick, of administration, of tongues. But no one should pride himself on his gifts (Rom 12:3-8; 1 Cor 12:27-30). In these texts, it is difficult to discern the priest who presides over the eucharistic celebration or to find for him a position of outstanding authority. Priesthood is one function among many and belongs to the category of service. In naming ecclesiastical offices, scripture deliberately avoids all the profane titles then available to indicate ministerial authority, as well as all the sacral and cultic titles that could be drawn from paganism or from the Old Testament. In their place, it simply indicates the various functions of service in the community. [1]

2. Only in the post-Constantinian period did the priesthood become a social status, with civil privileges and monopoly in

---

[1] Kasper W., *Glaube und Geschichte*, Mainz, 1970, pp. 361-365; Ortensio da Spinetoli, *Il sacerdozio ministeriale nel Nuovo Testamento*, in *Antonianum*, Rome, 1972, pp. 3-16; R. Laurentin, *Flashes sur l'Amérique Latine*, Paris, 1968, pp. 110-120 (Illich's attacks on the 'priestly aristocracy').

the cultic and administrative fields. Only at this point did a priestly caste develop, as in religions outside Christianity (precisely what Christ wished to avoid), with its claim to the obedience of the people and to respect in the name of God. Only then was the mystique of the figure of the priest as *alter Christus* promoted, as if every Christian was not another Christ in virtue of baptism. The more the Church was clericalized, the more the rest of the community was reduced to the rank of a Church that is passive and merely the recipient of teaching. It all led eventually to the idea that lack of priests would interrupt union with God.

In mission territories, this idea was reinforced by the importance of the priesthood in their former religions on the one hand, and by the combination of priest and superior white man in the missionary on the other. No wonder, then, that many native priests perpetuate this frame of mind, directing their devoted obedience upwards and dominating downwards. They demand respect and will not take any criticism, [2] especially when, owing to the old seminary regime, they have been educated to a lord's life and in some countries have been the first to enjoy the advantages of a European education. Something similar happened with us in the middle ages.

3. With an educated laity, with the spread of secularization and with theological rethinking in the light of the New Testament, there is a radical trend towards demythologization and, as a result, a crisis of identity for the priest in the Church.

The Council rejected the traditional picture of the Church as a pyramid with the various grades of the hierarchy at the top and the mass of the faithful at the base, although the preconciliar commission's schema certainly head to this. Instead it spoke of one people, consecrated to God although sinful and, at the service of this people, the ministers of the Church. This is now an assured theological datum and no one would presume to contest it. But, when we come to drawing conclusions, sociological and functional, from this datum, we are divided: some proceed wildly to reduce the priesthood almost to vanishing

[2] D.S. Amalorpavadas, *L'Inde è la rencontre du Seigneur*, Paris, 1964, p. 270.

point while others become all the more attached to traditional forms in order to save the priesthood. Ministry in the Church is now a burning issue. [3]

4. The spiritual crisis has already had measurable effects. Shortage of clergy is one of the most obvious worries of nearly all bishops. In traditionally Christian countries we are helpless onlookers before a rapid thinning in the ranks of the clergy and a rise in their average age. Lack of clergy in Latin America has been chronic, right from the beginning — although the very first secretary of *Propaganda Fide*, Mons. Ingoli wrote in 1638: 'Unless the Spanish religious start to ordain Indians, the Church there will remain an infant, with no strength of its own'. [4] Recent years have seen no alleviation of this chronic complaint.

If we consider one priest for every thousand Catholics to be a normal proportion, the following statistics will give food for thought: [5]

For every 10,000 Catholics, the Middle East has 14.2 priests, N. America has 12.6, Oceania 12.5, Europe 9.8, the rest of Asia 4.7, Africa 4.3 and Latin America has 1.8. The imbalance is actually getting worse from year to year.

Fr A. Hastings has worked out the figures for Africa. It is true that the number of students in major seminaries in the period 1964-1971 increased from 1807 to 2775, but the number of African priests finishing their studies still averages only 200 a year. Since the annual increase of Catholics is approaching 1.6 millions, we would need 800 new priests a year if we were satisfied with an average of one priest to 2000 faithful. [6] At

---

[3] Kasper, *op. cit.* (n. 1), pp. 355-441; R. Rahner, *Eine entklerikalisierte Kirche*, in *Strukturwandel*, pp. 61-65.

[4] K. Müller, *Propaganda-Kongregation und einheim. Klerus*, in Metzler, *Memoria rerum*, I/1, pp. 538-557, esp. 556; PMV-NS 23: *Les religieux de l'Amérique Latine;* Ageneau, *Chemins de la Mission aujourd'hui*, Paris, 1973, pp. 72-94. On the situation in recent years, see above, ch. 7.B.5, p. 157f.

[5] Secretary of State, *Ann. Stat.* 1970, 67.

[6] A. Hastings, *Ordinations and seminarians throughout Africa*, in AFER 1973, pp. 55-59; id., *Kirche und Mission im modernen Afrika*, Graz, 1969, pp. 255-320; (Eng: see bibliography); id., *Mission and ministry*, London, 1971.

present, we have about one priest for 2500 Catholics; we can foresee that, in 2000, there will be three times as many priests in Africa but the proportion of priests will be one for every 15,000 to 18,000 Catholics. Africa is in danger of going the way of Latin America both in regard to the socio-economic situation and also in its shortage of priests. The mathematics show that in both continents the number of priests is inadequate to provide for normal sacramental life. Here and there, we find isolated cases of vocations to the priesthood, as for example among the Ibo in Nigeria, at Moshi in Tanzania and especially in Kerala, India and in Japan. In 1970, Japan had 311,000 Catholics with 1901 priests (of whom 720 were Japanese) and 6516 nuns. [7] This means one priest for 163 faithful (or one Japanese priest for 432) and one nun for 48 faithful. A veritable hypertrophy of priestly and religious vocations! It is to be hoped that the salt and leaven of the gospel will penetrate still further into the laity within the mass of the Japanese people. But even here there are now signs of a regression. [8]

In India the small region of Kerala provides 60% of the 9500 Indian priests and 77% of the 35,000 nuns. Families with five or more vocations are not rare. Yet here too there is regression, with fewer vocations and more departures, though every effort is made to conceal this. An enquiry made among pupils of the middle schools revealed that priestly and religious vocations are thought of as opportunities of social mobility. For this reason, the percentage of aspirants diminishes with higher social class: 43% of young people belonging to poorer classes have aspirations towards the religious life and priesthood while only 16% of those belonging to the middle classes expressed similar aspirations. [9] Improvements in living conditions as a negative factor for priestly and religious vocations have not yet had much influence in the Third Church. But the other negative factor — criticism of the priestly state and the religious life and the consequent identity crisis — is spreading like wildfire through these countries.

[7] Secretary of State, *Ann. Stat.* 1970, 132, 180.
[8] PMV-CI 1970, 40.
[9] *Youth and vocations,* Mangalore, 1972, p. 26.

So far, Asia has remained in a relatively advantageous position, insofar as native priests represent 65% of the total (80% in India, 90% in Vietnam), while Africa still has only 25% native priests [10] and thus is threatened on both flanks, by the slow growth rate at home and by rapid diminution of foreign missionary aid.

5. All this presents a rather sad picture of the priesthood in the Third Church. In the past, the solution has been sought in continual appeals and calls on the resources of the older Christian countries. The Council stressed the need for vocations to the priesthood. Archbishop D'Souza made much of the extraordinary disproportion in priests' activities: the overwhelming majority devote themselves to the pastoral work of guarding the flock, a minority to recovering those who are lost and only 3% to 5% to the pastoral task of spreading the gospel, to mission, to 'the Church's most important task'. On this point we need a Copernican revolution in thinking and planning. Furthermore, he noted that France had more priests and nuns than all the missionary territories put together. [11] During his journey in East Asia in 1970, Pope Paul VI sent out a fervent appeal for the missions from Samoa. In 1965, W. Promper proposed that steps should be taken at the highest level: a supra-national centre should be set up in conjunction with an institute of pastoral sociology, to recruit priests in traditionally Christian countries and to share them out with the whole world in view. [12]

Today, we know we have little to share. The reserves are exhausted. Repeated urgent calls for help have failed to rouse a response. We must find other solutions.

B. *A salutary crisis*

1. Anyone who believes that salvation history has a meaning will be able to discover positive aspects even in this crisis of

[10] The figures are calculated approximately on the basis of the *Guida delle Missioni Cattoliche,* Rome, 1970; so far Propaganda have issued no new figures and the *Annuario Statistico,* Vatican, no longer distinguishes between native and foreign priests.

[11] Bühlmann, *Sorge für alle Welt,* 1967, p. 55.

[12] Promper, *Priesternot in Lateinamerika,* p. 289f.

the priesthood. We would do well to see this crisis not merely in the light of the present moment but also in the light of the ebb and flow of history, in relation to the whole of history. The Franciscan Order, as a whole, numbered 35,000 members in 1325, 80,803 in 1960, 142,064 in 1775, 25,336 in 1900, 46,604 in 1965.[13] One might assume, then, that the present decline will, at the appropriate moment, be reversed, although this time the roots of the crisis are much more profound. But we shall not reach a proper understanding of the crisis if we merely wait for another swing of the pendulum. The crisis is a form of external pressure leading to a necessary change in the Church which would not have taken place of its own accord, that is to say, the process of declericalization in the Church. The crisis in priestly vocation is the price that had to be paid if the universal priesthood of the faithful were again to be taken seriously, if the right value were to be placed on the Christian community as such. The sacred must no longer be the exclusive preserve of priests. The whole Christian life and the whole community of the baptized is to be sacralized, in the right sense,[14] thus releasing an unsuspected fullness of power and charisms.

In the same way the decline of religious vocations contributes, or at least should contribute, to closer relations between religious orders. How much isolation, introversion, rivalry, in fact how much downright strife there has been between various orders in the past. The history of the missions is full of such unpleasant traits.[15] Since Vatican II, there is less insistence on the particular originality of each order. All are following the spirituality of the Council and seeking to live in poverty, fraternity, availability for the service of the Church — in brief, in an evangelical attitude. In this way they come closer to one another and closer to lay people. With the losses they have suffered, some historical structures which used to have divisive effects have lost their importance.

2. Among the various measures to be taken the first would

---

[13] Hostie, *Vie et mort des Ordres religieux,* Paris, 1972, p. 348.
[14] Cf. suggestions below, ch. 12.4, p. 265.
[15] Metzler, *Memoria rerum* I/1, 34, 224, 574f, etc.

be a purification of function, that is, relieving priests of work which could be done as well or better by lay people. In the course of time, the priestly class has managed to corner all ecclesiastical posts, because it was thought to be uniquely capable of filling them and because this was an easy financial solution. So in the missions the opinion has gradually prevailed that religion is 'Father's business'. The institute of religious sociology in Santiago, Chile, in 1963 reckoned that only 20% of the priests working in the Chilean capital could not have been replaced by lay people. It seems that many priests could be spared or recovered by employing lay people.[16]

3. The renewal of the diaconate as a permanent ministry by the Council has awakened hopes which, however, have scarcely been satisfied so far. The matter has been pursued with great hesitancy. In 1970, in all Asia there were 12 deacons, 16 in Africa (7 of these in Cameroon), 98 in Latin America (53 of these in Brazil).[17] We are still looking for the real identity of the diaconate and it is said that, fundamentally, everything a deacon does can be done by lay people and that there is no need to start reclericalizing the Church. At all events, the introduction of the diaconate is not enough to solve the problem of our crisis.[18]

4. Minor seminaries, formerly the source of all vocations in the Third Church, are now the subject of discussion. Episcopal conferences do not know whether to keep them or close them down, particularly now that Rome has cut subsidies or even discontinued them. In Asia, their work is still satisfactory. In Africa, in the past, the proportion of students reaching ordination averaged one in four; this has fallen to one in eleven.[19] In Latin America, the situation is worse: here, the seminary

[16] Promper, *op. cit.* (n. 12), 292f; H. Küng, *Prêtre, pour quoi faire?*, Paris, 1971.

[17] Secretary of State, *Ann. Stat. 1970*, 175-180.

[18] PMV-NS 26: *Le diaconat permanent: son rétablissement et son évolution*, 17-20.

[19] So Archbishop Mihayo of East Africa, in AMECEA, *The priest in Africa today*, Lusaka, 1970, p. 59; cf. Hastings, *Kirche und Mission im modernen Afrika*, Graz, 1969, pp. 269-274.

system is in the doldrums. [20] Once, the seminaries were pioneering institutions: they were the only places to offer higher education. This is all changed. College and private boarding-school education has lost much of its attraction for it is recognized to have a softening effect on some of the pupils: knowing they are looked after, they lose their sense of responsibility and power of decision and are not obliged, like their friends in the world, to measure themselves up against some of the testing situations of life. Now vocations are sought principally from the upper forms in the public schools. Boarding facilities are in some cases being provided for students attending these state schools, yet many are afraid the students will nonetheless be exposed to contagious influences. Here we have a question of principle: we must choose between a method based on safeguards and one that is more testing. The second method is a more appropriate preparation for the life of the priest in the modern world. Of course, we cannot make the change until at least half the theologians come from sources other than the minor seminary — this, at least is the thinking of bishops in east and central Africa. But what assurances have we of this future?

As far as major seminaries are concerned, we can observe two opposite tendencies. Some would make seminary training less closed and remote from the world than it has been, and put it more in contact with the world, opposing the inevitable spread of secularization with the weapon of a more open theology. Others believe they must keep to the old style, removing 'dangerous' professors and nipping unruly tendencies in the bud by decisive action. It is not so much a matter of different methods but rather of different basic attitudes. I do not think one can act as if twenty years of rethinking in psychology, sociology and theology had changed nothing. We do not solve problems by ignoring them.

5. We come to the burning question of celibacy. From the Pauline directive that the bishop should be 'the husband of one wife' (1 Tim 3 : 12; Tit 1 : 6) to the law making an unconditional

[20] M. Schooyans, *Chrétienté en contestation: L'Amérique Latine,* Paris, 1969, p. 179.

connection between priesthood and celibacy, we have come a very long way. [21] This is not specifically a Third Church question, but the Third Church undoubtedly is concerned with it. African bishops are inclined to make this a 'political' issue: they do not want to countenance the idea that African priests might be less capable of celibacy than whites. Moreover, after fifty years fighting for the new idea of a celibate life for the sake of the Kingdom, they think it undesirable to abandon this value.

Talk of manipulation in this affair is not completely ungrounded. The synod of bishops at Rome, 1971, hardly took sufficient account of the extensive preparatory work that took place in some countries. Priests have said: 'They asked us questions but did not listen to our answers'. Sharp criticisms were raised in some Third Church territories (Zaire, India, Brazil). [22] Representatives at the synod were required to vote 'according to their conscience' that is, as individuals. This created a split between them and their colleagues in the episcopate, and also between bishops and priests in general. If in Zaire 83% of the 595 native priests spoke in favour of freedom from the obligation to celibacy, [23] one can question the rightness of disciplinary decisions to which the majority of those concerned no longer give whole-hearted assent.

A point of view to which too little attention is given is the question of the real value of celibacy as witness. The all too frequent transgressions in Latin America and certain regions of Africa have destroyed the faith of the people in priestly celibacy (if it ever existed). However, they show much understanding and do not take the matter too tragically. [24] Celibacy is in danger of appearing as an external sign of a ghetto community: as Jews and Moslems do not eat the flesh of pigs

[21] LThK 10, 1395-1401.

[22] For Zaire, PMV-NS 16; for India, S. Kappen, *Priestly celibacy in India,* in *Concilium,* oct. 1972; for Brazil, B. Kloppenburg, *O sinodo dos bispos de 1971,* in *Rivista Eclesiastica Brasileira,* 1971, pp. 891-929.

[23] W. Hoffmann, *Zölibatzdiskussion in Afrika,* in KM 1971, pp. 148-151.

[24] Schooyans, *op. cit.* (n. 20), p. 197f.

and many sects forbid alcohol and smoking, so Catholics do not eat meat on Friday (or used not to) and forbid their priests to marry. The real meaning of celibacy is not understood. In such a situation, celibacy is separated from its true basis and is maintained artificially for the sake of an ideology, or for incidental advantages such as the financial ones. The thing is unworthy. Gossips speak of the 'Italian solution': officially everything is according to regulations but each one makes his own arrangements. [26]

6. In this connection, we can raise the question of priests in religious communities. Community life, in many respects, creates favourable conditions for preserving freely chosen celibacy. This is in addition to other advantages: for example, the whole history of the orders and congregations makes for great missionary dynamism, and their world-wide extension is a sharing in the charism of the universal Church in face of more short-sighted local interests. For this reason Archbishop Pignedoli declared, in 1970, that *Propaganda Fide* had reconsidered its attitude and now tended to favour involvement of the orders and congregations in the mission field. [26]

7. A second proposal, specifically for Third Church situations (although not necessarily exclusively for them), is the possibility of ordaining married men. The question is not the disciplinary one: For or against celibacy? but primarily a pastoral one: How can we ensure Christian communities their right to have the Eucharist? If we take seriously what the Council said about the Eucharistic celebration being both source and climax of evangelization, [27] if we then take account of the fact that in Africa 80% of Catholics are deprived of the Sunday celebration and must be satisfied with monthly Mass at best [28] (things are even worse in S. America), and if there are also

[25] As reported by Thielicke, *So sah ich Afrika,* Gütersloh, 1971, p. 212.
[26] *Religious vocations of African priests,* in AFER 1971, p. 178f; cf. also P. van Stiphout, *De efformando clero indigeno in terris missionum* (thesis at the Gregorian, 1954).
[27] *Presbyterorum Ordinis* 5.
[28] Mihayo, *op. cit.* (n. 19), p. 27.

many countries with not very numerous native clergy and with missionaries facing the real possibility of being expelled at short notice — in these circumstances, we cannot be too choosey in looking for answers to our problem.

Besides this urgent pastoral concern, there is the general question of priestly training. Certainly, we have no cause to regret the fact that from the time of Benedict XV (*Maximum illud*, 1919) clear instructions have been given that native priests should have the same education as Europeans, so that we now have completely comparable standards among the African and Asian clergy. But is this the only thinkable solution? Or could we not allow for a certain pluriformity and combine the advantages of different systems? The Protestant Churches have ministers who are less well educated but who are good workers and very close to the people; they are now striving to build up, in addition, a fully educated class of ministers. We, on the contrary, already have fully educated clergy who, however, are increasing very slowly and are divided from the people by their European life-style. We could put those admirable men, the catechists, who already act as leaders of the more remote communities and are very largely maintained by them, into the position of being able to celebrate the Sunday Eucharist with their communities. As in primitive Christianity, bishops could 'call' men from the community and lay hands on them. 'Vocation' would then no longer mean some interior quality which a person has or has not in himself but a dynamic call which arises out of the circumstances and in which the will of God is made clear. It is well known that the wish to be a priest comes to many young people but only a few fulfil the desire; out of the remainder, it should be possible to find many candidates to satisfy the new conditions. An inquiry among Catholic university students in Nigeria revealed that 77% would like married men to be ordained and that 45% would be ready to offer themselves if the circumstances should call for it. [29]

This pastoral need is so pressing that we must certainly not reject out of hand any conceivable solution. The historical

---

[29] J. O'Connell, *Regards sur le christianisme*, in *Pertinance du christianisme*, 463.

tradition against the solution in question, and also the risks involved — among others, the risk of causing the collapse of the vocation to celibacy (although, surely, anyone who fears this has little faith in the power of the gospel), are so heavy that those who are responsible have declared themselves unable to consent. The bishops' synod in 1971 approved the more inflexible position with 107 votes. But the more 'open' position, according to which the Pope, taking account of pastoral needs and the good of the whole Church, could in special circumstances allow the ordination of married men, gained 87 votes. [30] This means that such a strong minority position cannot be considered finally disposed of; the last word has not been spoken.

Undoubtedly, it is good when something that has stood the test of time can continue as it is. But one needs to bear in mind that it *could* be otherwise, if ever, in changing circumstances, it *had* to be. History will be the judge whether we were wise not to yield on this point and whether, if after a certain time we *have* to yield, we shall then be too late for finding a solution we can control; too many questions of this nature could unexpectedly come to a head all at once for the Church to answer: the ordination of married men and of women, irregular marriages and many other matters besides.

At a bishops' conference (AMECEA) in Lusaka 1970, Archbishop M. Mihayo of Tabora in Tanzania made a proposal about the priesthood in Africa which received much attention. At the end of his speech, he recommended that catechists should be well educated and then entrusted with as much responsibiiity as possible in the service of their communities. The question will inevitably arise why these men cannot, then, be priests and celebrate the Eucharist every Sunday. The question is inevitable. The ministry of the word by itself is very precious but the sacramental nature of the Church demands that we should normally have the full celebration of the Eucharist. 'We cannot, *at this moment*, say what our response will be *when the occasion arises*'. In the meantime, there are

---

[30] AAS 1971, 918; B. de Margerie, *La pénurie de clergé en Amérique Latine. Faudra-t-il ordonner prêtres des hommes mariés?*, in *Nouvelle Revue Théologique*, 1970, pp. 468-504; Laurentin, *Flashes*, p. 20f; J. Dournes, *Après nous le clergé*, in SPIR 1971, pp. 47-66.

many things to change: we must go ahead with the best training possible for our catechists and with increasing their responsibilities. [31] For the present, nothing much more is being said on this question; but many more of the better catechists are being better educated and trained, in expectation of the appointed day and the response the Spirit will then give in the Church.

[31] So Archbishop Mihayo, *op cit.* (n. 19), p. 19-30, esp. p. 29.

Chapter 12

UNTAPPED POTENTIAL: THE LAITY

> *'You are a royal priesthood, a holy people.'* (1 Pet 2:9)

1. The honorific titles which Peter gave to the Christians of Asia Minor to strengthen them in their tribulation all derive from the Old Testament (Ex 19:5f; Is 43:20f). The chosen people, as well as Christians, are said not merely to *have* priests (and a king) but also to *be* themselves a kingly, priestly, holy people. They can all please God, approach God and 'proclaim the triumphs of him who called you out of darkness into his wonderful light' (1 Pet 2:9).

By a providential coincidence, as so often happens, Vatican II renewed the biblical theology of the people of God just as the crisis in the priesthood was becoming acute; it gave lay people a new position in the Church. Alongside the new openness to Protestants and to non-Christians, this openness to the laity must be counted among the great achievements of the Council: three factors, which were formerly misunderstood but are of great importance for the Church's understanding of herself, have now been put into true perspective.

From the middle ages, 'cleric' was synonymous with 'educated' and 'lay' with 'ignorant'. Some writers compared the two states with day and night, heaven and earth, soul and body.[1] Canon law itself, speaking of the laity, points out what they *cannot* do in the Church and what they should expect priests to do *for* them. The preparatory *schema* for the Council on the laity was put together by a commission which did not

[1] Y. Congar, *Priester und Laien im Dienst des Evangeliums*, Freiburg im B., 1965, p. 243f.

include a single lay person. (In contrast, the All Africa Conference of the World Council of Churches is composed in three equal parts of pastors, adult laity and youth.) It is generally known that the principal concern of the Catholic Church in southern countries has been the formation of a native clergy, while Protestant Churches have trained lay people who now fill important posts in business, politics and even the Church.

The greater awareness of lay people's co-responsibility in our Church was attributed by the Council to the 'unmistakable working of the Holy Spirit'. [2] A new impulse has been given, its theology formulated and the necessary structures devised (councils at parish, diocesan and national level). A broad and bright horizon has been opened up.

2. Putting all this into practice will be a long haul. The principles guiding the good lay person used to be: to go to Church each Sunday and the sacraments once a month; to recite morning and evening prayers; to be generous in responding to collections. Now that there is a demand for dialogue, discussion, participation and co-responsibility, many priests and bishops simply do not know where to start. They are used to making the decisions and to being in charge but do not know how to enter into dialogue with a group. To justify the fact that councils of lay people are still totally lacking in many countries, they say: 'Our people are not yet mature enough for it. They would soon be dictating to us. We must not make the same mistakes as the Protestants'.

Anyone who begins to dig in this lay field in the spirit of the Council soon finds to his surprise that it contains not only fertile soil as well as clay but often diamonds too. [3] Those who organize scripture study groups for families or young people remark how the laity find new interpretations and applications of scripture to their daily lives. Bringing parish problems before such groups reveals the richness of ideas, experience, suggestions

[2] *Apostolicam actuositatem*, 1; C. Leitmaier, *Der Katholik und des Recht in der Kirche*, Freiburg im B., 1971; A. del Portillo, *Gläubige und Laien in der Kirche*, Paderborn, 1972.

[3] R. Lombardi, *Terremoto nella Chiesa*, Turin, 1970, p. 73.

and inspiration which can be tapped for the good of the Church
when the parish priest stops insisting on doing all the thinking
for himself. Reports from many Third Church parishes experiencing renewal confirm this. To the objection that it can lead
to sectarian attitudes a Brazilian bishop has replied. He has
exactly seven priests (so smiles at talk of a shortage of priests
in Germany), and is in process of renewing his whole diocese
with basic groups of lay people. His answer was: 'Wherever
we talk of Christ, he is there in the midst of us and keeps us
united. But if we do not come together, the devil insinuates
himself among us'. If lay people are expected to practise a new
asceticism of commitment to the parish, then priests are called
to a new asceticism based on renouncing their formerly undis-
puted power to rule. What E. Zeitler said of India has a wide
application to the Third Church: 'Without the massive involvement of lay people the Indian Church will never be equal to
the immense task which the future will bring. With a minimum
of Church structure, personnel and finance but with a body of
laity fully aware of its own apostolic mission, we could probably
obtain better results than the whole costly apparatus of the
Catholic missions of the last few centuries'. [4]

Those who believe in the guidance of the Church by the
Holy Spirit will remain confident. The lay movement will continue. As the Council of Trent renewed the Church principally
by reforming the clergy, so one day Vatican II will be said to
have effected a complementary renewal by emphasizing the
importance of the laity; for this has imparted new realism and
efficiency to the Church in the world of today and tomorrow.

   3. Lay people are called to actualize in their own particular
way the mission of the Church in its double function: of
evangelizing and sanctifying people as well as of penetrating
and purifying the temporal order with the spirit of the gospel. [5]
By keeping these two functions too much apart in temporal

---

[4] E. Zeitler, *Indiens zwischen gestern und morgen,* in *Priester und
   Mission,* 1972, p. 108; *Church in India today,* New Delhi, 1969,
   pp. 535-539.
[5] *Apost. actuos.,* 2; on the relation between the two function cf.
   above, ch. 5.B.3.b., p. 109f.

succession and subordinating one to the other in theological valuation we have damaged both. They should pervade one another. In general the primary task of lay people (this includes, of course, evangelization and the proclaiming of Christian salvation) consists in their commitment to the temporal good of society. The temporal order should not be seen as the 'world', in contradistinction from the 'Church', and merely as aid and presupposition for salvation. It has its own intrinsic value in relation to human dignity and, therein, a direct relation to Christ himself. Many good Christians who collaborate zealously in pious associations but stand aloof from nation building have thereby brought discredit on the Church. Many prominent people in the new nations have not fallen away from belief in God but have abandoned the Church and religious practice because the connection between their task in the world and the faith of the Church has not been made clear to them, because the two have in practice been made to appear separate. Religion remains significant in proportion as it takes seriously, at the present time, the value and dignity of man (including, also, his eternal life) and prompts religious men more than others to promote this value and dignity. If she fails to do this, the Church will continue to lose her function in the community and will in the end be reduced to a mere ghetto of pious worshippers. On the other hand, she has a real chance, with her bands of priests, catechists, sisters and lay people, of becoming the vanguard of the movement towards a better world. This is what will make her faith credible. [6]

The special contribution of lay people to renewal in the Church (here understood as opposed to the 'world') does not necessarily consist simply in running the traditional 'societies' and 'associations'; it is much more a matter of exercising a positive critical function within the Church, of creating a genuine living unity, of being more outgoing, and of making a more courageous effort to de-westernise their Church. In fulfilling this task and in deepening their faith, they will certainly always

[6] J. Blomjous, *Christians and human development in Africa,* in AFER 1972, pp. 189-200; J. Vérinand, *Eveil de la jeunesse cath. indienne à la dimension politique,* in SPIR 1972, 397-412; T. Filthaut, *Politische Erziehung aus dem Glauben,* Mainz, 1965.

need the priest who is called to preach and make present the kingdom of God in word and sacrament.

4. Long before Vatican II had brought about this openness to the laity, the mission territories had a class of layman who can be counted as true helpers and firm pillars of the mission: catechists. We could say a lot of good things about them. But just as mission has recently been given a new look, so must the catechist be given a new status and function. This is particularly true of two aspects of his work.

In the past, the catechist was the last link in the chain within the monarchical system of the missions: one bishop — one missionary — one catechist, and then below that the more or less passive congregation. He was paid by his leader, was accountable to him alone, and was his one and only representative at the outposts. His service was directed to pastoral concern for individuals; he concentrated on instructing catechumens, preparing Christians for each of the sacraments and admonishing the lost sheep. But in the Council's new perspective, there is more emphasis on the communitarian character of the Church. The primary task now is not to win over individuals but rather to build up a living community. So the catechist becomes in the first instance animator of the community, which he must bring together and steer towards living its own life. [7] But even that smacks of paternalism. He really ought to work in collaboration with the community's council and even become a member of it. Where possible, he should be chosen by the community and sent by them to school, then employed and managed by them, receiving his pay from the community rather than from the bishop. At this second stage, he has become employee and servant of the community. But even this corresponds only to a transitory phase in growth. His work must be organized so that he can help the community to become gradually more mature and capable of shouldering by itself his various tasks and functions; an official, paid catechist would then be superfluous

[7] A. Shorter — E. Kataza (ed.), Missionaries to yourselves, *African catechists today*, London, 1972; S. Cong. pro Gentium Evang., *Catechists in Africa, Asia and Oceania*, Rome, 1972; PMV-CI n. 36: *les catéchistes;* Mgr van de Couwelaert; various reports.

in that community. In this process, we have much to learn from the Protestant Churches. [8]

Alongside this renewal of the formal structures, there has been a rethinking of the material content of training (in Africa much more than in Asia). Most schools for catechists are now designed to cater for young married couples. Man and wife together receive theoretical and practical instruction in both religious and profane matters (hygiene, domestic economy, agriculture. . .). So they return to their villages as the nucleus of a new life and animators of integral development, thus working out their salvation.

As far as laybrothers are concerned, we cannot report any great progress, although teaching brothers are relatively in the best position. This vocation does not appear as a real fulfilment but as a substitute for a failed priestly vocation, a reaction to frustration. That is the measure of our failure to declericalize the Church and our failure to make the vocation to a religious order familiar to Christians. We are still looking for the real identity of the laybrother. We could best find it, perhaps, not so much in works of service at home as in full commitment to development work for the whole people: communities of brothers could be engaged in community projects, as qualified workers such as builders, gardeners, nurses, or also in academic callings, and in these situations could bear witness to their evangelical life. [9]

5. Nuns have been much more successful. They represent an enormous potential for the Third Church. In Latin America they number 123,000, in Africa 33,360 and in Asia 72,373. [10] They have not, of course, escaped the crisis which has had its sharpest impact in Latin America. An inquiry has shown that the average sister does not know her role and her task in society: because of her consequent insecurity and anxiety, she is in danger

---

[8] F. Lobinger, *Katechisten also Gemeinderleiter: Dauereinrichtung oder Ueberganslösung?* Münsterschwarzach, 1973.

[9] Cf. the '*Kasita-Erklärung*' of the Capuchin Brothers in Tanzania, in ITE, Olten, 1970, pp. 100-111.

[10] Secretary of State, *Annuario Statist. 1970*, pp. 175-180.

of making mistakes in carrying out her mission. This is, once again, a typical crisis of identity. [11]

The tension between institution and charisma is particularly clear and painful in the case of nuns. They could be a ferment in the Church and do marvellous work, but they feel so imprisoned in a traditional way of life of foreign inspiration that, as soon as they attain a certain degree of awareness, they find things unbearable. In Latin America, one in four of those who took vows between 1965 and 1968 had left their congregation by 1972. One reason was the too strict observance of foreign forms in a life controlled by foreigners. In the whole of Latin America, where now only 25% of the nuns are foreign born, 72% of the local superiors and 75% of the provincial superiors are from abroad. In Indonesia, of 97 Institutes only 9 have native provincial superiors. [12] In general there is everywhere, including Africa and Asia, a great lack of originality and local creativity. On this account, R. Hostie can say, in his study on the Religious Orders, that the life of religious orders and congregations has remained an affair of the west. [13]

It would be wrong to conclude that it is better not to introduce international orders and congregations but to found only diocesan congregations. The latter formula predominates in Africa, the former in Latin America and Asia. Local diocesan congregations run the risk of being completely at the mercy of the bishop, of being too little adapted to changing circumstances and of having to struggle with material difficulties; when they have the courage and initiative to overcome these difficulties, then they do become much more autonomous. The bigger international communities offer the advantage of a much wider horizon but they need to give responsibility as soon as possible to native members and allow them the necessary freedom to attempt new and original ways. [14]

[11] CLAR, *La religiosa, hoy, en America Latina,* Bogotà, 1972; PMV-NS 23.
[12] PMV-CI 1971/35, *Religieux indigènes et étrangers en Indonésie,* 30.
[13] Hostie, *Vie et mort des Ordres,* p. 288.
[14] Interview with Mgr Zoa, in AIF 23.2.1972; cf. also the review of the international union of Superior Generals, Rome.

A particular difficulty arises out of the vow of poverty. The sisters live in big houses, wear clean and tidy clothes, receive a good education and so pass, necessarily, as rich people. At the same time they can do nothing for their poor relatives because they have no money, on account of their poverty. They are embarassed by it and the people can give no credence to such poverty. We need to break open this introverted attitude and identify evangelical poverty with a total commitment to be on the side of the poor, as the concrete situation may demand. [15]

A possible form of renewal consists in withdrawing from our institutions such as schools and hospitals so as to be free for direct contacts in the Church and in the world. The experience of sisters working in state schools and hospitals shows that this can provide opportunities for new relationships and ways of exercising influence, which can also help the sisters in their understanding of themselves. In 1962, the Brazilian episcopal conference published an 'emergency plan' which included possibilities for entirely new activities for the sisters. In fact, in a few years many things have been changed. Sisters who before had been completely occupied in teaching now form apostolic groups with their pupils and regularly visit poor districts, prisons, etc. Others, who had formerly only worked as medical nurses, now regularly exercise pastoral care of the sick, their relatives and the medical personnel. Yet others, who had been working merely as housekeepers in the minor seminaries, have begun to take part in the teaching and also preach to the students. Finally, a good number of parishes lacking priests have been entrusted to sisters. One of these may act as catechist, another as medical sister and a third as social worker. Each evening they celebrate a liturgy of the word and then distribute communion to themselves and to the parishioners. A priest from another parish comes on Sundays for the Eucharistic celebration. It is generally recognized that such parishes are better served than parishes with priests. To sum up, it can be said that nuns in Brazil have moved from the individual approach to group work, from the narrow point of view of the congregation to wider understanding of problems in the Church, from

[15] U.I.S.G. (Fr. ed.), 1970, n. 18, 22f.

lamenting the burdens of the past to a great hope for the future. [16] There are, of course, bishops who will not give up the former good, reliable, 'cheap' service of sisters or who will not allow them to take up this new 'dangerous' work. This contributes to the identity crisis we have referred to.

A native congregation of sisters in Uganda, *Banyatereza,* at their general chapter 1968–70, decided to allow foundations which would be distant from the centre and deprived of the daily spiritual assistance of a priest, so that they could live close to the people and be content with the same sort of housing as other Africans, sharing with them all they have, especially the word of God. In the meantime, they have also taken charge of some parishes.

The Indian national centre for catechetics and liturgy at Bangalore has held special courses for nuns on their work in the villages. Occasionally one meets sisters who have shortened their hours of teaching so as to spend the afternoons in the villages; they admit that this work is much more satisfying than teaching all the time. There are others who devote their whole time to the villages, living in a modest house: they are 'sisters' in the fullest sense and 'mothers' to the villages. Where formerly they had lived in their own institution and worked as teachers *or* nurses, now they work in a way much more appropriate for women, in a comprehensive approach where they are *at one and the same time* nurses, teachers, social workers, catechists (if the circumstances require it) and generally good neighbours to each and every one of the villagers in all their cares and aspirations. [17] This new approach is very promising both for the sisters and for the villages.

---

[16] I. Bastos, *In Brasile: rinnovamento del lavoro delle Religiose,* in CM 1966, pp. 140-145.

[17] Conference of Religious, India, General Assembly, 1969, pp. 111-153.

Chapter 13

THE COUNCIL'S DISCOVERY:
THE LOCAL CHURCH

*He who has ears to hear, let him hear
what the Spirit is saying to the churches.*
(Rev. 2:7)

A. *Back to the local Church*

1. Guided by intuitive sympathy and always open to the
promptings of the Spirit, St Paul travelled throughout the eastern
Mediterranean trying to found autonomous local Churches everywhere. His method was to remain only a short time in a city until
he had won for Christ a band of disciples able to stand on their
own feet. He refrained from tutoring them for long, still more
from dominating them. He simply started them off, visited them
again perhaps or wrote them a letter. For the rest, he confidently
left them to develop on their own. The communities were autonomous financially too; they sponsored local charitable activities
out of their own resources and also showed great generosity
towards the mother Church in Jerusalem. In spite of the considerable distances between them, the local Churches were acquainted
with one another and cultivated a strong group-consciousness;
they sent greetings (1 Cor 16:19) and exchanged the apostle's
letters among themselves (Col 4:16) and, regardless of geographical separations, understood themselves to be the one Church of
the saints and the elect (Rom 1:7; 1 Cor 1:2; etc.). But because
of their autonomy they developed particular characteristics. Every
Church had its individuality, with good and less good traits. Each
had to listen to the Spirit, who spoke *to it* not in general and
uncompelling terms but in concrete praise and blame for its
individual achievements and behaviour (as is obvious in the seven

letters to the Churches in Rev. 2 and 3). Thus, each revealed something of the riches and fullness of God; only the sum of them enabled the crown to shine forth in its full glory. This principle of the local Church remained, more or less, the model of missionary activity for the first millennium.

2. The modern system of missions came with the Age of Discovery. By then the Christian west had developed its superiority complex, the Church was clericalized, and there was no longer any question of the local Church doing missionary work in its own territory, for all the pagans now lived far off beyond the seas. So mission was delegated to groups of travellers to distant lands: the missionaries. Given the spiritual environment of their upbringing, these could not be expected to show Paul's unlimited confidence in his young Christian communities. They were going to 'uncivilized savages' who would need, as they thought, permanent aid and guidance. So mission ceased to be a matter of short stay only; it became colonization. This was the origin of missions (in the plural) — stations with churches, schools and hospitals, with the white missionary at their head, Pope and emperor to the village, remaining there indefinitely as the prop and stay of the whole community. In the course of time the *ius commissionis* was instituted, i.e. the Holy See granted certain missionary societies certain territories and missions for which they took full responsibility. [1] This led to efficient division of labour but also accentuated mission's tendency to become a thing apart: in the motherland the mission was no longer the whole Church's business but the special affair of the missionary societies; in the mission territory what ought to have been the local Church was committed to the rule of a group of foreign missionaries and became a faceless, passive community, a kind of dependency of the mother Church, a scaled-down version of a European Church.

3. Vatican II took a great step forward with its theology of the Church or, to put it better, a step back towards an earlier situation: it went back over a thousand years' historical development and rediscovered its connection with the primitive Christian

[1] M. Clementi, in *Bibliografia Miss. 1968*, Rome, 1969, 273-280.

local Church. By its teaching on the collegiality of the bishops and the importance of the local Church, it set alongside the historical development towards centralism and enforced uniformity of thought the necessary complementary aspect of legitimate pluriformity in the Church. We now understand that 'Church' in the New Testament could mean either the Church as a whole (the aspect which has been over-emphasized in traditional Catholic theology) or the Church in a particular locality (over-emphasized by traditional Protestant theology). The two aspects are really complementary not contradictory. Neither can exist alone. The whole Church is present in the particular Church; the latter is a complete realization of the Church, since Christ and his Spirit are really present in it. But *koinonia*, fellowship with the other Churches in the universal Church, is a constitutive element of the particular Church. So universal Church and local Church are equally fundamental. The universal Church is a reality only in virtue of the particular Churches, and these are true Churches only through being in communion with one another. [2]

This theology of the local Church was integrated into the Council decree on the missions, although this occurred at the last moment. Quantitatively, it left its mark: the word 'local Church' appears 25 times in *Ad gentes*, against 5 times only in *Lumen gentium;* but it was not thought through with all its consequences and it did not at the time determine the general bearing of the document. Later, the juridical consequences were worked out in the *Relationes* of 24 February 1969 and the *ius commissionis* for all dioceses in mission territories was abolished. [3] The theological and pastoral consequences are very far reaching and only slowly making themselves clear. They will bring about a fundamental change in the pattern of the missions. The bishops' synod in 1974 made clear how seriously the bishops of the young Churches view the right to be local Church — always, it should be understood, within the unity of the universal Church.

[2] W. Kasper, *Glaube und Geschichte,* Mainz, 1970, pp. 276-280; Rahner - Ratzinger, *Episcopat und Primat,* Freiburg im B., 1961, p. 28; JEE 1971, n. 4: Theology of the local Church.

[3] *Bibl. Miss.* 1968, pp. 245-250 with comment.

B. *The missions are coming to an end*

1. As far as measurable results go, the missionary task is far from completed. The majority of Asians and even Africans do not profess Christianity. (Here, we may accept Barrett's observation that evangelization is more widespread than Christianization and note that, in Africa, 237 million persons (65%) have been evangelized.[4]) From the qualitative point of view, however, we can say that in the last twenty years not only has the theology of the local Church been developed but also in most countries the local Church has become a reality with a more or less numerous body of native Christians, with native priests and a native bishop. That creates entirely new conditions for a further advance in missionary work.

2. As the local Church comes into existence, there will necessarily be a certain tension with the missionaries. I would ascribe this not to racial differences but to a generation problem. As with growing children, young Churches must go through phases of 'contrariness', in order to acquire their own personalities. It is easy for missionaries to let their concern and sense of responsibility degenerate into paternalism; they can unconsciously fall prey to a 'mothering instinct'. The young Church can and must defend itself against this.

Three phases in this process can be distinguished. In the beginning, when there are no native priests or only a few isolated ones and the missionaries have everything under their control, there seems to be no tension, apart from a certain passive or active resistance. Naturally, even at this stage, it is as well to be attentive to spoken or unspoken criticism so that it may not break out in a more violent form later. In the intermediate stage, where the native clergy form a distinct group but are still in the minority, these easily get the impression that they are being oppressed by the missionaries and prevented from developing their personality. They may be expected to react to this sooner or later, in a more or less outspoken way. In the final stage, when native priests form a strong group

---

[4] Barrett, *Frontier Situations for Evangelization in Africa*, Nairobi, 1972, p. 23; cf. above, ch. 6.B.4, p. 133.

and occupy the key posts, the tension is relieved. They hold the responsibility now, but they recognize that missionaries are still needed and under certain conditions make them welcome in the country. [5]

The degree of tension depends on a number of factors. In one mission, where the 19 native priests form only 25% of the clergy but belonging to an intelligent tribe, have almost all been to Europe to complete their specialist studies and are treated as full partners by the missionaries, there is no experience of tension. But in Zaire, where the missions have always been strong, there is all too much mistrust, lack of co-operation and Chauvinism on both sides — so much so that in 1968 some even spoke of a 'cold war'. [6]

3. In any case, a profound psychological change is required of missionaries who work in a young nation, and a new missionary spirituality is demanded of those who work in a young local Church. They must shed the mentality of founders of the Church together with the accompanying lifelong privileges (even religious congregations face a similar problem and similar tensions in relations to founders who are still living); they must willingly accept a more modest role as second or third rank auxiliaries. The theory of Church foundation must be accepted even when it begins to strike home: mission must die that the Church may live. To begin to dismantle one's own position can easily cause a defeatist attitude in the missionary; but this should not be so. It is necessary to reflect that the main objective has been more or less attained, that the operation can be broken off without leaving a vacuum behind and that the territory is not being handed over to the enemy but rather to the young Church. So, it is quite right to speak of a planned withdrawal; the order, 'Backwards march' is given in full confidence.

When Pius XI consecrated the first six Chinese bishops in 1926, it caused a shock to many missionaries and some resistance. They thought the Chinese were not yet ready for such responsibility and the Church would suffer harm. The Pope wrote energetically to the missionary bishops and the next year

---

[5] W. Bühlmann, *Die Kapuzinermissionen heute. Eine analyse,* in NZM 1973, pp. 161-189, esp. 175-177.
[6] PMV-CI 1970/32, 51f.

Propaganda wrote to mission superiors that this consecration was by no means merely a diplomatic move to please China but was consonant with the fundamental nature of mission; nothing could be finer than for foreign missionaries and bishops to collaborate with Chinese bishops and priests in brotherly union for the spread of the gospel and the good of the country. [7] A similar change in attitudes was to come about in one country after another, as increasing numbers of native priests and bishops were ordained and consecrated.

4. Similar conclusions from the change of circumstances have been drawn in the secular field. The Pearson Report is wholly concerned with 'partnership in development'. In multi-lateral aid, the world organizations (FAO, WHO, etc.) are turning away from grandiose plans (worked out in the centres but not carried out on the ground) towards 'country projects' based on felt needs in the localities. The needy country itself decides what form these shall take, and foreign aid is restricted to interventions for specific purposes accepted on strict conditions. Aid personnel do not seek to impose themselves but make good, dynamic offers and seek to respond to the wishes of the country receiving aid by sending carefully chosen technicians and advisers who are capable of adapting themselves and maintaining good relations. [8] To act otherwise would be neo-colonialism and would sooner or later lead to sharp reactions.

In this matter, the children of light must not fall behind the children of this world. With tact and with the necessary sense of the realities of politics, we must avoid all danger of neo-colonialism in the Church. To be sure, missionaries (unlike foreign technicians) are full members of the local presbytery and have the same rights as native priests. [9] But the juridical point of view is not the one that matters. They need to be sensitive enough to realize that they are *not* equally representative

[7] AAS 1926, 303-307; Propaganda Fide, *Sylloge praecipuorum documentorum,* Rome, 1935, p. 278.
[8] *La funzione delle collettività italiane nei paesi africani,* in S. Foderaro, *Africa nuova,* Rome, 1971, pp. 483-485.
[9] *Presbyterorum Ordinis,* 7, 8, 19, 29; LG 28; *Christus Dominus,* 11, 15, 28.

of the local Church and that they must not impose their own opinion, even if it is a better one. If they sincerely and honestly take the lower place, then they can win the friendship of the native priests and may be entrusted with responsible posts. [10] In the first place, then, they must 'resign' unreservedly in the interest of the Church, so that they may continue to collaborate in the mission of this Church.

5. With the Churches handed over to Africans and Asians, the missionaries must be prepared to renounce their European perfectionism in schools, hospitals and in pastoral care. What use is it to dot the i's and cross the t's, if it makes one odious to people? The high standards of the mission, which often caused envy rather than admiration, must be adapted to the ordinary levels of the country so as to permit a general growth. The loss in perfection, efficiency and organization will be compensated for by other values which may have escaped us and will allow the gradual development of a genuine African or Asian Church.

No doubt there is danger that, under the pretext of promoting 'African and Asiatic solutions', a local Church will become isolated. Some bishops want to shelter their Churches from the new theology and refuse to be used as an experimental station for western ideas. It could be asked how far this is not a cover for conservative attitudes, for an ostrich head-in-the-sand policy which pretends that the new ideas and new problems do not exist. We should not forget that the Orthodox Churches have stagnated in many respects since the break with the western Church. The English-language pastoral review for Africa (AFER) has reported that the number of subscriptions has remained stationary at 2000 for five years, in spite of the growth of the Church. In dioceses where africanization is going ahead, the subscriptions have diminished. [11] This is not a satisfactory state of affairs. It is to be hoped that the virus of renewal has infected the young Churches sufficiently to ensure its effects

[10] Cf. B. Joinet, *I am a stranger in my Father's house. The insertion of the missionary into a local community*, in AFER 1972, pp. 244-254.

[11] AFER 1972, p. 1f.

will be felt in due course. It is also to be hoped that the young native clergy will avoid the danger of isolation either by their own efforts or by further sharing of ideas with missionaries and specialists from the west, on whom now falls the clear responsibility for maintaining links with the universal Church.

6. This suggests certain concrete steps that could be taken by the missionary institutes which have borne the heat of the day in building up the local Churches. In virtue of the *ius commissionis,* whole dioceses and even whole regions came to be entrusted to a single mission institute. Today, it is recognized that this can easily lead to a narrow, regimented view of the Church — although obviously it has worked to the advantage of the native clergy, who have found themselves contending with a number of small enclaves rather than one solid front. But even the enclaves could now be broken up by exchanges between the institutions. Bishop J. Blomjous has proposed that mission institutes should offer their services not to individual bishops but to a bishops' conference and thus be employed according to the needs of a whole country. [12] Thanks to the Union of major superiors, the traditional separatism is being overcome in some countries and the institutes are becoming much more integrated in the local Church as a whole.

Should missionaries live and work together in the same parish with native priests? In favour of a positive answer is the advantage of thus avoiding all appearance of racial separation in the Church and bringing together complementary qualities. Practical experience, however, especially in Africa, has suggested that the best solution is found in brotherly collaboration but separate living. The little details of daily life, in eating, working and recreation, reveal many little differences that create tension. Living in separate places makes it easier to share work on an equal basis. It remains a necessary condition of sharing that the missionaries should reduce their living standards, that money from abroad should be equally divided among the stations, so that there should not be two categories of parish, the poor ones served by native priests and the rich ones by the missionaries.

[12] J. Blomjous - T. Agostini, *Le missioni domani,* Bologna, 1972.

Mission institutes are increasingly acting on the principle of not taking back parishes which have once been handed over to native clergy. It not infrequently happens that after some years the standard has fallen so much that the bishop would like to have the missionaries back. The request must be courteously declined. Missionaries must not appear to be a 'Deus ex machina'. It is better to face up to the harsh facts of the matter. Under the pressure of such circumstances, the native Christians should react in harmony with the whole body of their clergy and find an 'African solution' in the best sense.

7. Many mission tacticians go further and propose not merely that missionaries should take second place but that there should be a real, planned withdrawal of missionaries. They recall the saying of the pragmatic Englishman: 'Get in, get on, get out'. They speak of a phasing out, a progressive disengagement, to provoke a stronger reaction and force the local Church to become autonomous. [13] They assert that the most urgently needed aid today is interruption of aid both in personnel and in finance; today's missionary task is to go home. [14] They believe that, if missionaries withdraw suddenly or over a short period, the local Church would suffer a shock at first and a certain recession but then it would recover and, by its own strength, initiative and responsibility, build up a Church adapted to the conditions of the country. At the Bangkok conference of the World Council of Churches in 1973, there was talk of a 'moratorium', a temporary withdrawal of foreign aid, although no decision was taken. There was mention of the well known Church of Simon Kimbangu in Zaire, which arose without any help from abroad and now numbers 3 to 4 million enthusiastic Christians.

I do not think we are entitled to subject our young Churches to such violent treatment. We may not so provoke the Holy

[13] R. Ageneau - D. Pryen, *Chemins de la Mission aujourd'hui*, Paris, 1972, pp. 162-164; id., *Un nouvel âge de la mission*, Paris, 1973, pp. 158-166; id., *Les Sociétés miss. face à aujourd'hui et demain*, in SPIR 1970, pp. 48-69.

[14] Boberg et. al. (ed.), *Mission in the '70s. What direction?*, Chicago, 1972, p. 113.

Spirit or present him with a *fait accompli*. He will see to it at the right time. But we should be very sensitive to the often unexpressed wishes of the local Church. For example, missionaries who cannot easily adapt to changing circumstances could be left at home on the occasion of a vacation. In India, between 1968 and 1970, the number of missionaries went down from 6420 to 4903. In certain African countries, mission superiors think that next year 50% of the missionaries will stay at home for psychological or political reasons. [15] In some places, it is made clear in negotiations with the bishop that missionaries are at the disposal of the diocese from one vacation to the next; the bishop must ask for them again each time, if he so wishes. This removes the suspicion that the missionaries wish to establish themselves definitively.

The rapid fall in missionary vocations and the consequent ageing of missionary personnel, [16] the intensification of political pressure which is expected in many countries (it seems that the expulsion of missionaries from China marked the beginning of a movement which will bring the modern missionary era to an end) — these new factors are providing the necessary impulse to get the local Churches to stand on their feet. It is suggested that in certain places, where missionaries have been expelled or their entry made difficult, native priests and bishops were behind the government. We must be ready for many surprises. In Burundi in 1971 they were saying: 'We have such a shortage of priests. Send us any missionaries who are expelled from any other country'. But after the revolt in 1972, when some mission superiors sent a letter of protest to the bishops who had remained silent, the readiness to accept missionaries suddenly diminished. Similarly in Uganda they were saying in 1972: 'Here there is very good collaboration between the government and the mission, between white and black. All missionaries are welcome'. A few months later, President Idi Amin carried out his threats and about 50 missionaries had to go. It was a great shock but it stirred the Church in Uganda to put in hand an over-all pastoral plan with generous arrangements for exchanges

[15] Ageneau, *op. cit.*, (*Nouvelle âge*), p. 146.
[16] *Op. cit.*, pp. 268-276.

between dioceses. In countries where the administration, army, police and the Protestant Churches are africanized, it is scarcely tolerable that the Catholic Church should go on being mainly supported by foreigners. In one way or another a solution must be found.

8. One thing is clear: the only purpose of the present-day missionary is to further the movement towards making the local Church autonomous as rapidly as possible. Here and there, missionaries are speaking of the possibility of becoming superfluous or of being expelled as if it were a remote eventuality. But even in countries with few native priests there is nothing that guarantees the missionary a long future. It would be a good thing at pastoral conferences to explore the hypothesis that one is to be expelled from the country in three years. What ought one to do in the interval? A superior once told me that they had just successfully resisted the nationalizing of the schools but that they would now have to reckon with the possibility of being expelled within three years. 'What are you doing in these three years?' — 'We are trying to hold our positions'. — 'If you are expelled in three years, those positions will be useless. Have you thought of giving each family a New Testament and teaching them to find support for their Christian lives from Holy Scripture?' — 'No, indeed not'.

When in 1960 John XXIII asked all the major superiors in USA and Canada to send 10% of their priests and sisters to Latin America, Ivan D. Illich organized open resistance so as to limit the harm that could have been done to the Church in South America by a massive invasion of foreign missionaries. [17] Later, less passionate partisans stressed that such helpers would be welcome only on condition that they were entirely prepared to fit in with the local Church and able to work creatively to arouse its sleeping energies; they must prepare leaders so as to make themselves superfluous within a certain period. [18]

[17] I.D. Illich, *Almosen und Folter. Verfehlter Fortschritt in Latein-amerika,* München, 1970, pp. 43-55.
[18] E. Pironio, *Invio di personale apostolico in Am. Lat.,* in *Apporto* 21-34.

9. All these considerations make it clear that we are coming to the end of the missions, that is, of those enterprises which were put into operation in certain definite territories fixed by the Holy See. [19] They have been a special concern of the Church for 500 years — waves of missionaries supported by missionary alms from western to southern and eastern countries, the dedication amounting to heroism on the part of so many priests and nuns who left their home country without asking when or whether they would see it again, taking greater risks than the astronauts of today...

This ideal of total self-giving, 'for life' as the Council recognizes, [20] this constancy which constitutes the strength of the mission (whereas modern industry has an annual staff turn-over of 30% which brings with it many disadvantages in costing and delays) — all this will now have to give way to a more flexible plan, for both political and theological reasons. From now on we must recognize an equally high and no less demanding ideal in total readiness and willingness to diminish so that he, the Lord, may increase.

Already in 1851, H. Venn, one of the greatest Protestant mission pioneers declared that the aim of mission consisted in founding a native Church. Then, euthanasia for the mission must follow and the missionary should go on to a region not yet evangelized. [21] Protestant missionaries have worked more rapidly than we to attain this end and have been dismissed more hurriedly by the native Churches. Now the hour has struck for the more tightly structured Catholic mission, the hour to die deliberately and, with the same confidence as St Paul, to leave the young Churches to themselves and to the Spirit of Jesus.

C. *Mission goes on*

1. Although the missions, in the traditional sense of movement from north to south, are coming to an end, mission

---

[19] AG 6.

[20] AG 24.

[21] P. Beyerhaus, *Die Selbständigkeit der jungen Kirchen als mission-arischen Problem*, Wuppertal, 1956, pp. 31-44, esp. 41.

goes on and must go on in a new form under the guidance of the local Church. If 'the pilgrim Church is missionary by nature',[22] then every particular Church, since it truly represents the universal Church, should share in the universal Church's mission to 'all who live in the same territory but do not believe in Christ so that, by the witness of the life of the individual Christian and of the whole community, she may be a sign directing them to Christ. With that witness, the ministry of the word is needed for the gospel to reach everyone'.[23] The drive towards evangelization is the measure of Christian maturity in all the baptized, not only those in the west. At the time of St Paul and again in the Age of Discovery, mission meant going beyond the frontiers of the homeland. But today, now that the local Church exists in most places, we need to appreciate the value of mission to the distant parts of our own country and to forgotten corners of our own diocese, without excluding mission to other countries wherever the political situation allows. It is never a matter simply of maintaining a presence in the little local Church but rather of establishing the historically renewed presence of this Church 'even to the ends of the earth'. The advance of the Church into the Christian 'no man's land' is always comparable to the outward progression from Jewish Christianity to a Christian community composed of baptized pagans which appeared to the early Church as something new and creative and was attributed to an initiative of the Holy Spirit.[24] The idea developed by Vatican II that the local Church *as well* ought to be missionary (a new idea, given that formerly mission seemed a monopoly of the western missionary) has in the meantime become the only possible basis of mission in many countries.

2. The image we have formed of the missionary as always a westerner, and of the local Church as the passive recipient of mission, will not be so readily done away with. Mission demands something beyond the simple law of survival: it implies

[22] AG 2.
[23] AG 20.
[24] Rahner (ed.), *Handbuch der Pastoraltheologie*, Freiburg in B., II/2, p. 58.

an ever renewed dynamism. Even the old western missionaries rank the risk of a certain parochialism, limiting themselves to the care of 3000 to 6000 Christians (or in north India of 30 to 60) and not concerning themselves about the other 20,000 non-Christians (or in north India the two million or more). Missionaries ought to entrust the care of Christians to the community as soon as possible and make themselves free for first-time preaching of the gospel elsewhere; otherwise, they are pouring water into a bottomless barrel or, to change the metaphor, they fall into a snare and the gospel is trapped with them instead of running free (cf. 2 Tim 2:9; 2 Thess 3:1). The two vital functions of the Church, the pastoral and the missionary, must not be seen as rivals or as alternatives; they are interdependent and should stimulate one another. Only a missionary Church is a renewed Church and a renewed Church is necessarily missionary. [25]

So far, mission Christians have developed very little missionary initiative. An inquiry among Indian Catholics shows that the vast majority remain loyal to their faith: 73% attend Sunday Mass regularly; 50% (in the south) say family prayers together, and here the traditional rosary is giving way gradually to Bible reading. But few are interested in spreading the faith. [26] There is a similar report on the South Cameroons, where only two of the numerous native priests have gone to the very extensive non-Christian northern territories as missionaries. [27]

A partial explanation of this can be found in the fact that non-Christian religions are, by their nature, religions of the tribe and the people. You belong to them by birth not by conversion, and they are not on offer to foreigners. [28] The missionary efforts of eastern religions are of recent date and have been prompted by the model of the Christian mission. [29] In virtue

[25] W. Bühlmann, *Die pastorale Funktion der Missionskirche*, in KMJ 1968, pp. 29-34; id., *Zwischen Mission und Pfarrei*, in NZM 1953, pp. 21-40.
[26] KM 1972, 38; cf. ch. 7.C.5, p. 164f.
[27] Ageneau, *op. cit.* (n. 15), p. 61.
[28] J.S. Mbiti, *African religions and philosophy*, London, 1969, p. 4.
[29] J. Beckmann, *Weltkirche und Weltreligionen*, Freiburg im B., 1960, pp. 18-37.

of its fundamental constitution, Christianity is the first supra-national universal religion. It has been missionary from the beginning, and has had to demand freedom of religion in the sense of freedom to preach and freedom to change religion.

People who come from these non-Christian environments must first of all be made familiar with this dynamic aspect of Christianity. One of the important functions still remaining to the 'classic' foreign missionary is precisely to promote understanding of this. Various countries, since the Council, have set about founding national mission seminaries to meet their responsibilities in this field. We have come to a turning point throughout the world. Paul VI expressed himself as follows in Uganda in 1969: 'From now on, you Africans are your own missionaries. . . It is true the help of fellow-workers from other lands is still necessary. Accept this help with love and respect. Know how to insert it into your own pastoral work'. [30] In 1972 Father Arrupe formulated it as follows to Jesuits in Douala: 'The first page of the story of the evangelization of Africa was written almost exclusively by non-Africans; the second page, present-day events, is written in collaboration; the third page, on the future, will be very largely written by Africans alone'. The same things can be said of Latin America and Asia. By a coincidence on a world scale, the fall in missionary vocations and the nationalistic reaction in the southern lands have happened precisely when the local Churches founded in all three southern continents have been awakened to consciousness of themselves and of their own mission or, at least, can be awakened by the new situation facing them.

D. *Unity in pluriformity*

1. The character of the local Church is not primarily determined by geography but rather by anthropology and morphology and thus by its make-up and its theology. The decisive element is not the place but the people with their legitimate national pride and their culture, who are brought

[30] AAS 1969, 575; cf. the declaration of the African bishops after the synod, 1974, in AIF 16.11.1974.

together to celebrate the Eucharist and to shape *their own* lives strengthened by the word and the bread of Christ.

In temporal matters, decolonization has been a necessary condition to enable these people to free themselves of their alienation in cultural matters and gain respect for their own identity. In church matters, too, there is a demand for greater administrative autonomy than in the western oriented mission era, so that the local Church may breathe more freely, structure itself according to the circumstances and not be simply an executive organ for the central organization. The demand is in the interest of the universal Church as well as that of the local Church since they interact on one another. Decentralization of the power of Rome in favour of the local Churches would free the Pope of an oppressive burden. Greater freedom for the particular Church in dealing with the concrete situation in the country would bring out the particular qualities and original contribution of each Church; through unity in diversity, it would create true universality.

2. The history of the missions certainly does not show a single line of development concerning the problem of adaptation, but rather swings from one extreme to the other, and shows up a great gap between theory and practice. The first Christian centuries found spontaneous pragmatic solutions in close relations with the environment. Very soon there were Syrian, Greek, Latin, Coptic, Armenian, Ethiopian and Indian Churches with their own liturgies, theology and administration (in the form of patriarchates).

Propaganda Fide strongly emphasized in the well known 1659 letter to the first vicars apostolic of Indochina that there was no question of those peoples having to change their rites, customs and usages as long as these were not clearly against faith or morals: 'What could be more absurd than to try to transplant France, Spain, Italy or some other part of Europe into China? It is not these that you have to introduce but the faith, which will never despise or violate the rites and usages of any people provided they are not perverse but instead intends to safeguard and strengthen them'. [31] But practice was seldom

[31] *Collectanea SCPF,* Rome, 1907, I, 42f.

in accordance with this directive, not only because of the national and cultural narrowmindedness of missionaries but also because of diametrically opposite decrees from Rome itself. The contradiction came to a head in the rites controversy which had an inglorious outcome, doing untold harm to the work of the missions. [32] The Latinizing of the Malabar Christians of the Syrian rite was another scandal in mission history. [33] It is a general complaint that, throughout history, the missions have done too much ritualizing, dogmatizing, centralizing instead of simply evangelizing, [34] and that India and other places have been made to import all the distortions of the west — the Church structures that derive from the Roman empire, the traces of medieval feudalism, the polemical attitudes of the Counter-Reformation and post-Tridentine ecclesiology. 'Where can one find the courage to detect the true face of the Church and her evangelical nature behind all these disguises and distortions?' [35]

We have already seen that two of the principal grounds of criticism directed against the missions have been the spurning of native culture and the resulting 'foreignness' of Christianity. [36]

3. From the time of Benedict XV, encyclicals on the missions have had many fine things to say in favour of adaptation but they have remained dead letters; at the most, a few isolated enthusiasts have spoken up for the native values and have been ridiculed for their pains. Only the wave of nationalism has succeeded here and there in effecting a change of mentality; for example, native church music is now taken for granted in many places.

Vatican II says it is by the working of divine providence that particular Churches 'while safeguarding the unity of faith and the constitution of the universal Church, enjoy their own liturgical usages, their own discipline, their own theological and

[32] LThK 8, 1322-1324.
[33] B. Griffiths, *Christ in India*, N.Y., 1966, p. 237.
[34] J. Dournes, *Au plus près des plus loin*, Paris, 1969, p. 168f.
[35] Amalorpavadas, *L'Inde à la recontre du Seigneur*, Paris, 1964, p. 315.
[36] Ch. 8.A., p. 170ff.

spiritual heritage'. [37] It knows of growing masses of mankind 'who form great communities, bound together by the enduring links of a shared culture, by ancient religious traditions and by the strong ties of social relationships and yet have scarcely heard the message of the gospel or not at all... In order that all these may be offered the mystery of salvation and the life that comes from God, the Church must insert herself into all these communities as part of the same drive by which Christ himself, through his incarnation, allowed himself to be bound by the social and cultural conditions of the people with whom he lived.' [38]

4. These words are the key to our problem. 'Adaptation' does not mean altering our prefabricated laws in some matters of secondary importance, allowing some small changes in the historically conditioned shape of the Church or admitting a few rites and hymns taken out of their former cultural setting to be transferred into the Church (rather as if one were to collect an alpine flower and transplant it into the garden at home where it will wither). On the contrary, it consists in implanting Christ's message in that cultural environment, in a new creation springing from that way of life, an *incarnation* within an existing way of life — just as Christ was a Jew in the fullest sense, in facial appearance, in speech, in dress and in religious behaviour, and yet was more than a Jew, and so was able to renew and fulfil Judaism from within. With the same divine daring, and with Christ's *kenosis*, the Church needs to enter into the culture and religion of other peoples, take flesh and shape within them and allow her own message the chance to start a history of its own in each people. Only this can bring to birth a genuine pluriformity, taking due account of the creativity of God and of men. The universal Church is thus built up not through uniformity but in *koinonia*, in the sharing of experience, in mutual help where necessary, in the unity of faith, hope and charity, in the one life of Christ. [39] The speeches of the African

[37] LG 23.
[38] AG 10.
[39] A. Congar, *Initiatives locales et normes universelles*, Rome, 1972; Amalorpavadas, *Theology of evangelisation in the Indian context*, Bangalore, 1971, p. 17f, 29f.

287

bishops at the 1974 synod on authenticity were significant in this connection. The real questions facing the Church today are not about renewing the minor orders, or about who may, exceptionally, distribute Holy Communion, or whether four or more Eucharistic prayers are permissible; the only real question is: What is the absolutely essential kernel of the gospel which must be proclaimed to the Third World, and what are the fundamental structures of the Church without which the Third Church would not be Church of Christ?

5. This way of looking at things will certainly meet with resistance. Many have an instinctive fear of the consequences. They are afraid of the vacuum they will have to go through, if they give up the traditional forms, until they find new forms. They see an abyss open up before them into which their little Christendom will fall: 'The outlook for the Church here in India is black. The Protestant Churches are getting more and more lost in Hinduism. Only the Catholic Church can resist and survive' — as if the only meaning of our presence there were to eke out an isolated existence, to feel secure under the protection of fixed, human forms and, at least, to survive. Others warn us of the danger of pluralism and regionalism, as if this was the beginning of schism: they insist on 'fully belonging to the Body of Christ'. Many Christians and bishops are still affected by the fear of, or at least the contempt for, heathenism injected into them in the past. In India, for example, it happens that the majority of Christians originate either from the out-castes or from the Thomas Christians, both of whom will have nothing to do with Hinduism.

This last is a typical example, repeated in other countries, of how difficult it is to diverge from the traditional lines. About twenty years ago, the Art Centre in Poona began to develop an Indian Church art; but most Christians, priests and bishops prefer western art, and usually the more sugary catechism pictures, Christmas cards and statues. It is an instinctive defence reaction against a 'return to Hinduism', however much this attitude is openly abandoned by the Church. Indian oil lamps in place of candles on the altar look like Hinduism to many people and are considered dangerous: to use them would be to abandon one's identity. Supporters of change understand that these outward things do not make the Christian identity: Christ and his apostles did not carry any distinctive marks of their identity but simply proclaimed a dynamic message. The more this inner dynamic is lacking, the more one grasps at outward forms. [40] But gradually young Christians and young priests are taking up the new attitudes, which was encouraged by the All India Seminar. [41]

6. But, alongside these objections based on theological and pastoral considerations, there is also the phenomenon of the unitary technical culture which is beginning to impose itself throughout the world. All cultures are conditioned by technology, much more than people usually realize. What is taken to be African culture was characteristic of European culture 2000 years ago. But as the latter was transformed by the industrial era, so also the former must be. It would be an anachronism to try to introduce into the Church values which are vanishing and which really belong to the museum.

Following Paul Ricoeur, we can put forward the following considerations in this connection: in the technical field, we can no longer avoid the trend towards uniformity, towards standardization on a world scale (motorway construction is technically the same in Africa and Asia as in Europe). Similarly, politics, economics, speculative business all tend to develop along lines common throughout the world. This development is irreversible, even if it does mean the sacrifice of many traditional values. But must people who want to become citizens of the world, and nations who want to enter the world community, pay the price of giving up their own personality? The danger of such a death, such a terrible impoverishment of the world, is as serious as the danger of nuclear destruction. The danger must not be allowed to become reality; all men of good will must co-operate in preventing it. Beyond and above the world of technology lie the original personality of each man and the creative kernel

[40] M.R. Lederle, *Art India: Christian paintings in Indian style,* in JEE 1972, pp. 274-284.
[41] *Church in India today,* All India Seminar 1969, New Delhi, 344-351.

of each culture. Both can change, but can nevertheless retain their identity. Consequently, entry into the unitary technical culture need not mean death but can mean a new creation, just as in the course of history cross-fertilization of cultures has always proved fruitful. We find ourselves in a kind of cultural interregnum. The old dogmatism, the conviction that one's own culture was superior, is no more. The scepticism aroused by the meeting with other cultures and religions has not yet been mastered. A new healthy self-awareness in men and in peoples and the creation of a new culture for tomorrow's world are still only a hope. [42]

7. The incarnational adaptation required of us is not so much concerned with external forms and with modifying them to fit in with world civilization as with inserting our message into the spiritual world of the day — hence, with a new theology associated with the local Church. This is the basis and key to any further adaptation.

Present theology is itself the product of a long history. Revelation, though always under God's guidance and planning, was subject to historical development and dependent on contingency. In the development from Old Testament to New, from the preaching of Jesus to preaching about Jesus, from letters of apostles to the Acts of the Apostles and Revelation, the writers of Sacred Scripture were not merely writing history but making history. They not only handed on the gospel message but they made it actual and existential to men: they preach Jesus Christ as *present* Lord. The different books of Scripture were very much bound up with circumstances of the time. The 'synoptic' evangelists did not copy one another: they interpreted the same themes anew and with new emphases for the particular public that each had in mind. So the New Testament writings are not so much an unchangeable 'doctrinal system' as a seed that grows, an impulse that maintains faith in Jesus Christ in a multiplicity of life situations and spiritual worlds and, hence, in a multiplicity of theologies. So, indeed, it happened in the period subsequent to Biblical revelation, in the transition to the theology

[42] P. Ricoeur, *Histoire et vérité*, Paris, 1964, pp. 286-300.

of the Fathers, to medieval thought and finally to modern theology. [43] There is, then, no such thing as a 'theologia perennis' (still less a 'philosophia perennis'), only an 'everlasting gospel'. [44]

If we start from this historical and dynamic view of theology, it proves quite easy — almost something to be taken for granted — to promote and develop a local theology for the Third Church. Until a short time ago these regions were simply consumers of western theology. An Indian Jesuit once said to me: 'We are not going to go on chewing over the medieval and European theology we were taught in the seminaries. That kind of teaching destroyed our self-confidence and all our creativity. They made us into parrots. Now we have learned to express ourselves, to create a theology to suit our own problems, that is to say, the reality of our 500 million non-Christians, the poor and hungry, those for whom Christ cannot be a dogmatic formula in Aristotelian Thomistic terminology but must be an answer to *their* problems. Our problems are not inter-communion with Protestants but how we can practise a *communio in sacris* with our Hindu friends, since that is the only genuine form of communication'.

The call for a Latin American, African and Asian theology ought not to provoke a storm today. The real danger is of resting content with justifying such theology instead of getting on with producing it. As we have already said, it is not a question of preserving ancient traditions and vindicating them. But still, the many national religious traditions which leave their stamp on the present, as well as the whole spirituality and problematic specific to the continent, must be the object of study. All this must be set against the message of the gospel and interpreted in the light of the gospel. That is the way of

[43] J. Müller, *Missionarische Anpassung als theologisches Prinzip,* Münster i. W., 1973; id., in ZMR, 1-24; Kasper, *Glaube und Geschichte,* pp. 49-66, 159-186; International Theological Commission: *Die einheit des Glaubens und der theologische Pluralismus,* Einsiedeln, 1973.

[44] H. Gollwitzer, in *Die Zukunft der Kirche und die Zukunft der Welt,* EKD, München, 1968, p. 71.

the future to provide firm rooting for theology in the Africa of today and tomorrow. [45]

Instead of giving details of original work in theology in the Third Church, [46] I prefer to make three recommendations:

a) Priests of the Third Church who do doctorates in theology at Rome or elsewhere, and who for some years now have generally been doing theses on practical subjects (instead of the juridical subjects which used to be normal), should publish their theses. They should keep the urge to write and publish books in this field. Too many have failed to publish their theses or have published a truncated edition that does not bring out the consequences for ecclesiology and pastoral theology. [47] Again too many of them go into full time work in some pastoral or administrative field or even in government employment. That represents a spiritual loss which should not be inflicted on the Church. It shows that the right priorities are not being observed in the use of money and personnel.

b) Local theology needs to be worked out in ecumenical co-operation with Protestants and even with non-Christians. We have much to offer one another and learn from one another; we should find the way together.

[45] H. Häselbarth, *Die Auferstehung der Toten in Africa*, Gütersloh, 1972, p. 210; A. Shorter, *African culture and the Christian Church*, London, 1973.

[46] A. Camps, *Coup d'oeil sur las théologie chrétienne non occidentale*, in *Bulletin Secretariatus pro non christianis*, Vatican, 1970/5, 69-79; W. Henkel, *Das Echo einheimischer Theologen auf das II Vat Konzil*, in NZM 1972, pp. 95-107. — For Latin America: C.P. Wagner, *Latin America Theology*, Michigan, 1970. — For Africa: H. Bürkle, *Theologie und Kirche in Afrika*, Stuttgart, 1968; J.S. Mbiti, *New Testament eschatology in an African background*, Oxford, 1971, pp. 185-191. — For Asia: Kaj Baago, *Library of Indian Christian Theology. A bibliography*, Madras, 1969; C. Michalson, *Japan, Theologie der Gegenwart*, Gütersloh.

[47] Z.B.V. Mulago, *L'Union vitale bantu et l'union vitale ecclésiale* (see my observations in NZM 1956, pp. 296-304; 1958, p. 308): the published edition of this thesis (*Un visage africain du christianisme*, 1965) has very much abbreviated the ecclesial aspect. J. Komba, *God and man* (my observations in NZM 1965, p. 75). The same must be said of F.A. Arinze, *Sacrifice in Ibo religion*, Ibadan Univ. Press, 1970; the whole catechetical aspect of the thesis was omitted when it was printed.

c) The bishops and Rome both need to be open with regard to this area of concern and must show confidence in their theologians. Rome cannot prescribe for Africa and Asia what form their specific theology is to take, since they have to bring to light treasures of truth that have long lain hidden and must be allowed to enrich the Church. The bishops' conference of China, Japan, Korea and Vietnam in 1971 appointed a commission to elaborate an 'Asiatic theology', a synthesis of Asiatic thought with Christian revelation.

8. The effects of a local theology will first become apparent in a liturgy related to the locality. Liturgy is not just the carrying out of a ritual. It is a sacred, public happening for this particular people and *this* local Church; it is an event, a celebration, a privileged meeting place where a people, with all its riches and all its concerns, its own personality and its own features, encounters Christ and praises the Father. [48] It is no accident that among all the documents of Vatican II it is the Constitution on the Liturgy (especially nn. 36-40) that has found the strongest echo in the theological journals of Africa and Asia. [49]

The translation of the Roman liturgy into various local languages was certainly a big step forward and brought the liturgy significantly closer to the people. But this cannot be the end of the road. The next stage is the introduction of new gestures and forms as, for example, bows instead of genuflection in Asia, handclapping instead of a simple 'Amen' in certain places in Africa, etc., and also native hymns with native musical accompaniment. Then could follow extensions to the entry-, offertory- and communion-processions and the creation of new Eucharistic prayers. [50] Sacred texts from other religions are beginning to be used, not in place of the readings but to complement the Old Testament, principally in para-liturgical

[48] F. Dournes, *L'offrande des peuples,* Paris, 1967; J. Dupuys, *Planning the liturgy tomorrow,* in CLM 1972, pp. 93-105.
[49] Especially its norms concerning adaptation to the characteristics and traditions of various peoples: nn. 36-40; cf. Henkel, *op. cit.* (n. 46), pp. 95-100; B. Luykx *Culte chrétienne en Afrique après Vatican II,* Immensee, 1974.
[50] See above, ch. 9.A.1.9, p. 184.

celebrations but also occasionally in the liturgy itself.[51] Thus, we are beginning to recover some of the spontaneity and genuine prayer forms of Africa and Asia, which the Catholic missions had stifled in favour of the recitation of formulas (common morning and evening prayer, rosary, acts of the theological virtues).[52] We ought not to entrench ourselves in fortresses of prayer: it is better to meet God in freedom and joy.

The adaptation of religious symbolism to the conditions of particular countries is already being discussed. For so long we have passively accepted much that is not authentic and even imported it into other lands: plaster that looks like wood and wood that looks like marble. Similarly, for 2000 years, we have considered bread and wine as the only conceivable matter for the Eucharist. In the new liturgy, they are presented as 'fruit of the earth and work of human hands', even in countries where wheat and vines are nowhere to be seen and where the matter must be brought along every time Mass is offered (often the wine has to be specially prepared from pressed grapes). So the climax of the Christian community festival has to depend on imported goods. In Africa, such inauthentic 'signs' are in danger of being interpreted as magic. Only water for baptism is, fortunately, present everywhere. Did Christ really intend that certain typical Mediterranean products, wine, bread, oil, should be used as the only possible sacramental signs everywhere? Hardly. He was less concerned with bread and wine in themselves than with the meal and the sharing, which in other places might be better and more convincingly realized with other matter. It is time to renew the language of symbolism and restore life to mummified symbols.[53]

---

[51] D.S. Amalorpavadas, *Efforts made in the R.C. Church towards indigenisation,* Bangalore, 1971, p. 36f.

[52] W. Bühlmann, *Aufgabe der Gebetserziehung im christlichen Afrika,* in NZM 1965, p. 303f; J. Baumgartner, *Afrikan. Stundengebet,* in NZM 1972, pp. 44-62; J. Komba *Die Frömmigkeit des heidnischen und christlichen Mngoni,* St Ottilien, 1953.

[53] R. Luneau, *Une eucharistie sans pain et vin?,* in SPIR 1972, 3-11; W. de Mahieu, *Anthropologie et théologie africaine,* in RCA 1970, pp. 378-387; Hastings, *Kirche und Mission im modernen Afrika,* Graz, 1969, p. 91.

9. Many with pastoral responsibilities are frightened by this prospect. They should recognize the presence of the Lord, saying: 'Fear not. It is I, who am always present, speaking through these signs of the times'. It is not a matter of throwing everything on the scrap heap. But the green light must be given to small groups who will take the new theology on non-Christian religions seriously and who will try out the new pastoral approach by setting up local liturgies, always under the control of the bishops. People must be prepared prudently, but not in anxious trepidation, for pluralism in theology and liturgy, and led to an understanding of the profound meaning of unity in pluriformity. So many things could develop gradually through contact with the reality of life, instead of being determined once for all in centralized offices. In the 30's, Guardini and others had experience of the new liturgy in small groups, found it full of meaning and practised it at their own risk. At the time, many asked what it was leading to. Thirty years later, the Council recognized the new direction and recommended it to the whole Church. So, there is hope for an African and an Asian liturgy. The matter is not without dangers and risks. But Seeber asks whether those at the centre of the Church who are so quick to point out the dangers of the new style are equally aware of the danger of compromising the true nature of Christianity through a narrow, legalistic style. [54]

10. As so often in history, it could happen that external forces and the temporal power will come to the support of ideas. The storm signals are already visible. The vigorous advance of the Independent Churches continues. They are creating an African (and Asian) theology and liturgy, although only in a fragmentary way. They are teaching us not just to build the Church *in* Africa but rather not to rest until we have built the Church *of* Africa. [55]

The negative reactions are not new. In 1706, the noble Dame Beatrice was condemned to the stake. She had for years

[54] D.A. Seeber, *Paul, Papst im Widerstreit*, Freiburg im B., 1972, p. 15.
[55] D. Calarco, *Africani in Africa. Movimenti che contestano il cristianesimo e le missioni*, in *Fede e Civiltà*, Parma, 1970, n. 4-5, 47-64; Mbiti, *op. cit.* (n. 46), p. 186; D.A. Barrett, *Schism and renewal in Africa*, Oxford, 1968, p. 169f.

enjoyed the reputation of being a prophet. Her wish was to unify the Congo with one Christian but Africanized religion, so that Africans could be themselves and so that there could be African Saints. She seems to have worked miracles and had mystical experiences and was regarded by the people as a Moses. Then she gave birth to an illegitimate child and this was taken as an excuse to get rid of her. G. Balandier compared her with Joan of Arc, the poet B. Dadie wrote a play about her and the Congolese R. Batsikama thought this prophetess should be raised to the altars. [56]

Alongside such reactions within the Churches, we also have the sudden appearance of heads of state like Mobutu, demanding radical authenticity in the Church. He gives orders for the overnight abolition of Christian baptismal names, because they are European. In itself the matter is harmless enough, [57] although it has caused harmful confusion through its unexpectedness, for in India, for example, it is twenty years since native names were introduced as baptismal names. But who knows what other changes will follow this decree? We might do well to remember the Chinese national Church and think of it as a precedent for Churches which could be entirely autonomous but could possibly be still in union with Rome. [58]

The times are interesting. Those who have experience believe that the Church has never has such a good opportunity to become Church of the peoples. But she should lay aside her western defensive armament and be ready for encounter, ready for incarnation in the world.

[56] T. Filesi, *Nazionalismo e religione nel Congo all'inizio del 1700*, Rome, 1972.
[57] W. Bühlmann, *Taufname und Taufpatron bei den missionchristen*, in NZM 1952, p. 1-20.
[58] Cf. 4.A.12, p. 76f.

Chapter 14

FAITH, MAGIC AND MYTH

> *Not following cleverly devised fables did*
> *we proclaim the power and the coming*
> *of our Lord, Jesus Christ* (2 Pet 1:16).

A. *The biblical and catechetical renewal*

1. Doubts about the faith, mockery of the faith and moral decadence are no new phenomena. St Peter already knew by experience that among the Christians there were some who, 'after escaping the corruption of this world through knowing our Lord and Saviour, Jesus Christ, have let themselves be entangled anew', 'sneering mockers' who say, 'Where now is the promise of his coming? From the time our fathers went to their rest, nothing has changed'. They 'blaspheme what they do not understand'. Their 'eyes are full of adulterous desires'. Countering such false prophets, the apostle has only to aver the exact opposite: 'We were made eye-witnesses of his glory'. Precisely because of this, Peter is authorised to proclaim the 'prophetic word entrusted' to him. [1]

Jesus Christ, 'his power and his coming' (2 Pet 1:16), 'whom the Lord has raised, who will raise us with him' (2 Cor 4:14; cf. Rom 10:9; 1 Thess 1:9-10 etc.). There, in short, is the essential content of the faith to which the apostles bore witness, for which they gained disciples in every city and for which they died full of hope.

2. In the course of history, especially since the time of the Counter-Reformation, the faith has become complicated and

---

[1] The whole of II Peter is on this theme.

abstract. Complete abandonment to the Father who has accepted us in Jesus Christ has been replaced in the catechism by a doctrinal system of 200 or more little questions and answers. Christ has become one truth among many others. Much could be said of how catechists in Africa and Asia, who often cannot read or write but know the necessary questions and answers by heart, drill their catechumens until they can say it like clockwork, how the children before baptism or first communion are assembled a week or a month previously at the mission station to be crammed daily, morning and evening, with catechism definitions, how they learn the names of all conceivable sins including those that cry to heaven for vengeance but do not perceive that Jesus, on the sea at Genesareth, taught differently. [2]

Is it any wonder that such initiation produces semi-Christians, who have indeed accepted Christianity outwardly but have merely superimposed it on their former style of life, without harmonizing the two. [3] The first Catechetical Study Week for all Africa at Katigondo in 1964 brought painful surprises to many; from all sides they heard of shortcomings in the former methods of religious instruction which have led many Christians to change their outlook rapidly on leaving school and finding themselves in the freer atmosphere that decolonization has brought. [4] Anyone perceptive ought to have been aware of the rumbling dissatisfaction felt by so many students overfed with insufficiently credible religion. [5] A report from a west African state sums it up as follows: 'If the Church lost the working classes in the 19th century, it is now, as far as we can see, losing the élite. We have daily experience that a practical atheism is taking over among the higher functionaries and those who are well placed. A system of mistresses is replac-

[2] D.S. Amalorpavadas, *L'Inde à la rencontre du Seigneur*, Paris, 1964, p. 284f; T. van Bijnen, *Krankheiten der Afrika-Mission*, in *Priester und Mission*, Aachen, 1971, pp. 239-242; Bühlmann, *Afrika gestern, heute, morgen*, Freiburg, 1960, pp. 73-92; B. Häring, *Teologia nella protesta*, Brescia, 1972, p. 156-169.

[3] H.W. Mobley, *The Ghanaian's image of the missionary*, Leiden, 1970, pp. 100-139.

[4] W. Bühlmann, *The present catechetical situation*, in AFER 1964, pp. 341-353.

[5] Thielicke, *So sah ich Afrika*, Gütersloh, 1971, p. 33f.

298

ing polygamy. There is still some attachment to certain rites: baptism of infants, first communion and Christian burial. But beyond that there is no Christian practice, no Christian attitudes, and no Christian influence on life, on personal responsibility or on the future of the country. The Church seems afraid of this élite and unprepared to contact and evangelize it'.

3. If the Third Church has been carried along in the wake of unsatisfactory European catechesis, the missionaries being children of their time, still she can reap the fruits of renewal in the mother Church. Comparing modern religious literature on Africa and Asia with that of yesterday is like passing from theory to experience, from lecturing to working groups, from abstract timeless considerations to the concrete approach favoured in Africa and Asia. In content, modern teaching has developed successively the kerygmatic, anthropological and political implications of revelation.

In place of a doctrinal system full of commandments, prohibitions and warnings we have the *kerygma*, the good news that must be proclaimed before all the world; this, despite all harsh earthly realities, fills us with unshakeable confidence because Christ has overcome the world, has given meaning even to an event like the crucifixion and has shown us a way of release. The world, to be sure, remains full of sinners, but they can now believe and hope even when they have painful experience of their entanglement in a sinful situation: they can believe and hope that sin is already overcome and death is defeated, although these things must be endured so that they may experience the victory in their own flesh. Taking our cue from the New Testament, we must no longer speak of men's sins without speaking at the same time, and more loudly, of God's grace and mercy. So we must not rest content with inveighing against drink, sex, the twist, hashish, prostitution and other prevalent modern trends; we must try to understand these phenomena in the light of 'cultural shock', and realize that overcoming them will take time. Above all, we must recognize in addicts and in others who fall by the wayside creatures who are ripe for God's great mercy.

In saying this, we have already entered on the anthropological field of concern. The Christian is no longer to be thought of as the perfect man but as one who has to progress gradually towards self-attainment and is still only on the way. He must be given time and encouraged. Moreover, the doctrine of the kingdom of God must be allowed to grow; it should not be crammed into children's heads with a complete pocket-edition theology. Even in the case of adults, the hierarchy of truths of which the Council spoke [6] must be taken seriously: in concentric circles around the nucleus of our faith, that is, Christ and our saving relationship with him, lie other truths which are of more or less importance according to the closeness of their proximity to the nucleus. Fundamentally, life in Christ should be less complicated. Karl Rahner goes even further: 'Taking part in the life of the Church, with its meetings and discussions, etc., often leaves a frightening impression of the mass of quite secondary things about which the Church is busy and agitated. One asks if all this is necessary to attain the one thing necessary: a little faith in the incomprehensible God, a little love towards God and the neighbour, a hope of being accepted in an earthly life lived unselfishly and, finally, acceptance of death when it comes. These and no others are the things that matter'. [7] Theologians are trying to produce a 'short formula of the faith' in which to express to modern men in a modern way the thing that is central and decisive. [8]

Very recently, the political aspect too of religious teaching has been developed, to counterbalance the marked emphasis on individual salvation characteristic of earlier teaching and bring man into a living relationship with his contemporary material situation, to reveal the intimate connection between salvation history and the history of man and to induce man to play his part in history.

4. Comparing the catechetical situation today with that of twenty years ago, we notice an encouraging degree of renewal.

[6] UR 11.

[7] Interview for the tenth anniversary of the opening of the Council in *Vaterland,* Lucerne, 28 Jan. 1972.

[8] Rahner, *On the demand for a 'short formula of the faith',* in *Concilium,* 1967, 202-207; Kasper, *Glaube und Geschichte,* Mainz, 1970, p. 159-189, 308, etc.

International congresses, national and continental study weeks, the Council with the chain reaction it started, institutes, reviews and catechetical schools have fundamentally altered the whole situation. The Third Church, with the help of the Second, has made a great effort and has proved itself capable of change. Of course, there are still shortcomings and always will be. There are still too many priests who 'worship their golden calf: money, office work and hearing confessions', [9] and still give their students the traditional scholastic exercises with introverted themes, as if Vatican II had said nothing about the guidance of young Christians.

But there is also an increasing number of priests with both feet firmly planted in the Church and the world of today, who are making a new approach to men, not without success. An Italian missionary in Peru gave me his impressions while on leave: 'Our experience in Peru is the opposite of what is happening here in Italy. Here, in the countryside, only the old frequent the sacraments. In Peru, it is beginning to be the young. When a priest takes trouble with young people and knows how to lead them to genuine Christianity, he can do much more with them than with traditional Christians. Even those who keep away from religious practice are approachable, since they retain a religious sense and are curiously interested in religion. That is why I am an optimist, even though the masses still slip through our hands'. The experience could be matched in many other countries and it confirms that in the three southern continents the tightly knit official Church of the nation will be replaced by a Church freely chosen, by a *diaspora* Church, with all that entails.

B. *Secularization*

1. Secularization is to be met with neither sympathy nor antipathy but simply with realism. It has itself arisen out of realism, freeing the world from an unreal superstructure of myth and the sacral. In his impotence, primitive man turned

[9] Mgr. Zoa, in Ageneau et al., *Chemins de la mission aujourd'hui*, Paris, 1972, p. 62.

to superior beings and looked to them for good weather, good harvests, good health and good fortune in everything. In the middle ages, culture, economy and politics were still considered bound up with this sacral order and thus came under ecclesiastical authority. This integralist exaggeration was followed by a swing to the other extreme, rejecting the interference of the sacred and restoring independence and autonomy to the world. Modern science and technology now master the world in a worldly way and, with Nietzche, leave heaven to sparrows and old women.

After a phase of negative reaction, theology has recognized the basic concern of secularization and even seen it as a product of Christian impulses. In its opposition to pagan belief in spirits and gods, Christianity brought about a de-divinization of the world, restoring to man and creation their own dignity. [10] In the Christian sense, secularization means freeing religion from ideology and from myth, not setting men free from religion. The latter is secularism, the denial of religion, and itself an ideology. We have every reason to free ourselves of many myths based on Bible imagery and on the medieval world view (accounts of creation and the fall, miracle stories, descriptions of hell, heaven and purgatory) and thus to get religion accepted by men of today. Science helps us in this, and that is cause for gratitude not indignation. With John A.T. Robinson, we can say that the dismantling process is being undertaken not in any destructive spirit but in order to unblock the source of the living water which had become stagnant under the old ruins. [11]

2. In the Third World, secularization is doubly welcome. Religion has caused wide-spread human degradation. In Latin America more than anywhere, with the possible exception of old Russia, Christianity has offered consolation to the masses with the hope of heaven but has left them in inhuman conditions. In Africa, belief in spirits, taboo and sorcery established a régime of fear. In Asia, religion promoted a caste mentality

[10] J.B. Metz, *Zur Theologie der Welt*, Mainz, 1969; A. Auer, in LThK 9, 253f; Kasper, *op. cit.* (n. 8), p. 80, 226f, 269, etc.; *Kirche für andere*, 10-14.

[11] J.A.T. Robinson, *Honest to God*, London, 1963.

made up of gloomy resignation, world-denying pessimism or else fiery fanaticism. Harvey Cox thinks that India's future depends on the progress of secularization, since nowhere else has religious thought done so much to hinder progress or caused so much bloodshed as between Hindus and Moslems. [12]

In the Third World missionaries have been a principal cause of secularization, not usually intentionally. They pilloried paganism and thus slashed a world picture, and in so doing endangered also the biblical world picture. It was quite surprising, thirty years ago, how often Africans in the schools raised critical questions like: Was the tree of good and evil a real tree? Did the first men marry their sisters? Was it Jesus who told us to give money to support the Church, or was it the Church? Is the fire of hell real fire? Was the star at Bethlehem a real star? — and others. We have no need to look for the explanation in outside influences from the modern world: all this is sufficiently accounted for by the chain reaction started by the destruction of their former world picture. [13] The frontal attack on 'paganism' was supported by the natural sciences: it could be seen under the microscope that microbes were the cause of disease, not evil spirits or evil men, and that good harvests were to be obtained by fertilizers and selected seeds, not by magical means.

3. If anyone thinks that secularization is a European matter and that Africa and Asia should be left in peace, he is deceiving himself. It has, in fact, made itself at home in developing countries much faster than expected. Decolonization engendered a general feeling of freedom even from many traditional values and links. Progressive industrialization and the struggle for a better life pushed religious attitudes into the background. The numerous students show an outspoken spirit of liberal criticism; they detect pharisaism behind various religious systems, having seen that 'faithful' Hindus, Moslems and even Christians exploit their brethren.

Although communists have already described Africans as 'incurably religious' and although, in fact, religion in Africa does

[12] Cox, *The secular city*, N.Y., 1965, p. 100f.
[13] W. Bühlmann, *Psychologisch-religionspädagogische Erwägungen über Fragen von Negerschülern*, in NZM 1951, pp. 220-229.

penetrate the whole of life, this has not prevented secularization from spreading rapidly even there.[14] In 1972 a seminar on secularization was organised in Kampala under the patronage of the Secretariat for non-believers; it came to the conclusion that bishops must take the phenomenon seriously.

The process is going on much faster in Asia. The scholar, C.J. Blecker forecast that men of the west could safely say to those of the east that 'our experience today will be yours tomorrow'; religion was being thrown into the melting pot all over the world, even in the east, since modern culture was rapidly spreading to the ends of the earth and was undermining religious traditions.[15] Others have confirmed this prediction, a posteriori.[16] I saw with my own eyes written on a wall in an Indian city: 'There is no God. Go and live in a district where there are no churches or temples'. The priest accompanying me thought 99% of the people disagreed. Will he be proved right? In India, apart from foreign anti-religious ideologies, there are anti-religious movements directed against Brahmanism, on social, political and racial grounds; their open struggle against the theocratic and hierarchical tendencies of the Hindu social order constitutes one of the most far-reaching threats to Hinduism in modern times.[17]

4. No tree grows right up to the sky, not even secularism. Science, which released the forces of secularization, became a giant but has grown small again. The more mysteries it has explained, the more problems it leaves still unsolved. The more it makes miracles superfluous, the more it must recognize its

[14] V. Neckebrouck, *L'Afrique Noire et la crise religieuse de l'Occident,* Tabora, Tanzania, 1970; P. Day, *Secularization and Africa,* in AFER 1972, pp. 332-336; G. Casiraghi, *Le nuove società afro-asiatiche: secolarizzazione e svilluppo,* Turin, 1973. On Africa 'incurably religious' see above, ch. 7.A.5, p. 152.

[15] C.J. Blecker, *Christ in modern Athens,* Leiden, 1965, p. 139.

[16] L.S. Nagae, *Sécularisation au Japon,* in EV 1970, pp. 43-53; E. Piryns *La sécularisation au Japon,* in NZM 1970, pp. 40-50; A. Fonseca, *Secularization and evangelization in India,* in CIM 1972, pp. 178-188; S. Kappen, *Indische Studenten in der Glaubenkrise,* in KM 1972, pp. 121-124.

[17] H.J. Klimkeit, *Antireligiöse Bewegung im modernen Südindien,* Bonn, 1971, pp. 59-125, 152.

own weakness. J. Fourastié, one of the founders of futurology, felt obliged to write an 'Open Letter to four thousand million men' to tell them that science is not everything, that purely scientific solutions and decisions are rare, that usually decisions have to be made with many factors still unknown; this means that human judgement comes into play, interpretations by people; and the future of religion, written off in the 19th century, is now bound up with the fact that the man of today has not found peace and security in science but on the contrary has become a great deal more uncertain about his destiny than traditional man ever was. [18]

So man comes back to mystery. Once he has rid his house, his Church and his brain of myths which have been unmasked as unscientific (as he must do without restraint), he creates new ones, more acceptable to modern times but myths all the same. For he experiences so many things in his life that he cannot explain. In daily experiences like love, duty, death, faithfulness, sin, injustice, violence, forgiveness and hope, he can never come to an end of questioning. Without myth, man is nothing but flesh and bones. So, demythologizing does not consist in abolishing myth but in recognizing myth as myth, in asking what it really means and what meaning it gives to our lives. Anyone who thinks he is 'scientifically' opposed to religion has fallen victim to an ideology, a pseudo-religion. [19] For the rest, this confirms what Blecker asserts after the passage quoted: all the indications suggest that our times, so heavy with threats, will give rise to purer religion.

5. We must, then, see secularization as an opportunity to be put to good use pastorally. Secularization is a state of transition.

In the first place, it must be said that we render a false service to catechists and theologians by protecting them against 'new ideas'. This can perhaps be done successfully during the years of study; but then these people come unprepared into contact with the relevant literature and with the secularized

[18] J. Fourastié, *Lettre ouverte à quatre milliards d'hommes,* Paris, 1970, p. 144.
[19] Klimkeit, *op. cit.* (n. 17), pp. 149-151.

world, and their crisis can be all the more violent and disastrous. Instead of taking up the cudgels against secularization it is far more important to implant a genuine, renewed religion in secularized life.

All this is true of Christians in general, not merely of seminarists. Fourastié adds to his forecast the warning that religion will need new structures. In the foreseeable future, the average man will have the same world view as a Nobel prize winner and religion will have to be reconcilable with such a world view. It must not be concentrated on 'holy' places and times, surrounding with piety only the culminating points of life, birth, marriage and death. It must rather provide men with right attitudes in the autonomous spheres of politics and economics, attitudes that will make those spheres more human, brotherly and Christian. In this way, the whole of life is to be 'sacralized' and the whole of creation made transparent to the presence of the mysterious God. [20] It is a tragedy that, for example, in Japan which is perhaps the most secularized country of all, the Church has failed to be with the people in this way; we have made it more difficult psychologically than it need have been for Japanese of good will to give their adherence. All the Church's external forms, structures and way of preaching are badly adapted to the thinking of this modern country. 'The time must come soon when a Japanese synod will declare: "It has seemed good to the Holy Spirit and to us to lay no other burden on you beyond these necessary rules..."' [21]

We must say here another word on the popular piety which is widespread throughout Latin America and India, finding expression in innumerable processions, pilgrimages, novenas, offerings of candles and other things to various saints for all the necessities of life. In India, St Anthony is venerated by Christians and non-Christians, although almost all they know of him is that he 'works miracles'. Here, Francis of Assisi could

---

[20] R. Guardini, *Das Ende der Neuzeit*, Würzburg, 1965, pp. 100-116; H. Mühlen, *Entsakralisierung. Ein epochales Schlagwort und seine Bedeutung für die Zukunft der christlichen Kirchen*, Paderborn, 1971; S. Kappen, *The future of christian education and christian education of the future*, in JEE 1973/13, pp. 57-65.

[21] J. Spae, quoted by B. Willecke, in NZM 1970, p. 264.

be the inspiration for a more genuine mission and could be a model of fraternity, poverty, closeness to nature and peace. He could become a spiritual leader alongside Ghandi. While the Christian remains, in principle, open to the miraculous, to what takes us by surprise and cannot be fitted into our categories even in a world which is more and more subject to calculation, yet he must not debase God and his saints into automatic miracle-machines. God is much closer to us and much further from us than we think. Further from us because he is the first cause, Lord of all creation, and not a second cause force to be brought into play at our behest. Closer to us because he is our source, and in him we live and move and have our being; he is God who foresees all and has revealed himself in Jesus Christ as the mystery of life and of the world. [22] Certainly, the subjective faith of these people must be treated with understanding. This kind of piety can be psychologically therapeutic, a 'hope pill' for those whose life is no more than bare survival, so long as no other treatment is available. [23] God can ensure that they too 'return home justified'. But the younger generation knows quite well that it does not fall to St Jude to find you a well paid job or to St Isidore to provide sun and rain, or only to the angels in heaven to protect the animals or to scapulars and medals to provide all guarantees. Our prayers and petitions should not be the end but only a beginning, to renew us before God and give us new courage in facing life. [24] Certainly in a land like India, where even the Hindus go to their temples and sometimes our churches to implore graces and wonders, and where salvation is thought of in terms of earthly blessings as in the Old Testament, it would be wrong to make a frontal attack on this piety. But these people must be prudently prepared for secularization and given the insights of modern theology. In a state like Kerala, teeming with miraculous shrines but with social deprivation that cries to heaven, we certainly must not (with an eye to money in the collecting box) encourage

[22] Metz, *op. cit.* (n. 10), p. 68.
[23] Hollenweger, *Christentum,* 517-532.
[24] K. Kunnumpuram, *Worship in a secular world,* in JEE 1972, pp. 454-464.

them to look for miracles. The bishops have, in fact, spoken of the value of popular piety in their synod.

A last most important point: we must concern ourselves, with courage and initiative, with secularized man. The strength of the Church must be demonstrated not just in her care of good Christians but also in her approach to doubters, those who stand aloof, the 'godless' who nevertheless have a certain nostalgia for God; we must show how she can be near them and give practical and understanding help. J. Paillard, who worked as a professor and as a journalist in Scandinavian countries, sought deliberate contact with atheists, and found them full of religious questions; he regrets that priests generally concern themselves only with the few practising Christians. [25] In the future we shall have to deal with increasing numbers of 'post-Christian Christians' in western countries; in southern countries we shall be dealing with 'post-pagan pagans', who have given up their traditional religions without passing through the Christian phase. That creates pre-suppositions entirely new to the traditional concept of mission. Many people will be much more approachable on a secular basis than they were under the shadow of their religion.

On a flight in India, I entered into conversation with my neighbour, as I usually do. He was a business man in his prime. After I had expressed interest in his work and introduced myself as a Catholic priest he began, without preamble, to open his heart: 'I was brought up in a Catholic school. But, as students, we had no interest in religion. We only thought of money, business, careers. Now I have come to the point where I see it is not enough. I feel an emptiness in myself and every new success, every new pleasure leaves me with a feeling of frustration. What am I to do?' he asked me, as helpless as a child. After I had explained that this feeling was a grace, I asked if he had a Bible at home. He said he kept a Bible alongside the Hindu books. I did not advise him to read a page a day, which might have become a mere routine. Instead, when he felt this emptiness he should open the New Testament somewhere, read a few lines and think that, through this ancient document, the

[25] J. Paillard, *Christ unter Atheisten,* Frankfurt, 1971.

living God was speaking a word *to him at this moment* in his life. 'I will begin this evening'. God alone knows how far this man is meeting salvation through reading scripture. We need such secularized men, who master their earthly interests by their own efforts but, beyond that, hunger for true salvation.

In the Church, we are watching the phenomenon of secularization with anxiety. But anxiety is unprofitable and cannot alter reality. Asia is a clear case in which secularization is an opportunity for us. After centuries of presence, the Church has still made no impact on the ways of Asia's great religions. Today, millions are dropping out of those ways and losing, thereby, the security they gained from their religion with its myths and taboos. But they cannot escape the real questions of life. Without a religious interpretation, life leads sooner or later to frustration or even to absolute meaninglessness. Yet never was the question of the meaning of life presented with such urgency as at present. If men in the Church have the sensitivity to appreciate the *kairos* for each man, to be close to him then and offer him not a religious system but the message that lights up the darkness, then there is much to hope for.

We know by experience how the Secretariat for Christian Unity, under the impulse of John XXIII, 'discovered' Protestants as genuine believers in Christ and, in the course of a few years, built up an entirely different attitude to them in the Catholic Church. The Secretariat for non-believers now has the duty and the opportunity to discover 'saints' among secularized men, even communists and hardened atheists, who commit themselves heroically to justice on earth; if not 'saints', then men who are spiritually impoverished, sinners and seekers after truth. This must lead to a corresponding change in our judgement of them. We must change our defensive, fearful attitude into human and Christian love and our polemics into dialogue and a frank exchange of views on life. Secularization could become an open door to evangelization in today's world.

Chapter 15

FAMILY LIFE

Be fruitful and multiply; fill the earth.

(Gen 1:28)

A. *Traditional family problems*

1. God's words are not empty words. They are the foundation of all reality. With the words 'Let there be . . .' the world was created. With the word 'Multiply' the primitive force of the instinct for procreation was constituted. Man was to fill the empty world, subjugate it and cultivate it. In the biblical view, the problem of families and children is essentially connected with the politics of population. Under-population is dangerous: the land goes wild and man cannot protect himself against wild animals and his enemies. Therefore Israel aspired to have families rich in children for the sake of strength: 'Like arrows in the hand of a warrior, so are the children of one's youth. Happy the man who has so filled his quiver' (Ps 127). In the New Testament, which makes more of the dignity of the individual, the personal relation between man and wife is brought more into the foreground and set in the light of the great mystery, the relation of Christ to his Church (Eph 5:32).

2. This great mystery, never fully attained but always to be striven for as an ideal, has been reduced in the course of history to a set of individual ethical norms, fixed in canon law. This with all its details and casuistic interpretations has been exported, in rigid and immutable form, to the Third Church, so different in historical and social background. So nowadays there we face the reproach that Confucius' ethics seem nearer to the gospel

than what we have brought them. A reaction against this trend has set in, both in the Third and in the Second Church. The sexual sphere used to be regarded as something foreign to the personality, an adversary continually overpowering it, with which one came to terms in marriage but almost with a bad conscience. Now sexuality is being rehabilitated and re-integrated in the centre of the personality. [1] There is a move away from the purely static concept which regards the natural law as a solid immutable petrified object in the middle of the stream of history; instead, its relativity is being recognized honestly and realistically, and consequently also its dynamic nature. [2] Moreover this dynamic can very well be related to the dynamic and the imperative which belong to the gospel. The Christian, then, is not expected to be a perfect man in the observance of all commandments right from the beginning; in Church discipline there are both minimum demands and ultimate goals. Within the scope of positive morality, various steps towards perfection can be distinguished: this does not imply any justification of settling for the lowest steps but rather an obligation to continue on the way of moral improvement. This 'morality of the way' sustains hope and prevents the dissolution of public morality and of Church discipline. [3]

3. The incidence and typology of family problems vary from continent to continent according to the type of marriage which prevails among non-Christians. In India, for instance, Christian marriage does not seem to throw up any special problems, since living together before marriage is unknown in Indian society, divorce is rare and polygamy is not practised except by Moslems. In Latin America, migration and economic insecurity have produced a climate of opinion where marriage is considered a custom for the richer classes, who alone can afford the elaborate ceremonies. These factors are responsible for the fact that, in this Catholic continent, Christian marriage is by no means taken

[1] Cf. von Gagern, *Das neue Gesicht der Ehe,* Lucerne-München, 1966.

[2] F.M. Podimattam, *Relativity of natural law in the renewal of moral theology,* Rome, 1969.

[3] A. Röper, *Objecktive und subjecktive Moral. Ein Gespräch mit K. Rahner,* Freiburg, 1971.

for granted and the percentage of illegitimate births varies from 17.3% in Chile to 73.9% in Panama. [4]

In what follows, I restrict the discussion to Africa, where the marriage situation is quite specific. It has roots in tribal tradition, so the Church is hard put to it to alter it. [5] (Here, we must make a distinction between the patriarchal, pastoral cultures, which are roughly in the same state as in India, and the matriarchal, peasant cultures, with which we are particularly concerned.) In many regions of Africa, only the young and the very old can receive the sacraments. The others are excluded, though loyal to the Christian faith, because they are living according to tribal morality. When I asked a missionary about his work, he said: 'My work consists in refusing the sacraments'. There seems no prospect of improving matters for the time being. On the contrary, while baptisms are increasing nearly everywhere, the tendency to avoid Christian marriage goes on. [6] Did Christ really wish the average Christian to be excluded from the sacramental life of the Church? Fifteen years ago, Bishop J. Taylor wrote that the Anglican Church in Uganda, where the majority of adult members are excluded permanently from the sacraments (according to his figures, 75% are not canonically married), constitutes a monstrosity, requiring serious re-consideration of the pre-suppositions. [7] The fact that none of the encyclicals on the missions and not even the conciliar decree make any mention of this marriage problem which is such a burden for the missionary is taken as a sign of clericalism in the Church. [8] Marriage is the first of the three M's — marriage, ministry, money — on which, according to Hastings, the renewal and the firm re-structuring of the African Church will largely depend in the coming decades. [9]

4. We have, generally speaking, isolated the sacrament of

[4] *Ehe und Familie in Lateinamerika*, in HK 1968, pp. 536-541.
[5] This is developed further in Bühlmann, *Afrika gestern, heute, morgen*, Freiburg, 1960, pp. 131-148.
[6] Cf. the recent study by A. Hastings, *Christian marriage in Africa*, London, 1973.
[7] J. Taylor, *Die Kirche in Buganda*, Stuttgart, 1966, pp. 191, 196 (The English edition dates from 1960).
[8] Hastings, *Kirche und Mission im modern Africa*, Graz, 1969, p. 219.

marriage too much from life and made it too absolute. Significantly, in many places only the bridal couple and the witnesses come to church, the others staying at home for the 'proper' tribal marriage and to celebrate the feast. For us, the event of the sacramental rite marks the moment when the unmarried state ends and the married state begins. In the tribe, a marriage is formed little by little. We used to think that only the sacrament constituted the true marriage; but now we find that this 'marriage with a ring' has in many cases become a mere European-style ceremony, that it does not correspond, in any unqualified sense, with what Christ meant by marriage, and that pagan marriage can just as well express love and trust between God and men. At all events, a marriage contracted according to tribal customs is, for an African, a valid marriage, while a Christian marriage which ignores all native customs is worthless. So, the question can legitimately be raised whether the canonical form of marriage could not be more adapted to local conditions. Instead of being a complementary event separated from the tribal ceremony, could it not be understood as recognizing and blessing a tribal marriage contracted among Christians? [10]

5. One of the thorniest questions, here, is that of trial marriages. A young groom, after paying part of the bridal price, lives in the bride's clan for three or four years and co-habits with her. He must prove he can work, treat the girl decently and respect his parents-in-law. They must prove they can have children. Finally, when the bride-price is fully paid, the marriage is completed. Even boys and girls who have been baptized in our schools find it very difficult to go against tribal morality in this, and Christian parents seldom put themselves out to exempt their children from proceeding step by step. In the traditional Catholic view, they all automatically become open sinners and, as such, to be excluded from the sacraments. What the tribe takes for a prudent precaution is, for Christians, branded as

[9] Hastings, in AFER 1971, p. 203.

[10] M. Bonvin, *Gospel and Haya marriage*, in AFER 1972, pp. 18-27; B. Ebben, *Church marriage versus traditional marriage*, in AFER 1972, pp. 213-266.

sin, and these young people must do without the sacraments during the decisive years of their lives. Is there really no way out of this canonical impasse?

At the end of the 60's, Vandenberghe and F.M. Lufuluabo sought to hammer out a new way ahead. They thought sacramental marriage, like traditional African marriage, could be realized in stages, as used to be the case with baptism. There is a basic difference between co-habitation under the control of the tribe and casual affairs such as occur elsewhere. Those who live in trial marriages never accuse themselves of it when later they go to confession, although they do accuse themselves of any relations with other persons. No one treats this regular co-habitation as sin, except priests. These candidates for marriage must surely intend, in principle, to contract marriage in the full Christian sense; it follows that they have the necessary dispositions for penance and communion. The sacraments, after all, are not rewards for the good but help for those who are struggling.[11] But the theological week in Kinshasa, 1970, took a step back towards the traditional attitude. For all their pastoral concern, they felt they must not abandon the ideal of Christian marriage. The sacraments have a social character: those Christians may be right with God but not with the Church as a community. The Church must uphold an ideal and can only give the sacraments to those who are ready to live up to the ideal.[12]

Häring has come back to the proposal of Vandenberghe and Lufuluabo and taken it further. On his tour of Africa, he supported the idea of a marriage-catechumenate. Young people would sign up with a catechist or priest, attend instruction on marriage and promise to marry in canonical form after three or four years. Then they could co-habit and receive the sacraments. In the course of generations, this period could be reduced and finally allowed to fall into disuse. This, of course, would not be the last word but we must try to make a breach in the

---

[11] D. Vandenberghe, *Contribution à la pastorale du mariage en Afrique,* in *Orientations Pastorales,* Kinshasa, 1968, pp. 221-254; F.M. Lufuluabo, *Mariage coutumier et mariage chrétien indissoluble,* Kinshansa, 1969; id., in RCA 1969, pp. 189-258.

[12] RCA 1971, pp. 199-201.

unhelpful juridical stance; we must present the Church not as a club for the righteous but as a living sign of the merciful God. Various bishops have accepted the proposal as a possible line of solution. [13]

6. Another moral question is posed by wide-spread polygamy. We have been mistaken, up to the present, in our easy condemnations of this institution as a sign of unbridled sexuality. A considerable number of African bishops were born in polygamous marriages. Cardinal Otunga of Kenya, after the Consistory in Rome, told press representative that his own father, as a high chief, had a hundred wives. Polygamy in Africa has an economic background. It replaces a system of men and women slaves working the land. It provides a respite for women, enabling them to nurse their children for two or three years in peace. It is also based on the law of inheritance: when a man dies, his brother has to take his widow with her children, so that they will find social acceptance (as in the Levirate law of the Old Testament).

Missionaries could do no other than oppose polygamy. They gained a triumph when in 1948 it was forbidden under pain of punishment in the Portuguese territories as well as in the Congo, at least in the townships. The law remained a dead letter. Such social arrangements are not overcome by legislation but only through new insights, new strength and new social conditions. [14] If attempts are now being made in theology to be fairer to polygamy and even to 'baptize' it as a possible form of marriage, this implies no approval of the sort of polygamy which is coming back into fashion among newly rich and instructed Christians or the system that encourages marital freedom and is really based solely on uncontrolled instinct and selfishness. The universal trend from polygamy to monogamy is not to be reversed. But when men in a polygamous situation encounter the gospel and wish to be baptized, serious questions arise. Must they abandon their second and third wives and expose them

[13] M. Doucette, *A marriage catechumenate*, in AFER 1972, pp. 108-118.

[14] T. Filesi, *L'istituto della famiglia nelle Costituzioni degli Stati africani*, Milan, 1969.

to mockery? Is this the way to promote the 'dignity of women'? Might it be the case that, by the Pauline and Petrine privileges, we have gained individuals for the Church but exposed the values of marital and human trust to ridicule? African Christians seem in agreement that the practice of the missionaries in this matter did not seem fair. When a polygamous chief came to be baptized, as an exceptional case, the Christians said to the missionary: 'The gospel reached him as he is. He cannot drive away the mothers of his children. You baptize people much worse than he is. He is a good man'. [15] Knowing that Levirate marriage was strongly urged in the Old Testament (Gen 38: 8-10; Deut 25: 5-10) and still practised in the time of Jesus and in the primitive Christian community in Jerusalem, we should meet such situations in Africa with more comprehension. For some years now, E. Hillman has been concerned with this problem. It is a sufficient recommendation for his work that Häring has written a foreword for his book and urged that his arguments should at least be attended to, and that Rahner has done the same for his Concilium article. [16]

For the rest, there remains the task of using these new insights and energies to good effect. Traditional societies can be satisfied with a relatively good image of man. The gospel brings higher demands. The modern world, too, insists that equality of all, without distinction between races, religions or sexes, is at the core of the rights of man. In spite of reactionary movements in certain regions, it may be said that polygamy belongs to the Africa of yesterday, not the Africa of tomorrow. In proportion as education becomes general it will disappear as an official institution, since girls will refuse to be a man's second or third wife. [17]

7. I will not go into the problem of divorce and its pastoral consequences, since it is not a problem specific to the Third

---

[15] B. Häring, *Incontri con la chiesa africana*, in *Rocca*, Assisi, 1973, p. 40f; id., *Une contestation missionaire de la morale chrétienne*, in SPIR 1969, pp. 150-157, esp. 154f.

[16] E. Hillman, in *Concilium* 1968/3; id., *Church and polygny*, Cincinnati - Ohio, 1973.

[17] Bühlmann, *op. cit.* (n. 5), pp. 145-148; E. Dirven, *La polygamie admise par la philosophie?*, in RCA 1972, pp. 49-73.

Church, though it remains a general problems. The social revolution of our time is causing an increasing number of marriages to fail, so that in both Second and Third Church it is felt that we should not rest content with preaching loyalty to the marriage bond but should also seek pastoral solutions for those who have made a shipwreck of their marriage. Even here, there is one element of the gospel to preach. The two approaches are not to be related to one another simply as 'rule' and 'exception' but much rather as 'uncompromising requirement' and 'penitential order for cases of sinful falling short'. The sacraments could be administered, under certain conditions, even where the dissolution of the subsequent marital bond proves impossible or socially unjust, when those concerned do what they can by their good will to make reparation for the injustice committed. [18] According to an inquiry among Catholic university students in Nigeria 82% were in favour of allowing the sacraments in such cases. [19] In the bishops' conference in Indonesia in 1971, 24 out of 30 bishops declared their sympathy for this type of practice (by an expression of opinion not an official vote). [20]

B. *Future family problems*

1. For former generations the family situation could be expressed in the words 'Fear of childlessness'. Faced with a high child mortality rate, tribal warfare and epidemics, the community set its sights no higher than survival; consequently, the main purpose of marriage was the procreation of children. In the course of a few decades, the problematic has been altered and can now be expressed as 'Fear of too many children'. Thanks to charitable work by the missions and systematic action by governments and international organizations, child mortality has been reduced and diseases like malaria, smallpox and sleeping sickness have been eliminated in wide areas of the Third World.

[18] F. Böckle, in HK 1972, pp. 69-73; id., *Sexualität, Ehe und Familie,* in *Vaterland,* Lucerne, 18 Dec. 1971.
[19] RCA 1972, p. 461.
[20] *Summary report Indonesian Bishops' Conference,* Djakarta, 1971, 7.

The result is that people no longer need be anxious to have children and instead have become anxious to avoid having them. Moreover, modern conditions give rise to greater demands, demands that can be satisfied only if one has fewer children. Often it is a simple choice between a child and a bicycle. So the primary purpose of marriage changes automatically: what now comes first is a harmonious partnership in the marriage relationship. When this is assured, responsible parenthood can be expected.

2. Rather as if the heart had been allowed to rule the head, medical technology has outstripped economic development. Because humanity, ever increasing in number, has not been provided with correspondingly increased food supplies and employment opportunities, the bright hopes aroused by better health are now overshadowed by the spectre of the population explosion. This is dashing all hopes in developing countries, where the fruits of the 'green revolution' are currently swallowed up by the growth of the population and where consequently poverty is no less acute than before. [21] For millennia, the world population grew very slowly, reaching 1,600 million in 1900; then came a rise to 2,500 in 1950 and now it is apparently taking off. As far as we can foresee the figures will be:

in 1970 3,600 million
in 1980 4,400 million
in 1990 5,400 million
in 2000 6,500 million

Of these, 6,500 million, 10% will be in Latin America, 12.6% in Africa, 58% in Asia. So 80.6% will live in the southern continents [22] and these, because of the explosion, will continue to be poor for some time to come.

3. No one suggests that we should allow mortality to increase again. So there is only one way open — to reduce fertility. World organizations and many governments propa-

[21] Gunnar, *Polit. Manifest,* 138-162.
[22] World Bank, *Trends* 1.3; Banque Mondiale, *Planification démographique,* 1972.

318

gandize systematically in favour of birth control. In small, over-populated Japan, where this cause was promoted by every possible means, a paradoxical situation has been reached: the population has altogether ceased to expand, and one of the new religions, Seicho No Ie, has collected two million signatures for a petition to induce the government to mount a campaign *against* limitation of births. [23]

The biggest nation in the world, China, is a model in the matter of birth control. It managed to bring a population growth of 4.6% in 1963 down to 1.3% in 1970. (The world rate stands at 2.1%, the developed countries having a lower rate and the poorer developing countries a higher rate.) This meant that the 1970 population of 698 millions was already 60 million below that predicted in 1953. Experts call the Chinese experiment the best family planning programme in the world. The success is attributed to the 'barefoot doctors', who correspond to the Health Officers of English-speaking developing countries and the *assistants médicaux* of the French-speaking countries; they have had a great influence because their training is geared to the country's needs and their dedication to duty immense. [24]

India, the second biggest nation, cannot show any comparable results even though the government organizes birth control propaganda throughout the cities and the countryside using wall displays and slogans, and has even given presents of transistors to encourage people to undergo the necessary operations (sterilization and vasectomy). It did succeed in reducing the birth rate but, with the child mortality rate also falling and life expectancy increasing, the population increase is still 12 to 15 millions a year. [25]

Many countries in Africa and Latin America have strong objections to birth control, as was apparent at the world congress on population at Bucharest in 1974. They presume that the intense propaganda coming from the industrialized nations conceals a fear lest the southern countries grow too strong numerically. The pill is interpreted as an instrument of imperia-

[23] PMV-CI 34/1970, 10.
[24] F.B., *Bevölkerungsbewegung und Geburtenkontrolle in China,* in *Neue Zürcher Zeitung,* 1972, (suppl. ed.), n. 278.
[25] *UN Statist. Yearbook 1972.*

lism; it is rejected in order that the nation may advance into the future as a mighty people. [26]

4. Everyone knows that the encyclical *Humanae vitae*, 1968, did not definitively settle the attitude of Catholic people to this question; quite the reverse! The prophetic function of the document is not denied. In a world that no longer recognizes any ultimate values, it has upheld an ideal and launched an appeal to us not to be satisfied with easy solutions but rather, with a creative will and united action, to seek solutions that correspond fully to human dignity. *Humanae vitae* must not be separated from *Populorum progressio*. Vatican circles point out that the earth is still far from over-populated; the areas of the earth's surface that are capable of cultivation could support ten times the present population, so Cassandra-like prophecies are not justified. [27] Moreover, it should be honestly admitted that the contraceptive methods held to be illicit by the encyclical have clinical and psychological side-effects which can be harmful.

On the other hand it should be said that, with the advance of medicine, these side-effects can be diminished or eliminated. Also, human nature being what it is, ideal development plans are only slowly realized and are little use to the millions who are now suffering want in their huts with their children. After all, it is not just a matter of surviving but of living lives worthy of human dignity.

The World Council of Churches meeting at Sofia in 1971 claimed that the right of parents freely to determine how many children to have must from now on be counted among the rights of man, alongside the right of children to physical, social and psychological health and to an environment that will allow them to develop fully as persons. In India, a bishop once explained to me that, thanks to the 'green revolution' there was no more hunger. An hour later, in another context, he said that there were 20,000 engineers and as many doctors without work, and altogether 25 million unemployed in the country.

[26] L. Stucki, *Kontinent im Aufbruch. Südamerika auf dem Weg ins 21 J.H.*, Bern, 1971, p. 57f.

[27] Cf. the contributions of S.P. Theisen and C. Clark at the Eucharistic Congress in Melbourne 1973, published in OR 14.3.1973.

What is the use of surviving in such conditions? In most developing countries, unemployment is the greatest plague and the first big disappointment for young people leaving school. The situation gets worse year by year, since the increase in jobs does not keep pace with the growth of the population.

As things stand, can we allow people to remain in deprivation for the sake of an ideal, and obstruct measures designed to change conditions which *must* be changed, and quickly and effectively too? When the emergency is passed, we can again stress the ideal. The situation is in danger of getting worse and the gap between rich and poor wider. It is already a fact that young educated couples have two to four children, while the uneducated, 'primitive' masses increase rapidly, as formerly. In the USA it has been shown statistically that the better educated women become, the fewer children they have. The situation has been expressed in the paradox: the intelligent get academic degrees, the industrious get stomach ulcers, the poor who lack spiritual calibre beget children; so in the end mankind will be reduced a flock of sick, limited and weak human beings who cannot exist without outside help. [28]

The Church could never approve of certain methods such as direct killing or compulsory sterilization. For ordinary preventative methods, there is need for more tolerance, no matter what theological ground the tolerance is based on: either the doctrine of the lesser evil, or the teaching that married life as a whole, not each individual act, must be related to the aim of procreation. The root and branch opposition which has so far been maintained against most contraceptive methods has already squandered the moral force needed to mount a really effective protest against abortion. In many countries the Church's mission of salvation has been compromised, in that questions that are marginal in the hierarchy of truths have been made distinctive marks of the Catholic community, and there has been more preaching against birth control than on the Blessed Trinity. [29] We read that the papal legate, at a press conference, during

[28] G. Schwab, *Der Tanz mit dem Teufel*, Hannover, 1958, p. 454f.
[29] On all this cf. A. McCormack, *Population explosion, a Christian concern*, Commission for International Justice and Peace, London, 1971.

the Eucharistic Congress at Melbourne, 1973, 'had very severe things' to say about those who expected a change in the Church's attitude on the question of limitation of births [30] — hardly a preaching of the good news!

In the western world, many episcopal conferences naturally stand by *Humanae vitae* but go beyond it in pastoral applications. [31] In the Third Church, with few exceptions, a clear lead is wanting. The Indonesian episcopal conference declared, in a letter to the clergy in 1968, that the final decision must be left to the individual conscience, and that parents who, in their desire to respond to their mutual love and not to overtax the strength of their families, might reach a decision out of line with the encyclical must not be burdened by the thought of being in a state of sin. [32] The Mexican conference let it be known in December 1972 that they had come to an agreement with the government that they would accept the various methods of birth control but remained totally opposed to abortion. In other places the bishops seem curiously unable to reconcile the concept of responsible parenthood, as recognized both in *Gaudium et spes* and in *Humanae vitae,* with its application in practice. [33] That the bishops of India, a country facing the most tragic population problem of all, could do nothing to make their position clear except send a telegram of thanks to the Holy Father must be accounted a sin of omission. The result is that no helpful or clear line is taken in Indian Catholic hospitals but all sorts of opinions are expressed: there is no problem in the matter, or there is a real problem but the methods approved by the Church do not help and so one does nothing about it, or the whole matter is in bad taste and one will have nothing to do with it. *In private,* the advice given is to follow your conscience and choose whichever method helps you best; preference ought to be given to methods approved by the Church, but then people should be left to exercise the freedom

[30] OR 19/20.2.1973.

[31] J. Horgan (ed.), *Humanae Vitae and the bishops,* Irish Univ. Press, 1972.

[32] SEDOS 73/390f.

[33] Cf. e.g., *Pastoral perspectives in Eastern Africa after Vatican II,* AMECEA (bishops' conf.), Nairobi, 1967, 98f.

of conscience recognized by the majority of theologians. James S. Tong, Director of the Association of Catholic hospitals in India, after going through this list of opinions, concludes: 'In any case, we must evaluate all these possibilities and anticipate all the difficulties which will arise in 35 years, when India will have double the present population'. [34] The All-India Seminar in 1969 drew up a list of the difficulties arising out of *Humanae vitae* which they intended to submit respectfully to the Holy Father: families which did not understand the rhythm method or with whom it did not work either had an intolerable burden or lived with a continual sense of guilt and dared not approach the sacraments; doctors and nurses and others who came into conflict with the directives of the government programme for family planning risked their careers; Catholics, as citizens of a country which has an official policy opposed to the encyclical, find their minority situation is aggravated; the fact that different episcopal conferences have given different interpretations to the encyclical causes difficulties of conscience. The Seminar sought a clear lead from the Church towards a solution which would allow their mission to be effective. [35]

The episcopal conference of the Far East, in its first assembly in 1973, added the following sentence to its conclusions: the Church ought to present a positive programme in regard to birth control, although she cannot but continue to protest most energetically against abortion. [36]

5. In all this it is not merely a question of tactical retreats or advances. We are concerned with inner attitudes, with new and wider perspectives. It has already been said that the strength of the Third Church should lie in being present everywhere, in collaborating with the people so as to make progress with 'grass-roots' projects, in preparing men's hearts and minds, and in animation. [37] It ought to be possible for the Church to play this role also in population problems and to take appro-

[34] National Hospital Convention, Delhi, 1972, 81-83.
[35] *Church in India today*, 263f, 394f.
[36] AIF 6.10.1973.
[37] Cf. above, esp. ch. 5.B.3.a.3, p. 107f.

priate initiatives. It is possible that voluntary limitation of births will become the norm for mankind in future. Should it not be the task of Christians to see that this norm expresses values, which still need formulating but which would be the true justification of the norm? [38]

This throws a new light on the family apostolate, which perhaps should be renamed 'education for parents'. Presumably, parents will continue to go to the sacraments and teach their children to pray. But beyond that, they need to learn to see into the heart of things and to master their family problems constructively, whether these are the traditional ones or ones not yet met with. Marriage will never be without its problems. But they should be approached both realistically and in the light of the gospel; one must try to resolve them as best one can or at least bear them courageously. So in exactly the same way as the great Church, these little churches, the families which Vatican II calls 'domestic churches', [39] must not be apart from the realities of life, not the Church apart from the world but churches *in* and *of* the world, declaring the message of hope to all who need hope.

[38] PMV-CI 1972/40: *L'explosion démographique et l'avenir de l'Eglise,* esp. 26.
[39] LG 11.

Chapter 16

THE SHOW-PIECE: OUR SCHOOLS

Go, make disciples of all nations.

(Mt 28:19)

1. These words of the Lord's have often been mistranslated as 'teach all nations' and used as a proof of the Church's right to have schools. But Christ had no intention of advising, still less of ordering, schools as institutions in his Church. He wanted all nations to contain disciples who would believe his gospel and make its light shine out. For this, schools are helpful but not essential. Certainly there is a derivative sense in which this text can be taken to justify the aims of the schools: they set out to make the teaching and deeper understanding of the faith an integral part of the educational process; they are meant to help illiterate peoples to make progress and thus also lay the foundations for a mature Church (this aspect was strongly emphasized by Fr Charles, a former teacher of missionology at Louvain); they try to bring real comfort and support to deprived peoples by not only teaching Christian love but also giving this practical demonstration of it. However, since Vatican II there is less talk of the *rights* of the Church in regard to schools than of the simple service which she is ready to offer. What we now have to do is not dig ourselves in to defend what we have but try to reconnoitre the true needs of the people we are meant to help.

2. Foreign experts as well as native politicians have been lavish in their praise of the educational achievements of the Church in the three southern continents, and the list of men who have risen to prominence through the mission schools is a

325

long one. In many places it was the missions that started the very first schools. In difficult conditions they quickly laid the foundations of a viable school system, in spite of opposition from European interest groups and indifference to begin with from the people themselves. Lord Hailey introduces a study of African schools with the words: 'It is impossible to give a fair picture of the development of schools without acknowledging a debt of gratitude to the pioneer work of the missions'; he adds the statistical note that as late as 1945, 96.4% of all school pupils in British Africa were in mission school. [1] Wherever you go in the three continents, bishops and mission superiors point with pride to really magnificent educational centres built up in recent decades, and to crowds of happy students and throngs of priests, lay brothers, sisters and lay people all dedicated to teaching.

At the beginning of 1971, Catholic schools had the following numbers of pupils: [2]

	Primary	Secondary	Tertiary
Africa	5,937,353	455,201	9,595
Latin America	8,298,573	5,406,129	826,939
Asia	3,299,162	2,173,829	484,880

It is not only the numbers that are impressive but also the quality of teaching, for examination results showed the church schools to be the best in the country.

A particular and yet typical case is that of India. Here, Catholic schools have 2.5 million pupils (ten years ago it was 1.4 million) with 70,000 teachers, of whom 2000 are priests, 1000 brothers and 14,000 sisters). [3] There is a paradox: while leading Hindus and Moslems do everything they can to get their sons and daughters into these schools, they attack the Church for her schools and hospitals, restrict her activity and condemn her for proselytism. Their public speeches (expressions

[1] Lord Hailey, *An African survey*, Oxford, 1957, pp. 1133-1135; cf. also Bühlmann, *Africa*, pp. 45-51.

[2] Secretary of State, *Annuario Statistico*, 1970, 245-250.

[3] CIM 1972, 396.

of their nationalist spirit) and their private transactions are clearly contradictory. A well-known writer and a Brahmin, Ka Na Subramanyam, detects something very unsavoury at the bottom of it all: according to him, the situation can only be understood in the light of the chicanery of the politicians, who are ready to cast aspersions on anyone and everyone to keep the fire off themselves. He contrasts the incomparable dedication of the missionaries with the empty words of the politicians, rejects the anti-Christian Nyogi Report of 1958 as unworthy and unjust, and thinks that if Hinduism can be saved only by such means it is not worth saving.[4]

3. In assessing the merits of the mission schools we must not indulge in the old triumphalism about them, any more than we need give way to the root-and-branch type of criticism which has become fashionable. But we cannot avoid realistic criticism, especially from the social point of view. For Africa, in particular, where all schooling was begun by the missions, there has been a whole series of studies investigating the social changes provoked by it.[5] The schools, without intending it, have gone beyond their original purpose (the service of the Church) and set in motion far-reaching social changes. They laid stress on personal achievement — by the individual who then becomes distinguishable from society at large, until then homogeneous — and consequently made vertical mobility possible, that is, upward mobility for the educated. They also encouraged horizontal mobility, that is, migration; this led to the disintegration of the primary groups (traditional society) and the forming of secondary groups (Church, state and vested interest groupings).[6] None of that is, in itself, altogether reprehensible, but some concomitant

---

[4] Ka Na Subramanyam, *The catholic community in India*, Macmillans, 1970, reviewed in CIM 1971, pp. 154-156.

[5] J. Egger, *Missionsschule und sozialer Wandel in Ostafrika*, Bielefeld, 1970; N.V. Zanolli, *Education toward development in Tanzania*, Basel, 1971; P.V. Dias - W. Küper - H. Weiland, *Die entwicklungspolitische Bedeutung des christlichen allegemeinbildenden Schulwesens in Afrika*, 3 vols., Freiburg im B., 1971; J.W. Hanson - G.W. Gibson, *African education and development. A selected and annotated bibliography*, Michigan State University, 1966.

[6] Esp. Egger, *op. cit.* (n. 5), p. 276f.

phenomena are: schools isolated from the life of the village and contributing nothing to the progress of the village, a rootless class of young men who refuse to work on the land and want only office jobs with no sweat or dirty hands, an élite selfishly concerned for its own private interests and with no thought for the progress of the people. [7] President Nyerere, among others, has done what he can to eliminate the unhelpful effects of schooling. He has tried to build up a school system which will no longer breed parasites but servants of the people, one that will no longer pursue European academic aims (the mania for qualifications, as if qualifications were more important than persons) but will rather teach the way to self-help — a way far more in tune with the African situation. [8]

In Latin America and Asia, where there was already a two class society, the advantages our schools offered accrued predominantly to the privileged class, because of the high fees charged. Those we educated later became unscrupulous businessmen, career hunters in politics and exploiters of the people. There is no virtue in the fact that our schools gained us recognition and sympathy in these circles. The All India Seminar did not mince its words: the purpose of Church schools cannot be to 'rear idolators of success and security' [9] who, if they cannot get all they want in their own country, go swarming to the west in order to do well for themselves. This is the context in which we must understand the violent attacks of an Ivan Illich, with his demand for the 'deschooling of society'. [10]

4. If our schools rear spongers, they turn out to be a counter-witness. It is true that 80% of the increase in numbers of African Christians is due to the elementary schools. [11] But there is another side to the coin: religion can be simply a school subject, something over and done with at the end of

[7] Esp. Zanolli, and also Myrdal, *Politisches Manifest,* 170-190.

[8] J.K. Nyerere, *Freedom and socialism,* Dar es Salaam, 1968, pp. 267-290: *Education for self-reliance.*

[9] *Church in India today,* 291.

[10] I. Illich, *Deschooling society,* N.Y., 1970; H. von Hentig, *Cuernavacca oder: Alternative zur Schule?* München, 1971.

[11] Bühlmann, *Afrika,* p. 47.

school. Moreover, a disproportionately large share of the mission effort has been tied down in the schools. In many instances missionaries have been 'only' teachers, exercising little direct religious or social influence on their pupils or their parents. Further, the mission has carried the whole burden — buildings, administration, discipline and tensions between teachers and pupils — and has looked more like a monstrosity than a bearer of good tidings. Father Monchanin left a much deeper impression by his simple presence and mystical poverty than all our schools in India. No wonder an identity crisis has broken out among young members of religious orders dedicated to teaching: they are looking for new, more direct and modest forms of apostolate and social activity, and wish to be trained accordingly. In some places, they would like to see a nationalizing of the schools: after decolonization a kind of de-schooling could follow. [12]

5. Before throwing everything overboard, the necessary reforms, thrown up by brain-storming sessions as well as by friendly discussion, must be implemented regardless of ties with the past; our eyes must be on the present and future needs of the country and the Church. It is no use painting gloomy pictures of hopeless situations and shedding tears over the ruins. The Christian should be remarkable for always looking ahead and trying to make the best of every fresh opportunity offered.

In Africa, we must conquer our obsession with schooling (which some call 'school fetishism') and use our imaginations creatively to thrash out new ways of gradually improving the lot of the whole village community. [13]

In Asia, we must exploit the opening already achieved and, alongside the school, build up systematic contacts with the villages. We ought to decide once and for all not to build any more secondary schools. Knowing that in 1969 there were five

[12] Cf. e.g., the special number of JEE 1973, n. 13; further, the discussion in O.I.E.C., *L'enseignement catholique dans le monde et son rôle dans le développement*, Brussels, 1968.
[13] Cf. the interview with Archbishop Zoa of the Cameroons, in *La Croix*, Paris, 11.4.1971; cf. the community work described above, ch. 5.B., p. 106ff.

million unemployed with school education and, in 1974, ten million, [14] only the purblind would go on opening more high schools. But who has the courage to give a clear directive here? People who do not want to be awakened from their illusions seek education for their children and representatives of the Church increase the number of places in the schools — with a smile of satisfaction because it brings in the money. Any discussion of the matter comes up against a brick wall: emotional considerations are stronger than reason.

In Latin America, thanks to the influence of Medellin and of the Jesuit General Father Arrupe's message in 1968, a considerable change has already been accomplished. The sons and daughters of the rich oligarchy are no longer tacitly encouraged in their individual ambitions; instead the schools try to inculcate an attitude of service towards those who are on the margins of society, and places in the schools are reserved for such people. [15]

Christian schools everywhere must get rid of their excessively academic character and outlook and be more concerned to promote religious and social conscience formation. If Paulo Freire through his literacy courses can fill young people in Brazil and in the liberated territories of Portuguese Africa with the spirit of sacrifice, dedication to the people and the will to work, [16] and if experts from communist countries can achieve similar results in the Third World with slogans, rhythmical exercises and songs, then clearly the Church cannot just carry on placidly with her present school system.

6. The extent to which the Christian schools, through reforms such as these, become what they ought to be will determine the Church's right to take up a clearly defined position with regard to the nationalization of schools now threatened everywhere. Since the Church's heroic resistance in South Africa in 1956-57, there is a tendency towards becoming resigned. One state after another has nationalized the schools,

[14] A.J. Fonseca (ed.), *Challenge of poverty in India,* Delhi, 1971.

[15] G. Adler, *Revolutionäres Lateinamerika. Eine dok.,* Paderborn, 1970, 91-98.

[16] P. Freire, *Educaçao e conscientizaçao, Cuernavaca,* 1968.

without regard to the Church's wishes. Between the two extreme situations, one where the mission is not allowed to set foot again in the schools they built and the other where the teaching brothers and sisters continue as paid employees of the state and religious education is provided for, there are many intermediate positions. It is only a matter of time before the other states take the step of nationalization. An inquiry among Capuchin missions in the three southern continents has shown that

in 23 cases, the mission schools received some support from the state,

in 9 cases, they received no support,

in 10 cases, they were nationalized.

Of the 32 not yet nationalized, early nationalization

in 17 cases was thought probable,

in 9 cases was thought improbable;

in 6 cases, no answer was possible. [17]

The trend, therefore, has been and is away from a position of isolation, in which the mission alone built up a school system with great sacrifices, and towards co-operation, in which the state is ready to compensate the mission with subsidy, leading inevitably to ever greater dependence on the state and finally to total integration. State intervention is not necessarily meant as an attack on the Church as such. It is more of a reaction against anything that offends national feeling, that appears as a state within the state or promotes inequality of opportunity between rich and poor.

The Church should not obstinately defend her position but should rather offer the best possible service. She should seek to enter into loyal dialogue with the state, in an attitude of give and take. Some schools at least should be retained if possible, so that the Church may still have a voice in the field of education. We should stand firm about facilities for teaching religion in the state schools and support the right of parents to have the types of schools which meet their wishes. There

[17] Bühlmann, *Die Kapuzinermissionen heute. Eine analyse,* in NZM 1973, pp. 161-189, esp. 171f.

certainly ought to be a certain pluralism in education, because a genuinely pluralistic state can only exist when there are various ideological communities. Otherwise, we arrive at the monolithic state and dictatorship. In seeking this objective, the bishops should not enter the arena, still less the nuncio (it has been known for nuncios to try to hold certain positions against the will of the bishops, and to negotiate directly with the government). The hierarchy should certainly demand religious education; but the shape of the educational system is a matter for the whole Christian community, which should make its voice heard through representative laymen. Where the community is not mature enough for this (through deficiencies in the methods of former missionaries) or where the Church's good offices are at present neither recognized nor requested, we must 'shake off the dust that is on our feet' (Mk 6:11) and wait for better times.

It has been said that nationalization of the schools is the worst blow suffered by the missions since the 19th century, [18] but I cannot bring myself to subscribe to this without qualification. Experience has shown that, after the first shock, the Churches generally recover and manage to ensure Christian education by other means; they thereby gain in interior dynamism and now speak of it all as a providential liberation. [19]

7. The question remains: 'What are we to do after the schools are nationalized?' The loss of the schools should not lead to paralysis but should be a challenge. Just as once it was the mission schools that responded to a real need and were a visible sign of Christ's care for all men — and one cannot but admire the courage of the pioneers — so now we have to ask ourselves how Christ's importance to all men here and now can be made clear. Every age calls for a new response.

First and foremost there is the enormous task of regaining the youngsters who have left school. The saying goes that he who has the young has the future. But the saying becomes a gross

[18] Prof. Ayandale at the missionary congress in Driebergen, 1972.
[19] T. Balasuriya, *The Ceylonese experience,* in JEE 1973, n. 13, pp. 82-95.

self-deception if nothing is done for them after they leave school. The real problem begins then, and so far the Church has done much too little. In all developing countries, the situation of primary school-leavers amounts to a national tragedy. [20] The Church rightly does not want to give up external activities; otherwise she would be gradually reduced to a purely spiritual congregation without flesh. For this precise reason, it is necessary not to remain attached to the former school system. We must seize on the tasks that have been neglected. There is plenty of room for new initiatives: agricultural schools, technical schools (but not equipped with all the latest machinery, rather with the sort of tools that will be used in the villages), schools of domestic economy (not with electric ovens and all the refinements of European cooking), leisure activities, reading rooms, advice centres, schools for the blind and handicapped, the animation of self-help projects. Such initiatives would probably be very acceptable to the state as well. With some of the best potential released from the schools, we should also undertake to work among overseas students at western universities.

Apart from the young, we need to educate adults to understand the religious and social mission of the Christian. The transition from the Christian village and the closed Christian community to the 'world' is in full swing, and this calls for adequate training and formation for convinced Christians. It would be a betrayal of our predecessors in missionary work, who preached the gospel and founded local Churches, not to make sure that the Christians they baptized can remain Christian even now and be the light of the world of today.

Adult education in the sense of elementary instruction and state-sponsored literacy drives is an immense field in which there is a dearth of workers. In India, the intention is to reduce the 150 million between the ages of 15 and 25 who cannot read or write to 50 million in the course of ten years. Missionaries are not co-operating much in this and many do not even know the drive is on. [21]

---

[20] W. Küper, *op. cit.* (n. 5), II, p. 351, speaking of Tanzania; his words apply to other countries as well.

[21] G. Bellucci, *L'educazione degli adulti in India,* Milan, 1973.

Another enormous field that lies open before us is that of social communications. As we once invested the greater part of our money and the best of our resources in the schools, we now need to do likewise for these new means of preaching and of popular education. [22] Being relieved of our schools could provide us with the opportunity to exploit these new opportunities.

[22] See below, ch. 18.

Chapter 17

THE PERMANENT WITNESS OF CHARITY

Go and do likewise (Lk 10:37).

1. The Christian conscience has been stirred less by the Johannine theology of the new commandment — as a mark of Christ's disciples and of the dynamic unity of love between Father and Son, between the Son and Christians and between Christian among themselves (John, chapters 14 to 16) — than by the concrete models of love in Luke: the frightening example of Dives the glutton (Lk 16:19-31) and the encouraging example of the compassionate Samaritan (Lk 10:25-37). It is interesting to note the character contrasts in the second parable: on one side a priest and a Levite, both official ministers of the cult who, given their office, ought to be exemplary but are not; on the other side a Samaritan, a heretic worse than a pagan, who 'in himself' cannot be pleasing to God. It is the ministers who go wrong because of their cultic piety remote from the world, and the Samaritan who does what the circumstances demand. He pleases God by his love of the neighbour, because thereby he demonstrates the love of God at work. Finally, the parable addresses all hearers: 'Go and do likewise'.

2. Before speaking of institutionalized charity, we must put love in the foreground as the fundamental Christian attitude. It finds charismatic expression in the thirteenth chapter of First Corinthians and a modern expression in n. 8 of the Council Decree on the lay apostolate.

Recently we have become more honest and prudent about comparing Christian with non-Christian love. In the old Africa, morality was indeed tribe-centred, and strangers were not treated in the same way as members of the tribe. It is true that in

335

Hinduism the no-caste were left to their fate, and the poor and aged in the streets had a blind eye turned to them until Mother Teresa and her sisters took them home 'so that we may experience a little human love before we die'. It is true the rich oil sheiks do very little for the poor, and for prestige reasons some governments will refuse help from other countries in emergencies. But then we must honestly add that in Europe there is prejudice against migrant workers and that 'Christian' capitalists can be very hard with their fellow men; that many Christians, far from being Mother Teresa, pass the poor by without so much as a glance, and that the non-Christian religions can provide examples of love and dedication as genuine as any of ours. What is specific to Christianity is not something tangible; it is the coming of the kingdom of God and the fresh impulse released by the expectation of the kingdom.

3. For love to be really effective in the complex modern world, it must be organized. If development aid is not to be based on rivalry but is to be one aspect and one necessary expression of preaching, this is all the more true of charity and the activities of the various charitable organizations. In Christ's case, there was no opposition between his preaching and his curing of the sick; they confirmed and strengthened one another.

Since it is recommended, in this service of love, that 'the left hand should not know what the right is doing' (Mt 6:3), I will not give statistics on the charitable work of the Church. (Unfortunately, too many schools and hospitals have engraved on their walls the names of western institutions which have given financial aid.) Everyone knows how much the sisters have achieved by their never-ending hospital work. As one example out of many, I quote the words of President Nyerere, in 1965, at the opening of the new leprosy hospital in Mtwara: 'The opening of this new leprosarium is very much to be welcomed. For a long time there has been a centre for leprosy patients in this area, but it is Sister Lia Schwartmüller who is really responsible for the present fine development. Sister Lia came to this area in 1952 and for twelve years worked with the patients, helping them with what facilities she could find, and at the same time raising money in Europe for the extension.

During that whole time Sister took no home leave, and worked without thought for herself until last year she suffered a stroke and a heart attack. Her devotion to our service is an example to every citizen of this country and I am happy that she is with us today'. [1]

Besides such continuing work, occasional disaster work is still needed. This tragic world continues to provide us with floods, droughts and earthquakes, and people remain dependent on one another. It is astonishing how regularly Church organizations and others are on the spot in times of catastrophe, and one hopes that their supporters will never fall short in this brotherly duty.

4. Like everything human, charitable organizations need open criticism. They need to be careful not to lose the spirit of the gospel, not to become business or fall prey to a power and prestige mentality. Sooner or later this would provoke reactions and would destroy both the concept and the reality of charity. Another danger is lack of self-effacing co-operation. The All India Seminar in 1969 made an analysis of this danger which could be pertinent in other places: there is too much work done in isolation, without contact with other hospitals belonging to the Church or to the state, and this leads to a waste of energy and of resources; hospitals are not built in the right places and not enough use is made of the qualified personnel; a national ecumenical commission is desirable (as already exists on the international level in the contacts between Catholic organizations and the Christian Medical Commission at Geneva), and there is a need for co-operation with the government in regional planning and an extension of preventative medicine, so as to build a healthy society instead of treating endless queues of patients. The Seminar also remarked that a considerable increase in the number of children's homes, without any co-ordination, had been noted in recent years. This was far from being an urgent need, but it was defended on the grounds that it is easy to get overseas help for this sort of work and the work suits the sisters. [2] But today the trend is towards phasing out

[1] J.K. Nyerere, *Freedom and socialism,* Dar es Salaam, 1968, p. 57f.
[2] *Church in India today,* pp. 418-422.

orphanages and homes and reintegrating the inmates in society — even towards providing home area treatment for lepers, etc.

5. 'Rice Christians' are continually cropping up in literature. While the nobles and wealthy classes in pre-communist China, including prominent Christians, preferred not to notice the grinding poverty of the masses and regarded the orphanages and foundling-homes of the missions as an offensive intrusion, the western missionaries and sisters were exclusively occupied with the poorest classes. In some places, they even attracted people into the catechumenate by distributing rice (although the incidence of this has been much exaggerated). This sort of bribery certainly damaged the Church's reputation and provided arguments against the missions first for the old gentry and then for the communists. [3]

The missions in India are reproached for having done so much direct giving instead of assisting development. [4] Perpetual distribution of American 'surplus food' is no way out of deprivation. The Catholic communities of north India are predominantly, almost exclusively, poor people, aboriginals and no-caste. Is there any future for such a Church, people ask, given that it is psychologically as difficult for a caste Indian to enter such a Church as for a white in South Africa to enter a black congregation. The answer is that such a Church of the poor has nothing to be ashamed of. They are the 'blessed' of the Sermon on the Mount. [5] If wealthy and prominent citizens will not come into the Church because of them, that only proves that the revolution of the gospel has not yet touched them. In the time of the early Christians, slaves had to bring their masters to the faith.

In the state of Andra Pradesh in India, where there are congregations of caste Christians, I visited two villages. In one were the no-caste in poverty-stricken huts, landless and living on a minimal day wage. In the other were the landowners who

[3] J. Beckmann, *Die China-Mission,* Freiburg im B., 1959, p. 22, 26, 35.

[4] *Impact,* Manila, 1972, 389.

[5] Cf. the discussion of this point in *Conference of religious,* India, pp. 44-62.

with their own money have built a fine church of which they very proud. I asked the priest if he could not stir his congregation into action in favour of their poor neighbours who, after all, are more 'Church' than a stone building is. His answer was: 'They haven't got as far as that yet'. So something was lacking in their conversion from the beginning. What a courageous undertaking it would be to stop being content with caring for poor Christians and to confront the rich with the radical spirit of the gospel, to give them a new perspective on the world with the message of God's kingdom and to build bridges between the classes.

6. Defending the poor does not mean letting them stay poor and standing by them with regular handouts. That humiliates them and does not correspond to the dignity of man as image of God the creator. When the poverty of little groups persists after decades of missionary activity (though one is of course helpless to deal with the great masses), one can only conclude that the problem has been tackled in the wrong way. There needs to be a concentrated effort to lay the proper foundations and stimulate the energies of the whole community so that it becomes able to maintain and develop itself out of its own new-found resources. There will always be situations of acute need where quick and effective outside help is needed; but apart from that the best help is given when people are taught to help themselves. We must do all we can in this regard. Charitable work in the missions until now has been far too static and defensive, tied up in institutions. We dealt with the sick when they came to the hospital and then, after treatment, let them go back to unhygienic surroundings where the infection could strike them down again. We need to go over to a planned offensive, treating not only individuals but whole villages, fighting not only symptoms but their causes. Money invested in medicines can cure a sick man for a while; the same money invested in safe drinking water can protect a whole community from disease.

Nowadays charity must go into action not only when disasters and catastrophes occur calling for good-Samaritan-type succour, but must be willing to operate hand in hand with development workers within the framework of an agreed and effective policy — every helper retaining the degree of autonomy proper to his field. Charity, since it relieves suffering by providing food, education and housing, is certainly within the Church's competence and is her rightful duty. Socio-economic development on the other hand is a technical and scientific undertaking; it should, indeed, be brought under the influence of the gospel and related to the Church, though less to the hierarchical Church than to the Church as people of God; here it is a question not of jurisdiction but of competence, and here charity, of itself, is not competent either in principle or in fact.

Chapter 18

THE RESPONSE TO THE CROWD:
THE MASS MEDIA

They were all waiting on his words.

(Lk 8:40)

1. There is a leading idea running through the whole of the gospels of Luke and Mark: Jesus surrounded by great crowds, people flocking to him from all sides and claiming his attention, and he teaching and healing them (Lk 8:40; Mk 1: 45; 2:2; 3:7; 6:31; 6:55; 8:1 etc.). Although Jesus also showed solicitude towards individuals — Nicodemus with his questions (Jn 3:1-28), Mary with her spiritual hunger (Lk 10:38-42) and the sinner at Jacob's well (Jn 4:1-26) — still his message was for the people as a whole. So he spoke not only in the synagogues but also in the streets and the open market places, from rooftops, on open beaches, and from commanding positions on hills. The idea of the crowd is systematically developed in the gospels, since this teacher, this 'guru' is come for the many, for all.

2. It must be considered a providential coincidence that the techniques of the mass media have become available for social communication just when the population of the world has doubled in the course of a single generation. What could not have existed a few decades ago outside the futuristic novels of a Jules Verne has become a technical reality. When Christopher Columbus discovered America on 12 October 1492, the king of Spain learned about it five months later. When the American President Lincoln was assassinated, 14 April 1865, Europe heard the news twelve days later. Today? Whenever anything important happens anywhere in the world, everyone hears the

341

news by radio that same evening and next morning can read about it in the newspapers. Events like the Pope's visit to the Holy Land or the United Nations and major international sports championships can be followed live on radio and television throughout the world via satellite links. The time when there were 'distant lands' or 'forgotten corners of the globe', is over.

Developing countries too derive benefit from this state of affairs, even if they lag behind the rich nations in numbers of transmitting stations and receivers. In respect of resources, Latin America is an exception. Here, the mass media infrastructure is actually superior to that in Europe and only a little inferior to that in the USA. Since the western market for receivers is approaching saturation point, every attempt is being made to promote sales of transistors in the Third World. Even the UNESCO programme is explicable on the same commercial grounds, although it has higher motives too. One example, India illustrates the enormous progress made: in 1947, there were 275,000 wireless receivers and less than 10% of the country could receive transmissions; by 1968 there were five million receivers and 60% of the country or 75% of the population could receive transmissions; the number now increases yearly by 15 to 20% and there are thoughts of providing every one of the 500,000 villages with a communal television receiver before too long. [1] Japanese TV transistors will, it is said, soon be on sale at 20 dollars, and we shall all be able to receive regular programmes by satellite from New York, Moscow, Tokyo etc.

3. Although all this causes a terrible culture shock, penetrating even into the deepest bush, at the same time it affords the Church a tremendous opportunity. In traditional communities, children were brought up not by their parents but by the clan. The man of today is influenced not so much by his family or village as by public opinion, by the world. He belongs to the 'world village'. It is not for nothing that communist states always help the young nations by providing them with transmitting stations. He who holds the means of communication and has 2000 soldiers at his disposal controls the country. He

[1] UNESCO, *Communication in the space age,* 1968, esp. 111-128.

who uses these means can be the world's teacher. Whoever fails to use them will belong with his group to the illiterates of tomorrow.

Now that the technical problems are on the point of being resolved even in the Third World, the question of quality and of morality arises: what sort of knowledge is to be conveyed by these media? and what sort of community are they to build? For the Church, this is decisive. By her very nature the Church *is* communication; she *is* the mediation of a message to the world. Formerly, the missionary had laboriously to fight his way through the virgin forest and drag himself sweating from village to village. Personal contact between the priest and individual Christians will always remain an irreplaceable means of pastoral care, but today the priest can multiply a thousand-fold the strength and range of his voice. He can pass from micro- to macro-evangelism and proclaim the gospel not merely to individuals and villages but to the world community. There is a network of broadcasting centres throughout the world which can carry the gospel, by sound and image, to the furthest corners of the globe. If we can take full advantage of these technical achievements, we shall be in a position to make the world an auditorium for the gospel in the truest sense.

We are invited and urged to make our proclamation. What should we proclaim? The days of wordy catechism formulas are past; Christ himself is now the short formula of the faith and the entire content of preaching. [2] To whom? To the assembled masses of the world, to all who are 'waiting for Christ'. How? Through the mass media.

The conciliar decree (*Inter mirifica*) on the means of social communication was much criticized, [3] but the pastoral instruction *Communio et progressio,* 1971 which followed it up went a long way towards making up for its deficiencies. [4] Its practical effect is another matter. On the whole we have the impression that everywhere in the Third Church there has been much good

---

[2] W. Kasper, *Glaube und Geschichte,* Mainz, 1970, pp. 224-242: *Verkündigung als Provokation.*

[3] Rahner, *Kleines Konzilskompendium,* 1967, p. 91f. However: E. Baragli, *Difendo l'Inter mirifica,* Catania, 1974.

[4] AAS 1971, 593-656.

will, and in many places the conditions for making progress are there; but generous co-operation and decisive action seem to be lacking, in spite of the Papal Commission for social communications and the corresponding Catholic international organizations: OCIC for the cinema, UCIP for the press, and UNDA for wireless and television.

4. First, a short word on the cinema and the press. [5] With regard to films, the All India Seminar reported sadly that in the country which holds the second place in film production the Catholic contribution is insignificant. It is necessary at least to make a start by training people in film production and by dubbing any foreign Christian films. As for the press, it was said to suffer from lack of capital and trained specialists and to be poorly supported by lay people as well as by the hierarchy. And censorship, preventing free expression of thought, must be abolished. [6]

Concerning Africa, the Catholic Media Council (a means of communication between OCIC, UCIP, UNDA and the Catholic aid organizations) has called attention to the present crisis in the Catholic press. This continent is the worst served of all in written means of communication. English-speaking Africa has only eight copies of a newspaper for every 1000 inhabitants and French-speaking Africa barely 1.8. The papers founded by missionaries, some of which had become quite influential, have lost subscriptions; many have been forced to close because of difficulties with governments (this is the dilemma of religious journals: if you criticize abuses you are banned, and if you don't there is no reason for your existence), bad business management and lack of subscribers ready to pay. People spend money more readily on beer than on a quarterly subscription: so much for the will to read stimulated by the ability to do so! [7] No one would regret some restraint on the wild growth of reviews and periodicals: in India, there are 20

[5] Bühlmann, *Afrika*, 304-307; F.J. Eiler, *Zur Bedeutung der Publizistik in der Missionsarbeit von heute,* in NZM 1972, pp. 241-252.

[6] *Church in India today,* 347-383.

[7] *Le difficoltà per la stampa cattolica in Africa,* in OR 18.2.1972; F.J. Eilers, *Communicatio socialis,* Paderborn, 1968ff.

Catholic periodicals in Hindi, 26 in Konkani, 64 in Tamil and 73 in Malayalam. [8] But when reviews which played a guiding role before and during de-colonization go under then one must be sorry. The southern world seems to be on the point of skipping the reading stage and going straight into the age of hearing (radio) and seeing (television).

5. Bible distribution calls for special mention. In the last few decades truly remarkable efforts have been made, so that today the sound of the word can be said to echo to the ends of the earth. It has been calculated that by the year 1500 the Sacred Scriptures had been translated, in whole or in part, into 24 languages, by 1800 into 71, by 1900 into 567, by 1928 into 856 and today into 1350. 90% of the world population can, in theory, read part of Scripture in the mother tongue. The principal credit for this must go to the Protestant Bible societies who have undertaken systematic translation and distribution by means of Bible houses in almost every country, Bible Sundays and house to house visiting. For numbers of Bibles possessed, India is the second country in the world after America, and Japan is the third. Millions of Hindus possess the Bible and read it regularly. In Japan, an inquiry in a residential block in Osaka revealed that only 20% had a Buddhist or Shinto house-shrine but a good 60% possessed a Bible. [9]

The need is still immense. Since there were about 133 million children of school age in Asia (excluding China and Japan) in 1960 and only 3 million copies throughout the same region, we are clearly still very far from the objective of the Bible societies — a New Testament in the hands of every Christian. Moreover by 2000 the population of the world will have doubled and most will be able to read. One of the happiest developments of the present day is that the Catholic Church, after a century of hostility to the Bible societies, is committed in principle to

---

[8] Streit-Dindinger, *Bibliotheca Missionum,* vol. 28, Freiburg, 1971, 489-506.

[9] B. Willecke, *Der religiös-sittlicher Wandel in Japan,* in NZM 1970, pp. 253-265, esp. 264.

collaborating with them and already does so in many countries. [10]
Distribution of the Scriptures is genuine evangelization in the
sense of a first proclamation of the gospel and a sowing of the
seed over the widest field. We cannot follow this up or measure
its effects. Growth must be left to God's care and action. We
sleep and wake, night and day, and the seed sprouts and grows,
we know not how (Mk 4:27). We ought to be honestly grateful
to the Protestants for this pioneer work; we need to be a little
more generous and not just work where we can expect immediate
results. There are two distinct conceptions of the Church
hidden behind the two attitudes: the Protestant view, centred
on Christ, personal, salvation accepted and realized in faith,
and the Catholic view of missionary activity, tending to the
founding of Churches and visible and measurable results that
involve juridical structures. The two should be reconciled in a
sound comprehensive view.

6. In broadcasting, Latin America is in the lead, thanks to
private initiative and commercial publicity. Many states have a
choice of six to ten programmes. With 7% of the world population, they have 4021 transmitting stations, whereas Asia with
55.5% has only 2270 and Africa with 9.7% only 600. Catholics
in Latin America own 198 broadcasting stations, of which 126
are in Brazil, 16 in Peru, 11 in Guatemala, 6 in Colombia, etc. [11]
Apart from entertainment, they provide facilities for religious
and social conscience formation and amenities for human
development. In many places, radio schools have been set up.
The best known of these is *Accion Cultural Popular* founded
in 1947 by Mgr Salcedo. It conducts a literacy campaign over
its own transmitter, the most powerful in Colombia, as well as
more advanced education in agriculture etc. Twice every year,
150 girls and as many boys are trained as leaders so that they
can then organize village discussion groups based on the trans-

---

[10] J. Beckmann, *Die Hl. Schrift in den katholischen Missionen*,
Schöneck, 1966, esp. 3-6; W. Bühlmann, *Die Hl Schrift in den
kath. Missionen*, in H.J. Greschat (ed.), *Festschrift E. Dammann*,
Stuttgart, 1969, pp. 182-191; further, the annual reports of the
Bible societies.

[11] R. Aguilo, *America Latina: Communicacion*, Bologna, 1972, esp.
303, 319; id., *Catholic Media World Directory*, Rome, 1971.

missions. This *Accion* reaches a million serious students with its daily broadcasts. Even non-Catholic circles recognize that this has led to far-reaching changes in Colombia. [12]

7. In Africa, no great initiatives have been undertaken by Catholics. There are four local transmitting stations (2 in Angola and one each in Lesotho and Mozambique) and a few production studios (for example STAR in Kinshasa). Most national broadcasting stations put a certain amount of time at the disposal of religious bodies (in Dar es Salaam, religious broadcasts are transmitted by the Chinese built station!), but the use made of it varies in quality.

The broadcasting body 'Voice of the Gospel', set up at Addis Ababa by the Lutheran World League, is a considerable achievement. With an investment of two million dollars and an annual budget of 1.3 million, it maintains a network of local studios where the programmes are worked out in different languages as well as the central station (altogether 300 employees), and transmits the Christian message very attractively all over Africa and the Middle East. [13] Many Catholic missionaries encourage their faithful to listen to 'Voice of the Gospel', but unfortunately positive co-operation (with a single exception at Moshi) has not yet proved possible.

8. In Asia, the situation varies from country to country. The immense territory of India has one production studio in Bombay and that is all. Zeitler observes: 'As far as the missionary undertaking of the Church in India is concerned, we have to recognize that she has made no advance on methods tried with success at the beginning of the 20th century, although we have entered an entirely new world determined to an important extent by the mass media, whose importance has not yet been recognized by the Indian Church'. [14] Many Catholics and their priests listen to the Protestant station in Ceylon and appreciate its programmes.

[12] UNESCO (n. 1), 36; also a personal visit in 1970.
[13] Personal visits in 1966 and 1971.
[14] E. Zeitler, *Die indische Kirche im Zeichen des 1900 jährigen Thomas-Jubiläum*, in *Steyler Missionschronik*, 1973, 9-15, esp. 15.

In the rest of Asia, there is much more Catholic initiative in broadcasting — 16 undertakings in the Philippines alone. But again there is a lack of large scale planning and co-operation. The only project that began on a generous scale turned out miserably: Radio Veritas in Manila. Built in 1953 with German money and intended for all south east Asia, with China as a first priority, it remained limited to the Archdiocese of Manila, for reasons no one will state openly but which everyone knows. Now that the Cardinal has died (1973), collegial management and realization of the fine original plan may be possible, but the opening drive has slackened and the technical installations need renewing. [15]

With regard to China, nine resolutions were passed in 1967 and a four-year programme mapped out. In 1971, the records merely stated that nothing had happened but that the nine resolutions were still very practical. J.F. Hyatt, president of UNDA for Asia, called the fact that the greatest people in the world had been left without any Christian message the 'community sin of the Church'. A new five-year plan was projected. [16] Thank God it is no longer true that China remains deprived of the Christian message: three powerful Protestant stations transmit daily eighteen hours of excellent programmes from the Philippines, Okinawa and Korea, truly broadcasting the 'good news for the embittered'. [17]

9. Here again we must broach the question of ecumenical co-operation. We face the paradox that the 'one' Catholic Church has not managed to implement any large-scale well-planned collaborative effort, whereas the 'divided' Protestant Churches have shown themselves capable of working together towards this objective. They have constructed links round the southern hemisphere from Addis Ababa to the Seychelles, from Ceylon to the Far East. The most powerful group, the Far East Broadcasting Company, founded in 1945, possesses 17 stations

[15] UNDA/Asia, *The Catholic broadcasters of Asia,* Manila, 1971, pp. 36-39, 61, 306.
[16] UNDA, *op. cit.,* p. 55, 436, 439.
[17] See above, ch. 5.B.4,2, p. 123f. Cf. S. Mooneyham, *China: the puzzle,* Passadena, 1971, p. 52, 73.

and 77 studios in Asia, so distributed that they can reach two thirds of the population of the world. Their programmes are excellent. Behind everything one can sense the presence of specialists, and a deep Christian faith too. [18] So there can be no room for any parallel Catholic arrangements unrelated to the Protestant initiatives, much less for any rivalry; the only thing that will do is courageous collaboration. [19] If there is any domain where ecumenism imposes itself peremptorily, it is this one of making contact with the mass of humanity. Through the mass media — book stores, Bible distribution, radio and television — we can make a common witness to Christ. The doctrines that divide us can be kept for private religious instruction. The ether must not become a battleground for the various Christian denominations but should be filled with the unique message of salvation, as happened once in the heavens round Bethlehem.

10. At the centre the Vatican, with its own means of social communication, does not give the entirely good example to the periphery that might be expected. From the technical point of view there is nothing to complain about. But one does sense the stifling influence of absolute monarchy, as well as the effects of clericalization precisely where good journalists are needed rather than good priests. We could do with less of the incense-laden atmosphere and more in the way of comprehensive information. We still remember how, during the Council, the world press had to fight for even moderately satisfactory information. Things are certainly much improved but there is still too much secrecy. Quick, complete and competent information should be the rule and secrecy the exception. [20] Some foreign reporters who know Bonn and Washington find the Vatican press service closed and ill at ease; they have the impression that information is only given under compulsion and that there is no positive approach to the press as a useful tool. *L'Osservatore Romano*

[18] PMV-CI 1970/30, 18f.

[19] *General criteria for ecumenical collaboration in the area of social communication,* 15.11.1971, from the Papal Commission for social communication (not published in AAS).

[20] E. Baragli, *Segreto di informazione nella Chiesa,* in *Civiltà Cattolica,* 1973, 347-358.

is criticized for its one-sidedness; on burning questions, it gives only decisions and fixed positions and covers up the real theological problematic. An information service that was more open and penetrating would be more effective. Even in fidelity to its own line, and with its justifiable loyalty to a group interest, it could still allow more freedom and give the reader more scope to make his own judgement.

Radio Vatican, with its 260 employees and magnificent resources continually improved ever since 1931, does wonderful work for the Church. But the complaint of many people, not only the young, is that it is so solemn and pious. It does not use the right language for the medium. Its news is unexciting and uncommunicative, too concerned with the Vatican (papal speeches and decisions and visits to the Pope), and it does not mirror the reality of the Church in the wider world. If one compares the different language services, there appears to be no common programming. So one deduces that co-operation is minimal and that the editors of the different language programmes do not sit round a table to ask themselves what they ought to tell the world, at this moment, by this means of communication. The newly appointed director, Fr Tucci, has promised to review the programmes, so that this splendid broadcasting station may send out equally splendid programmes. [21]

Similar things could be said about the international agency *Fides*. It seems the question of its identity has not yet been put. The differing categories of press service (communiqués, articles, commentaries, documentation), are apparently not appreciated, for the service offered often falls between two stools. Comparison between the different language editions betrays a lack of co-operation here too. The agency speaks for five independent editors, not for a single centre for the evangelization of the nations.

A few years ago, a courageous enterprise saw the light of day — an ecumenical commission for satellite communication (ECUSAT) comprising representatives of Catholic organizations and of the World Council of Churches. The intention was to negotiate together with governments in the planning of satellite

[21] OR 1/2.10.1973.

350

communications and to put forward our own progamme needs in good time before everything is booked up. [22] Unfortunately, the project has been left in cold storage since 1972. Financial difficulties are partly responsible but also the ecumenical crisis.

11. We are faced by a challenge. Either the Church makes her voice heard in the media or the voice from the pulpit will be lost in the din of the world and we shall become a silent Church. Both at the centre and at the periphery we need to make bold strides into the age of the mass media. We must plan and act now so that we can accomplish something in five years' time. In principle, there is recognition that these means are useful for the apostolate and that the appropriate steps should be taken, but there is hesitation over the necessary investment in money and personel. S. Bamberger, president of Multimedia International, an organization in Rome which promotes ideas for the mass media among institutes and religious orders and congregations, thinks that a local Church of 300,000 Christians (half of them Catholics) in a population of two million needs a team of four to five trained specialists — a journalist, a publicity man, a speaker, an assistant for audio-visual catechetical aids (all of whom need not be priests) — to ensure the presence of the Church in the press, radio and television, making use of the existing mass media infra-structure in ecumenical co-operation. [23] There is no reason why this should not be possible after the relinquishment of the mission schools. It must be said that, in view of the wide potential of such a team, the proposed investment of four individuals is a very modest one.

12. It is important to take these big steps, but small step tactics are indispensable too. Social communication is not, primarily, a matter for specialists but one aspect of all apostolate. Even if nothing is happening at the highest level, something can be done in the average parish to speak to the faithful through drama, photographic slides and films; people can also be brought together to discuss particular programmes from the national broadcasting stations, and can be encouraged to write to the

---

[22] UNDA, op.cit. (n. 15), 404-408. On the ecumenical crisis mentioned here, see above, ch. 10, A.3, p. 218.
[23] SEDOS-JV, Mar. 1973, 11f.

press, etc. [24] The east African episcopal conference (AMECEA) decided to make study of the media an essential part of the course for theology students. Fr Healey of Nairobi was made responsible for this and has already given courses and practical exercises in various seminaries.

[24] O. Kaspar, *Der 'Medien-Missionar' als neuer Berufstyp,* in *Communicatio Socialis,* Paderborn, 1972, 130-133.

Chapter 19

CITY AND COUNTRYSIDE:
PROBLEMS OF URBANIZATION

Come, let us build a city...

(Gen 11:4)

1. Between Genesis 2, where the story of salvation begins in the garden of Eden, and Revelation 21, where we arrive at the goal of the heavenly city, there lies a long series of psychological and sociological experiences which offer us rich material for a dialectical theology of the city. The Israelites came from the desert. They cherished an inborn preference for the life of the beduin and the open countryside which reminded them of the state of paradise before the fall. The sedentary culture of the city seemed, by contrast, an incarnation of evil. Sodom and Gomorrah were proof of this (Gen 18-19) as also the story of Babel (Gen 11), the first evidence of a hostile attitude to the city. Here is the classic example of the ambitions of the proud city-dweller brought to nothing by God: 'Come, we will build a city and a tower'... The Lord came down to see the city and the tower and they ceased to build the city. 'Let us build a memorial to ourselves, that we may not be scattered over the whole earth'... The Lord scattered them from there over the whole earth. 'The whole land then spoke one language and used the same words... Let us go down and confound their speech, so that a man will not understand his neighbour's speech'. All the intentions of the men of Babel were thus foiled.

After the founding of Jerusalem, the attitude changes and the glorification of the city begins. The image of the 'perverse city' comes to be applied to Babylon, the world power that had subjugated Israel, and later to the Rome which persecuted Christians. Revelation 18 has a sarcastic lament over the fall of

353

Babylon-Rome, the great whore. Jerusalem is correspondingly idealized. From now on, nostalgia for the lost paradise of Eden is replaced by longing for the city that God has prepared for us (Heb 11:16), our fatherland (Phil 3:20), where God will abide with us (Rev 21:2).

2. This dialectic developed in the opposite direction in the course of Church history. Paul began his mission with a pronounced emphasis on the city. He did not visit the villages but the metropolis, the major road junctions and ports, the commercial, political and religious centres. This gave him the opportunity to bring the gospel to the largest possible and most influential public. There was also the hope that the Christians he gained would radiate their faith into the pagan hinterland. [1] This clearly did not happen to a sufficient extent, so that the inhabitants of the villages and the countryside remained for a long time outside Christian influence. Hence the expression pagan (= dweller in the country or in a village) came to mean a non-Christian.

In the early centuries and right up to the middle ages the city, a concentrated and autocratic human community, provided the basis also for the community of the Church, the local Church. The whole formed a parish under a bishop. With the feudal system came country parishes, where the landowner built a church for himself and his fiefs and maintained a priest. But the Church's centre of gravity remained in the city with its proud cathedral, built not by the bishop nor by the prince but by the urban population. It was only with the Enlightenment and the Industrial Revolution that the cities began to slip from the Church's grasp while the good country people remained loyal: only then did a clear preference for the country, and antipathy and fear with regard to the city, develop. [2]

So the messenger of the faith, as he continues to exist in our imagination, is the missionary sent to the bush, the forest and the villages. In Africa, at any rate, the missionary did

[1] O. Hass, *Paulus der Missionar*, Münsterschwarzach, 1971, p. 85f.

[2] A. Bundervoet, *La théologie de la ville*, in SEDOS-JV 1973/11, 16-23; the whole number is devoted to the problems of urbanization and contains a select bibliography.

concentrate on the country. The cities were still small, the domain of government and business people who showed no interest in the Church (and vice versa). The mission centres were set up in the interior, and there the numbers of Christians increased. But, since the Second World War and decolonization, cities have sprung up on the missions' shoulders and this urgently demands a reaction from the Church.

3. Whether we like it or not, urbanization is a pronounced trend in modern society. It is true that in western countries after the flight from the land there is now some talk of a flight from the city. Some cities are losing population as people try to escape from the concrete and asphalt jungles and look for homes in the green belt communities. But in the Third World urbanization is in full spate. The country with its boredom and poor prospects loses all attraction and the city seems to offer hope. The following table shows the foreseeable development of urbanization in the Third World: [3]

City dwellers (in millions)

	1960	1970	1980	1990	2000
All developing countries	310.7	464.3	693.4	1013.0	1437.1
South east Asia	27.7	42.9	66.8	106.3	162.4
South central Asia	76.6	113.5	168.9	244.8	343.9
Tropical Africa	13.9	22.6	37.2	62.3	105.6
Southern Africa	5.7	8.6	13.1	20.3	28.7

The figures make it clear that, both for the total and for each of the regions, the city population more than doubles itself in each twenty years (1960-1980; 1980-2000). The 1,437,100,000 city dwellers in the year 2000 will make up about 30% of the total population of the Third World. Latin America leads the way in this trend. Its 1975 urban population of 195 million already constitutes 59% of the total and, by 1985, the 290 million people in cities will be 67% of the whole. [4]

[3] UN, *Study: growth of world population,* N.Y., 1970, 133.
[4] UN, *Statistical Yearbook 1972,* 10, 82.

4. The bad effects of urbanization endured by the migrants can be seen by any visitors to the cities. In most regions there is hyper-urbanization: the influx of migrants is much greater than the slowly increasing supply of jobs. This brings unemployment, disintegration, frustration, revolution. [5] In western cities, the boundaries have almost disappeared, and in the southern hemisphere slums, *favelas*, shanty towns dominate the picture. The people living there multiply alarmingly, as if in protest against the inhuman living conditions. In Caracas, for instance, the upper and middle classes have a population increase of 1.5 - 2%; the increase in the slums touches 4.5 - 5%. This means that, quite apart from any new migration, the population will double in 14 years.

Cities are islands of wealth, symbols of power, but at the same time breeding grounds for poverty and desperation. Behind the façade of the main streets with their sky-scrapers, hotels, banks, department stores and administrative centres, the slums lie hidden with their distinguishing marks: primitive housing, overcrowding, lack of sewers and rubbish disposal, children who get no more than a few years' schooling at most and so have no prospects and easily fall into juvenile delinquency. [6] But even those who live in high apartments and in the sun have to pay their toll to the city. The pessimist, Spengler, has a penetrating description of the 'soul of the city'. He notes that the peasant is, indeed, without history, and that the village stands outside world history because world history is the history of city dwellers. But here is the toll that must be paid: 'The stone Colossus, named 'world city', stands at the end of the life span of every great culture. The man of culture, who is spiritually formed by the land, will eventually be seized by his own creation, the city. He is possessed by it, becomes its creature, its executive organ and, finally, its victim'. [7] We almost hear an echo of the drama of Babel.

[5] L. Voye, *La ville, creuset des révolutions*, in SML 1972, 26-44.

[6] UNICEF, *Social development in peri-urban areas: a study of the needs and problems of children and youth in 4 slums in Bangkok*, Bangkok, 1972.

[7] Spengler, *Untergang des Abendlandes*, II, 101-131, esp. 117.

5. The Church must not be content to repeat, 'Woe, woe for the great city' (Rev 18:16). She must accept facts for what they are and make the best of things. She is the all-embracing sacrament of salvation, and certainly in the city too. She must strive to attain a positive attitude to the city. It is not merely that here she has the opportunity to meet so many men in her immediate surroundings and in areas she can directly influence. She also finds them enjoying greater human freedom now that they are liberated from the bonds of tribe and tradition; in the pluralism of the modern world they are thrown back on their own personal decisions. Young people feel at ease in this freedom. Here the Church needs to proceed otherwise than in the interior of the country. Pressure and paternalism will not do. She must appeal to freedom as the supreme human value. In this way, we can hope to establish a fruitful symbiosis between Church and state. [8]

Then it will become apparent that the city is not just a fairground where evil is on sale in bars and night-clubs, not just a laboratory where Promethean man develops his science and technology, not just the arena where cheer-leaders and demagogues seek their laurels and their careers, not just a treasure house where the financial magnates guard their mammon. In this same city, we can find those 'little ones' to whom God has revealed the secrets of his kingdom. Even among the 'great' there are some with the mind of Nicodemus, who in their hearts long to know something of the secrets.

6. Harvey Cox thinks that the Church, as the vanguard of hope, is called to exercise her triple function in the 'godless city' more than anywhere: *kerygma* — making men aware with new methods of preaching that the powers and principalities have certainly been defeated, but that we have to pass through the unavoidable crisis of urbanization and secularization and shoulder responsibility for ourselves and others; *diakonia* — serving by healing, helping, reconciling rich and poor not by old-fashioned charity but through genuine acts of justice, bringing them together in shared tasks and a common effort; *koinonia*

[8] Bundervoet, *op. cit.* (n. 2), p. 22f.

— leading men out of isolation and the anonymity of the city, making them part of a genuine human community and so making possible the coming of the kingdom of God. [9] Then it will be seen that the human problems are more urgent than the architectonic problems (though these are important), and that the cities need not only Le Corbusier but also the evangelical man, priest or layman, if life in them is to be healthy, worthy of humanity and meaningful. The godless city of yesterday can become the Church of tomorrow.

7. We must pluck up courage and get down to the first task, which is seeing things as they are and devising plans. Lamenting the flight from the land is not helpful. It is quite true that country districts are being impoverished by the move, not only financially but in quality of life. This is a consequence of schooling, [10] which encourages the abler and more dynamic part of the population to migrate. Should we preach against this? It would be no use; at most, social action to improve living conditions in the country could help. But the main question is to see how we can welcome these people in the city and build up a dynamic Church with them.

In Africa, there is no mission from the city to the interior but rather the city is faced with Christian immigration from the interior. The migrants went to school and so became Christian. Consequently the proportion of Christians in the cities is rising rapidly. Dar es Salaam in 1967 had 81,000 Christians (55,000 of them Catholics) which was 30% of the population, compared with 15% in 1957. Within 20 years it will probably be half a million, that is, 50% of the population.

In the first phase our experience is that the Christian from the country, going to his *diaspora* in the city, is not equal to the adventure of freedom. He does not contact his new parish and new priests. He 'takes a holiday from the faith', as many Christians say when they make their confessions on returning to the village some years later. The conclusion is obvious: we should build up structures in the interior that ensure as far as possible

[9] H. Cox, *The secular city*, N.Y., 1965, pp. 137-160.
[10] See ch. 16.3, p. 327f.

continuity between the country and the city. After a team of Canadian experts had studied the demographic development of Dar es Salaam and had prepared a development plan, an inter-denominational working party formed on the initiative of L.W. Swantz of the Protestant Council of Churches in Tanzania examined the consequences for the Churches. It came to the conclusion that 80 new Churches (for 5000 new Christians each) are needed in the next 20 years; so four new Churches should be built each year. [11] Will we have the courage to look the new facts in the face, and accept new solutions too?

8. If we are to master these immense problems to any appreciable degree, we must move with them and take action. The centre of gravity of our commitment in personnel and financial resources must be transferred to the cities. It would be worth while to make a study of how priests were distributed in relation to Catholic population in the country and in the city ten years ago and how they are distributed now. [12] All the dioceses should share in providing the capital with a sufficient number of priests, as does happen here and there. After all, the work in the country leads nowhere to speak of if Christians continually leave first the land and then, in the city, the Church. In the more stable country parishes, we can hand over a lot of responsibility to lay people (parish councils, elders, teachers) and reduce the necessity for priestly presence to a minimum. In the less stable city parishes, the priest is much more urgently needed as a catalyst; not that he should do everything, but within the large parish he should give strong support to basic groups and act as animator to the animators. Then there would be hope that, in the long run, the cities would cease to be cared for by priests from the country: instead we might get the necessary vocations out of active urban communities. In India, 68 out of 78 dioceses get more than half their seminarists, and 58 more than 90%, from the country districts. We must make more energetic efforts to tap the resources of the city. [13]

[11] Unfortunately, the study has not been published.
[12] W. Bühlmann, *Die Kapuzinermissionen heute,* in NZM 1973, pp. 173-175.
[13] C.B.C.I., *Survey of vocations in India,* New Delhi, 1969, 12.

9. A practical example will illustrate more effectively than any theory the urgency of the situation and will stimulate city pastors to look for their own solutions.

Sao Paulo in Brazil contained

636,000 inhabitants in 1920
3,825,351 inhabitants in 1960
5,901,533 inhabitants in 1970.

For 1980 the statistics anticipate 11,200,000 and for 2000 about 29,000,000. At present, the immigration rate stands at 300,000 and the yearly excess of births over deaths at 120,000: in all, almost half a million more people each year, the majority of whom are Catholics. So there ought to be fifty new parishes founded each year. The priests and the church buildings this would entail cannot possibly arrive in time to meet the need. Traditional methods for the care of souls are not equal to the situation. In the course of recent years, Cardinals A. Rossi and E. Arns have organized 380 social centres where sisters and volunteer workers teach mothers hygiene, baby care, cooking and sewing, and help youths and men to fill in application forms for jobs and try to help them to get professional training. Buildings for these purposes are being put up in all the new quarters. This is a form of immediate presence. The aim is to establish small communities, basic groups, centred on these buildings. In this way, men can feel they belong to one another and contribute something to the community. The Church can become a ferment of unity and a sign of hope. [14]

10. Here again it is evident that such tasks can only be undertaken in ecumenical co-operation. The World Council of Churches has a study commission on the problems of rapid social change and its consequences for the Churches. This has already provided inspiration for many study seminars in local Churches, from which we could learn. [15] In east Africa, an

[14] Interview with Card. E. Arns, in *Kontinente,* Essen, 1972, Feb., p. 6f; Card. A. Rossi, *Organizzazione dell'apostolato d'insieme a S. Paolo,* in CM 1971, 23-27.
[15] E.g., *The Church and the problems of the town,* by Tanganyika Rapid Social Change Study Commission, Dar es Salaam, 1964.

inter-disciplinary and inter-confessional course on urban and industrial problems has just come to an end; forty men and women from various Churches were prepared for Christian service in the present situation in African cities. The Roman Secretariat for non-believers showed interest and is proposing to finance the employment of a Catholic expert (in theology and sociology).

Chapter 20

STONE AND SPIRIT:
THE PROBLEM OF BUILDINGS

*There will not remain a stone upon a
stone...* (Mk 13:2)

1. 'Master, see! What stones! What buildings!' Jesus
reacted unexpectedly and said: 'Not one stone will remain
upon another. All will be destroyed!' The disciples' admiration
for the temple prompted him to speak of the fall of Jerusalem
and the end of the world. Instead of being impressed by the
magnificence of the buildings, Jesus perceived rather their
transitory nature and the dangers inherent in them. He put
himself in the company of the prophets who repeatedly foretold
the destruction of the temple as a punishment for the wrong-
headed trust of the Jews. What use was it to pride themselves
on 'the temple of the Lord' if they would not improve their way
of life? Jeremiah showed up this trust for what it was: self
deception and lying. He paid for his words. The priests and
the whole people seized him and cried, 'Thou must die' (Jer
7:4; 26:7f). One of the charges against Jesus was that he had
said, 'I can destroy the temple of God and in three days build
it up again' (Mt 26:61).

2. There is a temptation, in visiting mission stations,
sometimes to react as Jesus did. The missionaries, sisters and
bishops are proud of their buildings, schools, hospitals, seminaries, mother houses, some in process of construction and some
completed; every corridor and every room must be seen before
you can sit down to a talk over a cup of tea.

These efforts and achievements certainly are admirable. They
are the fruit of untold labours. Money had to be begged and

the plans were brought to fruition in very primitive conditions. Some buildings are quite astonishing — like the cathedral at Dar es Salaam which Brother Seitz built at the turn of the century; he was the only specialist mason and had with him 300 black workers. The churches and monasteries established by Spain and Portugal in the new world are still to this day worthy of admiration; their splendid ornamentation and abundance of gold express deep faith (in the artistic idiom of the time). [1] For centuries the mission stations served the people as centres of culture and of Church life; formerly, they also served as fortresses in case of uprisings. But they cannot escape the fate of today's radical questioning.

3. These constructions lent the whole mission undertaking the character of a *powerful* Church. Natives never guessed with how much difficulty the money was collected from benefactors, themselves usually poor. They only saw that the money was there and that it was invested in fine buildings while they themselves remained as poorly housed as before. The mission buildings were not outshone by the governor's residence — quite the contrary. Both were seen as foreign institutions and both had the effect of isolating people, not binding them together. [2] J. Leclercq wonders what an African or Asiatic feels as he stands inside or in front of Notre Dame in Paris. He will certainly have an impression of magnificence and, hence, of the majesty of God, but not of humility and of God's closeness to us in Jesus. Such buildings are hardly the Sermon on the Mount in stone. [3] The same must be said of many mission stations which began poor but became what they are through the drive for development and through the many needs they served.

4. The native effects, psychological and pastoral, of this involvement with buildings are serious. That many bishops are better builders than pastors is a complaint often heard. They

---

[1] J. Baugartner, *Mission und Liturgie in Mexiko,* Schöneck, 1971, pp. 92-99.

[2] H.W. Mobley, *The Ghanaian's image of the missionary,* Leiden, 1970, 73-80.

[3] J. Leclerq, *De l'Eglise des princes à l'Eglise des pauvres,* in PM 1964, pp. 355-369, esp. 355.

find themselves in a trap: they feel they *must* build in this or that place and then have difficulty in keeping their heads above water financially so money becomes their first concern. For direct pastoral work they have neither time nor, apparently, taste — and certainly no money. Something similar threatens many missionaries and native priests. They do not know what it is to earn a living. Native theologians were brought up in a seminary without having to worry about money. They live on alms, on other people's sweat not their own. They are, therefore, more extravagant with money than lay people. Many a congregation in the Second Church has taken as long as a generation to pay off its building debt, but in the missions churches are no sooner built than paid for. So it happens that building is undertaken too precipitately and on too grand a scale; the buildings may not fulfil the function that was imagined for them. [4] It is much easier to construct buildings, and so lull oneself into a sense of false security, than to solve serious personal problems and confront hard reality. An experienced missionary in India explained: 'A genuine guru prays and fasts by the side of the road. Gradually people gain confidence in him, give him money and build him an *ashram* and later a temple. We have got money too easily and built too many buildings, but we lack gurus'.

5. We are back to the crucial question of the Church of the poor, so difficult to achieve. [5] Pope Paul VI, who has this question at heart, explained that the Church must not only be poor but look poor. [6] However, although no one doubts that he himself lives frugally inside the Vatican palace, it is difficult for the visitor to believe that the Church of Rome is poor. So too with the native sisters: they may be poor in their personal lives but their mother-houses, often the biggest buildings for a considerable distance, hardly bear witness to poverty. A magnificent seminary was opened at Recife in 1965 but was soon out of commission for want of theologians and remains empty and abandoned like a medieval ruin. Archbishop Helder Camara made a speech at the inauguration which began: 'The Holy

[4] Cf. the empty seminaries of Latin America, ch. 7.B., p. 158.
[5] Cf. above, ch. 5.B.3.d., p. 120-122.
[6] OR 2/3.5.1969.

See wanted this seminary and built it. . . But the priests and seminarians must never forget that they are to preach the good God to people living in subhuman conditions. These people must have got the impression that religion is a theory that has no influence on life. . .' [7] For this reason, he himself abandoned his traditional bishop's palace and lives in a modest annexe alongside a church.

Again, a missionary in Asia said: 'No church building should infringe the limits of social justice. The Church means nothing to the great mass of the poor; for them she is voiceless and faceless. They do not know that the sisters teach in schools because these schools are not for their children. We must not let western institutions impose these buildings on us. We should be wise to decline them'. One day I was met at a station in India and taken by rickshaw to the mission station where I found a modest building in cement blocks. Before I could express my approval, the superior said apologetically: 'This is only temporary. We shall have a two-storied building soon'. The same superior was later to argue with the rickshaw driver over a half rupee fee! In the course of history, the Church has been too bound up with the rich and powerful and has been paying the penalty for this over the last century. And now, in the poor countries, her buildings tie her down in the camp of the rich. It is going to be very hard to repair the damage done.

6. Those who object that what I have been saying betrays a 'European', not to say 'communist', mentality quote the psychology of Africans and Asians: so far uncontaminated by secularism, they are proud of their fine churches and say, 'we may be poor wretches but at least we have a beautiful church'. At this, one may ask how many fail to come to the beautiful church because they have no beautiful clothes. There is also the question of how long it will be before this medieval mentality dies out and loyal communists turn these beautiful churches into grounds for accusations against the Church. But quite apart from tactical considerations: anything triumphalist and anti-conciliar cannot be justified by a reference to the clothes worn

[7] H. Camara, *The Church and colonialism,* London, 1969, pp. 18-20.

365

by African chiefs or by any appeal to pluriformity. On this point, we should not be tolerant of the 'psychology of the Africans' but we must prudently and carefully reform it. But it is difficult to exorcize the curse of past bad actions. Since the missionaries built on a generous scale, the native bishops and sisters do not want suddenly to begin living in poor houses. But I seriously think that anyone, after Vtaican II, who builds palatial residences or monumental churches must very earnestly ask himself whether he is not betraying the Lord and his message for thirty pieces of silver. Obviously, there can be no compulsion; one can only hope that individuals may begin to make prophetic gestures, as does happen here and there.

There are many concrete stumbling blocks to mention. One Sunday morning I visited the cathedral in Rio de Janeiro. Inside I saw the cardinal (now dead) celebrating solemn Mass amid a sea of candles, flowers and lights but with fewer than fifty faithful present. Later, I was taken to a place a few kilometres away where the new cathedral stood nearly complete; it was circular, 105 metres in diameter. A few days later, I mentioned it to a Brazilian archbishop and asked: 'Why such a new building when the existing cathedral is too big?' He answered: 'There are occasions on which we are glad to have such a building'. I objected: 'But on such occasions, national feasts, eucharistic congresses and the like, which only happen once a year or every two years, you could use the national stadium'. But there were difficulties: 'In the stadium, you never know; it might rain or be baking hot'. 'Still, on every sporting occasion, there are 50,000 there'. His last word was: 'It is not the same thing'. I thought: with a man like that there is nothing to be done; he hasn't caught up with the times. It should not be left to the communists to protest against such scandals; it is up to good Christians to do so too.

In Uganda, a martyrs' memorial was to be built as a centre of pilgrimage — to serve as a rallying point from which religious energy could then radiate. The building had to correspond to African aspirations and yet avoid accusations of triumphalism and extravagance. An international fund-raising committee was set up and the Swiss architect, Dr J. Dahinden found a splendid compromise solution; the result was something both original and functional. But many bishops wanted something more magnificent and reproached the architect for using brick instead of marble and wood doors instead of metal, saying it all represented a retreat towards the primitive. [8]

In Kerala, where there are already too many churches and shrines and too little social action, Catholic students protested against the buildings of four churches in the same place for different rites, but in vain. [9]

We must ask ourselves what precisely is the Church's task in the world and decide, once for all, which image of the Church to preserve: the sacral, monumental and archaic, or the simple, evangelical and in tune with the times.

7. This poses the real problem of sacred buildings. What we have come to regard as natural and unquestionable turns out to be no more than a phenomenon of history (recent history at that) which finds no support in the gospel. In Judaism and in all pre-Christian religions, the sacred was a central concept: it could be a particular place or person set apart for the divine, holy, powerful, associated with reverence, fear, and taboo. But Christ desacralized the domain of the sacred or, better, he sanctified the whole world and all men (Jn 17:17). No longer only in the temple, or on this or that hill, but in every place will the Father be worshipped in spirit and in truth (Jn 4:21-24). The temple is replaced by the person of Christ, for 'here is one greater than the temple' (Mt 12:6) and by the congregation, the people of God. The apostles drew further inferences: *'We are the temple of the living God... Do you not know that your flesh is a temple of the living God?'* (2 Cor 6:16; cf. 1 Cor 6:19) — 'Let yourselves be built up as living stones into a spiritual temple' (1 Pet 2:5). Consequently, Christians built no temple but assembled in their own houses, then in community buildings and finally in basilicas designed as assembly places. Gradually, the tendency towards resacralizing grew. But even in the middle ages the church of the people of God was often available for all purposes and not just for worship: for the

[8] J. Kraus, *Kirchenbau-Probleme in den Missionsländern,* in NZM 1970, pp. 137-147, esp. 141.
[9] *Concilium* 1971/8, 94f.

agape, for trials, for political assemblies and for markets (leading, of course, to abuses). Until 200 years ago, churches were nearly always multi-purpose buildings, in which the whole life of the congregation was played out. Only since then has worship and the rest of the life of the congregation been separated. 'This is not an ideal; it is rather a warning sign'. [10]

Nowadays, instead of churches designed exclusively for worship, we are beginning to build community centres where the Christian community can again be found with all its preoccupations, hopes and activities. At the heart of it all, and as the climax, is the Sunday celebration of the Eucharist. It is an idea that should be spread in the Third Church. How can we use foreign money to build churches in poor countries to be used only on Sunday mornings and then, a few years later, write to another address to finance a parish hall which will be used on a few evenings in the week? No institution in the world could allow its resources to be so badly utilized as the Church. We should, therefore, plan buildings for more than one purpose, especially in the country and the outskirts of the cities. I would even go so far as to say that it could be a sin against the Church to build a church.

The first reaction of Africans and Asians, bishops, priests and people, will be negative. They have a pronounced sense of the sacred. They point to the Hindu temples and the Moslem mosques and want to compete with the other religious communities (even other Christians) and have a church as big or bigger that they can call their own. Here, we must go along with the New Testament idea, taking pride not in a beautiful house of God but in a living people of God. The opposition ought to be overcome by proposals to build a multi-purpose centre in place of a church and presbytery and use the money saved for social purposes, for the good of the living Church. The realization that Catholics in Africa are likely to increase from 45 million in 1970 to 175 millions in 2000 [11] should make us abandon quickly

[10] G. Rombold, *Brauchen wir 'sacrale' Kirchen?*, in *Fastenopfer der Schweizer Katholiken, Kirchenbau*, Lucerne, 1971, 9-13, esp. 13 (Eng. and Fr. editions).
[11] Ch. 1.D.5, p. 22.

the ambition to build a proportionate number of traditional churches.

Here are two sketches from the plans drawn up by the architects, H. Oberholzer and O. Scherer for a Swiss Catholic action group. They show how a multi-purpose building can be devised with very simple means. A partition separates off a space for daily Mass, prayer and meditation and marriages. The bigger space serves during the week for film projections, discussions, etc. On Sundays the partition is opened and the whole building becomes a place of worship.

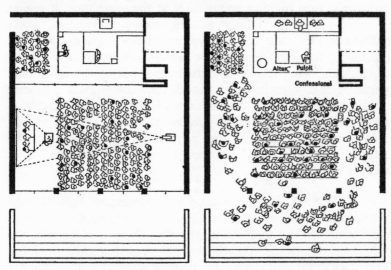

Under the heading 'Heretical building programme', a working party of the World Council of Churches writes: 'As there can be heretical structures, so also there can be heretical buildings. They must be considered heretical if they encourage in the congregation a feeling of religious security within the walls of an isolated holy place. They must be rejected if they suggest introversion and flight from the world and lead worshippers to long for the joys of heaven far away from all the labours of this world and thus to overlook the fact that heaven is only realized on earth when day-to-day relations between men are made holy both in the congregation and outside it'. [12]

[12] *Kirche für andere*, ORK, Geneva, 1967, 32.

8. Recently, the Congregation for the evangelization of the peoples and the pontifical mission societies have recommended modesty in setting up new buildings and made it a condition for new subsidies. [13] Rome itself has not set a good example of this modest line in either its secular or ecclesiastic history. The building of new churches and religious houses since the Second World War has continued in the triumphalist style and now rightly disturbs critical observers [14] as well as many residents in Rome. *L'Osservatore Romano* is very inclined to print photographs and descriptions of magnificent new churches and cathedrals, thus inviting imitation; [15] at the same time, it speaks of multi-purpose buildings as 'impersonal, polyvalent, polycultural places' and as an 'uncomforting diagnosis' for the future. [16] The new Directory for bishops comes down in favour of churches being modest and functional but at the same time warns against anything that can disturb the 'sacred character of the place'. [17] From discussion with Italian architects it is clear that the idea of multi-purpose buildings has simply not been considered. More's the pity, since it shows that the external signs of a gulf between worship and life remain as marked as ever.

9. We need to be continually re-examining the question of the true nature of mission. Christ did not commission us to build churches but to build up the Church, that is, to heal the sick, cast out devils, preach the gospel and gather disciples. This does demand a degree of space or some building; but the problem can be solved quite simply along the lines adopted by Christians of the early centuries and by the Independent Churches today. In Latin America, especially, but also in Africa and Asia, we come across free space everywhere in the cities,

---

[13] S.C.P.G.E., *Acta Pontificalium Operum,* Rome, 1972, 42.

[14] E.g., *Lettera ai cristiani di Roma,* from 13 priests living in the migrant quarters, in IDOC, Rome, 1.4.1972, p. 15-23. Further, the statements of Abbot Franzoni, Card. Pellegrino, etc.

[15] *La moderna Cattedrale di Barranquilla,* in OR 1.1.1972; *Monumentale tempio in Polonia alla Madonna,* in OR 28.10.1972.

[16] OR 7.7.1972.

[17] Directory for bishops, Rome, 1973, 116f.

often the inner courtyard of houses where on Sundays a dozen or perhaps a hundred believers assemble; they pray, sing, clap their hands, listen to the gospel, meditate in silence, open themselves to the gospel (and sometimes speak in tongues). They go out renewed, as people 'sent', confidently returning to their daily lives. We call them sectarians; but we have much to learn from them in renewing the Church, and we have already learned much. We learn from pastoral experience that monumental buildings stand in an inverse relation to liveliness of worship.

10. We may leave what is well founded in peace. Each age has its own style. But for the time to come, we make the following recommendations, in the spirit of Vatican II:

— We should look for new, dynamic but more modest activities, which are not tied to rigid institutions or to ambitious building programmes.

— We must one day give up building as a habit, and only allow new building in unavoidable exceptional cases.

— When we have to build, we should look for architects capable of taking a middle way between the traditional, often ponderous mission style and the modern expensive techniques, and who can unite simplicity with beauty, solidity and a functional style.

— We should promote the idea of multi-purpose buildings which, depending on the environment, can be anything from a hut to a community centre in concrete.

— Our money must first and foremost be put into work which is plainly religious and social, e.g., catechists, Bibles, the mass media, founding co-operatives. We should invest also in means of improving living conditions.

— Our big buildings must be thrown open to the poor, so that we can welcome them and give them the help they need; then the buildings will cease to excite criticism.

— Once the buildings needed as bases for church action are available, then our brothers and expert lay helpers in them should be placed at the disposal of the people and even the local government.

371

Chapter 21

MONEY AND THE SPIRIT:
FINANCIAL PROBLEMS
IN THE LOCAL CHURCH

The labourer is worthy of his hire.

(Lk 10:7)

1. The Lord's missionary discourses (Lk 9:1-6; 10:1-24) have something fascinating about them: committed and yet care-free; a hazardous and yet confident going forth to announce the coming kingdom of God; a return full of joy that even the evil spirits had trembled before the disciples; and finally the Lord's exultant cry: 'I bless you Father...' Francis of Assisi was particularly attracted by this passage in the gospel. Today's apostles must continually examine their own attitudes in its light. A fundamental aspect of it is serene poverty ('Take nothing with you on the way, neither staff not wallet, neither food nor money') and, correspondingly, a readiness to accept hospitality because one service deserves another: the receiver of the message should support the messenger.

Paul's economic theory seems to deviate a little from this. In some places, he declined all support and lived by the work of his hands to prevent any misunderstanding that he preached the gospel for gain. Elsewhere, he accepted alms and defended the principle that preachers of the gospel should be able to live by the gospel (1 Cor 9:14). Further, he insists that the community should face up to their own financial problems and develop charitable activity even beyond their own boundaries. When need prevailed in Jerusalem, he organized a collection in various communities, although those Christians largely belonged to the ranks of the poor themselves. There must have

372

been rivalry in giving: 'It was to the limit of your strength and even beyond, I am witness, that you spontaneously begged us to let you share in the grace and the fellowship of this service to the saints' (2 Cor 8:3-4). In the sequel are some of the finest considerations ever written on the subject of Christian charity. [1] It is clear that it was not a case of the mother Church helping her daughters but of poor communities helping those who were poorer still.

2. History decreed that mother and daughter Churches should belong to countries with very great differences in culture and wealth, and this almost inevitably led to the principle of financial dependence on help from abroad. First, the courts of Spain and Portugal covered the costs of the missions; then came the various kinds of missionary associations and the appeal sermons preached by missionaries. The latter got themselves sent baggage trains of supplies: clothes for themselves and the naked children, provisions and medicines, machines and tools, candle-sticks and thuribles, vestments and every kind of sacred and profane accessory. [2] This must not be ridiculed. The people were genuinely poor and needed help with everything. What we can recognize and regret as we look back on it, although we did as much ourselves, is this: Christianity was cheapened in this way, because 'What costs nothing is worth nothing'; and the communities we founded were immature and dependent, because he who pays the piper calls the tune. The financial autonomy of the missionary was transposed onto the spiritual level. He was in every way the active element; the congregation was passive.

3. After political decolonization, the young Churches need structural changes not only in personnel but also in financial matters. They must not continue to be dependent on foreigners. Only children, the halt and the lame have the right to live at other people's expense. That is not what the young Churches are. Or is it? An African priest, B. Nkuissi from the Cameroons, writes in his unpublished thesis: 'The mission Churches find

[1] O. Haas, *Paulus der Missionar,* Münsterschwarzach, 1971, pp. 51-53, 70-72.
[2] Bühlmann, *Afrika gestern, heute, morgen,* Freiburg, 1960, pp. 113-120.

themselves in a situation which we must unhesitatingly call dramatic. They are alive only through artificial feeding. They are like patients whose vital organs — heart, lungs — are artificial, who breathe through an oxygen mask and can survive only with regular blood transfusions. Our young Churches are alive only thanks to continual injections of money and personnel, with the consequence that our theological thinking, liturgical reforms and pastoral methods are also injected from abroad'. [3]

A great number of young Churches are in fact financially dependent on help from abroad to the extent of 70 - 90%. This is an abnormal and humiliating condition. It is well known and sorely felt; it is discussed at episcopal conferences but a way out is hard to find. The Tanzanian Pastoral Institute at Bakumbi proposed in 1970 that parishes each year should find 20% more of their own expenses so that they would be self-supporting in five years; in the following five years, they should take on themselves 20% more of diocesan commitments as well. Thus in ten years, the dioceses too would be self-supporting in ordinary commitments and would need foreign help only for new projects. A splendid plan, but carrying it out is hard indeed.

The young states, in their first enthusiasm, contracted debt after debt, so that they are now up to the neck in it and complaining about the evils of neo-colonialism. Only a few heads of state have had the foresight not to get chained up like this, not to be beggar-nations but to promote self-reliance. One of these is President Nyerere. With the slogan, 'Live more simply, work harder', he raised the national product, between 1960 and 1970, from £22 millions to £100 millions and kept overseas loans below 10% of that. [4] The 'Do it yourself' tried by the Chinese and recommended by them to the young states should also be applied in the Third Church.

4. They must discover how best to pay their own way. A tax on Church members imposed by the state, which still exists

[3] Partially published in EV 1968, pp. 33-44, 97-105.
[4] E. Steiner, *10 Jahre unabhängigkeit Tansanias,* in ITE, Olten, 1971, p. 106-116.

in some western countries although it is criticized, is out of the question in countries where Christians are in the minority. Contribution under pain of exclusion from the sacraments, as has been tried in a few places, cannot be justified. There is only one way — and that is to grow and develop oneself under the guidance of the Spirit. In the Church, financial problems can be solved only by the Holy Spirit, insofar as Christians filled by the Spirit give to the Church what belongs to the Church, and the Church for her part refrains from pretentiousness and is ready to live poorly according to the gospel.

Stole fees (offerings made on the occasion of the administration of the sacraments and sacramentals) have led to too many situations little in accord with the gospel. For many priests in Latin America, pastoral work consisted in baptizing and saying Mass on Sundays, since that brought in the money. They opposed division of parishes since it would reduce the number of baptisms and the size of the collections. They refused to follow the new instructions to renew the faith of parents on the occasion of the baptism of their children, since that could have led to many parents not bringing their children to baptism. Some had funerals of first, second and third class with different fees, depending on the number of bells rung and on whether the priest blessed the body at the altar, accompanied it to the door of the church or as far as the cemetery. The new Directory for bishops, 1973, ordered the abolition of stole fees, with the exception of Mass stipends. [5]

Mass stipends from Europe and America provide many Third Church priests with the only ready money they have. Even in countries where the priest has a secure position in society, the system can be questioned on theological and practical grounds; but in the Third Church it is clearly bad because the poor peoples' mass collections are of necessity very small. So priests are tempted or even forced to let these mass stipends go on coming, in spite of constant prohibitions from the Vatican. [6]

---

[5] Nos. 88 and 182; on the problems of Latin America: L. Stucki, *Kontinent im Aufbruch. Südamerika auf dem Weg ins 21 Jahrhundert,* Bern, 1971, p. 69f.

[6] AAS 1971, 841; 1974, 308-311.

Other possibilities are the Sunday collections, tithes and offerings in kind, and parish bazaars which have the advantage of involving a number of people. In many places, bishops have recently introduced a Church tax, equivalent to about a day's wage every year, to be collected at a suitable time by members of the parish council.

5. The goal of gradually gaining financial independence should be pursued with certain priorities in mind. A first claim on the congregation is the support of their own catechists: 'The labourer is worthy of his hire'. There is today a tendency to employ fewer full-time and more part-time catechists, which means less of a burden for the congregation. It would be considered a betrayal of one's own local Church to turn to European and American Churches to pay them; [7] at most, foreign contributions towards the initial investment (the training costs) could be justified. Next in priority would come the regular expenses of worship, the maintenance of priests and those sisters who are no longer in paid employment in the schools but directly at the service of the congregation. Of course, their standard of living cannot much exceed that of the people; we can hardly expect the poor to contribute to the support of the 'rich'. Thirdly, the parish's connection with the whole of the local Church should be made clear by annual collections for the minor seminary and other diocesan works. Besides meeting all these regular expenses, special collections will be needed when repairs have to be undertaken or when some contribution to larger projects is called for from the local community. Pastoral experience teaches us that only by such joint efforts can a community realize its own identity and acquire not merely a building but also self-confidence and a sense of belonging together.

6. Native priests and missionaries must be on the same financial footing. Insecurity has an oppressive effect on many priests. Not all have the courage to take up the challenge of poverty in common with the masses of their people and work

[7] So says Hastings, *Kirche und Mission im modernen Afrika*, Graz, 1969, p. 304; cf. also S.C.P.G.E., *Catechists in Africa, Asia and Oceania*, Rome, 1972, pp. 45-51.

part-time so as to contribute to their upkeep by the work of their hands (this could be a relaxation, or just a good example, or even ascetical exercise). Furthermore, some feel under a special obligation to their relatives. Education is seen not as a contribution to national development but rather as an investment which is expected to bring returns to the whole family, even where the family has not contributed to the costs. Not a few native priests are too free with parish money and with offerings for the mission; if we were to press the point, it could be called diverting funds.

Until now missionaries from different institutes have worked under various contracts with bishops. Institutes specializing exclusively in missionary work have been worse off than other societies which, with stronger home bases, can support their missionaries and so relieve the bishop's burden. A fair compromise is being sought in Tanzania. A missionary should cost the bishop or congregation no more, but also no less, than a native priest. What he does *as a missionary* to assist the local Church (his living and the expenses of his apostolate), should be paid for by that local Church; the expenses he incurs *as a foreigner* (his journeys home for vacation, his care in sickness and old age), should be covered by the institute or the home Church. [8] Not until the financial arrangements are similar in all countries shall we be able to consider exchanges of personnel which could be advantageous on occasion.

7. It is not utopian to make such demands of the local Church, as is proved by the example of the Protestants. They have anticipated us in calling for local financing by about a century. The famous trio of self-support, self-government and self-propagation derives from H. Venn (1796-1873) or, more probably, R. Anderson (1796-1880). These were the three steps to the founding of new Churches. [9] Now, every observer can see that the Protestants are a long way ahead of us in making these demands felt, everywhere from Indonesia to India, Africa

[8] Religious Superiors' Association of Tanzania, *Contracts of Missionary Institutes with Local Ordinaries,* Dar es Salaam, 1973.

[9] P. Beyerhaus, *Die Selbständigkeit der jungen Kirchen als missionarisches Problem,* Wuppertal, 1956, p. 46.

to South America. We still tend to do everything for the poor Christians and, out of sincere concern for their salvation, to enrol them in the Church without making any demands of them. But the members of the sects make real sacrifices in their joyous faith. Pentecostals often require their adherents to contribute 10% of their income. As one appeal puts it: 'Give until it hurts. Then go on giving until it stops hurting. Salvation is free but not cheap. There are many who put nothing in the collection and then are surprised at the coldness of the worship'. [10]

Something similar occurs in the messianic movement. Fuchs studied the question in India and discovered how among the lowest classes and the non-caste a great number of enthusiastic leaders had arisen, able to arouse optimistic hope in a most pessimistic situation. They gave life to a movement towards self-help, created solidarity and sense of community and achieved astonishing results both in work undertaken and money collected. Most of the movements ended in disappointment, since they were not, after all, able to change the situation by their own efforts alone. Both the government and the missions, instead of joining in with these movements and guiding them to success, have worked out their own plans from above and kept all the responsibility to themselves. In so doing they have deprived these people of their self-respect and kept them in beggarly status. Then they complain about their lack of co-operation. [11]

8. There is no doubt that help from abroad is still needed. But it must take the form of *helping people to help themselves*. Pearson accepts that, according to the most optimistic calculations, developing nations will still need substantial foreign aid at the end of the present century. This will be true also of those Churches which are no longer 'missions' but are still young Churches in need of help, 'developing Churches'. The help given must not perpetuate dependence but must, as quickly as

[10] W.J. Hollenweger, *Enthusiastisches Christentum,* Zürich, 1969, p. 448.

[11] S. Fuchs, *Rebellious prophets,* Bombay, 1965, IX–XIV, 284–290.

possible, create the conditions for the young Churches to stand on their own feet. The pontifical works for the propagation of the faith distributed in 1971 about 30 million dollars, 69.33% of which was for regular works and 30.67% for extraordinary purposes. So far, the regular works have been supported by grants equally distributed among the ecclesiastical divisions under *Propaganda*. Efforts are being made, with the greatest tact and diplomacy, to persuade the better-off dioceses to renounce part of their grants in favour of the poor districts. [12] This surely is an obvious step to take. But we ought to go further and adjust the allocation between the ordinary and extraordinary grants by five to ten per cent in favour of the latter. We ought not to be continually setting up new works which will need permanent financial support. We ought instead to set up some economic basis for the Church as it now is — rather in the manner of benefices, livings and foundations. [13] This could take the form of small farms and enterprises (without too much of the flavour of modern capitalism) which could bring in a yearly income for the Churches; together with the contributions of active congregations — their efforts must never be allowed to flag because capital becomes available — they could make the Churches independent of foreign aid. The long term solution would also have to include juster prices for raw materials and national social and economic development. Then the better-off Christians, in so far as they preserve the spirit of Christ, will be able to contribute in the most appropriate way to the support of their Church on a world-wide scale.

9. If only evangelization could be kept independent of money, as it was when the Lord sent out his disciples. Money always brings tensions and temptations. But, with things as they now are, such an ideal is unattainable. Nonetheless, the impression that the Church is a great economic enterprise should be erased. The 'rich' western Church must find ways of improving its image to conform better with the gospel. In some regions, the mission has at its disposal larger buildings and many more jeeps and lorries than the government; and this causes

[12] *Acta Pont. Operum,* Rome, 1972, p. 53f, 44f, 66f.
[13] LThK 2, 196-200.

resentment. In the postwar years, quite a number of lay helpers came out to assist in development work but in fact spent most of their three years installing electric light, water pumps, refrigerators, washing machines and hygienic improvements in the houses of the missionaries and sisters. We need more genuine solidarity with the poor and more equality of opportunities for all.

A native Church which is really poor need not necessarily saddle itself with all the works set afoot by the missionaries. She is in no way obliged for ever to have her own nurseries, schools, workshops, maternity clinics, hospitals and private cemeteries, thus appearing as a state within the state. Her principal contribution is animation and Christian commitment. What the western Churches contribute for development should not be invariably channelled through the native Church (through its hierarchical and clerical structures). We need to form more committees of responsible lay people of the locality (on which the 'Church' should certainly *also* be represented, since the priests are after all responsible men), to work in collaboration with the local government people.

10. In spite of the trust which the Church enjoys, in contrast with the international organizations and other secular institutions, there is a growing *malaise*. Christians who pay out money expect to see the accounts. It is certainly desirable, in accordance with post-conciliar views of the Church, that the money should be spent sensibly, with due regard for priorities and within an overall plan. But when the charitable organizations make such stipulations, the other side reacts badly and complains of mistrust, bossiness and neo-colonialism. People on the spot object to having decisions made for them. [14]

To avoid such friction, the bishops' conference should set up a co-ordinating body in each country, to examine and approve all projects seeking overseas aid. This could help to ensure more effective pursuit of national aims and avoid ecclesiastical egotism. It would bring better planning for the local Church and more positive dialogue with overseas organizations

[14] Interview with Mgr. Zoa, in *Peuples du Monde,* Paris, June 1970.

leading to agreement on common principles of aid for development. Since 1967, the Evangelical Lutheran Church of Tanzania, formed in 1963 out of seven local Churches, has directed all contributions from abroad, all new missionaries and all student grants through its central administration. [15] This kind of centralization does not stop the free-lances and the 'charismatics' from going their own way regardless. But overseas bodies do now know who they are dealing with in each case.

11. Perhaps here, as elsewhere, external pressure may engineer a breakthrough for new ideas. Many states turn a covetous eye on the Churches. They keep material in their archives to be used when opportunity offers: records of duty-free imports for distribution, such as milk powder and clothing, which later came to be sold; financial transactions which circumvent rules and damage the state; buildings erected without tax (because they are for education purposes), which in fact become motherhouses. They know the money is not diverted to private advantage but is used in the service of the people (in India, an illustrated review stirred up a lot of interest by revealing how in mosques and Hindu temples offerings were systematically and cynically diverted into the pockets of a small group of corrupt people in league with one another. It was said that the Churches seemed to be the only religious institutions free of these abuses [16]), but in spite of this the strong position of the 'rich' Churches gives offence.

Here and there, legislation is planned to control all overseas aid and with it all church finances. The Indian parliament has been discussing a 'Foreign Aid Bill' since 1972. We must expect that before long church money from abroad will be blocked or subject to heavy taxation. Then the local Church is bound to find a way of living out of its own resources at the ordinary living standards of the country; it will be as good a Church —

[15] S. Hertlein, *Aufbau der Kirche in Tansania*, Münsterschwarzach, 1971, p. 147f. The same tendency is apparent in the secular field in Latin America: Stucki, *op. cit.* (n. 5), pp. 264-67.

[16] J. Malhorta, *Corruption in the houses of God*, in *The Illustrated Weekly of India*, New Delhi, 3.9.1972, 8-17.

perhaps a better Church — when that happens. But it would be wiser to make preparations in advance for the day.

In the meantime, we ought immediately to cease infringing any state regulations in the matter of remittances, not only to avoid scandals but also, in all loyalty, to render the state its due.

Chapter 22

FROM HEGEMONY TO PARTNERSHIP:
SERVICES BETWEEN CHURCHES

> *Many will give honour to God when they see how you obey the gospel of Christ and how generously you share with them and with all others* (2 Cor 9:13).

1. With the key word *koinonia* (fellowship, sharing, communion), that fine ecclesiologist Paul put his finger for all time on the crux of all Christian existence. While in the Old Testament the word referred to the link existing between those who share the same life and calling, in the New Testament it becomes a central theological concept. In the vertical sense (or, to change the image a little, in the direction of the centre), it connotes being one with Christ, in his passion, death and resurrection, with his body, with his Spirit; in the horizontal sense (or in the direction of the periphery), it connotes union with those who believe in Christ with whom we are gathered around Christ in celebrating the Eucharist. It leads to spontaneous sharing of goods within the community, as well as with other Churches with whom the bishop is in communion. The service in love to which it leads is proof of obedience to the gospel of Christ and induces others to praise God, pray for one another, feel drawn to one another and wonder at the abundant grace of God (cf. 2 Cor 9:13). [1]

2. This theology is now again become extremely topical. After centuries of dependence and subordination, local Churches have sprung up everywhere. *Koinonia* shows how the missionary

---

[1] LThK 6, 368f; J. Müller, *Missionarsiche Anpassung als theolog. Prinzip*, Münster i. W., 1973, pp. 242-244.

nature of the Church should today be understood and manifested both in the old Churches and in the young ones.

All must remain open to all around, since individual salvation and that of the neighbour are bound up together. The one does not exist unless it is linked to the other. A Church which is introvertedly concerned about its own maintenance, a mere service station for its own clientèle, is developing into a pseudo-Church. Its structure obstructs the progress of the gospel instead of clearing a way for the gospel in the world: 'Mission is not a peripheral concern. It is not an optional activity but rather the heart of the Church. The Church stands or falls with its missionary élan, with its liveliness, causing movement and disturbance all around'. [2]

But this missionary élan which has always belonged to the Church is not to be exercised simply in the north-south direction. It is not to find expression in a one-sided tutelage and in one-way traffic but must include an awareness of the political, economic and churchly interdependence between all peoples in the modern world; it means we must all put ourselves at one another's disposal in a kind of osmosis and complementary mutual aid, so that we may all grow into the fullness of Christ. No more godparents and godchildren but partners all. 'It would be false to suggest that the non-western Churches must attain full independence without delay. No Church, western or not, is called by God to be independent. Rather, each is called to manifest an identity which is unique and cannot be repeated by others or interchanged, while at the same time all are to enrich one another by exchanges and mutual help, thus co-operating in a more credible and effective way towards the full liberation of mankind within the framework of Christ's saving plan'. [3]

[2] H. Lagerberg, *Strukturen der missionarischen Gemeinde,* in Van der Linde (ed.), *Neue Perspektiven nach dem Ende des konventionellen Christentums,* Freiburg, im B., 1968, pp. 429-462, esp. 436; Bühlmann, *Sorge für alle Welt,* Freiburg im B., 1967, pp. 30-41; H. Tenhumberg, *Die missionarische Verantwortung der Ortskirchen,* in *Ordenskorrespondenz,* Cologne, 1972, 2-12. Häring, *Teologia nella protesta,* Brescia, 1972, pp. 169-172.

[3] J. Kerchofs, *Situationsanalyse der Kirchen die nicht zum nordatlantischen Raum gehören,* in ZMR 1972, pp. 161-171, esp. 167.

3. Mission no longer relates merely to people in geographically distant lands who are 'far from Christ'. [4] The Church is missionary everywhere both in the passive and the active sense: 'mission in six continents'. [5] Every Church today faces need and crisis; every Church is either still in the diaspora situation or has returned to it. Everywhere there are increased numbers of doubters, onlookers and alienated; the nucleus of believers will be renewed, *can only* be renewed, when they give their full attention to all these who are 'far from Christ'. [6] Home and foreign mission are not in competition with one another; they do not deprive one another of money, people or energy. Rather, they stimulate one another. Experience teaches that those who are most zealous for the 'missions' are also those who best serve the community at home, whereas those who cannot see any big task ahead of them give themselves up to cavilling criticism and eventually leave the Church. Gheddo formulates the principle that contestation within the Church varies in inverse proportion with the missionary commitment of the Church. [7] The fact that many groups are slipping towards Marxism seems to show that young people have lost hope that the Church can still offer the world a real message of liberation.

4. Since our views have been dominated by the picture of the western Church as benefactor and the southern Church as beneficiary, before elaborating the demands of service between Churches it may help to indicate briefly what the southern Church has to give. [8] She can help the western Church towards understanding herself as 'a sign raised among the nations', as 'Church for the others' rather than being satisfied with her own life. She can show us what conversion really entails. In Biblical usage, conversion is a definitive change of direction and an orientation of life according to the message of the kingdom. It

[4] AG 23.

[5] On this call to mission, see ch. 1.A.4, p. 5.

[6] AG 37.

[7] P. Gheddo, *Quale il futuro dell'animazione missionaria?*, in *Mondo e Missione*, Milan, 1972, pp. 368-395, esp. 384.

[8] W. Bühlmann, *Mission und Geneinde*, in *Lebendige Seelsorge*, Freiburg im B., 1968, pp. 245-252.

means, primarily, that first conversion which takes place quite frequently in the southern Church, where adults hear the message, are astonished at it and say: 'Yes, if that is so, I will be baptized'. For ourselves, baptized unresisting in infancy and confirmed as school children, we need to share their experience of the meaning and the shock of biblical *metanoia*. They provide us with pastoral inspiration. During the Council and since, the urgency of their situation has led to new practices, for instance the renewal of the catechumenate and ecumenical openness. Many things described in this book can provide the Second Church with a mirroring of her own problems, and she may see a better way to their solution. For our growing shortage of priests, the Third Church offers us the model of the 'mission station' where two or three priests live together and serve a region with 30,000 Christians, with out-stations of 500 to 1000 faithful. These out-stations are visited once or twice a month by the priest; for the rest they live their religious life as a congregation, hold Sunday worship without a priest and receive communion. They are responsible for the catechumens, for administering the Church tax and are much more active than Christians in our congregations for whom the priest has always done everything.

The Third Church also enriches our theology. In their seminaries, today, it is not only scholastic theology that is taught but at least the beginning of an original encounter between revelation and this particular local Church with its own environment. This new orientation does not mean opening the way to a deceptive universal theological synthesis. Rather, it takes seriously pluralism in theology and leads to an experience of theological richness in the Church. It raises healthy doubts about the obviousness of one's own theological approach and can open up new horizons by framing questions in a fresh way. [9]

5. The first effect of *koinonia* should be communication, that is, sympathetic understanding, feeling for one another,

[9] F. Kollbrunne, *Der Ort der Mission in der Theologie*, in J. Baumgart (ed.), *Vermittlung zwischenkirchlicher Gemeinschaft*, Schöneck, 1971, pp. 247-263, esp. 262; Müller, *Missionarische Anpassung als theol. Prinzip*, 1973, pp. 154-161.

suffering with one another. It should mean real interest, in the sense of sharing the common ground between us, leading us to take the affairs of another Church as seriously as those of our own. In making us sensitive to these needs, mission preachers and missionaries on leave will play an important role but not the only one: parents will begin to open their children's eyes to the needs of other Churches; teachers, in their various subjects (for example, geography, world history and literature), will refer to the presence of the Church in other lands and to foreign Christian literature; priests, in religious instruction, will open up their pupils' horizons 'to the ends of the earth'; letters from missionaries who come from the parish will be used in preaching and reproduced in parish newsletters; the needs of the Third World and the Third Church will be brought into the bidding prayers — 'Among the sick and suffering, pastors will encourage those who with generous heart offer prayers and penance for the evangelization of the world', [10] after the manner of St Thérèse of Lisieux, patron of the missions; teachers in seminaries and universities 'in the way they present dogmatic, biblical, moral and historical disciplines, will bring out the missionary aspects in them, so as to form a missionary consciousness in future priests'; [11] journalists (not only in missionary reviews, which in recent years have been significantly improved) will no longer make headlines of the Third World only when a new war has broken out but present a realistic picture of their daily needs, their aspirations and the progress they make... [12]

6. But let us not lose ourselves in dreamland: we are far from this ideal. Instead of a new missionary breakthrough after the Council, we are facing the great crisis of the missions and the gap in missionary information has not been filled. True, in comparison with twenty years ago when the German catechism did not mention the missions at all, [13] there is now a mention; but it is only a marginal one, as if mission were merely an

[10] AG 38.
[11] AG 39.
[12] Bühlmann, *op. cit.* (n. 2), pp. 45-57.
[13] *Op. cit.*, p. 29f.

optional extra and certainly not the commission given us by the Lord to be the overriding motivation affecting our view of the future and our attitude to the making of history. [14] The same is true of preaching. [15] In study days and national synods, working parties on mission awaken little interest even when they include consideration of ecumenism, peace and justice. Development aid and mission have as yet failed to find their due place in the consciousness of Christians, although an interesting distinction can be observed: aid for development is regarded as quite important by men and by well-educated people in general, while mission is of great interest to women over sixty who have had only elementary education and are regular church-goers. [16]

Much depends on the way things are presented. There is an old image of the missionary, now quite out of date but persisting for psychological reasons. Can it be renewed and seen within the framework of the whole problem of the young local Church? There are grounds for hope. Here and there, groups of young people do seek information about the problems of the Third World and the Third Church and inquire about the appropriate response from committed Christians. Their ecumenism thus does achieve a world dimension, since they seek not only to overcome the 'ecclesial underdevelopment' of the western world by sensitizing it to these issues but also, indirectly, to help the southern Church. [17]

The same should happen in the reverse direction, sensitizing the Third Church to the problems of the Second and First.

7. It has become clear that information, however much it is stepped up, is so much water on a duck's back unless interest in the subject is already alive. Interest is aroused through personal relations. In this light we can see the importance of

[14] J. Vattkattasser, *Das Verständnis der Mission in den deutschsprachigen katechet. Lehrbüchern der Gegenwart,* reviewed in VSVD 1971, pp. 159-161.

[15] M. Linz, *Anwalt der Welt,* Stuttgart, 1964.

[16] L. Wiedenmann, *Die Mission auf der deutschen Synode,* in KM 1972, pp. 76-79.

[17] E.g., *Politisches Nachtgebet in Köln,* Mainz, 1969; H. Weber, *Schalom,* Freiburg, i. Ue., 1972.

exchanges of personnel. Certainly, it is still a highly-principled and unselfish act of service, on the part of countries Christian for many centuries, to place at the disposal of the Third Church such resources as can be mustered in response to the latter's wishes. But these efforts should be thought of as bridge-building, as embassies between the Churches and guarantees that the universality and unity of the Church are not just ideas, as catalysts and signs of genuine mutual interest. When a family, a youth group or a parish have a missionary working in some part of the world, they follow the events of that country and Church with a new interest.

Journeys made by priests and bishops could also fit into this scheme. Formerly, priests made it a point of honour to visit the Holy Land at least once in their life-time. Now, in addition, they could make it a point of honour to visit the Third Church at least once. Now that intercontinental tourism is making such strides, why not promote journeys for contact between Churches?

To supplement the missionaries who go out 'for life', thought is being given to sending people to the missions for a limited number of years. I would suggest as a solution (not to be taken literally): 'Every priest to serve a few years in the Third Church'. Missionary institutes, with their stable organization, could provide the employing agency. A priest could serve for four or five years without arousing fears of colonialism and afterwards could keep his home Church in live contact with the Third Church. Teachers of theology especially are needed in many seminaries. They could make their own theology more fruitful by getting to know and understand the situation of the Church they visit.

Priests and students from overseas also help to strengthen these links when families and parishes open their doors to them. Could it not fit into the logic of this service between Churches that these priests should serve for a few years in parishes in western countries? The expectation that one day African priests will come to convert Europe will remain utopian for many years, in view of the growing shortage of priests in Africa and South America. It is easier now to conceive such a movement coming from India or from Vietnam. We are not suggesting that these countries give up their priests for us, but they could serve in the Second Church for a few years, thus making the universality of the Church more visible; then, instead of carving a niche for themselves in Europe, they could return home enriched by their impressions and experiences.

8. Another form of *koinonia* is economic aid. There is no calculating the amounts of money that have gone from western to southern Churches in the course of centuries and especially in recent decades. God knows all the hidden good will and sacrifices it has meant. The Catholic Church in West Germany despatched 401 million DM, in 1970, by various channels to the Third World and needy Churches. [18]

On the whole, there is still too little done by Churches and states to lay the foundations of a better future. Incomparably more is done out of motives of necessity, self-defence and aggression than out of concern for the neighbour. The war in Vietnam, even before it reached its climax, cost more in half a day than a year's budget for UNESCO. The Arab-Israeli war in 1973 used up ten million dollars an hour. Here is tangible evidence of original sin in the world of today.

The custom of begging for the missions is gradually dying out. Without wishing to minimize the importance, financial and spiritual, of traditional systems of alms-giving, one can say that it hardly appears consonant with the 'most important and most holy task of the Church' [19] to live entirely on alms. It should not be necessary for newly consecrated missionary bishops to set out on six months' begging tours or for missionaries on leave to go begging for their poor Churches. The links of service between the Churches require us to find a solution better suited to the times. In any case, the young generation will not accept the old-fashioned way of supporting the missions but will insist on structural solutions.

Missionary institutes, which will no longer be in charge of 'their' mission but will be at the service of the local Church, will cease to treat home parishes as a hunting ground in which to compete for alms and instead will put forward their needs in

[18] PMV-CI 1973/44, 38.
[19] AG 29.

390

ways agreed between them. The seven Protestant missionary societies in Switzerland have set us an example by forming a body for 'Evangelical Mission Co-operation': they combine in approaching parishes, make plans in common and have a combined postal account. The money received is shared according to budgets worked out in advance. [20]

Most western countries now have Church organizations and institutions like Misereor, Family Fast, etc., which use planning and modern publicity methods (and slogans like: 'We don't need milk powder: we need education' — 'People are not suffering famine because we eat too much but because we think too little' — 'What are we to do to make sure 40 millions die of hunger? Nothing'). By fully involving lay people, these organizations get results.

Although in managing development aid and disaster funds co-operation has been sought at the highest level and attained to some extent by CIDSE (*Coopération internationale pour le développement socio-économique*, based in Brussels) and *Cor Unum* at the Vatican, we still lack a similar planning body for inter-Church missionary assistance. The pontifical missionary works have a part to play here in conjunction with diocesan and national missionary councils. Many documents stress their prominence in the framework of aid organizations and they have, indeed, good reasons for stating their case: their universality, their multilateral constitution and their function as equalization funds. [21] But it is less important to emphasize their own priority than to prove the value of their work and to bring lay people in, not just as contributors but also to share responsibility. In some countries the pontifical mission works remain marginal to the Church while in others they have gained ground by new initiatives and modern methods of work. Since the system of contributions by individual associate members is bound to give way to a more communal response, one of the first tasks is to induce parishes and dioceses to 'pay their dues' according to the mind of the Council and provide a yearly contribution

[20] E. Blum, *Die Mission der reformierten Schweiz,* Basel, 1965, p. 41f.
[21] Mgr Kempeneers, *L'aide aux Missions et les Oeuvres Pont. Miss.,* in *Seminarium,* Rome, 1973 (Nov.).

to the needs of sister Churches as a matter of course. [22] For this purpose, specialists need to present a general view of the real needs of local Churches and earmark contributions according to a global financial plan. This could at least start on a regional basis. The pontifical mission works face the need to make themselves into an efficient central office for multilateral aid. The congress at Lyons in 1972 tried to show the way. [23]

9. Inter-Church service (which in principle ought to have absolute priority in all allocation of aid both financial and personal but which in practice has not been sufficiently expounded), could become not an authoritarian but a realistic and theologically based way of dealing with arguments about whether local Churches can be true Churches and therefore whether true *koinonia* is possible.

Vatican II was fortunate in that a new, pastorally-oriented theology had already been laboriously worked out; the Council gave it recognition and acceptance. This did not happen to the same extent at the subsequent bishops' Synods, as was particularly evident at the recent one on evangelization in the modern world. To be sure, there was no lack of speeches and discussions, case studies and sociology; what was lacking was real illumination of the new horizons, fresh theological guidelines capable of providing either a firm basis for the many opinions expressed or a criterion for discernment. It was not that the post-conciliar theology was found wanting; it was simply not taken into consideration. It is significant that in the whole discussion on theological pluralism nobody — as far as the record shows — made any reference to the fundamental study on this theme undertaken by the International Theology Commission. [24]

Once one has opened the door to fresh understanding of the Church's nature and being in this world, one must take the consequences. Europe is no longer the world; the Church

[22] AG 38; *Ecclesiae Sanctae*, III/8.

[23] *Les Oeuvres Pontificales Missionaires. Sous le signe de la collegialité apostolique,* Lyons, 1973, esp. pp. 229-235, 281f, 288-295.

[24] Commissione Teologica Internazionale, *Pluralismo. Unità della fede e pluralismo teologico,* Bologna, 1974 (the study itself dates from 1972).

is no longer a Church of the west. At the last synod, the majority of bishops came from the Third Church and two thirds of the speeches were made by them — facts which are a cause for rejoicing that the Church has made such progress. Now is not the time to draw back, terrified by our own daring. We must not stand in the way of young Churches in their search for new experiments, new methods and a 'native' theology. To date, only a small part of mankind has engaged in theologizing: the west has had a virtual monopoly. Now the other regions of the world are meeting Christ and his message and are beginning to make theology on the basis of their own history and their own insights, so we must expect a springtime burst of fresh theologies in bud. It would be unchristian to hinder this growth by shutting out the light — blanketing everything with a ready-made system of teaching as has happened in the past. What God has revealed through his prophets and finally through his Son to illuminate the meaning of our existence must be passed on without any restriction to the whole of mankind. Mankind is in a new situation in salvation history since Christ has come, and should not have to start time and again from scratch in dealing with its problems. The young Churches must have room and air to breathe, and should not be suffocated by all the panoply of western structures and western history. Fear is a very poor counsellor in this matter. Restrictive provisions, aiming to preserve 'unity' as the west understands it at all costs, risk losing more than they gain. It is only when we relate our theologizing to history, starting from the gospel, and so gain the broadness of vision needed to face the situations that present themselves that we can hope to preserve and reconcile everything.

The draft of a document containing the conclusions of the 1974 synod was rejected (except for the first section) by a large majority because the text seemed too novel and dangerous to some and too tame, abstract and non-committal to others. So polarization of thesis and antithesis carried the day. Instead of making a synthesis of mission and dialogue, general and parti-cular history of salvation, Christian and non-Christian religion, instead of being serious about co-operation with all men of good will, many wanted to retire into their own fortress behind a moat. Instead of welcoming the Third World requests for theology to be made relevant to the full liberation of man, and for stress to be laid on the unity of the two aspects ('Humanizing through the gospel. Evangelizing through human development'), many returned to dogmatic insistence that the other things are not the Church's business. Instead of treating Vatican II, with its ideas of the collegiality of the bishops with the Pope and of the autonomy of the local Church with regard to 'its own discipline, liturgical usages and theological and spiritual heritage', as the completion of Vatican I and so making section 23 of *Lumen Gentium* the foundation of the local Church, many put all the stress once again on the primacy of the Pope and on the universality of the one Church; and so, when it came to practical detail, they took back all they had previously agreed in theory. [25]

These syntheses must take their proper place in theological teaching in the Second Church as well as in the Third Church so as to remedy a certain time-lag in the mentality of the average bishop, priest and layman; people should not live in their imagination in a world that no longer exists (the cultural lag) nor must they do theology for a Church that is no longer *the* Church (the theological lag).

The bishops of the western Church had to admit in this last Synod that they had lost the leadership; one of them, afterwards, admitted it had been a lesson in humility (not humiliation). If that is so, it seems that there is no more important task for the Second Church, in view of the coming of the Third, than that of preparing herself for this new era by pausing for some open and creative theological thought.

[25] Typical of this centralizing tendency is D. Grasso, *I problemi trattati al Sinodo dei vescovi,* in *Civiltà Cattolica,* 1974, pp. 435-446.

Chapter 23

WHAT NOW? THE CHURCH OF THE FUTURE

Waiting in blessed hope (Tit 2:13).

A. *The Church of planning*

1. Orientation towards the future, 'waiting in blessed hope' defined the fundamental attitude of the first Christians. They had little to gain or lose in this world. So their gaze, quite ignoring the vast plain deep in gloom, was fixed on the glistening snow-covered heights that seemed so close from which they expected 'the manifestation of the glory of our great God and Saviour Christ Jesus' (Tit 2:13). Their invocation in their vigils and their watchword among themselves was: 'Maranatha — Come, Lord Jesus' (Rev 22:20). With the appearance of Jesus, everything had been set in motion: in the first phase, the shepherds in the night, the wise men from the east, the Holy Family in the flight to Egypt; in the second phase, the pilgrim band of a teacher with his disciples, the crowds that came from near and far, the angry synagogue authorities stirring up intrigue; in the third phase, the Easter morning that broke through all the darkness and all laws of nature, the sending of the disciples to the ends of the earth, the tumultuous intervention of the spirit... It could not all end in a calm return to the status quo, to a period without any more surprises. The climactic end to the series of events must be at hand: 'Come, Lord Jesus'.

2. Since that time, we have learned to effect a juster evaluation of the vast plain and to know the *this-worldly future* as our immediate task. This future is not just something that comes upon us. In contrast to the past and the present, it does

395

not yet exist for us except in man's guesses and the prognoses of the futurologists. We can and must project forward the habits and developments which mark the recent past and the present so as to foresee the proximate future, while being ready to add necessary corrections. The future, in fact, grows. It is newly created out of the present moment and, in that same moment, is condensed into something unchangeable. But this is not a mechanical process like a stalactite growing through the incessant dripping of water. At each fleeting moment of the present, man is free. He is, indeed, shaped by his past but he has the power to create something entirely new, as through the present moment he lets the future become history. If in doing this he denies all links with the past, he is floating on the clouds of utopianism. But if, on the contrary, through anxiety he represses the availability of the future, and sees it only in terms rigidly determined by the past, he becomes a reactionary. [1] The Church too must shape her future in continuity but also in creative freedom, finding a middle way between these two extremes.

3. The case is quite different with the *absolute future*, as we Christians know it. This does not grow out of the past. It comes as something absolutely new, in no way shaped by the present moment or by human history; it is the 'day of the Lord' (1 Thess 5:2) which, against all expectation but according to revelation and Christian hope, brings the resurrection of the flesh, the judgement of the world and the transformation of the universe into the new heaven and the new earth (however we may imagine these realities which transcend all imagination). [2] Of course this distant event is not simply added on to our history as a last act. Jesus Christ will not rise like a meteor. He is already present in our history as its alpha and omega, and his second coming will be only the final effect and final revelation of his continuous saving activity. This belief gives the Christian perseverance, invincible confidence and inner freedom in meeting all

---

[1] A. Darlapp, in LThK 10, 1411f; Y. Congar, *Priester und Laien im Dienst des Evangeliums,* Freiburg im B., pp. 277-284: *Der christliche Begrriff der Geschichte.*

[2] W. Theurer, *Der neue Himmel und die neue Erde. Die Zukunft in der Sicht der christl. Theologie,* in A. Resch (ed.), *Welt, Mensch und Wissenschaft morgen,* Paderborn, 1972, pp. 267-325.

actual social situations, so that he is able continually to create new this-worldly utopias as models for shaping a better future. [3]

4. This hope, which will never be disappointed, provides no dispensation from human striving and planning. On the contrary, every present moment must be freely and responsibly used for the good of the Church and of mankind. In this intermediate time, it is never enough to 'wait in blessed hope' *only*. Although the final eschatological event is entirely in God's hands, we ourselves have to leave our mark on all the preceding events. We are not allowed piously to say, 'God will provide' until we have done all that is humanly possible to direct the Church, in matters big and small, along the right course. The providence of God did not ward off the fall of the Church of North Africa, torn apart by conflicts and feuds; it did not prevent the Reformation which, because of the political and disciplinary state of the Church, 'had to be'; nor did it check the Church's loss of the working class in the 19th century, since the Church was too closely connected with capitalism.

Against an all too human type of missionary activity, continental Protestant theology has for decades been defending the opposite extreme position (the eschatological): mission is regarded as a free act of God who fulfils all his plans for humanity according to his own sovereign will. Both secular history and Church history are simply the stage and the wings where God enacts his eschatological event. To this there is the most valid of objections: it is equivalent to evacuating the incarnation and, consequently, it diminishes the reality of the Church and radically devalues man (the basic principle and the fundamental error of the Reformation): human labours lose their significance in face of God who does everything. [4]

The orientation towards God as our absolute future does not remove our responsibility for this world but makes it more radical. He who knows that God will one day wipe away all tears will not resign himself to letting the tortured go on suffering.

[3] Congar, *op. cit.*, p. 284; Rahner, *Die Frage nache der Zukunft,* in *Schriften* 9, 519-540, esp. 537.
[4] L. Wiedemann, *Mission und Eschatologie. Excerpta,* Paderborn, 1964, pp. 34-40.

He who knows that one day sickness will be at an end does all that is necessary at the present time to heal the diseases of individuals and of society. He who knows that the enemy of mankind, the devil, is already overcome, opposes him and all his trickery with ever renewed confidence, in spite of all temporary reverses. Either hope with anticipatory realization now in this world created and loved by God, or no hope at all! [5]

5. The present moment, as connecting link between the past and the future we have to shape, cannot be mastered with a simple flick of the wrist. Among the complications of the modern situation, progress is possible only with serious planning. It will not do to proceed piecemeal, merely dealing with each particular case as it occurs. Anyone doing that will one day have to tell a story of missed opportunities; we can seize our opportunities and exploit them only if we have a comprehensive view and plans. We need to weigh up the particular cases already dealt with and work out guidelines for future cases, so as to align them with the sort of future we are aiming at and not just any sort of future. Although we cannot swear by this type of planning, we must not despise all planning out of a false sense of superiority which is the result of ignorance and incompetence. God, who has given man understanding and a share in his providence, wishes these gifts to be used not only in the technical, economic and political fields but also in the field of Church matters.

6. Planning starts with collecting data and taking stock of the situation. At parish and diocesan level, in pastoral councils or clergy councils, it should be possible to undertake an examination of the present situation, perhaps on the basis of a good article from a pastoral review or a chapter of this book; it would not be just a matter of collecting figures for the yearly statistics but of looking for actual problems and trends, for instance, the degree of secularization among the young, of missionary dynamic in the parishes, how Christians are exerting influence on public life and the development of the country, etc.

It would also be interesting to establish a typology of dioceses

[5] Hollenweger, *Christentum,* p. 477, based on Moltmann.

and regions for countries and continents, or even for the whole Third Church. This has not been attempted for Catholics. Barrett has made a start in this direction by estimating the degree of evangelization of a population, basing his study on how long and how closely the Church has been present in a region and, particularly, on how much of the Bible has been translated and distributed; he has thus devised an index of evangelization for African tribes. [6] It would be possible to draw up a more detailed set of significant factors: the people's degree of openness to the Christian faith, the government's attitude to the Church, the social conditions in the region, methods of preaching used, number of catechumens, the stage of dialogue reached and the influence of Christians on their neighbours, Church structures (proportion of priests to Christians, of foreign to native priests, involvement of laity in parish and diocesan councils), etc. One to four points could be allocated to each of these indicative factors and the priority of each diocese for personal and financial help could be reckoned. Something similar is done by the United Nations: with the help of an index of illiteracy, industrialization, level of exports, average income, etc., 25 countries have been reckoned to be the least developed in the world and, in consequence, they receive particular attention in the second decade of development aid. [7]

7. After the data have been collected they need to be digested. Through the 'see - judge - act' technique, they can lead to recommendations and plans of action. It matters little whether they are called three- or five-year plans or mission strategy or something else. [8] The essential thing is to decide on definite priorities based on concrete data and pastoral consideration. Since means and resources (quantitatively and qualitatively) are not everything that could be wished for, we must seek to achieve the best and quickest results possible with the means and resources available. Naturally, every decision on priorities

[6] D.A. Barrett, *Frontier situations for evangelization in Africa*, Nairobi, 1972.
[7] Bühlmann, *Die Kapuzinermissionen*, in NZM 1973, pp. 183-189.
[8] J. Schmidlin, *Katholische Missionsstrategie*, in ZMR 1915, pp. 101-119; T. Ohm, *Vom Missionsplan und von der Missionsplanung*, in ZMR 1961, pp. 1-15.

hurts, because we have to postpone objectives that are less important but important for all that. Without the courage to make hurtful decisions, there is no planning. Those adversely affected must show understanding in the common interest. Besides, choice of priorities does not mean excluding anyone for there can be no exclusiveness in the kingdom of God: every local Church, even the smallest, has the right to develop. It is simply a question of more or less, now or later.

Priorities can be understood, in the first place, geographically. While the Church must go to every corner of the globe, there is no necessity always to be present with the same intensity everywhere. Simple Christian presence, the witness of life according to the gospel even without the prospect of immediate success, is not to be undervalued. But when it is realized that for a particular region the time of grace is clearly not at hand, fewer resources can be invested there and new missionaries sent by preference to places where the fields are ripe for the harvest, leaving those other peoples in all confidence to the grace of God which is present everywhere and is more powerful than the Church. Moreover, the Church's presence should be strengthened where there is greater historical potential for the future of the world: so, for instance, it is preferable to preach the message in Japan than among the Eskimos, even if greater immediate results can be expected among the latter. [9]

There should be no playing off one continent against another, since each of the three southern continents has its 'hour'. But within continents and individual countries, it ought to be possible to work out fairer priorities. This kind of planning is lacking among the Roman congregations. Each case is taken in isolation, urgent backing is given to requests for personnel from bishops and nuncios but no attempt is made to set up a scale of priorities. Missionary institutes are not easily allowed to run down their establishments or to give them up for more urgent tasks. In Cairo and Alexandria, for example, a few hundred nuns work in schools and hospitals. The young sisters would prefer to live in small communities in dialogue with the Moslem

[9] Rahner, *Strukturwandel,* 54; id., in *Pastoraltheologie,* I, 225f; II/2, 76f.

world (which would accord with the views of the Secretariat for non-Christians) or else go to the missions (which would suit the Congregation for evangelization). However, the competent Congregation for Oriental Churches will not agree to any change of the status quo. There is congestion of institutions in many cities of the Third World, often with schools competing against one another, but no bishop wants to let them go from 'his' city. 'Poor' bishops urge fairer shares in finance and personnel on a country basis but the 'rich' oppose the change. This kind of ecclesiastical egotism must be laid aside and *koinonia* must be practised on the basis of the pastoral priorities of the country.

8. Besides geographical priorities, there are priorities with regard to content and method. More important than all individual tasks is the question of the right fundamental pastoral attitude which should correspond to historical trends (what the French call *'tendances lourdes'*). These might be expressed by the following key-words: *for* freedom, equality, brotherhood, dialogue, subsidiarity, decentralization, participation, collegiality; *against* all kinds of discrimination, (theocratic) authoritarianism, institutionalism.

Burgalassi has given a good account of this change of mentality among perceptive Christians. [10] He describes a change

— from a juridical mentality to one more spontaneous, based on love;

— from impersonal systematizing to spontaneity and personal liveliness;

— from submission to routine to awareness of purpose;

— from individual, self-regarding activity to community and social activity;

— from the approach which goes from the world to God to an understanding of God coming to meet the world;

— from a spirituality of renunciation and segregation to a revaluation of earthly reality and of the part it plays in man's pilgrimage towards God;

[10] S. Burgalassi, *Le cristianità nascoste. Dove va la cristianità italiana?*, Bologna, 1970, p. 303.

401

— from order to conflict;

— from passivity towards the hierarchy to the necessary forms of collaboration and co-responsibility;

— from pastoral policies based on dispositions made from on high to practical experience;

— towards desacralization;

— from 'religion is all' to 'all is religion';

— from a Manichaean view of life to a more open and trustful one;

— from the ghetto mentality to ecumenism;

— from power to service;

— from external institution to the prophetic view.

We should not rest content with becoming aware of these trends, still less should we fight against them; we should welcome them as a dispensation from God and as fully compatible with the dignity of man.

There can be no either/or in regard to the great aims — evangelization and work for development, individual conversion and building up the community; we must have a comprehensive view and proper co-ordination, although the emphasis may need to be adjusted to circumstances. However, as far as our immediate tasks are concerned, the education and development of people must take precedence over building programmes, adult education over education for children, decentralized action in the villages over great mission centres, direct action over institutions, work in teams and groups over activity under one man in charge. We should prefer to work with cadres rather than with the crowd, because well trained cadres multiply our influence on the crowd. We must put the city before the country, mass media before the care of individuals, and first preaching of the gospel before regular parish work.

9. At this point, the many suggestions and recommendations in this book may cause the reader to take fright. But the flashes recorded here in black and white can only become reality if they ignite a spark in the reader's mind. The worst that could

happen would be for the book to be read over without its causing any shock (in the sense of annoyance and impulse to react). Many suggestions have been put in a deliberately provocative way, so that they can be considered by the reader or by a working party, in the hope that what truth there is in them may be recognized and that even better ideas may emerge from discussion. If the considerations presented here are followed up in concrete situations, tested, corrected and assimilated, then the ideas may become ideals and build up the necessary driving force to get something moving and assist renewal in the Church.

B. *The Church of hope*

1. If — as is desirable but improbable — renewal in the Church continues with an accelerating tempo, and if all the bishops' conferences of the Third Church work out a thorough planning programme in co-operation with pastoral centres (although we western perfectionists continually see men of the Third World getting themselves out of impossible situations by improvising, so that the Church too survives in poverty stricken situations and perhaps realizes the gospel better than many of our highly organized western parishes), even so there will always be plenty of room for the factor of uncertainty. We have seen this factor at work even in the compilation of cold statistics, so there is no hope of eliminating it from the present and future of the Church. Apart from the quite real threat of total atomic war hanging like Damocles' sword over mankind, which could bring world progress back to scratch, [11] (in fifth century Rome there were six-storied buildings and the children had tops working by steam power; contemporary futurologists might have predicted 20-storied houses for the sixth century, and steam power for industrial purposes; instead, goats were grazing over the ruined Roman forum, by then!), we must always allow for the unknown factor X that always keeps history in tension — the incalculable freedom of man. For a long time modern science thought it had analysed man as a physical and chemical

[11] G. Anders, *Endzeit und Zeitende. Gedanken über die atomare Situation*, München, 1972.

403

product and seen to the bottom of him as a psychological mechanism. But now, after all this scientific research, we find ourselves more than ever up against the incomprehensible mystery of man. [12] How much more is the Church a mystery, out of whose depths there is always rising the creatively new, unexpected and unplanned, as well as the devilishly inexplicable. We must always be ready for surprises in both directions. God can lead men to true piety through trashy Church art. He can bring the wisdom of the wise to nought (1 Cor 1:18f) and he praises the farmer who ceased to worry after sowing the seed (Mk 4:26-29). But he pitilessly unmasked those who were responsible for perverting religion, the Pharisees and those learned in scripture, and he castigated the servant who buried his talent in the ground instead of putting it to profit (Mt 25: 26-30). So we must practise planning and futurology and yet know that the future of the Church is not a matter for futurology but the object of a hope against all hope. [13]

2. Hope, then, is a fundamental attitude of the Christian in this world. In the midst of the complete absurdity that life can produce, rather as it is described in the books of Solzhenitsin, the Christian believes life has a meaning. He knows that salvation history is realized not only in the mighty works of God for his chosen people and in the recorded actions of Jesus so long ago now. To believe in salvation history, we need not to study archaeology but to involve ourselves in the activity and movement God inspires today, as he reveals himself to the world. God's involvement in the history of man is found in the risen, living, present Christ. In the Bible we do not find the one and only exclusive source of revelation but rather precedents which teach us how to experience events in the present as possible forms of God's action. [14] We cannot accept that there is a vacuum in salvation history between the Ascension and the return of the Lord.

[12] Resch, *op. cit.* (n. 2), pp. 121-173: *Der mensch in der Sicht der Psychologie von morgen,* esp. p. 170f.
[13] Rahner, *Strukturwandel,* 7, 49f; Ratzinger, *Glaube und Zukunft,* München, 1970, p. 109f.
[14] H. Cox, *The secular city,* N.Y., 1965, p. 159; cf. also *Espérance miss.,* in SPIR 1970, no. 40, 1-92, esp. 7f.

Hope must not be identified with human wish (and plan) fulfilment. By its nature, hope is bound up with the dramatic, disturbing phases in the development of history. If hope ceased to be the hidden meaning of a reality that is outwardly meaningless it would be in danger of falling to the level of rational thought and of dying. [15] We are still, as we always have been, totally dependent on the incomprehensible mystery of God who reveals and conceals himself in history. Only when we can find no more answers to our questions, only when we have destroyed all the idols of our supposed answers, do we begin to have some inkling of what God really means. [16] Then hope really begins. Then we are ready with Francis of Assisi to lay aside money and clothing and even, if needs must, good name, freedom and life itself. Like him we can go on to say: 'Our Father, who art in heaven'. Hope does not fail us even when Christ accompanies us only *incognito* in our sufferings, as he accompanied the discouraged disciples at Emmaus (Lk 24:13-35), or even when he sleeps — and really sleeps — in the storm-tossed boat (Mt 8:24). So although insecurity is the fundamental feeling of man as he faces the future, and the Christian is to 'endure without illusions' in this world, [17] nonetheless we do believe that God (whom we cannot in any way manipulate) is faithful in his own way, and that Christ has overcome the world precisely by his defeat in this world. 'Fear not' was Christ's injunction to his disciples on their way, both before and after the resurrection (Lk 12:7; 12:32; 24:36 etc.).

A great deal is said at the present time about the malaise among missionaries and their feeling of worthlessness. [18] Similar things could be said about many Christians in the First, Second and Third Church. To overcome this depressive phase we must first, as in psychiatric treatment, accept the situation for what it is — a typically Christian *diaspora* situation (being scattered in the world) and also a *paroikia* situation (being away from home, among strangers). It is the situation of a pilgrim or

[15] P. Ricoeur, *Histoire et vérité*, Paris, 1964, p. 98.
[16] Rahner, *Die Frage nache der Zukunft*, in *Schriften* 9, 526.
[17] Metz, *Theologie der Welt*, p. 41f.
[18] T. Ohm, *Vom, Selbstwertgefühl des Missionars*, in ZMR 1958, pp. 177-185.

nomad. Bound up with this situation is a certain lack of calm and security which must be accepted. We need faith that God moves salvation history forward with us just as he did with Abraham and Moses, and that he does so with all men through us. We must believe that beyond all our horizons God awaits us with his promise. For God is always the God of the Exodus and of the resurrection; he is always ahead of us on our way, leading us out of the captivity of the conditions we have come to terms with into the land of freedom. [19]

3. This theological hope can be verified in history — not, of course, with mathematical certainty. Compare the workings of evolution attaining its ends with incredible precision from primitive beginnings. Then take a quick glance at the history of the missions, how the initial impulse through Jesus Christ was carried on by apostles, bishops and monks, how the Franciscans and Dominicans broke through the barrier of Islam during the middle ages and penetrated through Asia, how in the 16th century, after the upheaval of the Reformation, the Jesuits moved out into the newly discovered worlds, how in the 17th century a new impulse came from the founding of *Propaganda Fide*, how in the 19th century, after the French Revolution had destroyed the home base, many new missionary institutes arose and missionary activity truly attained its high point of achievement. Whenever the Church seemed on the point of death, there came a renewal movement, and even while the tide was ebbing the signs of new forward movement were already apparent. Latourette followed the working of this principle through his history of the missions and was amazed by the immense vitality of Christianity even though, when he wrote the last volume in 1944, we were only at the beginning of ecumenism, the beginning of the birth of local Churches and the beginning of modern times with their challenges and opportunities. In a later work he condensed his reflections on the theology of history in the words: 'Much in the history of the missions can cause us bewilderment, but there is nothing in it that can make Christian hope evaporate as an illusion'. [20]

[19] Moltmann, *Umkehr zur Zukunft*, München, 1970, p. 10.
[20] K.S. Latourette, *Christianity in a revolutionary age*, N.Y., 1958/

4. All this gives us courage to face the future. The African peoples knew only two dimensions of time: a long past and a dynamic present. The future, as such, had no value in their thought. For them, history did not move towards a point in the future but strove to re-establish the origins, to adapt the present to the past. [21] Asiatic religions remain trapped in the cycle of birth, marriage, death and rebirth. The neighbours of the people of Israel, the Babylonians and Canaanites, believed in gods that had fixed the world at the beginning for all time. They had no new horizons towards which a people could journey. In contrast to all these, the God of Israel was a God of nomads who must ever continue their journey. Christ has once for all broken the barrier of death (*hapax*: Rom 6:9) and through the breach has opened up for us an everlasting future. [22]

So we have only to make our way with confidence and remain open to new situations. We are at the end of one world, not at the end of *the* world. Life goes on. Forms may change, often more than we would like, but the realities remain. Nothing damages the Church and her mission more than the desire to cling to historically conditioned forms. If we have the courage to let go of structures that are out of date, God will enable us to find new structures through observing the signs of the times. In doing this, we have to allow for a certain insecurity. It is not necessary to have a map of the Promised Land before we leave Egypt. [23]

The Third Church is coming. I dare to hope that the reader will now agree with what I said in the introduction: by a providential coincidence with world events, a new Pentecostal wind is sweeping through the Church which has never faced a greater challenge and never had a better opportunity to become Church for the world.

1962, V, 534; cf. J. Kraus, *Missionsgeschichte als Heilsgeschichte,* in VSVD 1971, pp. 177-186.

[21] J.S. Mbiti, *New Testament eschatology in an African background,* Oxford, 1971, p. 24f (referring to the Akamba).

[22] J. Daniélou, *Vom Heil der Völker,* Frankfurt, 1952, pp. 82-103: on the mission and the return of the Lord.

[23] Cox, *The Secular city,* p. 246.

SELECT BIBLIOGRAPHY

Note. Owing to the broad scope of the theme, it is impossible to give a comprehensive bibliography. The books listed here have been chosen because they seem basic and have been regularly used in the composition of this work. The footnotes throughout refer to the editions given here. Other books and articles used in specific connections are also referred to in the notes as occasion demands.

For reviews and journals see the list of abbreviations, p. viii.

(Where convenient, English editions, translations and originals, are given in brackets. But this is by no means a complete list of available English translations.)

Achariya F. (Br Mahieu), *Kurisumala Ashram*, Blois, 1972.

Adler G., *Revolutionäres Lateinamerika. Eine Dokumentation*, Paderborn, 1970.

Ageneau R. and Pryen D., *Chemins de la Mission aujourd'hui*, Paris, 1972.

— *Un nouvel âge de la Mission*, Paris, 1973.

Amalorpavadas D.S., *L'Inde à la rencontre du Seigneur*, Paris, 1964.

— *Theology of evangelization in the Indian context*, Bangalore, 1971

Amalrik A., *L'Union Soviétique survivra-t-elle en 1984?* Paris, 1970.

L'apporto dei religiosi italiani nella Chiesa dell'America Latina, Rome, 1972.

Ayandale E.A., *The missionary impact on modern Africa*, London, 1966.

Baeta C.G., *Prophetism in Ghana*, London, 1962.

— (ed.), *Christianity in tropical Africa*, Oxford, 1968.

Barrett D.A., *Schism and renewal in Africa*, Oxford, 1968.

— *AD 2000: 350 million Christians in Africa* in IRM 1970, pp. 39-54.

— *Frontier situations for evangelization in Africa*, Nairobi, 1972.

Baumgartner J., *Mission und Liturgie in Mexiko*, Freiburg i. B., 1960.

Beckmann J., *Die China-Mission*, Freiburg i. B., 1959.
— *Weltkirche und Weltreligionen*, Freiburg i. B., 1960.

Beyerhaus P., *Die selbständigkeit der jungen Kirchen als missionarisches Problem*, Wuppertal, 1956.

Blecker C.J., *Christ in modern Athens*, Leiden, 1965.

Boberg J.T. and Scherer J.A. (ed.), *Mission in the '70s. What direction?* Chicago, 1972.

Böttcher W. (ed.), *Das grosse Dreieck Washington-Moskau-Peking*, Stuttgart, 1971.

Brunner H.T., *Kirche ohne Illusionen*, Zürich, 1968.

Bühlmann W., *Afrika*, Mainz, 1963.

— *Afrika gestern, heute, morgen*, Freiburg, 1960.

— *Sorge für alle Welt*, Freiburg i. B., 1967.

Burgalassi S., *Le cristianità nascoste. Dove va la cristianità italiana?* Bologna, 1970.

Camara H., *The Church and colonialism*, London, 1969.

Casty A. (ed.), *Mass media and mass men*, New York, 1968.

The Catholic Broadcasters of Asia, UNDA, Manila, 1971.

Church in India today, All India Seminar 1969, New Delhi, (no date).

Cohen P.A., *China and Christianity*, Cambridge, 1967.

Cone J.H., *Schwarze Theologie*, Mainz, 1971.

Conference of Religious, India, General Assembly 1969.

Congar Y., *Priester und Laien im Dienst des Evangeliums*, Freiburg i. B., 1965.

— *Initiatives locales et normes universelles*, Conference, Rome, 1972.

Cox H., *The secular city*, New York, 1965.

Dhavamony M. (ed.), *Evangelization, dialogue and development*, International Theol. Conf., Nagpur, 1971, Rome, 1972.

Dammann E., *Die Religionen Afrikas*, Stuttgart, 1963.

Daniélou J., *Vom Heil der Völker*, Frankfurt, 1952. (E.T. *The Salvation of the Nations*).

Directory of vocation promoters, Kerala, 1971.

Dournes J., *Aux plus près des plus loin*, Paris, 1969.

— *L'offrande des peuples*, Paris, 1967.

Edwards M., *A history of India*, London, 1967.

Emmerich H., *Atlas hierarchicus*, Mödling, 1968.

Filthaut Th., *Politische Erziehung aus dem Glaube,* Mainz, 1965.

Folliet J., *Le temps de l'angoisse et de la recherche*, Lyons, (2nd ed.), 1972.

Fonseca A.J. (ed.), *Challenge of poverty in India*, Delhi, 1971.

Fourastié J., *Lettre ouverte à quatre milliards d'hommes*, Paris, 1970.

Fuchs St., *Rebellious prophets*, Bombay, 1965.

Garaudy R., *L'alternativa*, Assisi, (3rd ed.), 1973.

Gheddo P., *Cattolici e Buddhisti nel Vietnam*, Milan, 1968.

— *Processo alle Missioni*, Milan, 1971.

Goodall N. (ed.), *Bericht aus Uppsala 1968*, Geneva, 1968.

Greiwe M. (ed.), *Herausforderung an die Zukunft*, München, 1970.

Griffiths B., *Christ in India*, New York, 1966.

Groves C.P., *The planting of Christianity in Africa. IV: 1914-1954*, London, 1958.

Guardini R., *Das Ende der Neuzeit*, Würzburg, (9th ed.), 1965.

Guariglia G., *Prophetismus und Heilserwartungs-Bewegungen als völkerkundliches und religionsgeschichtliches Problem*, Vienna, 1959.

Le Guillou M.J. and Mercier G., *Mission et pauvreté*, Paris, 1963.

Haas O., *Paulus der Missionar*, Münsterschwarzach, 1971.

Häring B., *Teologia nella protesta*, Brescia, 1972 (ET Theology of Protest, Vision Press).

Hastings A., *Kirche und Mission in modernen Afrika*, Graz, 1969. (Eng. original: *Church and Mission in Modern Africa*, A. Clarke).

Herburger G., *Jesus in Osaka. Zukunftsroman*, Berlin, (2nd ed.), 1970.

Hoekendijk J.C., *Zur Frage einer missionarischen Existenz in Kirche und Volk in der deutschen Missionswissenschaft*, München, 1967 (p. 297-354).

Hollenweger W.J., *Enthusiastisches Christentum*, Zürich, 1971.

— (ed.)Auf den Spuren dynamischer Gemeinden, Zürich, 1971.

Holzer W., *26 mal Afrika*, München, 1968.

Hostie R., *Vie et mort des Ordres religieux*, Paris, 1972.

Illich I.D., *Almosen und Folter. Verfehlter Fortschritt in Lateinamerika*, München, 1970.

Italiaander R., *Profile und Perspektiven*, Erlangen, 1971.

Jahn J., *Geschichte der neoafrikanischen Literatur*, Düsseldorf, 1966.

Jalée P., *Il Terzo Mondo in cifre*, Milan, 1971.

Jungk R. and Mundt H.J. (ed.), *Der Weg ins Jahr 2000*, München, 1968.

Kahn H., *Bald werden sie die Ersten sein. Japan 2000*, Vienna, 1970.

Kasper W., *Glaube und Geschichte*, Mainz, 1970.

Kaunda K.D., *Humanismus in Zambia*, Freiburg i. Ue, no date (cf. id *Humanism in Africa. Letters to Colin M. Morris*, Longman, 1966).

Kerkhofs J. and Henry A.A. (ed.), *Dialogue d'aujourd'hui — Mission de demain*, Paris, 1968.

Kirche in den Völkern. Missionsstudien-Tagung in St. Gabriel-Wien 1971 in VSVD n. 13, 1972.

Kirche in Not, XIX: Christentum und Atheismus heute, Königstein T., 1971.

Die Kirche für andere in Ringen um Strukturen missionarischer Gemeinden, ORK, Geneva, 1967.

Klaes N., *Stellvertretung und Mission*, Essen, 1968.

Klimkeit H.J., *Antireligiöse Bewegungen im modernen Südindien*, Bonn, 1971.

Küng H., *Structures of the Church*, London, 1965.

Kurzrock R., *Asien im 20 Jahrhundert*, Berlin, 1972.

Latourette K.S., *A history of the expansion of Christianity, I-VII*, New York, 1937-1945.

410

Laurentin R., *Flashes sur l'Amérique Latine*, Paris, 1968.

Le Saux, *Indische Weisheit — christliche Mystik*, Lucerne, 1968.

Lefringhausen K. and Merz F., *Das Zweite Entwicklungsjahrzehnt 1970-1980*, Wuppertal, 1970.

Lombardi R., *Terremoto nella Chiesa*, Turin, 1970.

Margull H.J., *Theologie der missionarischen Verkündigung*, Stuttgart, 1959.

Mbiti J.S., *African religions and philosophy*, London, 1969.

— *New Testament eschatology in an African background*, Oxford, 1971.

McCarthy Ch., *Le Filippine e l'evangelizzazione dell'Asia* in *Civiltà Cattolica*, Rome, 1970 (pp. 360-369).

Mehnert K., *China nach dem Sturm*, Stuttgart, 1972.

Metz J.B., *Zur Theologie der Welt*, Mainz, 1969 (ET *Theology of the World*, Herder, 1969).

Metzler J. (ed.), *Sacrae Congregationis de Propaganda Fide memoria rerum, 1622-1972*, Freiburg im B., 1971ff.

Mobley H.W., *The Ghanaian's image of the missionary*, Leiden, 1970.

Moltmann J., *Umkehr zur Zukunft*, München, 1970.

— *Die ersten Freigelassenen der Schöpfung*, München, 1971.

Mooneyham St., *China: the puzzle*, Passadena, 1971.

Mulders A., *Missionsgeschichte*, Regensburg, 1960.

Müller J., *Missionarische Anpassung als theologisches Prinzip*, Münster i. W., 1973.

Myrdal G., *Politisches Manifest über die Armut in der Welt*, Frankfurt, 1970.

Neckebrouck V., *L'Afrique Noire et la crise religieuse de l'Occident*, Tabora, Tanzania, 1970.

Nyerere J.K., *Freedom and unity*, Dar es Salaam, 1966.

— *Freedom and socialism*, Dar es Salaam, 1968.

Ohm Th., *Asiens Nein und Ja zum westlichen Christentums*, München, 1960.

Pannikkar K.M., *Asien und die Herrschaft des Westerns*, Zürich, 1955; (ET *Asia and Western Dominance*, Allen and Unwin, 1959).

Pannikar R., *Kerygma und Indien*, Hamburg, 1967; (cf. id *The unknown Christ of Hinduism*, Darton, Longman and Todd).

Parrinder G., *Religion in Africa*, New York, 1969.

Pearson L.B., *Partners in development*, New York, 1969.

La pertinence du christianisme en Afrique, VIe Sem. Théologique, Kinshasa 1971, in RCA 1972.

Petsch H.J., *Religion aus dem Untergrund*, Freiburg i. Ue., 1972.

Pin E. and Cavallin G., *La religiosità dei Romani*, Rome, 1970.

411

Rahner K., *Schriften zur Theologie I-X*, Einsiedeln 1954/72; (ET *Theological Investigations*, Darton, Longman and Todd).

— *Strukturwandel der Kirche als Aufgabe und Chance*, Freiburg im B., (3rd ed.), 1973.

— (ed.) *Handbuch der Pastoraltheologie I-IV*, Freiburg im B., 1964-69.

— (with H. Vorgrimmler) *Kleines Konzilkompendium*, Freiburg im B., 1967.

Ratzinger J., *Glaube und Zukunft*, München, 1970.

Renouveau de l'Eglise et nouvelles Eglises, IVe Sem. Théol. Kinshasa 1968, in RCS 1969.

Resch A. (ed.), *Welt, Mensch und Wissenschaft morgen*, Paderborn, 1972.

Rétif A., *Un nouvel avenir pour les Missions*, Paris, 1966.

Richardson W.J., (ed.), *The modern Mission apostolate*, New York, 1965.

Ricoeur P. *Histoire et vérité*, Paris, (3rd ed.), 1964.

Robinson J.A.T., *Gott ist anders*, München, 1964 (from the English).

Rüstow A., *Ortsbestimmung der Gegenwart I-II*, Erlenbach ZH, 1950/52.

Rütti L., *Zur Theologie der Mission*, München-Mainz, 1972.

Schmitz J. (ed.), *Das Ende der Exportreligionen. Perspektive für eine künftige Mission*, Düsseldorf, 1971.

Schooyans M., *Chrétienté en contestation: l'Amérique Latine*, Paris, 1969.

Schütte J. (ed.), *Mission nach dem Konzil*, Mainz, 1967.

— *Die katholische Chinamission im Spiegel der rotchinesischen Presse*, Münster i. W., 1957.

Sedlmayr H., *Verlust der Mitte*, Salzburg, (7th ed.), 1955.

Seeber D.A., *Paul, Papst im Widerstreit*, Freiburg i. B., 1972.

Secretary of State, *Raccolta di tavole statistiche 1969*, Rome, 1972.

— *Annuario statistico della Chiesa 1970*, Rome, 1973.

— *Annuario statistico della Chiesa 1971*, Rome, 1973.

— *Annuario statistico della Chiesa 1973*, Rome, 1975.

Silone J., *L'avventura di un povero cristiano*, Mondadori, (13th ed.), 1971.

Southern African Catholic Bishops' Conference, *Pastoral Letters*, Pretoria, 1970.

Spengler O., *Der Untergang des Abendlandes*, I, Vienna, 1918; II, München, 1922.

Stucki L., *Kontinent im Aufbruch. Südamerika auf dem Weg ins 21. Jahrhundert*, Bern, 1971.

Taylor J.V., *Die Kirche in Buganda*, Stuttgart, 1966.

Thielicke H. *So sah ich Afrika*, Gütersloh, 1971.

Traber M., *Das revolutionäre Afrika*, Freiburg, i. Ue. 1972.

The United Nations, *The next 25 years*, New York, 1970.

— *Statistical Yearbook 1972*, New York, 1973.

— *1970 Report on the world social situation*, New York, 1971.

— *1971 rapport sur la situation sociale dans le monde*, New York, 1972.

Van der Linde H. and Fiolet H. (ed.), *Neue Perspektiven nach dem Ende des konventionellen Christentums*, Freiburg i. B., 1968.

Van de Pol, *Das Ende des konventionellen Christentums*, Freiburg i. B., 1967.

Weber H.R., *Gottes Arithmetik in der Mission* in *Kirchentreu und kirchenfern*, Wuppertal 1967 (p. 63-72).

Wei Tsing-Sing L., *Le Saint-Siège et la Chine*, Allais, 1971.

West M.L., *In den Schuhen des Fischers*, Vienna-Basel, 1964 (English original: *The Shoes of the Fisherman*, London).

World Bank, *Trends in developing countries*, New York, 1971.

Die Zukunft der Kirche und die Zukunft der Welt, EKD München, 1968.

GENERAL INDEX

abortion, 321
absolution, general, 183
Abyssinia, see Ethiopia
Accion cultural popular, 62, 346
accountability, 380
adaptation, missionary, 286ff
Addis Ababa, broadcasting, 347
— theological faculty, 223
Africae terrarum, 154
African religious tradition, 171, 292n
African socialism, 64, 127
African spirituality, 184, 293
Aggrey, Dr., 151
aid for development, 57, 390, 399
— by China, 75
— by missionaries, 106f, 339f
Alexander VI, 43
Algeria, 132
All India Seminar, 164, 193, 235, 237, 289
— on service, 95, 337
— on birth control, 323
— on films, 344
— on schools and competition, 328
All India Association of Cath. students, 111
All India consultation on evangelization, 165
Amalorpavadas, 132, 172
AMECEA, 352
Amin, Press. I., 279
Ammann, Bp. J., 194f
Anderson R., 377
Andhra Pradesh, 338f
Angola, 104
animation, 113, 266, 333
apartheid, 35ff, 103
architecture, 370
Arinze, F.A., 292n
Arns Card. E., 360
armaments, 33
Arrupe, P., 284, 330
Arusha Decl., 108
ashrams, 164, 243f
assimilados, 38

atheism, 308
Augusta Conf., 190
Auschwitz, 92
Ayandale, E.A., 171

Bambaren, Mgr., 62
Bamberger, S., 351
Bantu prophets, 204, 223
Bantu religions, 292n
Bantustan, 37
Bangkok conf., 278
Bangla Desh, 32
Banyatereza, 269
baptism of infants, 146
baptismal names, 49, 296
Baptists in Russia, 11
'barefoot doctors', 319
Barrett, D.B., 20f, 143n, 153, 204, 399
basic groups, 157, 205, 208, 360
Beatrice, Dame, 295f
Benelli, Archbp., 190
Benin, 29
Berlin Congress, 33
Bible distribution, 345
Bloch, E., 123
Blomjous, J., 277
Boers, 36
Borneo, 49
Brazil, 159f, 346, 204, 254
— rich and poor, 60
— diplomacy and prophecy, 102
— new pastoral policy, 263, 268
Brunner, H.H., 16
Buddhism, 236f, 246
Burke, F.H., 223
Burgalassi, S., 401
Burma, 50
Burundi, 32, 279

Camara, H., 57, 62, 102
— on anti-Communism, 122
— on seminaries, 364f
Cantin, Archbp., 193
Capuchin mission schools, 331
Cameroons, 153, 254, 283, 373
catechetics, 300f, 306
catechists, 113, 265, 298, 376

414

415

416

marriage-catechumenate, 314
married clergy, 259
mass stipends, 375
Maurer, Card. J.C., 121
Maximum illud, 191, 258
Medellin, 156, 330
meditation, 164, 244
messianic movements, 88f, 378
Mexico, 170, 322
Mexico City, 1963, 5
Mihayo, Arch. M., 259
mission, 5, 97f
— by eastern Churches, 9
— working hypothesis, 7f
mobility of the Church, 7
mobility, social, 327f
Mobutu, Pres., 296
Mobley, H.W., 170
Moltmann, J., 202
'moratorium' on missions, 278
Moshi, 347
Mott, J., 143f
Mozambique, 36, 104
Muaca, E., 106
Mulago, Z.B.V., 292n
Multimedia International, 351
music, 287
Myrdal, G., 60

Namibia, 35
nationalization of schools, 330ff
négritude, 30, 151
Neill, S., 5n
neo-colonialism, 275, 374, 380
New Delhi, 1961, 226
Nigeria, 153, 171, 317
— expulsion of missionaries, 49
— vocations in, 251, 258
— Ibo religion, 292n
Nijmegen, 1959, 176
Nkrumah, 32
Nkuissi, B., 373f
non-violence, 115ff
nuncios, 195f, 332
nuns, 266f
Nyerere, Pres. J., 26f, 51
— on corruption, 61
— on missionaries, 108, 336
— on self-reliance, 374
— on religious freedom, 46n
— on socialism and Christianity, 126f

— school policy, 328
— and Portugal, 38f
Nyogi Report, 327

OAU, 32
oriental studies, 85
Orissa law-suit, 46
Otunga, Card., 315

Pacific, new world centre, 83f
padroado, 105
Pakistan, 245
Pannikar, K.M., 29
Pannikar, R., 43
Paths Marga liturgy, 185n
Paton, A., 40
patriarchates, 285
patriotism, 61f, 99, 156
Paul VI
— in Africa, 45, 284
— message to China, 77
— in Samoa, 252
Pearson Report, ix, 275, 378
Peking, 124
Pentecostalists, 144, 204
— Church finance, 378
persecution, 49, 163
Peru, 62, 156, 301, 346
Peter, L.J., 186
Pezzoni, A., 162
Philippines, 54, 68, 111, 211
— broadcasting in, 347
piety, 306f
Pignedoli, Card. S., 95, 193, 257
Pillard, J., 308
PIME, 166n
Pius XII, 44f, 77, 154
polygamy, 315
Pontifical Mission Works, 379, 391
Poona Art Centre, 288
Populorum progressio, 100, 107, 115, 320
poverty of spirit, 120f, 268
prayer, 184
priesthood of the faithful, 253
priorities in mission work, 399f
promocion popular, 63
Propaganda Fide, 131
— founded 1622, 190f
— and rites controversy, 285
— and religious, 257

417

— and nationalism, 43, 250, 275
— distribution of funds, 379
— on economies, 370
proselytism, 221, 326
Pueblos Jovenes, 62

Radio Vatican, 349f
Radio Veritas, 78, 348
Radhakrishnan, 171f
Rahner, K., 17, 120, 173, 179,
    184n, 225, 316
— on poverty, 122
— basic communities, 208
— on hierarchy of truths, 300
— on non-Christian religions,
    230
— on 'horizontalism', 111f
Recife seminary, 364
religious attitude, fundamental,
    238
religious orders and congrega-
    tions, 253, 257, 267
Rerum Ecclesiae, 191
retiring age for bishops, 200ff
revolution, 63, 102, 114f, 356
— theology of, 116ff
Rhodesia, 36f, 40, 103
Riberti, Mgr., 76
Ricoeur, P., 289
Riobé, Bp., 15
Rio de Janeiro, 125, 366
rites controversy, 286
Roma, Lesotho, seminary, 223
Rome and centralization, 78f,
    178f
Rosmini, 213, 224
Rossi, Card. A., 193, 360
Roy, Card. M., 212
Ruanda, 32

Salcedo, Mgr., 62, 346
Sales, Card. E., 102
salvation, integral, 91, 113, 144f,
    230
Sanon, A., 6n
Sao Paulo, 159, 360
scholarship in Third Church,
    292
— in India, 243
schools, mission, 152
— and urbanization, 358
Schütte, J., 70f

Schütz, R., 206, 219f
Schwartzmüller, Sr. L., 336
secularization, 153, 166, 203
— and secularism, 302
— Kampala conf. on, 304
— due to missionaries, 303
SEDOS, x
self-support, 71, 377
seminaries, 158, 254
Senegal, 56
Senghor, L.S., 233
Shraddhananda Sr., 245
Sikhs, 240
Singapore, 56
slavery, 150
Smith, I., 36
Snow, E., 73
SODEPAX, 218
Sofia, 1971, 319
Sollicitudo omnium, 195
South Africa, 36f, 40, 103, 330
— theology in, 223
— violence in, 118
Spengler, O., 11, 18, 40, 356
spontaneity, 171, 202f, 247
sport, 124
STAR, Kinshasa, 347
stole fees, 375
Streit, R., 191
Sunramanyam, K.N., 327
sunsidiarity, 180
Sudan, 29
Sundkler, Bp. B., 151, 204
Sutatenza study centre, 62
Swantz, L.W., 359
symbolism, 294
Synod of Rome, 1971, 101, 104,
    116, 125, 256, 259
Synod, 1974, 24, 113, 272, 284n,
    392f

Taiwan, 77
Taizé, 206
Tanganyika, 153
Tanganyika Nat. Union, 26
Tanzania, 40, 64, 126, 223, 251
— railway in, 75
— church building, 359
— church finances, 374, 377,
    381
Taylor, B.J., 312
technology, 289f